Readings in Persuasion

ASPEN COURSEBOOK SERIES

Readings in Persuasion

Briefs That Changed the World

LINDA H. EDWARDS

William S. Boyd School of Law
University of Nevada, Las Vegas

 Wolters Kluwer

Law & Business

Published by Wolters Kluwer Law & Business in New York.

Wolters Kluwer Law & Business serves customers worldwide with CCH, Aspen Publishers, and Kluwer Law International products. (www.wolterskluwerlb.com)

To contact Customer Service, e-mail customer.service@wolterskluwer.com, call 1-800-234-1660, fax 1-800-901-9075, or mail correspondence to:

Wolters Kluwer Law & Business
Attn: Order Department
PO Box 990
Frederick, MD 21705

Printed in the United States of America.

1 2 3 4 5 6 7 8 9 0

ISBN 978-0-7355-8775-5

Library of Congress Cataloging-in-Publication Data

Edwards, Linda Holdeman, 1948-
Readings in persuasion : briefs that changed the world / Linda H. Edwards.
    p. cm.—(Aspen coursebook series)
  Includes bibliographical references and index.
  ISBN 978-0-7355-8775-5
  1. Legal composition.   2. Legal briefs—United States.   I. Title.
  KF251.E39 2012
  349.73—dc23
                                    2012026656

About Wolters Kluwer Law & Business

Wolters Kluwer Law & Business is a leading global provider of intelligent information and digital solutions for legal and business professionals in key specialty areas, and respected educational resources for professors and law students. Wolters Kluwer Law & Business connects legal and business professionals as well as those in the education market with timely, specialized authoritative content and information-enabled solutions to support success through productivity, accuracy and mobility.

Serving customers worldwide, Wolters Kluwer Law & Business products include those under the Aspen Publishers, CCH, Kluwer Law International, Loislaw, Best Case, ftwilliam.com and MediRegs family of products.

CCH products have been a trusted resource since 1913, and are highly regarded resources for legal, securities, antitrust and trade regulation, government contracting, banking, pension, payroll, employment and labor, and healthcare reimbursement and compliance professionals.

Aspen Publishers products provide essential information to attorneys, business professionals and law students. Written by preeminent authorities, the product line offers analytical and practical information in a range of specialty practice areas from securities law and intellectual property to mergers and acquisitions and pension/benefits. Aspen's trusted legal education resources provide professors and students with high-quality, up-to-date and effective resources for successful instruction and study in all areas of the law.

Kluwer Law International products provide the global business community with reliable international legal information in English. Legal practitioners, corporate counsel and business executives around the world rely on Kluwer Law journals, looseleafs, books, and electronic products for comprehensive information in many areas of international legal practice.

Loislaw is a comprehensive online legal research product providing legal content to law firm practitioners of various specializations. Loislaw provides attorneys with the ability to quickly and efficiently find the necessary legal information they need, when and where they need it, by facilitating access to primary law as well as state-specific law, records, forms and treatises.

Best Case Solutions is the leading bankruptcy software product to the bankruptcy industry. It provides software and workflow tools to flawlessly streamline petition preparation and the electronic filing process, while timely incorporating ever-changing court requirements.

ftwilliam.com offers employee benefits professionals the highest quality plan documents (retirement, welfare and non-qualified) and government forms (5500/PBGC, 1099 and IRS) software at highly competitive prices.

MediRegs products provide integrated health care compliance content and software solutions for professionals in healthcare, higher education and life sciences, including professionals in accounting, law and consulting.

Wolters Kluwer Law & Business, a division of Wolters Kluwer, is headquartered in New York. Wolters Kluwer is a market-leading global information services company focused on professionals.

*To the scholars whose work is represented here
and to those on whose shoulders they stand.*

Summary of Contents

Contents

If you are reading this book, you have probably already learned a great deal about legal writing. You already know how to use authority, organize a typical legal argument, draft the customary parts of a legal brief, write clearly, and cite correctly. Learning these fundamentals has been important, no doubt about it. But that basic knowledge only enables you to make the team. The next challenge is becoming the best player you can be. So now it is time to think more broadly and deeply about written legal persuasion.

This book is organized into two parts. Part One provides a set of readings covering some of the most important topics a lawyer must consider in writing a brief—topics like imagination, voice, tone, order, emotion, reasoning, and framing. Part Two introduces the briefs in some of the ground-breaking cases of our shared past—literally, briefs that changed the world. The readings in Part One are certainly important but only when and if they actually work in the push and pull of real lawyering. The briefs introduced in Part Two give us a chance to see whether and how skilled lawyers have used these abstract ideas when there is a great deal at stake.

The briefs introduced here are not perfect. Some of them are truly masterpieces, and others are more workmanlike. Some will surprise you. Some will prompt strong reactions from different readers. But all of them were instrumental in achieving a critically important legal result. Some of them even saved lives. So read them in order to learn what they can teach us about what to do and occasionally about what not to do.

Before proceeding, I should first acknowledge two important limitations on this project. First, these briefs were filed in the United States Supreme Court and dealt almost entirely with issues of law rather than fact. Therefore, some of the strategies and characteristics of these briefs might not work as well in a trial court or even in an intermediate appellate court. A skilled legal rhetorician always evaluates the setting, issues, and forum as part of choosing her strategies.

Second, the ability to critique these briefs will be limited by our incomplete understanding of the rhetorical situation at the time they were written. To do a more thorough and accurate analysis, we would have to study much more than we will be able to cover here. At the very least, we would need to understand the cultural, historical, and political context of each case; the personalities and jurisprudential leanings of each justice on the Court at the time; the histories of all the related cases that preceded our case; the trial court record; all of the opinions below; the petition for certiorari and the replies; the briefs of all the parties and *amici*; the oral arguments; the interpersonal relations on the Court; and the impact of the work of the justices' law clerks. Because we will have time for only a fraction of this material, our assessments of the briefs must be tentative. Still, these briefs can teach us a great deal, despite our limited understanding of the rhetorical settings in which they operated. So let's plunge in and see what we can learn.

If you're intrigued by the cases and articles discussed in the book, please visit www.aspenlawschool.com/books/edwards_readings for additional materials. Here, you'll find briefs from the cases discussed in the book, as well as full versions of the articles excerpted.

Acknowledgments

> *"In the end, all books are written for your friends."*
> —Gabriel Garcia Marquez

And this book is no exception. I am indebted to a large and vibrant scholarly community of people interested in legal language and persuasion. I claim each and every one of them as friends, whether or not I have had the privilege of meeting them face to face. The work of some of them is represented in this book, but restrictions on length and scope prevent inclusion of all the interesting work being done by members of that community. I hope only that this book will make a small reciprocal contribution in their honor.

I am indebted to many other generous friends and colleagues, most especially Matthew Wright, Jeanne Price, Nettie Mann, Catherine Bacos and her team, and Aaron Mayes, all of whom saved the day countless times. Christine Hannan and Jay Harward provided expert editing, and Carol McGeehan was, as usual, a source of support and inspiration. Thanks also to my ever-patient husband, Dan, for once again listening, suggesting ideas, and reminding me of what's truly important.

Finally, I thank the following copyright holders and others who have kindly permitted the use of their material in this book:

PART ONE

Chapter 1: Imagination

Mary R. Falk, *The Play of Those Who Have Not Yet Heard of Games: Creativity, Compliance, and the 'Good Enough' Law Teacher*, 6 J. ALWD 200 (Fall 2009). Reprinted with permission.

© The New Yorker Collection, Bruce Eric Kaplan, 4/23/2001. Used by permission. All rights reserved. http://www.cartoonbank.com.

Carol Parker, *A Liberal Education in Law: Engaging the Legal Imagination Through Research and Writing Beyond the Curriculum*, 1 J. ALWD 130 (Fall 2002). Reprinted with permission.

Chapter 2: Voice and Self

Justice Oliver Wendell Holmes, Jr., circa 1924, Library of Congress.

Mark Osbeck, *What is "Good Legal Writing" and Why Does it Matter?* 4 Drexel L. Rev. _____ (2012). Reprinted with permission.

J. Christopher Rideout, *Voice, Self, and Persona in Legal Writing*, 15 J. Legal Writing 67 (2009). Reprinted with permission.

Speaker with megaphone, photo provided by University of Nevada, Las Vegas, used by permission.

Kathryn M. Stanchi, *Resistance is Futile: How Legal Writing Pedagogy Contributes to the Law's Marginalization of Outsider Voices*, 103 Dick. L. Rev. 7 (1998-1999). Reprinted with permission.

Nathan Straus, Chief of the U.S. Housing Authority, speaking before the Annual Conference of the U.S. Conference of Mayors, Nov. 17, 1937, Harris & Ewing, Library of Congress.

Chapter 3: Rhetoric

Linda L. Berger, *Studying and Teaching "Law As Rhetoric": A Place to Stand*, 16 J. Legal Writing 3 (2010). Reprinted with permission.

Michael Frost, *Introduction to Classical Legal Rhetoric: A Lost Heritage*, 8 S. Cal. Interdisc. L. J. 613 (1999). Reprinted with permission.

Yvonne M. Jones, "The Orator Speaks," Jan. 1, 2008, used with permission.

Robin Madden, "Demosthenes," Sept. 2, 2008, used with permission.

Chapter 4: History

Suzanne Ehrenberg, *Embracing the Writing-Centered Legal Process*, 89 Iowa L. Rev. 1159 (2004). Reprinted with permission.

Michael Frost, *Brief Rhetoric—A Note on Classical and Modern Theories of Forensic Discourse*, 38 Kansas L. Rev. 411 (1990). Reprinted with permission.

Shayla M. Gladney, "Amicus Brief," March 7, 2012, used with permission.

Joseph D. Kearney and Thomas W. Merrill, *The Influence of Amicus Curiae Briefs on the Supreme Court*, 148 U. Pa. L. Rev. 743 (1999-2000). Reprinted with permission.

Belva Lockwood, Nineteenth-Century Lawyer, Library of Congress.

"A Negro Lawyer," circa 1942, Library of Congress.

Chapter 5: The Court

Elizabeth Beske, *Perspectives of a (Fleeting) Insider.* Printed with permission.

McConnell Center, "U.S. Supreme Court Chief Justice John Roberts," April 18, 2009, speaking at the University of Louisville, used with permission.

Dbking's photostream, www.flickr.com, "U.S. Supreme Court," 2004, used with permission.

Harris & Ewing, "U.S. Supreme Court Courtroom," Library of Congress.

Chapter 6: Language

Bruce Ching, *Things in Threes—Utilizing Tricolons—a Linguistic Look*, The Law Teacher 18 (Fall 2008). Reprinted with permission.

Shayla M. Gladney, "Shhh," March 7, 2012, used with permission.

Harris & Ewing, "Justice Benjamin Cardozo," Library of Congress.

Hopeandmegan's photostream, www.flickr.com, "Bong Hits 4 Jesus," July 4, 2007, used with permission.

"Make-Up Artist," 1961, Library of Congress.

Bret Rappaport, *Using the Elements of Rhythm, Flow, and Tone to Create a More Effective and Persuasive Acoustic Experience in Legal Writing*, 16 J. Legal Writing 65 (2010). Reprinted with permission.

Stephen E. Smith, *The Poetry of Persuasion: Early Literary Theory and Its Advice to Legal Writers*, 6 J. ALWD 55 (Fall 2009). Reprinted with permission.

Chapter 7: Tone

George Eastman House, "O.W. Holmes," July 31, 2008, Library of Congress.

Elizabeth Fajans & Mary R. Falk, *Shooting from the Lip: United States v. Dickerson, Role [Im]morality, and the Ethics of Legal Rhetoric*, 23 U. Haw. L. Rev. 1 (2000-2001). Reprinted with permission.

Learned Hand, circa 1900-1915, Library of Congress.

Stephen Masker, "Supreme Court Justice Antonin Scalia," 2010, used with permission.

Andrea McArdle, *Teaching Writing in Clinical Lawyering and Legal Writing Courses: Negotiating Professional and Personal Voice*, 12 Clinical L. Rev. 501, 510-514 (2005-2006). Reprinted with permission.

Bret Rappaport, *Using the Elements of Rhythm, Flow, and Tone to Create a More Effective and Persuasive Acoustic Experience in Legal Writing*, 16 J. Legal Writing 65, 99-107 (2010). Reprinted with permission.

Chapter 8: Freedom and Form

James R. Elkins, *What Kind of Story Is Legal Writing?*, 20 Legal Studies Forum 95-135 (1996). Reprinted with permission.

Shayla M. Gladney, "I Will Follow IRAC," March 7, 2012, used with permission.

Teresa Godwin Phelps, *Tradition, Discipline, and Creativity: Developing "Strong Poets" In Legal Writing*, 20 Legal Stud. Forum 89 (1996). Reprinted with permission.

Statue, photo provided by the William S. Boyd School of Law, University of Nevada, Las Vegas, used with permission.

Chapter 9: Order

Shayla M. Gladney, "Foot in the Door," March 7, 2012, used with permission.

Kathryn M. Stanchi, *The Science of Persuasion: An Initial Exploration*, 2006 Mich. St. L. Rev. 411 (2006). Reprinted with permission.

Chapter 10: Involvement

Brandon C. Diaz, "Three Kinds of Involvement," March 20, 2012, used with permission.

Carol M. Highsmith, "Oil Rigs, Galveston, Texas," Library of Congress.

Oleg.Skl's photostream, www.flickr.com, "Skepticism?," Nov. 20. 2009, used with permission.

Kathryn M. Stanchi, *The Science of Persuasion: An Initial Exploration*, 2006 Mich. St. L. Rev. 411 (2006). Reprinted with permission.

Aidan Whiteley, "Uninvolved," Oct. 12, 2009, used with permission.

Chapter 11: Emotion

Terry A. Maroney, *The Persistent Cultural Script of Judicial Dispassion,* 99 Cal. L. Rev. 629 (2011). Reprinted with permission.

Stephen Masker, "Supreme Court Justice Antonin Scalia," 2010, used with permission.

Talk Radio News Services photostream, www.flickr.com, "Supreme Court Nominee Sonia Sotomayor," July 13, 2009, used with permission.

John Valery White, "Contrasting Emotions," provided by the William S. Boyd School of Law, University of Nevada, Las Vegas, used by permission.

Chapter 12: Disagreeing

AJC1's photostream, www.flickr.com, "Influenza Vaccination," April 28, 2009, used with permission.

Mark DeForrest, *Introducing Persuasive Legal Argument Via The Letter From A Birmingham Jail,* 15 J. Legal Writ. 109 (2009). Reprinted with permission.

Carol M. Highsmith, Statue of Policeman and Dog, Library of Congress.

Warren K. Leffler, "Martin Luther King, Jr.," Library of Congress.

Thomas J. O'Halloran, Civil Rights March 1963, Library of Congress.

Melvin Schlubman, "Disagrees," July 26, 2010, used with permission.

Jan Smith, "Through the Window," Feb. 25, 2011, used with permission.

Kathryn M. Stanchi, *Playing With Fire: The Science of Confronting Adverse Material in Legal Advocacy*, 60 Rutgers L. Rev. 381 (2008). Reprinted with permission.

Chapter 13: Legal Theory

401K's photostream, www.flickr.com, "Money," Nov. 8, 2011, used with permission.

Brandon C. Diaz, "Realism," March 20, 2012, used with permission.

Linda H. Edwards, Legal Writing and Analysis 227-243 (3d ed., Aspen Publishers 2011). Reprinted with permission.

Shayla M. Gladney, "Rule Book," March 7, 2012, used with permission.

Harris & Ewing, Louis Brandeis, Library of Congress.

Aaron Mayes, Photo of Clouds and Sun, 2009, used with permission.

Chapter 14: Constitutions

Ian C. Bartrum, *The Modalities of Constitutional Argument: A Primer.* Printed with permission.

Conducting, photo provided by the University of Nevada, Las Vegas 2012, used with permission.

Brandon C. Diaz, "Equal Protection," March 20, 2012, used with permission.

Ian Gallacher, *Conducting the Constitution: Justice Scalia, Textualism, and the Eroica Symphony*, 9 Vand. J. Entertainment & Tech. Law 301 (2006). Reprinted with permission.

Noaman's photostream (Flickr), "One Person, One Vote, One State," July 22, 2006.J Valas Images, "No Taxation Without Representation," Aug. 27, 2010, used with permission.

Justin Valas, "No Taxation Without Representation," 2010, used with permission.

Chapter 15: Categories

Bridge, photo provided by the William S. Boyd School of Law, University of Nevada, Las Vegas, used by permission.

Brandon C. Diaz, "Box," March 20, 2012, used with permission.

Brandon C. Diaz, "Journey," March 20, 2012, used with permission.

Adam Foster, "Cute Penguin Couple," Nov. 8, 2009, used with permission.

Mark L. Johnson, *Mind, Metaphor, and Law*, 58 Mercer L. Rev. 845 (2007). Reprinted with permission.

Karl Llewellyn, Used courtesy of The University of Chicago Law School.

Barbara Miers, "Sure Sign of Spring," March 4, 2012, used with permission.

Chapter 16: Metaphor

Linda Berger, *What Is the Sound of a Corporation Speaking? How the Cognitive Theory of Metaphor Can Help Lawyers Shape the Law*, 2 J. ALWD 169 (Fall 2004). Reprinted with permission.

Timothy Boyd, "Coffee," June 10, 2005, used with permission.

Lucille A. Jewel, *Through a Glass Darkly: Using Brain Science and Visual Rhetoric to Gain a Professional Perspective on Visual Advocacy*, 19 So. Cal. Interdisciplinary L. J. 237, 263 (2010). Reprinted with permission.

Carol Parker, *The Perfect Storm, the Perfect Culprit: How a Metaphor of Fate Figures in Judicial Opinions*, 43 McGeorge L. Rev. _____ (2011). Reprinted with permission.

The Perfect Storm © Warner Bros., a division of Time Warner Entertainment Company, L.P. All Rights Reserved. Used by permission.

Nalini Prasanna, "Pencil Art," May 4, 2007, used with permission.

Markus Ram, "Ice-Cold Gin and Tonic," July 19, 2010, used with permission.

Robert Sapolsky, "This is Your Brain on Metaphors," From the New York Times 11/15/2010. © 2010 The New York Times. All rights reserved. Used by permission and protected by the Copyright Laws of the United States. The printing, copying, redistribution, or retransmission of this Content without express written permission is prohibited.

Gary and Anna Sattler, "Homemade Cleaning Wipe Supplies," Aug. 17, 2007, used with permission.

Jerry Wong, "Cockroach," Oct. 14, 2009, used with permission.

Chapter 17: Storytelling

Kenneth D. Chestek, *Judging by the Numbers: An Empirical Study of the Power of Story*, 7 J. ALWD 1, 10-22 (2010). Reprinted with permission.

Brandon C. Diaz, "Side-shadowing," March 20, 2012, used with permission.

Linda H. Edwards, *The Convergence of Analogical and Dialectic Imaginations in Legal Discourse*, 20 Legal Studies Forum 7, 20-27 (1996). Reprinted with permission.

Philip N. Meyer, *Vignettes from a Narrative Primer*, 12 Leg. Writing 229, 229-230 (2006). Reprinted with permission.

Jennifer Sheppard, *Once Upon a Time, Happily Ever After, and in a Galaxy Far, Far Away: Using Narrative to Fill the Cognitive Gap Left by Overreliance on Pure Logic in Appellate Briefs and Motion Memoranda*, 46 Willamette L. Rev. 255, 259-263 (2009-2010). Reprinted with permission.

Chapter 18: Clients' Stories

Franck Chicot, "Once Upon a Time ... ," June 14, 2008, used with permission.

Brandon C. Diaz, "Plot," March 20, 2012, used with permission.

EpSos.de's photostream (Flickr), "Lifesize Religious King Statue with Spear," Dec. 2, 2009, used with permission.

Harris & Ewing, "Tornado," Library of Congress.

Philip N. Meyer, *Vignettes from a Narrative Primer*, 12 Leg. Writing 229, 241, 250-251, (2006). Reprinted with permission.

Ruth Anne Robbins, *Harry Potter, Ruby Slippers, and Merlin: Telling the Client's Story Using the Characters and Paradigm of the Archetypal Hero's Journey*, 29 Seattle L. Rev. 767 (Summer 2006). Reprinted with permission.

Chapter 19: Law's Stories

Daniel Carter Beard, "Tilting at Modern Man," Library of Congress.

Construction Scene, photo provided by the University of Nevada, Las Vegas 2012, used with permission.

Linda H. Edwards, *Once Upon a Time in Law: Myth, Metaphor, and Authority*, 77 Tenn. L. Rev. 885 (2010). Reprinted with permission.

David Hoffman, "Late September Road, Maryland," Oct. 28, 2008, used with permission.

John C. McRae, "My Child, My Child!" Library of Congress.

Chapter 20: A Life in the Law

Chris-Havard Berge, "Shaking Hands," June 5, 2010, used with permission.

James Boyd White, *An Old-Fashioned View of the Nature of Law,* 12 Theoretical Inquiries L. 381 (2011). Reprinted with permission.

Wirawat Lian-udom, "Two Businessmen Shaking Hands," Aug. 22, 2006, used with permission.

PART TWO

Chapter 1: *Muller v. Oregon*

Protesters, circa 1909-1923, Library of Congress.

Chapter 2: The Voices Briefs: *Thornburgh*, *Webster*, and *Gonzales*

Lynn M. Paltrow and Marcia Nieman, On the Steps of the Court, 1985, used with permission.

Chapter 3: *Brown v. Board of Education*

Justice Thurgood Marshall, Library of Congress, 1976.

Travis S.'s photostream, www.flickr.com, "Desegregation," March 26, 2011, used with permission.

John Valery White, "*Brown v. Board of Education*," 2012, printed with permission.

Chapter 4: *Loving v. Virginia*

Stanzak's photostream. www.flickr.com, "Loving," May 6, 2008, used with permission.

John Valery White, "*Loving v. Virginia*," 2012, printed with permission.

Chapter 5: *Hernandez v. Texas*

Elvert Barnes, "06.Juror.SW.WDC.24feb06'" Feb. 26, 2006, used with permission.

Charles R. Calleros, "*Hernandez v. Texas:* A Milepost on the Road to Civil Rights for Latinos," 2012, printed with permission.

Sarita Kenedy East Law Library, St. Mary's University, San Antonio, Texas, "Carlos Cadena."

Chapter 6: *Meritor Savings Bank v. Vinson*

Catharine MacKinnon (photo provided by and used with permission of Professor MacKinnon 2012).

Ann C. McGinley, "*Meritor Savings Bank v. Vinson,*" 2012, printed with permission.

Chapter 7: *Griswold v. Connecticut* and *Eisenstadt v. Baird*

Brizzle born and brd's photostream, www.flickr.com, "London at War—Birth Control," circa 2941, used with permission.

Library of Congress's photostream, www.flickr.com, Margaret Sanger, circa 1910.

Kathryn M. Stanchi, "Introduction to *Griswold v. Connecticut* and *Eisenstadt v. Baird,*" 2012, printed with permission.

The U.S. Food and Drug Administration's photostream, www.flickr.com, "Recalled—Oral Contraceptives," Feb. 1, 2012, used with permission.

We News's photostream, www.flickr.com, "Planned Parenthood," Feb. 26, 2011, used with permission.

Chapter 8: *Bowers v. Hardwick* and *Lawrence v. Texas*

Carlos A. Ball, "LGBT People and the Constitution: *Bowers v. Hardwick* and *Lawrence v. Texas,*" 2012, printed with permission.

Barack Obama's photostream, www.flickr.com, "Laurence Tribe in Des Moines, IA," Nov. 19, 2007, used by permission.

Quinn Dombrowski, "Holding Hands," May 28, 2009, used with permission.

Michael Hayes, "Bedroom Door," Feb. 7, 2007, used by permission.

Holy Outlaw's photostream, www.flickr.com, "Gay Rights," May 12, 2006, used with permission.

Kathleen Sullivan, photo furnished by Professor Sullivan and the Stanford Law School 2012.

Chapter 9: *Miranda v. Arizona*

Shayla M. Gladney, "Interrogation Room 2," March 7, 2012, used with permission.

Gary L. Stuart, "*Miranda v. Arizona*: The Story of America's Right to Remain Silent," 2012, printed with permission.

Vectorportal's photostream, www.flickr.com, "Hands Behind Prison Bars Vector Art," March 18, 2011, used with permission.

Chapter 10: *Gideon v. Wainwright*

Abe Fortas, photo by Marion S. Trikosko, Library of Congress 1965.

Penny J. White, Introduction to *Gideon v. Wainwright*, 2012, used with permission.

Chapter 11: *Furman v. Georgia* and *Roper v. Simmons*

Ken_Mayer's photostream, www.flickr.com, "Prison Bars" (and empty bed), Dec. 25, 2006, used with permission.

Sean D. O'Brien, "Introduction to *Furman v. Georgia* and *Roper v. Simmons*," 2012, printed with permission.

PART ONE

Readings in Persuasion

Ourselves

This first section focuses on ourselves as writers. Writing—any kind of writing—is a profoundly personal activity. That is part of why a course in writing can be so difficult. It can feel like someone (usually a teacher) is intruding into your own very personal space.

These first two chapters include thoughts of some veteran legal writing professors reflecting on the work they have been doing with generations of law students. You may be surprised to see that some of these reflections question the foundations of that work, raising a paradox that may have troubled you as well. But the reflections also provide a look at the Self behind the computer screen and offer some helpful thoughts about reclaiming your own writing.

1. *Imagination*

"I was always my own teacher."

—Eudora Welty

"I don't think good huffing and puffing can be taught."

Not long ago, you were a beginning law student. You took the introductory courses in legal writing and first encountered a new discourse community—one peopled by lawyers, judges, and, of course, law professors. Those early courses gave you a basic introduction to how to read cases and statutes; how lawyers reason and persuade; how briefs are divided into sections and what those sections usually contain; how a traditional legal argument is structured; how to use authority. They gave you the foundation for becoming a competent legal writer, so in an important sense, good legal writing can be (and is) taught.

But now you are ready to move from being a novice to taking the first steps toward true expertise. That expertise will come, in part, from deepening your knowledge of such important topics as rhetoric, voice, tone, readers, emotion, categories, metaphor, and narrative. The academic principles of that deepened knowledge can be taught, and hopefully you will begin that study in this course. But only you can learn to use those concepts in your own writing. In that sense, good legal writing cannot be taught by someone else. The responsibility for becoming an expert is your own.

With expertise, you earn the freedom to make more choices about how you write, what arguments you'll make, and how you'll put together a persuasive document. And with that freedom comes the chance to be more creative and to refine your own professional voice. The more skilled you become, the more your writing style will be uniquely your own. The more skilled you become, therefore, the more responsibility you will be taking for your own writing. This book invites you to take the first steps toward true expertise and to exercise the responsibility and judgment that true expertise requires.

The freedom and responsibility that come with true expertise may sound daunting, but don't be discouraged. As Steven Winter has written, "Most of us were brought up to believe that we spoke prose and that poetry, creativity, metaphor, and the like were special gifts. One of the truly wonderful aspects of the recent developments in cognitive theory is the democratization of imagination, the discovery, in Alasdair MacIntyre's words, of 'that part of the ability of every language-user which is poetic.'"[1]

> "Imagination is more important than knowledge."
> —Albert Einstein

To begin our journey deeper into the world of legal persuasion, here are short excerpts from articles by two very experienced legal writing professors sharing their thoughts about the kind of creativity and imagination that seems to be missing from much of traditional legal education. We will need this creativity and imagination if we are to become experts at legal persuasion. You may notice that both of these authors quote Professor James Boyd White, one of the most influential law professors of the modern era. We will hear from Professor White again in Chapter 3 and return to him in the final chapter of this book, as he reflects on a well-lived life in the law.

Excerpt from

Carol Parker, *A Liberal Education in Law: Engaging the Legal Imagination Through Research and Writing Beyond the Curriculum*

1 J. ALWD 130 (Fall 2002)

In his essay, *Doctrine in a Vacuum*, James Boyd White describes a bleak vision of . . . law school after the first year:

> The case method . . . is likely to be seen no longer as a method of exploration and dialectic, a technique for discovering what is problematic in the law or in life, but as a way of distancing oneself from that—a way of reducing experience to the level of the Gilbert's Outline. The implied contract between the student and teacher shifts its focus: [the teacher's] insistence to the student, "You are responsible for these texts as you have never been responsible for anything in your lives," all too frequently becomes the acceptance of a

correlative, "and responsible for nothing else in the world." The focus on discrete texts, which is the key to the concentration of attention in the first year, thus becomes a focus on doctrine in a vacuum. . . . The [course is reduced] to the black-letter law, either through the hornbook or the more laborious method of reading the cases, or to the application of a theory; the teacher cannot prevent it, and his examination in any event often seems to ask for nothing that a bright student cannot provide on the basis of hornbook reading.

Does this description of legal education match your experience?

Law school on such terms trivializes law and education alike. The traditional casebook . . . presents severely edited opinions as if they were all that one needed to know, and often does the same with other writers as well—a paragraph each from Bentham, Kant, and Plato, for example. The whole thing feels to some like a charade, a complex way of doing something that is at heart rather simple and unimportant. . . . Legal education seems no longer to be learning to think like a lawyer but learning to think like a bar exam.[2]

The vision of lawyers trained to think like bar exams in turn trivializes legal thought so as to suggest one (or both) of the stock caricatures of the nature of law: (1) that law is simply the mechanical application of rules; and (2) that law is simply the vehicle for the exercise of power by the powerful. If those statements do not define our sense of the nature of law and legal thought, then the passage must raise the question, "How do lawyers think—or how do we hope they think?"

An answer may be glimpsed in Professor White's idealized version of a graduate course in British nineteenth-century history, offered in contrast to the specter of law school at its worst. In this history class, the professor

would not assume that everything that counted would be said or referred to—"covered"—in class, but rather that the class would treat a set of questions, chosen for their interest and importance, as examples of the historical mind at work. The students would be assumed to know much more, and to learn much more, about this period and its history than was ever said in class. Bibliographies too large for anyone to read would be circulated. The idea would be that each student was different; that each was engaged in an educative process for which he was responsible. . . . Such a history course would not teach facts or themes or doctrine in a vacuum: it would take place in a context, partly of the student's making, including his prior reading, his contemporaneous reading and independent thought, and his imagined future intellectual life.[3]

If we [students and teachers alike] were to so conceive a law school class, what questions might we choose "for their interest and importance" to exemplify the *legal* mind at work? How does it work? If the sort of individual engagement in learning envisioned in that history class—the ability to "ask questions that will generate new material; and the capacity to organize it all in new ways"[4]—is what legal education seeks to foster, then [how should we describe that activity? Perhaps we should say,] not lightly but quite seriously . . . : Use your imagination.

Each word in that short sentence is essential to its message. First, "imagination" represents a conception of legal thought that not only animates White's writings but also finds support in cognitive theory. Second, the word "use" states an educational imperative that practice is the path a novice must travel in seeking expertise. And finally, "your" recognizes the unique contribution that each [of us] can make to the cultural enterprise—which is the core premise of liberal education, that is, an education that seeks to develop [our] individual capacities. Those words offer a lens through which to envision a curriculum, in Professor White's words, not as "professional training alone but as the education of the individual mind."[5]

In this next excerpt, Professor Molly Falk struggles with a fundamental question about legal education: how to find a place for the kind of imagination Professor Parker just described. Let's see what Professor Falk has to say here. We will return to this topic again, in another context, in Chapter 8.

Excerpt from

Mary R. Falk, *"The Play of Those Who Have Not Yet Heard of Games": Creativity, Compliance, and the "Good Enough" Law Teacher*
6 J. ALWD 200 (Fall 2009)

Every year, a colleague and I choose four students from the top 10% of our law school's third-year students. Our job is to supervise them as they create the appellate record and bench brief for the moot court competition that our school hosts each spring. Their job is to create a larger-than-life hypothetical that gives rise to novel legal issues that call for novel arguments—in essence, to play, to make believe. Mainly, they can't, they have lost the knack of play. They are baffled by this change in the rules, this abolition of rules. "But there are no cases on point," they object patiently to our proffered suggestions, or "all but one of the circuits reject that argument," or "no court has ever so held." After a while, they get into the spirit of the enterprise to the extent of playing with narrative, creating fact patterns based on highly inventive wrongdoing. But playing with ideas comes harder to these very smart authority junkies, and that's a shame, because it's through play that we find creative solutions and new directions.

Some lawyers come to playing with ideas on their own, those who love thinking about the law. And some learn through mentors or in the process of writing a law review note or moot court brief or working in a clinic. But if there is creative thinking out there in the law offices and courts of our country, it is present not, in the main, because law school does a good job of teaching that skill. Not surprisingly, employers of new law graduates believe [that law school] could be doing a better job of turning out creative thinkers.

I'm all the more distressed by my third-year students' fear of flying because as a teacher of basic legal skills to first-year students, I reward obedience to the rules with A's and I sanction non-compliance with lower grades. I have done so now for almost twenty years. In approximately the words of Pogo Possum, I have met the enemy, and I am it.[6] Worse still, I have known it for a long time.

Does it surprise you to hear this veteran professor's critique of a lifetime of her own work?

I used to tell myself that my strictness is mitigated by the freewheeling Socratic dialogue in my students' doctrinal courses, but I'm less sure about this than I used to be. I have also told myself—and this is probably true—that without a substantial knowledge base and without traditional analytical skills, it is difficult . . . to think useful new thoughts about the law. It is also true, however, that once these skills are mastered, they in fact may master the student or lawyer, who finds it nearly impossible to think creatively and critically about the law, to have new ideas about it.

To some extent, the solution to this problem lies in recognizing it, in communicating candidly to [my] students the paradoxical nature of an education that threatens to destroy their ability to engage in the very activity it should prepare them for. Surely, a competent lawyer must be able to recognize, tolerate, and even thrive on paradox. But is notice enough? Do [law teachers] have a responsibility to do more . . . ? If so, what would that "more" look like?

These are problems that I have been thinking about and writing about these past 15 years—all the while teaching [my] students in their first year to toe the intellectual line and then trying to convince them as upper-class students to think new thoughts about the law. Recently, I've been led to consider these issues in a different light. That light is cast for me by the work of developmental psychoanalyst D.W. Winnicott.

The article then introduces some concepts from Winnicott, especially the term "good enough mother." Surprisingly, Winnicott does not mean something like "good enough to get by." The standard is, instead, quite high, with a key characteristic being the quality of knowing when and how much to leave the child alone, thus encouraging development without causing trauma. Winnicott applied this quality to the relationship between psychotherapist and patient, advocating the "good enough therapist."

Professor Falk's article then considers how this key quality might apply to the process of transitioning from novice to expert legal writer. The process should provide "a safe space in which opposites are always in equilibrium—insecurity with reassurance, new with familiar, paradox with certainty."[7] It should provide a place for risk-taking, uncertainty, and temporarily forgoing control, but it also should provide a good mix of passion, challenge, toughness, and empathy. Then the article ties the idea of the "good enough law professor" to another concept from Winnicott, the idea of play.

"The Play of Those Who Have Not Yet Heard of Games"

The notion of "good enough" and its implications for law teaching and lawyering initially led me to Winnicott, but as I read him and some of his commentators, I was equally drawn to his understanding of play and playing. Winnicott came to believe that healthy individuals develop in infancy through play. . . .

"Play" in Winnicott's sense is an inventive "free play" of ideas and feelings engaging the whole individual—it is emphatically not playing games with rules or conventions; thus, he calls it "the play of those who have not yet heard of games."[8] Playing is first and foremost a mental state: "To get the idea of playing, it is helpful to think of the *preoccupation* that characterizes the playing of young children. The content does not matter. What matters is the near withdrawal state, akin to the *concentration* of older children and adults."[9] Play takes an infinite number of forms. Winnicott's examples include a two-year-old child using a piece of string in different ways and an adult connecting random passages of poetry.

Winnicott saw play as a lifelong necessity of the healthy and creative individual. "It is in playing and only in playing that the individual child or adult is able to be creative and to use the whole personality, and it is only in playing that the individual discovers the self."[10]

For Winnicott, play in this sense is the ground of both culture and creativity. Just as the transitional object exists between the me and the not-me and play is experienced in the potential space between inner psychic and external reality, so creativity exists between originality and tradition. "The potential space between baby and mother, between child and family, between the individual and society or the world . . . can be looked upon as sacred to the individual in that it is here that the individual experiences creative living."[11] Importantly, Winnicott's notion of creativity is not that of "successful or acclaimed creation," but rather, "a coloring of the whole attitude to external reality."[12]

"The thing about writers that people don't realize is that a lot of what they do is play. You know, playing around. That doesn't mean that it isn't serious or that it doesn't have a serious meaning or a serious intention."
—*Margaret Atwood*

Here, the article summarizes thoughts from Barbara Stark, professor of law at Hofstra, in *The Practice of Law as Play*.[13] Professor Stark notes that the lack of play in law school can interfere with the ability to maintain paradox, one of the most important of all lawyering skills. Stark writes that the law "draws on deeply rooted values ... but at the same time, each case exposes more ... ambiguity. Each lawyer argues that resolution of that ambiguity in her client's favor is required by the same deeply rooted values ... relied on by the other lawyer to support the opposite conclusion.... The lawyer unable to maintain paradox is unable ... to truly grasp the law."[14]

"To control what is outside, one has to do things, not simply to think or to wish, and doing things takes time. Playing is doing."
—*D.W. Winnicott*

Stark has found that, once in practice, lawyers may discover that law practice offers—even demands—possibilities for play.[15] Stark is thinking of lawyers "who put in long hours because they love what they do—because practicing law gives them the kind of profound satisfaction they once knew as children deeply immersed in play. They like winning cases and making money, of course, but for them practice itself is rewarding—not always, but enough of the time for them to feel lucky in their choice of work."[16] As Falk explains, they may find their time for play in "a quiet hour alone in the office, back from court or at the end of the day. It can be a solitary walk or run, a museum visit, or even a long shower."[17]

Stark's two examples of lawyer play are role playing and storytelling. Good lawyers role play in order to understand the "motivations, interests, and perspectives" of the parties, of opposing counsel, of the court, "to negotiate the terrain between these multiple realities."[18]

> It is an internal, intermittent exploration, over the course of the case. ... Like a child at play, the lawyer conjures up other selves. ... The lawyer adept at this sort of play is the lawyer whose deep, sometimes startling insights often provide the key to intractable disputes.[19]

Storytelling is another form of play that good lawyers engage in, finding the core narrative that will inform their work on a case.

> A litigator ... must shape the facts into a coherent and compelling story. She must transform mountains of documents—or, conversely, a bare record—into a story that rings true, that accounts for the facts, and that is amply supported by them. The story must be flexible enough to accommodate new facts as the case unfolds, but firm enough to resist an adversary's attempt to turn it against her client. ... [T]he stories emerge as the case evolves, shifting and changing as new facts are discovered and new theories considered.[20]

In addition to Stark's two related examples of role play and storytelling, I would add another important form of play in which creative practitioners engage—play in which ideas rather than plot and characters are manipulated at will. Anything can be analogized or contrasted or equated to anything. Boundaries—between civil and criminal, between law and economics—dissolve. There is no one to disapprove, to note dismissively that no court has ever so held. With no responsibility to espouse one idea, the lawyer can play flirtatiously with many.[21]

Compliance: "Caught Up in the Creativity of Someone Else, or of a Machine"

There is no quarreling with Stark's conclusion that traditional methods of teaching law, and, indeed, the very enterprise of legal education itself, militate against play. Even though she also is correct that some lawyers and law students will nevertheless always find ways to play in Winnicott's sense, I think it would be selling [law] students and [the] profession short to accept . . . that three years of studying the law will be an almost entirely play-free zone.

The impetus for this conviction came as I continued to read Winnicott, and particularly, from his description of what happens when individuals are deprived of play; without play, life is compliance. Indeed, for Winnicott, "the opposite of play is not work, but coercion."[22] He believed that play was necessary to healthy development, that without play, infants tended to become compliant, unhappy individuals. Indeed, Winnicott believed that play was necessary for the development of the individual's "true self," and that play deprivation fostered the dominance of a compliant "false self." Without play, there is no "creative apperception" of reality, only rote, often sullen, obedience to the authority of what is.

> It is creative apperception more than anything else that makes the individual feel that life is worth living. Contrasted with this is a relation to external reality which is one of compliance. . . . Compliance carries with it a sense of futility for the individual and is associated with the idea that nothing matters. . . . In a tantalizing way, many individuals have experienced just enough of creative living to recognize that for most of their time they are living uncreatively, as if caught up in the creativity of someone else, or of a machine.[23]

In brief, Winnicott's "theory includes a belief that living creatively is a healthy state, and that compliance is a sick basis for life."[24] Believing as he did that play was a life-long necessity, Winnicott was convinced that its absence had negative implications not just for individuals, but for society as well. . . .

James Boyd White has explored this connection between intellectual compliance, or as he puts it, "acquiescence," and inauthentic legal writing. "[M]ore fully than we should wish," he writes, our minds are "full of a repertoire of standard moves, received ideas and images, ways of thinking and writing . . . acquired by imitation from those whose approval matters."[25] He goes on to say that "[t]he temptations of acquiescence are present whenever we speak or write; resisting them means the struggle to emerge as a mind saying something true or real or valuable, something you can really mean, in the law and in the rest of life."[26] Acquiescent writing is "conclusory writing, cast in terms that bury argument and thought in one's premises, reducing it all to a set of unargued assertions."[27] In contrast,

> [t]he key element present in good legal writing, missing in bad legal writing, is a certain kind of life: the life of the mind, of thought and argument, that is generated by the recognition that we live in a world in which there are many valid things to say, many points of view, with which it is the task of the legal mind to come to terms.[28]

The "life of the mind" that White describes sounds much like play in Winnicott's sense—there are no rules, no authority figures to please, just the writer playing with multiple perspectives in the potential space between psychic reality and external reality. In the introduction to one of his most original papers, Winnicott thus describes his own writing process.

> I shall not first give an historical survey and show the development of my ideas from the theories of others, because my mind does not work that way. What happens is that I gather this and that, here and there, settle down to clinical experience, form my own theories, and then, last of all, interest myself to see where I stole what. Perhaps this is as good a method as any.[29]

In short, Winnicott resisted White's "temptations of acquiescence." He played with ideas, "gathering this and that," integrating new experiences into older ideas and coming up with fresh theses— and when he was done, he acknowledged his debts. In *Playing and Reality*, Winnicott notes that the "interplay between originality and the acceptance of tradition [i]s the basis of inventiveness" and that "in any cultural field *it is not possible to be original except on a basis of tradition.* Conversely, no one in the line of cultural contributors repeats except as a deliberate quotation, and the unforgivable sin in the cultural field is plagiarism."[30] Thus, it is in the potential space between psychic and outer reality that the playing mind of the writer manipulates originality and tradition to create fresh ideas and resist the temptation of acquiescence.

Discussion Questions

1. Do you notice an undercurrent of revolution in these readings? Is it a little rebellious to use our imaginations? What are we rebelling against and why?

2. When you began law school, did you feel like you were, in Winnicott's words, "caught up in the creativity of someone else, or of a machine"? Do you still?

3. Professor Falk describes talented law students who protest "no court has ever so held." Can a lawyer make an argument with no citation to authority?

4. The Falk excerpt quotes James Boyd White speaking of resisting the imposition of rules and the tyranny of authority figures. But lawyers must write for judges. How can we learn to "play" as we write and still hope that our final written product will persuade a particular judge?

5. Notice how personal these readings are. Is good persuasion as much about a lawyer's own self as about ideas and strategies? In his fascinating book, *Win Your Case*,[31] Gerry Spence begins with a section titled "Gathering the Power to Win."[32] Chapters in that section include "The Power of Discovering the Self," "The Indomitable Power of Our Uniqueness," and "The Power of Fear—Ours and Theirs." Spence says, "After fifty years . . . I've learned one thing for certain: *It all begins with the person, with who each of us is.*"[33] Has law school encouraged you to learn more about yourself? Should it? How?

Endnotes

1. Steven L. Winter, *A Clearing in the Forest: Law, Life, and Mind* 21 (U. Chi. Press 2003) (quoting Alasdair MacIntyre, *Whose Justice? Which Rationality?* 382 (Notre Dame U. Press 1988)).

2. James Boyd White, *Doctrine in a Vacuum*, in *From Expectation to Experience: Essays on Law and Legal Education* 8, 13-14 (U. Mich. Press 1999). (Note that White cautions that the description is a caricatured view of law school life.)

3. *Id*. at 15-16.

4. *Id*. at 20.

5. *Id*. at 17.

6. In the eponymous comic strip created by Walt Kelly, Pogo famously said (on Earth Day in 1971, referring to polluters), "We have met the enemy and he is us." Kelly derived that pronouncement from his 1952 introduction to *The Pogo Papers*, where he wrote "there is no need to sally forth, for it remains true that those things which make us human are, curiously enough, always close at hand. Resolve, then, that on this very ground, with small flags waving and tiny blasts of tiny trumpets, we shall meet the enemy, and not only may he be ours, he may be us." Mrs. Walt Kelly & Bill Crouch, *The Best of Pogo* 224 (Simon & Schuster 1982).

7. Falk, 6 J. ALWD at 204.

8. D.W. Winnicott, *The Place Where We Live*, in *Playing and Reality* 135 (2d ed., Routledge 2005).

9. Winnicott, *Playing: A Theoretical Statement*, in *Playing and Reality* 69 (emphasis in original).

10. Winnicott, *Playing: Creative Activity and the Search for Self*, in *Playing and Reality* 72-73.

11. *Id*. at 139.

12. Winnicott, *Creativity and Its Origins*, in *Playing and Reality* 87.

13. Barbara Stark, *The Practice of Law as Play*, 30 Ga. L. Rev. 1005 (1996).

14. *Id*. at 1015-1016.

15. *Id*. at 1017.

16. *Id*. at 1005.

17. Falk, 6 J. ALWD at 209, n.44.

18. Stark, 30 Ga. L. Rev. at 1018.

19. *Id.*

20. *Id.* at 1018-1019.

21. One litigator describes this process thus:

Sherlock Holmes solves problems that Scotland Yard cannot when he sits in his armchair and thinks. There are some things we can do to help us think more productively. Just as it is better sometimes to skim than to read, so it is often better to flirt playfully with problems than to obsess upon them. And we need to learn to listen to our intuition . . . [to] our minds trying to communicate something we already dimly sense.

Tom Galbraith, *The Joy of Motion Practice*, 24 Litig. 15, 16-17 (No. 2, 1998).

22. Adam Phillips, *Winnicott* 145 (Harv. U. Press 1988).

23. Winnicott, *Creativity and Its Origins*, in *Playing and Reality* 87.

24. *Id.* at 88.

25. James Boyd White, *Meaning What You Say*, in *Law in the Liberal Arts* 136 (Austin Sarat ed., Cornell U. Press 2004).

26. *Id.* at 137.

27. *Id.* at 124.

28. *Id.*

29. Phillips, *Winnicott* 16 (quoting D.W. Winnicott, *Primitive Emotional Development*, in *Collected Papers: Through Paediatrics to Psycho-Analysis* 1435 (Tavistock 1958)).

30. *Id.* at 134.

31. Gerry Spence, *Win Your Case* (St. Martin's Press 2005).

32. *Id.* at 7.

33. *Id.* at 11.

2. *Voice and Self*

—Peter Elbow[1]

This chapter covers the closely related topics of voice and self. Professor Andrea McArdle defines "voice" as "the combinations of word choice, tone, structure, and syntax, and the unconscious influences contributing to them, that inform and help to distinguish individual writing."[2] While there are a number of other definitions, some of which are contradictory, here is a workable set of definitions for our purposes: "Voice" is what your writing says about who you are. Closely related, "tone" is what your writing says about your attitudes—attitudes toward your audience, your topic, and the parties about whom you are writing. Since tone is best addressed by careful attention to language, we will cover tone in Chapter 7, as part of the section about language.

Our primary question for this chapter is how "voice" relates to "self." What kind of a person are you (or can you be) when you write a brief? In our first reading, Anthony Kronman, Sterling Professor of Law and former Dean of Yale Law School, offers an inspiring vision of the kind of transformation of one's self that can come from submitting to the discipline of the practice of law, with all that it entails.

Excerpt from

Anthony Kronman, *Living in the Law*

54 U. Chi. L. Rev. 835, 873-874

To the question, then, of why one would ever choose to spend a lifetime in the law the following answer might be given. To live *in* the law, rather than *off* it, is to submit to its discipline and to accept its ideals. Among these ideals is the attainment and exercise of good judgment or practical wisdom. To possess good judgment, however, is not merely to possess great learning or intelligence, but to be a person of a certain sort, to have a certain character, as well. It follows that to aim at practical wisdom can never simply be to aim at the appropriation of a skill whose mastery leaves its possessor fundamentally unchanged. To aim at practical wisdom is to aim at a

particular conception of character and at the way of life associated
with it. To the extent one's aim is true the result is likely to be what
Socrates in the *Republic* describes as a turning about of the soul, a
transformation of one's own self, the development of a professional
persona. Unlike some, I do not regard this as a cause for regret or
fear. Instead I see it as a source of pride, for the character that lawyers achieve if they live up to their professional ideals is itself an
accomplishment of value marked by the attainment of a central
human excellence.

Dean Kronman waxes eloquent in this first reading, and there is much truth
to what he says. But the development of a professional voice is a complex
matter, and it can be a delicate negotiation. In fact, it can be fraught with
personal frustration or even profound distress. And it can raise deeper and
potentially problematic systemic questions, as this excerpt from Professor
Stanchi reminds us.

Excerpt from

Kathryn M. Stanchi, *Resistance Is Futile: How Legal Writing Pedagogy Contributes to the Law's Marginalization of Outsider Voices*
103 Dick. L. Rev. 7 (1998-1999)

Language is powerful. It is not only the method by which human
beings communicate, but it also reflects and creates human social
relations. As a reflection of society, language can function as a
marker—as an indicator of the speaker's class, gender, or position
in society. In addition, language [contributes to] the creation and constitution of social relations. Indeed, language has the power to regulate human social relations in subtle ways that are difficult to see. It is a
powerful tool of social conditioning—because language and words
encompass cultural norms and conventions. What does it mean to
act like a "lady"? Is it a sign of rudeness or interest to interrupt someone who is talking? Is the use of a qualifying word or phrase (maybe,
I'm not sure) a way to be more accurate or a sign of weakness?

[Learning] a new language [includes learning] not only a new
vocabulary, but a new culture, with history, rules, customs and conventions. Whether interrupting is a sign of interest or rudeness may
depend on a variety of factors, including the culture of the speaker
and audience, the geographic region, and the interrupter's tone.
To communicate effectively, the speaker must understand the customs and culture of the language. Otherwise, use of the vocabulary,
however accurate, will be ineffective.

In the first year of law school, legal writing is the course dedicated to [learning] to communicate effectively using the language of

law. . . . But, because legal writing pedagogy reflects the biases in legal language (including legal reasoning), its effectiveness in "socializing" law students comes at the price of suppressing the voices of those who have already been historically marginalized by legal language. Law is a species of language that some linguists call a "language of power" or "high language"—a prestigious type of language that must be used if the speaker is to function effectively and to which only the most powerful members of society have access.[3]

Linguists have identified a tension associated with languages of power and those traditionally excluded from them: should the marginalized embrace the language of power, and risk being coopted by it, or reject the language of power and risk not being heard? . . . Of course, the risk of cooption involves more than the loss or compromise of the individual's voice, which itself is no small thing. But, because language is such a powerful social tool, encouraging "socialization" means that legal writing pedagogy is contributing to the suppression of certain unique and valuable voices, cultures and concepts in law, and ensuring that law remains a language of power and privilege. On the other hand, if [writers] are not socialized, have legal writing teachers "set up" already marginalized students to fail in legal practice?

In subsequent passages, Professor Stanchi's article makes the case that legal writing contributes to the marginalization of outsider voices in the law. She shows some of the ways this happens and considers some solutions. Inherent in all of the proposed solutions is the idea that law school should expressly recognize the inherently personal linguistic transition that law study and practice demand and should value and help preserve the more "personal" voices we all brought with us to law school.

The excerpt from Professor Stanchi raises serious questions. Does the requirement to write in a traditional lawyer's voice silence the "real" or "authentic" voices of some writers? Or as Professor Rideout explains in this next excerpt, is the idea of a single "real" self a misunderstanding of both the human psyche and of the writing process?

Excerpt from

J. Christopher Rideout, *Voice, Self, and Persona in Legal Writing*

15 J. Legal Writing 67 (2009)

What Do We Mean by Voice?

[A] survey of recent scholarship on voice . . . finds that the terms "voice" and "self" are still almost automatically linked to a third term, "authentic voice."[4] Voice remains a matter of authentic voice, and of presence in the text, because of the enduring appeal of the idea of the writer as an independent subject, autonomous and unshaped by the text or its discourse conventions. [The survey's author] traces this link to a long-standing tradition in Western humanistic thought, at least since [the] time of the Oracle at Delphi. Central to the Western liberal tradition is a sense of human agency within history: "[T]he Western liberal humanist tradition has accepted belief in a central core of stable, unified, transcendent, even transcultural self, a belief which served as a matrix out of which definitions of citizenship and ethical behavior and creativity are thought to evolve."[5] A writer's voice, even if it is inescapably metaphorical, remains well-anchored in the idea of a real self and in voice as the authentic expression of that self.

Personal Voice and Self Expression

In the contemporary literature, much of the discussion of voice in writing has focused on personal voice, partly because of this continuing link between voice and presence. Voice continues to be seen as a way of asserting the presence of the "real" writer in the text. . . . This school of thought goes back to the 1960s, as part of a shift from product to process approaches to writing instruction and to notions of writing as an act of self-discovery. . . . [A] prominent textbook [of that period] affirms the link between [writing and self:] "The development of an authentic voice is a natural consequence of self-discovery. As you begin to find out who you are

and what you think and to be comfortable with the person you are, you learn to trust your own voice in your writing."[6]

One of the most prominent of the voice advocates has been Peter Elbow, who sees each writer as having his or her own unique voice. In describing that unique voice, Elbow—not surprisingly—uses speech metaphors: "in your natural way of producing words there is a sound, a texture, a rhythm—a voice—which is the main source of power in your writing."[7] The goal for the student writer, and the writing classroom, is to draw this voice out. If the writer can do so, the effect will be to inject a kind of "magic" into that person's writing.[8] The magic comes from an authenticity to writing that has found that resonating voice.[9] By the early 1980s, Elbow had become the leading spokesperson for a movement that links voice to self and that finds "real voice" and "real self" to be almost synonymous.[10]

Because of the link of voice to self and to the expression of that self, this school of writing instruction became known as expressivism. It encouraged writing that "resonates" with the individual, "real" voice of the author, partly because writing like this would be empowering. Voice, in writing, was an engaged personal voice. . . .

Expressivism [, however,] has been subject to critique since the late 1980s or early 1990s, partly because its proponents seemed to inadequately respond to questions like [whether writers writing in the traditional language of a discourse community, like law] have no "real" voice and therefore no self. If voice is linked to self and if [traditional legal writing has no personal] voice, then it follows that such non-personal, non-expressive writing also lacks a self. Certainly in non-expressive prose, like [a legal document], what

we would call the real author is effaced. But that does not mean that the real author is absent, or that the author . . . is not struggling to establish some relationship between himself and the text, and perhaps even to locate himself in that text.

Philosophically, the critics of expressivism point out that the self in an expressivist view is overly simplified. Expressivism seems to presume a stable, unitary, and unchanging self, one that is independent of the discourse and bears no necessary relationship to it. Locating voice in this central self, then, relies upon a false epistemology. The author's self is independent of and prior to the text, and that author can choose—or choose not—to "voice" herself in the text. But perhaps part of this "voicing" occurs, not independently of the text, but through the text itself, and through the discourse in which the text is located.

The article continues here, showing how the language we use for different kinds of writing—that is, language not common in the broad culture— usually did not originate from an autonomous self. Instead, we learned that language from others. When we use that learned language, we are not "voicing" the words (as words from our autonomous self) but rather "revoicing" them from the sources in which we originally encountered that language.

In that sense, the self and voice . . . are "discoursal"—they are a product of the discourse in which that writing is located as much as they are a product of an independent, a priori self. . . . That voice may not be the personal voice allowed by the expressivists, but viewed differently, it is a voice. Given its close relationship to the language of the law, it may be what is meant by professional voice in legal discourse.

Professional Voice and Personal Voice

Although the literature on voice in legal discourse is limited, what literature there is, not surprisingly, discusses voice in terms of a professional voice. In a colloquy on voice in legal discourse, Julius Getman observes that establishing this professional voice is a primary goal of law school. "The great bulk of legal education is devoted to inculcating 'professional voice.' The magical moment at which the 'light dawns' and bewildered first-year students are transformed into lawyers occurs when this voice becomes the student's own."[11] Getman does not use the term "revoicing," but the process that he describes sounds remarkably similar.

Getman lists some of the features of this professional legal voice: it is objective and registers at a high level of generality; its style tends to be formal, erudite, and "old-fashioned"; it contains both terms of art and Latin phrases; and it situates itself at a distance, "as though its user were removed from and slightly above the general concerns of humanity."[12] All of these features entail an erasure of the personal from what we would consider professional voice in the law.

Elizabeth Mertz mentions voice in her discussion of legal language, but she takes her analysis one step further than Getman, tying the features of a professional legal voice such as those of objectivity and generality, above, to what she describes as the underlying epistemology of legal discourse and to the legal persona that emerges from that epistemology[13] [the study of knowledge; how we "know" what we know]. The core trope of most legal discourse, according to Mertz, is that of argument. Accordingly, the legal narratives contained within that trope convert the persons involved in those narratives into "speaking subjects whose primary identity is defined by their location in an argument," or defined by the doctrinal requirements of that argument.[14] The roles of these speaking subjects, or characters, within the argument are narrowly shaped by the limits of the corresponding legal doctrine, and speaking about them requires distance and a stripping away of emotional and moral content. In the role-playing setting of law school, law students in turn internalize the limits of those roles, learning themselves "to speak in the voices of persona defined by the demands of . . . legal discourse."[15] They acquire the professional voice of a lawyer, and doing so is a powerful measure of their success at learning "to be and think like a lawyer."[16]

Both Mertz and Getman acknowledge the importance of acquiring the professional voice of a lawyer, but both also lament the narrowness of that voice. Mertz calls the process "double-edged."[17] She acknowledges that stepping into the legal persona of a lawyer, including its professional voice, can be "liberating" for students in that it allows for a more neutral and objective approach to human conflict. But at the same time, that objectivity can erase some of the more important emotional and moral underpinnings to such conflict.[18] This in turn, can be alienating. In a somewhat cruel twist, the very process of acquiring the voice of a legal professional can also unavoidably alienate the [writer] from some other, more personal voice. . . .

Getman offers a similar analysis . . . [and] adds that this distanced professional voice even detracts from some of the most important activities that lawyers undertake, such as counseling and negotiating.[19] He concludes that legal education, and the law, undervalue what he calls "human voice," a voice that would analyze legal issues using "ordinary concepts" and without "professional

Does Professor Mertz's description of "professional legal voice" ring true, in your experience?

ornamentation."[20] . . . By "human" voice, . . . Getman . . . seems to advocate something more authentic and personal, perhaps akin to the expressivist voice mentioned above. Neither, however, offers a model for capturing this kind of voice within the law and legal discourse.

More recently, Andrea McArdle argues that [legal education should] "preserve some sense of individual voice and ownership of . . . writing." . . .[21] In her view, new law students lose a part of their writing self—the very personal voice that Elbow and others . . . try to inculcate in their student writers. McArdle [advocates using] reflective writing . . . as a way of . . . [maintaining] individuality.[22] . . . I am not sure, however, that [this] methodology fully bridges what I see as an inevitable gap between the more individual voice allowed by expressive or reflective writing and the professional voice that . . . lawyers uniformly adopt in practice. In my view, this gap is difficult and problematic because the different voices that I have discussed so far—personal and professional—emerge, in a sense, from different selves, or different identities. That is, from a certain perspective, it is not just one unitary self that is negotiating back and forth between these personal and professional voices. I would call this perspective "discoursal." . . .

Kathryn Stanchi offers another recent critique of professional legal voice in her article, *Resistance Is Futile*.[23] . . . Stanchi carries her analysis one step further, however, by noting the effects of this assimilation on marginalized groups and "outsider" voices.[24] . . . *[Here Professor Rideout describes the point made in our earlier excerpt from Professor Stanchi.]*

[So far, we have seemed to assume] that a personal voice is a more authentic voice, and therefore of value. By "authentic," at times [the literature seems] to mean "real" or "true," or something that comes from inside. And even when outsider voice is discussed as emerging from the different experiences and values of an outsider group—as being situated differently—it still seems valued in part for being a more personal voice. But so long as authentic voice means personal voice, and vice versa, then any discussion of professional voice in legal discourse will be problematic and, in my view, incomplete. . . . [I]f voice is viewed as a social and discoursal phenomenon, [however,] this dichotomy between professional and personal voice may begin to collapse. . . .

The Social View and Discoursal Voice

[Viewing voice as social and discoursal means that we] view it not as personal or as the expression of an individual, or as coming from within, but rather as social, as coming from outside the writer—from the discourses and the uses of language in which the writer is embedded. . . . In this view, voice in writing is not so much a matter of looking within and trying to express what is there, but rather of trying to control or appropriate the voices that surround the writer in a given writing context. This view, I think, has promise for looking at the voice of legal writers.

In this more social view, voice in writing is intertextual. That is, the language that a writer uses—the words and phrases—do not spring from within, but rather are a "revoicing" of other words and phrases that the writer has encountered. All uses of language are a borrowing from other uses of language, prior uses that the writer has encountered and appropriated for a new writing occasion. In this sense, language becomes "dialogic"—any effort to produce a piece of written discourse is influenced by prior, similar discourses that the writer has encountered and through which those discourses are mediated, as well as by the immediate context for the writing task. This is by now a well-rehearsed view of language, most usually associated with the work of Mikhail Bakhtin and what is known as "dialogism."[25]

Because most of us are attached to personal, individualistic notions of voice, the social view can be disconcerting at first. . . . In this notion of voice and writing, the individual act of writing and the context in which it takes place are "co-constitutive."[26] Any individual act of writing takes place within a speech genre (e.g., an appellate brief) and a context (e.g., . . . law practice), but the act of writing that individual appellate brief is not merely a rote exercise in creating a typical appellate brief. . . . Rather it is also a situated occasion that generates, along with all the other instances of writing of appellate briefs, the genre of the appellate brief. In Prior's words, in any individual instance of writing, "the person is socialized and the social is personalized."[27] . . .

Under the social view, then, voice includes the personal or the individual, but the personal or individual as redefined. If the individual act of writing and the context in which it takes place are co-constitutive, then the subject at the center of this act (and the voice that metaphorically represents that subject) is also both constituting and constituted. . . . Under this view, the writer's self is discoursal—a product of discourses and discursive practices.

[Thus, the social, discoursal view is distinguished] from the Cartesian, or expressivist accounts of the writer's self—where the self is autonomous and unitary. . . . [*The article here continues discussing a discoursal view of voice and a writer's identity.*]

[The discoursal view is] important for legal writing and voice. . . . [I]t accounts for part of the struggle that [we all] encounter . . . when [we] . . . attempt to "become" a legal writer. That "becoming" is in part an effort . . . to negotiate with the available discoursal voices of legal writing and to construct a new identity—a new self-representation . . . as a legal writer. That self-representation must include the voice of a legal writer, and . . . that voice is largely the product of a discoursal self that must be constructed and then represented.

The article next discusses the concept of a "persona" (roughly, a "role") and the voice of that persona—e.g., a legal writer. Professor Rideout identifies a legal persona, with its own voice, which emerges from a constructed self-representation of the author—a discoursal self-representation.

Professor Rideout's original conclusion was written to legal writing professors, offering advice about how to help their students think about their own voice. With his kind permission, I have revised the conclusion to speak directly to readers of this book.

Conclusion: Inculcating Voice and Persona in Legal Writing

As you become a legal writer, you are, among other things, developing a voice—the voice of a legal writer. This voice is not a personal voice, at least not in the sense in which we commonly understand that term. But to call it a professional voice—the voice of a lawyer—is not to diminish its importance, because in a certain way that professional voice still belongs to you. It represents the legal persona that you have constructed for yourself. In the other types of writing that you did before law school, you have also constructed a persona, although beginning early on in school, you may have constructed a persona that has remained with you for a long time and with which you probably feel very familiar—the persona of student-as-writer. The legal persona you are constructing may be new to you, and it may be more difficult to construct because it is more fully positioned within a particular discourse and because that discourse—legal discourse—can seem overly constraining.

Constructing this legal persona entails a complex negotiation between who you think you "really" are as a writer and how you are learning to position yourself in legal discourse. You may find that this understanding of voice eases the transition into legal writing, especially if your writing experience has been shaped by expressivist assumptions or if your language experience lies outside dominant discourses. The concept of a persona can be useful beyond your legal writing classroom as well. Often, in internships or judicial clerkships, you are expected to write in the style and voice of someone else—a judge or law partner. It may be useful to see that taking on that voice is a matter of adjusting or reshaping your writing persona—but not necessarily of losing your self.

Tying voice to a persona, and to the positioning of that persona, also allows you to sometimes assert an authorial presence—that part of your persona that represents the self-as-author. Insofar as the typified voice of much legal writing requires an effacing of the self-as-author, or a submerging of it to the discoursal self, you probably receive the message that in its objectivity, neutrality, and distance, that voice leaves no room for you. But you are always authorially there in that persona, although not always represented in the voice. And at certain times, the self-as-author can emerge, even if subtly. You will certainly have the occasion to write in legal settings in which you are positioned with more authority, with the ability to assert more authorial presence—in a voice and through a persona that are larger than the merely discoursal. In that sense, you would possess a public voice, not the same as a personal voice but perhaps more engaging than what is commonly meant by professional voice.

Finally, in understanding both that you are acquiring a voice in legal writing and that this voice is tied to a discoursal identity, to a persona, you can understand how your individual writing contributes to the professional voice of the law. Your contribution will not be direct—within a discoursal view, no autobiographical self speaks directly in a text. But the legal persona that you construct can assert an authorial presence through a public voice, one that in turn becomes a small part of the professional voice of the law.

Even the small choices you make about your discoursal identity shape the professional, typified voice of the law. For example, most modern lawyers increasingly choose to avoid blatant legal archaisms. They may do so because someone has taught them to, or because they want their legal prose to be more readable; but I think they also do so because the demographics of the legal profession are changing, and they no longer identify with the stuffiness that legal archaisms lend to both their prose style and the voice of that prose. In much the same way, choices you will make about your discoursal identity contribute as well to the voice of the profession.

Both through these small conceptual changes, then, and in the much larger task of constructing a legal persona, you can understand who you are as you become a legal writer and how that construction entails voice. You may be using the words of the law, but those words are never voiceless. Neither are legal writers.

Part of Professor Rideout's point is that in traditional legal writing, an "authentic" voice is the voice of a professional persona rather than the voice of a stable, unified, transcendent, personal self. If that is true, we may not need to worry quite so much about the personal consequences of adopting a traditional professional voice. But should we stop searching for an "authentic voice," or is there some other meaning for the term "authentic voice" in the context of legal writing? Perhaps we still want our writing to reflect some sense of human personality and agency in the text—to sound alive and interesting, as if a human being wrote it. How might we achieve that kind of "authentically human" voice? In the final excerpt in this chapter, Professor Osbeck helps us answer some of these questions.

Excerpt from

Mark Osbeck, *What Is 'Good Legal Writing' and Why Does It Matter?*
Forthcoming at 4 Drexel L. Rev. _____ (2012)

The writer's *voice* . . . contributes significantly [to producing writing that engages a reader]. If the writing style seems stilted, overly casual, or artificial, the writer's ability to connect with the reader is diminished. . . . Some [writers] seem to emulate the style they see in older cases. . . . [T]he result is writing that is artificial-sounding and lifeless, full of legal jargon and stilted constructions. . . . [I]t sounds "intelligent," but it is ponderous and dense. . . . [It] fails to engage the reader because [it] employs[s] a voice that is not authentic. The writing style comes across as artificial[, lacking] character and individuality. J.B. White, one of the principal figures in the law and literature movement, describes the development of an authentic writer's voice as central to the enterprise of becoming an effective lawyer:

> Law, as you can see, is for me a kind of writing, at its heart less of an interpretive process than a compositional one. The central task of the lawyer from this point of view is to give herself a voice of her own, a voice that at once expresses her own mind at work at its best and as a lawyer, a voice at once individual and professional.[28]

It is difficult to define the concept of voice. Basically, though, it refers to a style that comes naturally to the writer, so that a glimmer of the writer's personality reveals itself through the text. A writer's authentic voice, in other words, lets the reader see that there is a real person behind the document. Consider, for example, Justice Holmes' infamous pronouncement in favor of forced sterilization in *Buck v. Bell*:[29]

> It is better for all the world, if instead of waiting to execute degenerate offspring for crime, or to let them starve for their imbecility, society can prevent those who are manifestly unfit from continuing their kind. The principle that sustains compulsory vaccination is broad enough to cover cutting the Fallopian tubes. Three generations of imbeciles are enough.[30]

The reasoning and result of this decision may be open to question, but is there any question as to its authenticity? Holmes' voice is likely a factor in why only one member the Court dissented from such a dubious holding.

Library of Congress

Justice Oliver Wendell Holmes, Jr.

Of course, in the context of legal writing, individuality is constrained to some extent ... [but] there is room for individuality. And the legal writer who is able to project an authentic voice while still maintaining a professional tone will produce a more engaging style of writing.

Occasionally, as in a work of fiction, the writer may make effective use of a voice that is not the writer's own, but rather a character the writer wants the reader to identify with. Chief Justice Roberts' amusing dissent in *Pennsylvania v. Dunlap*, for example illustrates this technique. There, in reciting the facts, he cleverly employs the point of view as well as the voice of the arresting officer in order to help the reader appreciate the officer's perspective on whether there was probable cause to make an arrest:

> North Philly, May 4, 2001. Officer Sean Devlin, Narcotics Strike Force, was working the morning shift. Undercover surveillance. The neighborhood? Tough as a three-dollar steak. Devlin knew. Five years on the beat, nine months with the Strike Force. He'd made fifteen, twenty drug busts in the neighborhood.
>
> Devlin spotted him: a lone man on the street corner. Another approached. Quick exchange of words. Cash handed over; small objects handed back. Each man then quickly on his own way. Devlin knew the guy wasn't buying bus tokens. He radioed a description and Officer Stein picked up the buyer. Sure enough: three bags of crack in the guy's pocket. Head downtown and book him. Just another day at the office.[31]

For the most part, however, the most effective voice in legal writing is the writer's own. It is not precisely the same as the way the writer would normally speak. But it does reflect a style that comes naturally to the writer, rather than a style that the writer mimics or assumes for effect.

Discussion Questions

1. Professors Anthony Kronman and Kathryn Stanchi seem to agree that the development of a professional persona can be and often is transformative. Professor Kronman sees this transformation "as a source of pride," however, while Professor Stanchi raises concerns about what is or may be lost in the transformation. What do you think about these two positions?
2. Professor Rideout offers what we might call a middle ground. He suggests that there is no such thing as a single "authentic" self. Rather, all "voices" are learned, and each of us has multiple "voices" appropriate for various audiences and contexts. The professional voice of a lawyer (the professional persona) is one of our voices, to be used when we are doing a lawyer's work. But when we develop a lawyer's voice, are we changed in some fundamental way? Do you feel different after a couple of years of law study? If so, how? Have you gained something important? Do you think you are in danger of losing something important?
3. Notice that Professor Osbeck's two engaging examples are both from judicial opinions written by Supreme Court Justices. Do these examples translate to the kind of writing lawyers can do? Are lawyers constrained in ways that judges are not? Or are lawyers actually less constrained than many of them think they are?
4. Imagine the "voices" of the two speakers on pages 18 and 19. Describe what you imagine about those "voices." What effects do you think each voice would have on particular kinds of listeners? What would be appealing about each voice? What would be irritating or otherwise less effective? What does your imagination say about a desirable voice for a brief writer?
5. As you read the briefs we will study, notice the individual differences in the voices of the authors. How would you describe those voices and the writers themselves? How do those voices work for the purposes they are employed to serve? Develop the habit of noticing the voice of each writer you read, so you can become sensitive to the quality of voice in legal writing.

Endnotes

1. Peter Elbow, *Writing with Power: Techniques for Mastering the Writing Process* 287 (Oxford U. Press 1981).
2. Andrea McArdle, *Teaching Writing in Clinical, Lawyering, and Legal Writing Courses: Negotiating Professional and Personal Voice*, 12 Clinical L. Rev. 501, 503 (Spring 2006).
3. Deborah Cameron, *Feminism and Linguistic Theory* 199, 205 (2d ed., Palgrave Macmillan 1992).

4. Randall R. Freisinger, *Voicing the Self: Toward a Pedagogy of Resistance in a Post-modern Age*, in *Voices on Voice: Perspectives, Definitions, Inquiry* 242 (Kathleen Blake Yancey ed., Natl. Council of Teachers of English 1994).

5. *Id*. at 244.

6. Donald C. Stewart, *The Authentic Voice: A Pre-Writing Approach to Student Writing* 2 (W.C. Brown Co. 1972).

7. Peter Elbow, *Writing Without Teachers* 6 (Oxford U. Press 1973).

8. *Id*. at 282.

9. *Id*. at 286.

10. *Id*. at 293.

11. Julius G. Getman, *Colloquy: Human Voice in Legal Discourse: Voices*, 66 Tex. L. Rev. 577, 577 (1988).

12. *Id*. at 578.

13. Elizabeth Mertz, *The Language of Law School: Learning to "Think like a Lawyer"* 97-101 (Oxford U. Press 2007).

14. *Id*. at 100.

15. *Id*. at 126.

16. *Id*. at 127.

17. *Id*. at 101.

18. *Id*. at 133-134.

19. Getman, *Colloquy* 578.

20. *Id*. at 582.

21. Andrea McArdle, *Teaching Writing in Clinical, Lawyering, and Legal Writing Courses: Negotiating Professional and Personal Voice*, 12 Clinical L. Rev. 501, 501 (2006).

22. *Id*. at 520-526, 538-539.

23. Kathryn M. Stanchi, *Resistance Is Futile: How Legal Writing Pedagogy Contributes to the Marginalization of Outsider Voices*, 103 Dick. L. Rev. 7 (1998).

24. *Id*. at 9-10.

25. *See e.g.*, Mikhail Bakhtin, *The Dialogic Imagination: Four Essays* (Michael Holquist ed., Caryl Emerson & Michael Holquist trans., U. Tex. Press 1982), and M.M. Bakhtin, *Speech Genres and Other Late Essays* (Caryl Emerson & Michael Holquist eds., Vern McGee trans., U. Tex. Press 1986).

26. *See* Paul Prior, *Voices in Text, Mind, and Society: Sociohistoric Accounts of Discourse Acquisition and Use*, 10 J. Second Lang. Writing 59, 71 (2001).

27. *Id*. at 72.

28. James Boyd White, *The Legal Imagination* xv (abr. ed., U. Chi. Press 1985).

29. 274 U.S. 200 (1927).

30. *Id*. at 207 (citation omitted).

31. 129 S. Ct. 448, 448 (2008).

Our Heritage

This second section provides an overview of the long and well-established tradition we inhabit when we write a brief. Rhetoric, the art of civic persuasion, became a respected area of study over 2,500 years ago, and principles established by philosophers such as Aristotle, Cicero, and Quintilian constitute the foundation of legal persuasion to this day. We have roots closer in time as well, in the forms of advocacy we inherited from the English legal system. We've made the system our own in some important ways, as the chapters in this section will show, but we still adhere to traditions that harken back to the early days of the nation, as the chapter on "The Court" describes.

3. *Rhetoric*

"The law is not smooth and pure like distilled water. It is instead a wild river, fed by tributaries which arise from myriad wellsprings."

—Wilson Huhn[1]

At heart, a lawyer's job is rhetorical. Becoming an expert in brief-writing is becoming a rhetorician. Every topic in this book is part of the study of rhetoric. If we think of "rhetoric" as the term is commonly misused today, that statement may be alarming. Today, in common usage, the term is thought to mean "a lot of hot air: inane spoken language usurping the place either of silence or of meaningful discourse and indicating some sort of moral fault in the speaker (and perhaps even in the audience), either because the speaker has nothing to say, or wishes to evade the truth. Colloquially, 'bullshit.'"[2]

This understanding of "rhetoric" might describe the facetious huffing and puffing image at the start of Chapter 1, metaphorically picturing lawyers as growling and gesticulating at each other. But "rhetoric" does not imply either untruth or lack of reason. It does not call for overly charged emotional language. What is legal rhetoric, then? Once again, we turn to Professor James Boyd White to begin our inquiry:

Excerpt from
James Boyd White, *Imagining the Law* in *The Rhetoric of Law*
35-36 (Austin Sarat & Thomas R. Kearns eds., U. of Michigan Press 1996)

The lawyer's task is not just to apply rules in a mechanical way, then, but to learn how to think and argue about their meaning, not simply as words but as texts given significance by their context. What the lawyer is to learn in law school is not merely a structure of rules—in fact that is a very small part of what she learns—but how to engage in argument of a certain sort, especially in argument about the meaning of a set of authoritative texts: constitutions, statutes, judicial opinions, regulations, contracts, and any other text that may be called upon as legally authoritative in a case. . . .

For the lawyer, all this is a radically rhetorical process, in precisely the sense in which Aristotle defines the term in his treatise

How to engage in arguments of a certain sort

- Knowing how lawyers and judges think. so that they can learn how to speak w Them effectively.

on rhetoric: It is the art of "finding out the available means of persuasion in a given case." What is to count as a means of persuasion
is to be determined not by "logic" but by knowledge of the relevant
audience and its culture. This too Aristotle knew, and much of his
treatise is devoted to a catalogue of the argumentative claims that
were, in his judgment, effective in his world. The lawyer, therefore,
must learn the ways in which lawyers and judges think, so that he
can speak to them effectively. This is what law school is about.

Next we read an excerpt from Professor Michael Frost, from whom we learn
that rhetoric as an art worthy of study began in the ancient classical worlds
of Greece and Rome. Key components of this ancient study were logos
(logical argument), pathos (appeals to emotion), ethos (the character of
the speaker), context, and audience. As our study progresses, we will see
that all five of these key elements are as relevant to legal persuasion today
as they were in the ancient world.

Excerpt from

Michael Frost, *Introduction to Classical Legal Rhetoric: A Lost Heritage*
8 S. Cal. Interdisc. L.J. 613 (1999)[3]

In 400 A.D. if an ordinary [Greek] citizen of the educated class had a
legal dispute with another citizen, he usually argued his own case
before other [Greek] citizens and did so without the advice or help of
a lawyer. Even so, he analyzed and argued his case with a near-
professional competence and thoroughness. In preparing his case,
he first determined the proper forum for his argument and identified the applicable law. He then determined which facts were most
important, which legal arguments were meritorious, and which
arguments his adversary might use against him. When choosing
his strategies for the trial, he also decided how he would begin,
tell the story of the case, organize his arguments, rebut his
opponent, and close his case. Before actually presenting his arguments, he would carefully evaluate the emotional content of the
case and the reputation of the judges. And finally, he would assess
how his own character and credibility might affect the judges'
responses to his legal arguments. In effect, he was analyzing and
preparing his case in a lawyerly fashion.

In making these preparations, he was not depending solely on
native intelligence or good instincts. Instead, he was relying on a
lengthy, highly structured, formal education in the art of rhetoric
which featured the most comprehensive, adaptable, and practical
analysis of legal discourse ever created. In fact, the art of rhetoric
was originally created as a flexible technique for training advocates

to present cases in Greek and Roman law courts. Moreover, for nearly 1,000 years, the study of rhetoric was at the core of both Greek and Roman education and, in one form or another, has been part of most formal education since that time.

However, in the years since its creation . . . classical rhetoric has continuously transformed itself in response to dozens of social, political, educational, religious, and philosophical forces. In the course of these transformations, rhetoric has lost its close identification with legal discourse. Instead of being regarded as the most coherent and experience-based analysis of legal reasoning, legal methodology, and argumentative strategy ever devised, the term rhetoric is now usually associated with meaningless political exaggeration or mere stylistic embellishment. Although this association is unfair and reductive, it is not [surprising]. Throughout history classical rhetoric has always suffered from misunderstandings concerning its meaning, value, scope, and purpose.

But because classical rhetoric is an adaptable and, above all, a practical discipline, it always manages to survive and re-establish its original identity as an extremely effective tool for analyzing and

Photo by Robin Madden. Used by permission.

Demosthenes

creating legal discourse. In fact, with some adaptations for modern stylistic taste and legal procedures, Greco-Roman rhetorical principles can be applied to modern legal discourse as readily as they have been to legal discourse in any other period.

However, to understand how classical principles apply to modern legal discourse, it is first necessary to understand their original form and how, by virtue of several important historical transformations, these principles are connected to modern rhetorical theories and practice. . . .

Professor Frost here describes the principal features of classical rhetoric and follows its history through the Middle Ages, the Renaissance, the English Neoclassical period, and nineteenth-century America, bringing us to the role of classical rhetoric in twentieth-century America:

Current-traditional rhetoric predominated in the American educational system until the late 1930s and the early 1940s. Then, prompted by student demand for practical training for business contexts, speech departments and English departments began emphasizing a combination of speaking, writing, listening, and reading skills in ways that restored "basic rhetorical principles into composition classrooms."[4] In effect, they were restoring classical coherence and completeness to the teaching of rhetoric. Soon, they returned to the classical texts for inspiration and guidance.

Most modern rhetoricians who draw on the classical texts concentrate on a single topic like "invention" or the discovery of arguments; sometimes they attempt to apply all the classical principles to modern topics. Occasionally, classical rhetoric is used as a starting point for a "new" rhetorical theory loosely based on classical principles. Kenneth Burke, for example, seeks to discover a "generating principle" for discovering the available arguments using a methodology that differs from but echoes the classical topics of invention. Burke's "dramatistic" principle uses five "master terms": Act, Scene, Agent, Agency, Purpose. By systematically employing these terms, a writer or advocate will discover "what is being done (the Act); under what circumstances or in what situation (Scene) the act takes place; what sort of person (Agent) does it; by what means (Agency) he does it, and for what end or Purpose."[5] Burke's "master terms" provide a shorter list, but serve a similar purpose to Cicero's list in *De Inventione* which examines a topic in terms of: name, nature, manner of life, fortune, habit, feeling, interests, purposes, achievements, accidents, and speeches made.

In almost all cases, modern rhetoricians are primarily interested in applying classical rhetorical techniques to meet the many practical requirements of modern discourse. Their applications depend on their theoretical point of view or purpose. . . .

Only rarely, however, do modern rhetoricians or scholars devote much attention to how classical rhetoric applies to modern judicial or legal discourse. One exception is Chaim Perelman, a widely respected, legally trained Belgian philosopher, whose *The Idea of Justice and the Problem of Argument*[6] analyzes judicial uses of legal precedent in order to illuminate connections between classical and modern methods of legal argument. Perelman's *The Idea of Justice* and his *The New Rhetoric: A Treatise on Argumentation*[7] emphasize, in ways that are reminiscent of the classical techniques of legal argument, modes of "nonformal logic which [can] 'induce or increase the mind's adherence to these presented for its assent.'"[8] Perelman's work, however, is a notable departure from the general neglect of the topic of legal discourse.

Despite this neglect, a growing number of modern lawyers, judges, and legal academics have begun employing classical rhetorical principles in their analyses of legal discourse. For example, Robert F. Hanley refers to the classical concepts of *ethos* (an advocate's credibility) and *pathos* (the emotional aspects of a legal argument) when making recommendations regarding courtroom argumentative strategies.[9] In his treatise on legal logic, Ruggero Aldisert examines modern legal arguments using the classical rhetorical concept of enthymetic proofs (an *enthymeme* is a syllogism in which the major premise is only probable, or in which one term is omitted).[10] Richard Posner's treatise on law and literature contains a section on judicial "style as persuasion" in which he states that "it is an open question whether the style of judicial opinions is better studied from the standpoint of linguistics and rhetoric or from that of literary criticism...."[11] Anthony G. Amsterdam and Randy Hertz' analysis of the rhetorical structure of closing arguments includes quotes from Aristotle, Cicero, and Quintilian.[12] Most of these commentators are interested in how classical rhetorical principles help discover or explain the internal logic and persuasive value of legal discourse....

[L]awyers ... could certainly benefit from a greater familiarity with the comprehensive, coherent, and experience-tested classical system, which offers detailed advice for handling a legal case from the initial issue and fact determinations to the final courtroom techniques and strategies. As this essay demonstrates, rhetoric has always been an educational tool geared to meet the practical demands of the legal profession. For 2,450 years it has survived and adapted to those demands and can certainly do so again.

In his summary of twentieth-century rhetoric (above), Professor Frost introduces Chaim Perelman, perhaps the most influential modern rhetorician. In the introduction to a translation of Perelman's work *The Realm of Rhetoric,* Carroll C. Arnold describes some of Perelman's major claims: (1) Argument is informal rather than being limited to deduction and induction. (2) It is always addressed to one or more audiences. (3) To be successful, argument must start with premises that are already acceptable to the audience. (4) It uses strategies that emphasize key ideas in the minds of its audience. (5) It uses language and therefore cannot entirely eliminate ambiguity. (6) It uses certain key kinds of moves, including quasi-logical arguments, real life consequences, examples and illustrations, analogy and metaphor, distinctions, amplification or abridgment, and imposing particular structures on ideas.[13] Having summarized Perelman's rational justifications, Arnold explains Perelman's claim that all such argument is rhetorical rather than logical, describing the distinction as follows:

Chaim Perelman and *The Realm of Rhetoric*

First, most of the claims we make in arguing are not self-evidently true; they must be *made* to seem reasonable. They cannot be "proved" completely; they must be *judged to be reasonable* by those to whom the claims and their supports are presented. But this means that what the audience knows or thinks it knows must be . . . rendered consonant with the claim being made. What is said in arguing *and* what the audience knows and feels must, together, seem reasonable. Moreover, since the claims we argue for cannot be demonstrated to be totally and finally true, we cannot hope that the adherence we win . . . will be total and irrevocable. [One can seek only] a *degree* of acceptance. . . .

Implicit in what we have just said is a second crucial condition of all argument. . . . [A]n audience's choices and judgments are affected not only by their knowledge and experience but by their situations at the time of confronting our arguments. Thus methods of arguing must shift as the nature and conditions of the audience shift. Argument that is addressed to a particular audience . . . cannot be the same as argument addressed to another particular audience. . . .

A third, constraining condition of all argument . . . is the ambiguity of the language we must use. The relationships between linguistic terms and the concepts or images they symbolize are never entirely stable. . . . [E]very definition implicitly admits that some other definition is possible; otherwise, there would be no need to define [at all]. Likewise, every evaluative term or statement implicitly admits that one *could* give a different evaluation and make some defense of it. Were it not so, we would have no need to express *our* evaluation.

Fourth, Arnold introduces Perelman's idea that advocates create liaisons between ideas. Arnold explains that in Perelman's native language (French), the term "liaison" connotes a joining together. In French cooking, it implies thickening, such as in a sauce. Ideas can be joined temporarily but not irrevocably because they address matters about which we cannot discover absolute proof.

So what does all this have to do with studying and practicing law? We turn now to an excerpt from Professor Linda Berger, in which she discusses the linguistic transformation of the first year of law school and rhetoric's potential role in that transformation.

Excerpt from

Linda L. Berger, *Studying and Teaching "Law as Rhetoric": A Place to Stand*

16 J. Legal Writing 3 (2010)

[Each year as] they begin law study, [new law] students "undergo a linguistic rupture, a change in how they view and use language."[14] The change affects not only their understanding of language use, but also their ideas about how the law works and its place for them.[15] Their ideas are influenced by pervasive legal conversations reflecting the positions of Socrates and Callicles: the law is all rules or all power. Against these versions of the legal conversation, I propose in this Article to offer [these new] law students a rhetorical place to stand, between reason and power.

[The study of] rhetoric makes it possible . . . to envision [the lawyer's] role . . . as constructive, effective, and imaginative while grounded in law, language, and persuasive rationality. . . . [R]hetoric provides a strong counter to the constrained view of the life of lawyers offered by popular depictions of formalism [the law is all rules] or realism [the law is what a judge will do]. In the typical description, proponents of legalism or formalism are said to believe that the meaning of legal rules can be "found," the true version of facts can be established, and logic can be applied to yield certain results. Contrasting their theory with this version of formalism, political realists argue that even though meaning is often indeterminate and facts are frequently ambiguous, judges must still decide. To do so, realists claim, judges will necessarily turn to their personal, political, or ideological beliefs.

Set next to these depictions, rhetoric looks at how the law works by exploring a meaning-making process, one in which the law is "constituted" as human beings located within particular historical and cultural communities write, read, argue about, and decide legal issues. Studying and teaching "law as rhetoric" treats rhetoric not as tool or technique, nor even as the art or craft of persuasion, but instead as an interactive process of persuasion and argumentation that is used to resolve uncertain questions in this setting and for the time being. Such treatment rescues rhetoric from being viewed as a grab bag of literary devices, language tricks that put a gloss on legal reasoning but add little of substance. Instead, it focuses on the rhetorical process as being central to perception, understanding, and expression. . . .

[In this view] "rhetoric" [is] a study (of the effects of texts), a process (for composing texts), and a perspective (for invention in the classical rhetorical sense). . . . [R]hetoric recognizes [lawyers'] power and ability to affect outcomes in their rhetorical communities. . . . In their traditional guises, formalism and realism appear to doom lawyers to lives of "quiet desperation":[16] if "rules" or "politics" compel outcomes, the work of lawyers will have little effect. Rhetoric recognizes a constructive role for . . . lawyers by acknowledging that the law is often being interpreted and that interpretations are often contestable. From the rhetorical point of view, law students, law teachers, and lawyers are human actors whose work makes a difference because they are the readers, writers, and members of interpretive and compositional communities who together "constitute" the law.

Photo by Yvonne M. Jones. Used by permission.

The orator speaks

But their power is not unrestrained. Unlike political realists, rhetoricians suggest that there are reasonable constraints on what lawyers argue and how judges decide and that the constraints come from the rhetorical process itself. These constraints emerge from language, history, and culture, and, in particular, from the norms and customs of judging and of law practice. Although rhetoric does not promise certain answers, it can promise results that are, in Karl Llewellyn's term, reckonable[17]—they are certain enough that lawyers can make judgments about their likelihood and appellate lawyers can feel comfortable charging clients for their work.

Finally, rhetoric may help [lawyers] to move more effectively between the law and life, between the legal language of abstraction and their future clients' words describing individual human conflicts and dilemmas. If law school pedagogy carries the message that the "law's key task is effective translation of the 'human world' using legal categories," [lawyers] may find themselves poorly prepared for the realities of legal practice.[18] The language of law school may even distance [them] from individual voices they will need to be able to hear.

To sum up, studying the "law as rhetoric" allows [us] to take part in the many-voiced and open-ended rhetorical process through which the law is made. [Studying] the law as rhetoric [encourages lawyers] to bring in pluralistic and complicating forces, including their own experiences, values, and senses of themselves. Studying legal arguments as rhetorical performances helps [lawyers] become more aware of the effects of language and symbol use and meaning frames. This growing awareness makes them more rhetorically effective speakers and writers. Beyond improving their skills, engaging in law as rhetoric may help conjure and channel [the] natural ability to imagine and invent, and it may enable [lawyers] to better listen to alternative views and to speak in their own voices.

Discussion Questions

1. As you may have noticed, the theme of imagination has carried over from Chapter 1. Are you beginning to have a sense that our work will call into question the idea that law can be "boiled down" to a set of rules or propositions? That law is instead "a wild river"? Is that thought unsettling? Why or why not?

2. How does it feel to be continuing an ancient tradition? Does that role come with responsibilities? Responsibilities to maintain the tradition or to update it or both? In what ways might we need to maintain the ancient traditions about logos, ethos, pathos, context, and audience? In what ways might we need to update them?

3. Perelman says that most argumentation is rhetorical rather than "logical." What is the difference? Does that difference apply to legal argument? How?

4. Is language inherently ambiguous, as Perelman says? If so, what does that mean for law and for the work of lawyers and judges? Does it mean that law is hopelessly unpredictable?

5. Professor Berger quotes Elizabeth Mertz as saying that new law students "undergo a linguistic rupture, a change in how they view and use language." What does that mean? Did you experience something like that? How is your use of language different now from before you began law school?

6. Many debates in recent years have been between the view that law is all rules and the view that law is all power. What do those two views mean?

What problems do these two views raise? One of the most important benefits of realizing that law is rhetorical is the idea that there is a third option, one that frees us from many of the difficulties of the other two. Professor Berger calls this a "place to stand." How is it that rhetoric avoids some of the problems of viewing the law as all rules or all power?

7. Professor Berger says that law is not a preexisting set of rules we inherit but something we, together, "constitute." What does that mean?

Endnotes

1. Wilson Huhn, *The Five Types of Legal Argument* 3 (2d ed., Carolina Acad. Press 2008).

2. John Hollander, *Legal Rhetoric*, in *Law's Stories* 176-177 (Peter Brooks & Paul Gewirtz eds., Yale U. Press 1996).

3. Reprinted with the permission of the Southern California Interdisciplinary Law Journal.

4. Robert J. Connors et al., *The Revival of Rhetoric in America*, in *Essays in Classical Rhetoric and Modern Discourse* 8 (Robert Connors, Lisa Ede & Andrea Lunsford eds., Southern Illinois U. Press 1984).

5. Kenneth Burke, *The Five Master Terms: Their Place in a "Dramatistic" Grammar of Motives*, in *Landmark Essays on Rhetorical Invention in Writing* 1 (Richard Young & Yameng Liu eds., Hermagoras Press 1994).

6. Chaim Perelman, *The Idea of Justice and the Problem of Argumentation* (John Petrie trans., Routledge & Kegan Paul 1963).

7. Chaim Perelman & L. Olbrechts-Tyteca, *The New Rhetoric: A Treatise on Argumentation* (John Wilkinson & Purcell Weaver trans., U. Notre Dame Press 1969).

8. P.J. Corbett, *Classical Rhetoric for the Modern Student* 629 (2d ed., New York: Oxford U. Press 1971).

9. Robert F. Hanley, *Brush Up Your Aristotle*, Litig., Winter 1986, at 39.

10. Ruggero J. Aldisert, *Logic for Lawyers: A Guide to Clear Legal Thinking* 54 (National Institute for Trial Advocacy 1989).

11. Richard Posner, *Law and Literature: A Misunderstood Relation* 270-271 (Harvard U. Press 1988).

12. Anthony G. Amsterdam & Randy Hertz, *An Analysis of Closing Arguments to a Jury*, 37 N.Y. L. Sch. L. Rev. 55 (1992).

13. Carroll C. Arnold, *Introduction*, in Chaim Perelman, *The Realm of Rhetoric* x-xi (William Kluback trans., U. Notre Dame Press 1982).

14. Elizabeth Mertz, *The Language of Law School: Learning to "Think Like a Lawyer"* 22 (Oxford U. Press 2007).

15. *Id.* ("As in other forms of language socialization, new conceptions of morality and personhood are subtly intertwined with this shift to new uses of language.")

16. *See* Charles A. Bird & Webster Burke Kinnaird, *Objective Analysis of Advocacy Preferences and Prevalent Mythologies in One California Appellate Court,* 4 J. App. Prac. & Process 141, 149 (2002) ("The . . . lawyer's life would be one of quiet desperation if the work consisted merely of delivering a list of issues and a record to a court that would decide cases without regard to the quality of advocacy.").

17. Karl N. Llewellyn, *The Common Law Tradition: Deciding Appeals* 4 (Little, Brown, & Co. 1960).

18. Elizabeth Mertz, *Inside the Law School Classroom: Toward a New Legal Realist Pedagogy*, 60 Vand. L. Rev. 483, 505 (2007).

"A negro lawyer," circa 1942

Belva Lockwood, nineteenth-century lawyer

41

In Chapter 3, we saw that writing a brief places us in an ancient tradition. But our history is a bit more recent as well. This excerpt from Professor Ehrenberg describes the tradition we inherited from England and an important way in which our path diverged.

Excerpt from
Suzanne Ehrenberg, *Embracing the Writing-Centered Legal Process*
89 Iowa L. Rev. 1159 (2004)

One of the great popular misconceptions about the U.S. legal system is that it is propelled by the collective breath of half a million lawyers orally arguing their cases in court. According to this myth, the central role of the lawyer in our legal system is that of oralist. The news media, the entertainment media, and even members of the legal profession all celebrate those activities of lawyers that involve oral communication. The lawyer making an impassioned plea to the jury, sparring orally with judges over points of law, or belligerently cross-examining witnesses—these are the "heroic acts" of the legal profession we invariably see portrayed on television, in movies, and in the news media.

But this portrait of the legal profession, while ripe with dramatic possibilities, does not reflect the reality of legal practice in our country. Behind every display of oral pyrotechnics in a courtroom, one will likely find a carefully crafted set of written arguments. Any attorney who has practiced law for more than a few months recognizes that writing, not speaking, is the preferred medium of communication in the U.S. legal process, even if it is not the most celebrated.

What may not be as obvious to many practicing lawyers is that our legal system is unique in its emphasis on the written over the spoken word. No other common law legal system, past or present, has relied so persistently on the written word as a vehicle for legal communication. Our commitment to the written expression of ideas influences not only the way in which lawyers communicate with judges, but the way in which judges decide cases and communicate their decisions to others, and the way in which lawyers communicate with one another.

The fact that writing occupies a status superior to speech in our legal system is truly revolutionary when viewed from both a cultural and an historical perspective. One of the persistent themes in Western thought since Plato is that speech is a superior form of communication to writing. Moreover, the English, from whom we derived the most salient characteristics of our legal system, have a long tradition of orality in both trial and appellate courts, which continues to this day. In England, and in most other common law countries, appellate argument is still predominantly oral, and there is no role at all for a written brief at the trial level.[1]

Lawyers in the United States, however, began to reject that oral tradition from the early days of the Republic and developed a unique document known as the "appellate brief." Over the past 150 years, appellate courts (and more recently, trial courts) have increasingly limited the role of oral argument, and have relied more heavily on written briefs in their decision-making processes.

The written judicial opinion, as well, is a salient feature of legal practice in the United States. Our reported opinions are written by the judges themselves, after lengthy deliberation. This practice provides a stark contrast to the English tradition, in which appellate judges historically issued the majority of their judgments orally from the bench at the conclusion of oral argument. Emphasis on written expression is also a distinguishing feature of legal practice within U.S. law firms and other legal practice settings. Lawyers in the United States tend to memorialize their research and share ideas with one another in writing to a far greater extent than do foreign lawyers.

Why is it that so much more ink is spilt by U.S. lawyers and judges than by their counterparts in other common law countries? Does all of this scribbling, in the end, result in better common law and better resolution of legal disputes? This article will attempt to answer those questions. . . .

Professor Ehrenberg here begins a historical comparison of contemporary English and U.S. legal systems, showing how they came to differ on the question of the importance of writing. We will pick up with the discussion of the history of changes in the U.S. system.

B. The Ascendance of the Written Tradition in the United States

The first sign that the new nation was charting its own course in developing a legal system was its decision to adopt a written constitution with a catalogue of individual rights. The English constitution is "unwritten" to the extent that its provisions do not appear in any single document and are an amalgam of customs, cases, statutes and judicial writings. Our written constitution is arguably an outgrowth of the written charter which had governed the colonies prior to the formation of the republic. Because the colonies had been governed for generations by the terms of written instruments, which established and regulated the structure of government, "the conviction had been bred that only through matter of record could the metes and bounds of the fundamental law be secured."[2]

The United States did not diverge immediately from the English tradition, however, in its litigation practice. Early appellate practice in the United States was conducted almost exclusively on an oral basis, as it had been when the colonies were subsumed under the English legal system. Oral arguments lasting several days were not uncommon. The early rules of the United States Supreme Court mention neither oral argument nor written briefs, but the Court expressly adopted the practice of the English courts and Chancery as a blueprint for its own practices.

Nevertheless, a convergence of circumstances made it difficult for the oral tradition to take hold in the United States as it had in England. First, the new nation lacked a significant body of trained barristers to carry on the tradition. In the seventeenth and early eighteenth centuries, many of the colonies enacted legislation hostile to professional lawyers and initially sought to conduct their legal proceedings with all litigants acting pro se. Ironically, this attempt to lock out professional attorneys forced litigants to turn to untrained officers of the court, "sharpers and pettifoggers," to perform their legal work.

By the beginning of the eighteenth century, most of the colonies recognized the need for responsible, trained practitioners of law and had set up a formal system to admit lawyers into practice. A significant number of colonists became qualified as barristers by studying in England at the Inns of Court, but they were not sufficient to handle the case-load of the colonial courts. Although English-educated barristers were regarded as the best . . . , qualification as a barrister was not a pre-requisite to practicing before a colonial court. Most colonial attorneys were trained by merely "reading the law" in the office of a practitioner. Such was the nature of the legal profession at the time of the Revolution. Litigation was being conducted by attorneys who lacked the classic education and legal training of the English barrister, and who had no political motive to preserve a system based on oral advocacy; thus, the oral tradition was ripe for reform in the new nation.

Another major factor that contributed to the demise of orality in the U.S. legal system is the sheer size of our country. Because individuals had to travel great distances in order to attend political meetings and participate in government, the written and printed word were becoming an important means of political and governmental communication. The development of the commercial printer facilitated such communication. It was natural, therefore, that the courts would eventually come to rely on the written or printed word as a means of communication between lawyers and judges who were separated by significant distances.

The first sign of a writing requirement in the United States Supreme Court appeared in 1795, when the court promulgated

Rule 8 requiring that attorneys submit "a statement of material points of the case."[3] Supreme Court Rule 30 expanded this requirement in 1821 to "a printed brief or abstract ... containing the substance of all the material pleadings, facts and documents ... and the points of law and facts intended to be presented."[4] Although this was probably the first instance of the word "brief" being used to refer to a legal document submitted to a court on appeal, briefs submitted pursuant to this rule did not resemble our modern appellate briefs; they generally contained only a list of points with no actual argument. Such submissions could only serve as a preview of, rather than as a substitute for, oral argument. There is only one known surviving example of the statements required by Supreme Court Rules 8 and 30, and the cases suggest that non-compliance with the rules was a problem.[5]

In 1833, the Supreme Court first gave parties the option of submitting a case on the basis of a written argument in lieu of oral argument.[6] This rule apparently was instituted at the request of attorneys because the Court stated that "it has been represented to the court, that it would in many cases accommodate counsel, and save expense to parties, to submit causes upon printed argument."[7] The Court later clarified that such cases "shall stand on the same footing as if there were an appearance by counsel."[8] Written arguments submitted in lieu of oral argument were most likely more extensive than those submitted merely as a supplement to oral argument, but examples of briefs from the early nineteenth century are virtually non-existent.

Perhaps the clearest sign that the United States was abandoning the oral tradition in appellate advocacy was the Supreme Court's promulgation in 1849 of Rule 53, which limited each attorney in the case to two hours of oral arguments.[9] The Rule reiterated that in order to be entitled to a hearing, an attorney was required to submit a printed abstract, with a list of points and authorities to be raised; an attorney waived his right to oral argument if he failed to submit such an abstract and the case was heard ex parte for the other side.[10] Now, however, there was an additional incentive to file a written brief containing substantive legal argument; it was arguably necessary in order to make up for the time lost in oral argument. Oral argument was further curtailed in 1858 by a rule that imposed a limit of two attorneys per side, thereby reducing oral argument to a maximum of eight hours.[11] In 1871, total argument time was cut in half, to a maximum of two hours per side.[12] As the written brief assumed more prominence in the appellate process, the Court set forth more specific content requirements for written arguments. A Rule promulgated in 1884 required "a brief of the argument, exhibiting a clear statement of the points of law or fact to be discussed, with ... reference[s]."[13]

The historical decline of the oral tradition in many of the state courts follows roughly the same pattern. . . .

In some instances, the imposition of time limits on oral argument provided a clear catalyst for attorneys to submit more sophisticated written arguments. The State of New York, for example, limited oral argument to two hours in the middle 1850's. Prior to this time, the typical brief submitted to the New York Court of Appeals was only one or two pages long and contained a number of broad assertions with no citations, or citations without explanation. These briefs evidenced few of the persuasive techniques that we have come to associate with good appellate advocacy; they made no effort to build an argument or establish a connection between cited authorities and the specific facts of the case. . . .[14]

By 1860, however, the standard written submission to the New York Court of Appeals resembled a fully-developed modern appellate brief. The brief ranged in length from eight to fifteen pages, began with a statement of facts of the case, and was organized in outline form with main propositions subsuming a series of narrower points. The arguments were written in fully developed sentences and paragraphs rather than brief, cryptic statements, and they sought to apply general legal principles to the facts of the particular case.[15]

. . . [M]ost of the written briefs filed in appellate courts by the end of the nineteenth century became more sophisticated, more intellectually rigorous, and more persuasive. They engage in serious discussion of legal authorities, and make use of narrative techniques, hypotheticals and policy arguments, as well as emotional appeals.[16]

The history of appellate practice in nineteenth-century America, therefore, shows a movement from the use of oral argument as the court's principal means of learning about a case, with the brief as a supplement, to the use of oral argument as a supplement to the brief. As noted above, the most likely explanations for this transition are the absence of a distinct class of attorneys trained as oral advocates, the practical difficulties of traveling to appear in court given the size of the country, and the increasing availability of typewriters and commercial printers.

The history of appellate practice in twentieth-century America shows a similar (although less dramatic) movement toward reliance on written briefs and curtailment of oral argument. The Supreme Court continued to reduce the time allotted for oral argument, ending up in 1984 with a rule restricting oral argument to one counsel per side and limiting each argument to one half-hour.[17] In addition, the decision to allow oral argument at all has been discretionary in the Supreme Court since 1954.[18]

Similarly, the federal Courts of Appeal began adopting procedures for disposing of cases without oral argument around the middle of the twentieth century. Federal Rule of Appellate Procedure 34 currently permits disposition of an appeal without oral argument where "1) the appeal is frivolous; 2) the dispositive ... issues have been recently authoritatively decided; or 3) the facts and legal arguments are adequately presented in the briefs and record, and the decisional process would not be significantly aided by oral argument."[19]

Along with the rejection of the oral tradition in appellate argument, came a rejection of the oral tradition in rendering judicial opinions. Almost from the beginning, the written opinion has been a prominent feature of appellate review in the United States.[20] U.S. appellate judges, unlike their English counterparts, had little or no experience rendering oral opinions as trial judges and were not necessarily skilled as oral advocates. In addition, when our legal system was in its infancy, there was no binding precedent on which judges could rely. Thus, there was a strong incentive to produce well-reasoned written opinions and publish them.[21] ...

Thus, it is the oral component of the appellate process, rather than the written component, that has been curtailed more consistently in the interest of achieving greater judicial efficiency. In the U.S. legal system, it is deemed more palatable to eliminate oral argument than to eliminate a written opinion articulating the reasons for a court's decision. Just as the English have resisted opportunities to incorporate more writing into their legal process, so we have resisted opportunities to move our legal process toward greater orality. ...

Here Professor Ehrenberg discusses the impact of the writing process on legal reasoning, showing that an emphasis on writing improves the reasoning process and the quality of judicial outcomes. After a thorough discussion on the significant implications of our emphasis on writing, Professor Ehrenberg concludes:

Perhaps we will never see a time when the media extol the writing of a compelling appellate brief as a heroic act. But lawyers and law professors themselves should celebrate the written word, and should recognize that the power of the written word to deepen and refine legal analysis carries with it the power to shape and improve the common law.

We learned in Chapter 3 that rhetoric—the art of persuasion—originated in the ancient world. In this short excerpt from Professor Frost, we learn that, amazingly, the specific components of a modern appellate brief originated there as well, over two thousand years ago.

Excerpt from

Michael Frost, *Brief Rhetoric—A Note on Classical and Modern Theories of Forensic Discourse*

38 U. Kan. L. Rev. 411 (1990)

By necessity, instinct, and design, modern lawyers organize and write appellate briefs according to rhetorical principles that would be familiar to Aristotle, Cicero, and Quintilian. Although classical organization patterns, rhetorical strategies, and writing conventions are evident in many types of legal writing, they are particularly evident in modern appellate briefs. Lawyers submitting briefs to the United States Supreme Court, for instance, follow rules for forensic discourse that Cicero and other classical rhetoricians formulated over two thousand years ago. . . . Supreme Court Rules 15 and 34, for example, which stipulate how briefs must be organized, require that briefs begin with the legal questions presented for review, state the facts upon which the case is based, provide an argument based on those facts, and conclude with a description of the remedy sought.[22]

Both rules emphasize that substantive sections of the brief must be organized exactly in the order just described. In all important respects, these organizational requirements are the same as those first formulated in the fifth century B.C. by Corax of Syracuse, who divided forensic discourse into the "Introduction," the "Narration," the "Argument," and the "Peroration."[23] These sections served roughly the same purposes in classical legal arguments as the "Question(s) Presented," the "Statement of the Case," the "Argument Summary," the "Argument," and the "Conclusion" sections serve in a modern appellate brief. . . .

I. Historical Development

Rhetoric, sometimes defined as the use of language to inform or persuade, has always had strong links to judicial and forensic discourse. Rhetoric texts devoted to forensic discourse were well developed in Sicily by the fifth century B.C. and were subsequently refined by Greek and Roman rhetoricians. Since their inception in fifth century Sicily and their use and development in the public assemblies of Greece and Rome, rhetoricians involved with forensic discourse have been particularly concerned with the most effective and persuasive ways of organizing an argument.

Corax, a Sicilian whose teachings were admired by classical Greek rhetoricians, divided argument into "*proem*" or "Introduction," "Narration," "Argument," and "Peroration" or "Conclusion,"[24] These divisions, with some additions and modifications by Aristotle, Cicero, Quintilian, and other rhetoricians, have survived substantially intact for over two millennia.

Although Aristotle maintained that an argument actually contains only two essential parts, the "Statement of the Case" and the "Proof," he conceded that in practice orators usually added two more parts, the "Introduction" and the "Conclusion."[25] Romans like Cicero, Quintilian, and the anonymous author of the *Rhetorica ad Herennium* developed and refined the divisions first described by Corax. They added an argument summary section thus creating a five-part division—"Introduction" *(exordium)*, "Statement of Case" *(narration)*, "Argument Summary" *(partitio)*, "Proof of the Case" *(confirmation)*, and "Conclusion" *(peroratio)*— which survived virtually intact throughout the classical period.[26] This five-part organization of the substantive parts of a legal argument is the same as that required by the United States Supreme Court Rules.

Professor Frost's article then demonstrates the ancient roots of the key components of a modern appellate brief: the questions presented; the statement of the case; the summary of the argument; the argument sections; and the conclusion.

In the prior two excerpts, we have been looking at our distant past, glimpsing our roots in the ancient world and in the historical development of brief-writing in the United States. This final excerpt deals with our more recent past and the largest change in Supreme Court brief-writing in our own time.

Excerpt from

Joseph D. Kearney & Thomas W. Merrill, *The Influence of Amicus Curiae Briefs on the Supreme Court*
148 U. Pa. L. Rev. 743 (2000)

The last century has seen little change in the conduct of litigation before the United States Supreme Court. The Court's familiar procedures—the October Term, the opening-answering-reply brief format for the parties, oral argument before a nine-member Court—remained essentially as before. The few changes that have occurred, such as shortening the time for oral argument, have not been dramatic.

In one respect, however, there has been a major transformation in Supreme Court practice: the extent to which non-parties participate in the Court's decision-making process through the submission of amicus curiae, or friend-of-the-court, briefs. Throughout the first century of the Court's existence, amicus briefs were rare. Even during the initial decades of [the 20th] century, such briefs were filed in only about 10% of the Court's cases. This pattern has now completely reversed itself. In recent years, one or more amicus briefs have been filed in 85% of the Court's argued cases. Thus, at the close of the twentieth century, cases without amicus briefs have become nearly as rare as cases with amicus briefs were at the beginning of the century.

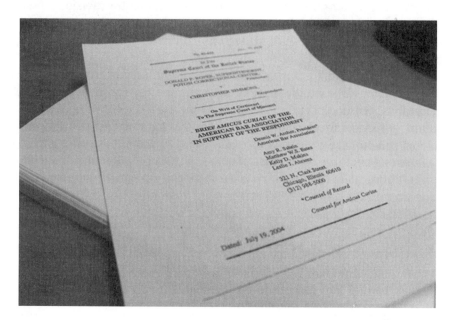

Attitudes within the legal community about the utility and impact of amicus briefs vary widely. . . .

Here the article identifies three attitudes toward amicus briefs: moderately helpful (the most common attitude); unnecessarily duplicative of the parties' filings and therefore a nuisance (articulated by Judge Richard Posner); and expressions of self-interest by amicus filers (articulated by Justice Scalia).

The critical but unstated variable that divides these different perspectives is the model of judicial decision making adopted by each commentator. Each of the three positions corresponds to a different model of judging, which in turn suggests a different pathway of influence that amicus briefs may have on the outcomes reached by courts.[27]

The first or moderately supportive view of amicus briefs implicitly adopts the conventional legal model of judicial decision making. Under this model, judges are regarded as seeking to resolve cases in accordance with the requirements of law, as understood by professional actors in the legal community. Amicus briefs are assumed to have an impact on this process insofar as they contain new information—legal arguments and background factual material—that would be relevant to persons seeking the correct result in light of established legal norms.

The second or sharply negative view is often associated with what political scientists call the "attitudinal model" of judicial behavior.[28] This model posits that judges have fixed ideological preferences, and that case outcomes are a product of the summing of the preferences of the participating judges, with legal norms serving only to rationalize outcomes after the fact. Under this view, amicus briefs should have little or no impact on the outcomes reached by a court, because each judge's vote in a case is assumed to be the product of his or her preestablished ideological preferences with respect to the issue presented. A judge can obtain all the information needed to determine his or her vote, the attitudinal model would suggest, by reading the "Question Presented" and the statement of facts contained in the parties' briefs. To the extent that amicus briefs provide additional legal arguments and factual background, under this model they offer information of no relevance to judges.

The third view . . . implicitly adopts an interest group theory of the judicial process. In contrast to the attitudinal model, the assumption here is that judges do not have strong ideological preferences about most issues. Rather, they are empty vessels who seek to decide cases so as to reach those results supported by the most influential groups in society that have an interest in the question at hand. Amicus briefs on this view should be important to the judicial process because of the signals that they convey about how interested groups want particular cases decided. If . . . the groups filing amicus briefs all want a case to come out a certain way, this tells the judges how to rule if they want to secure the approval of organized groups. . . .

In this [a]rticle, we present empirical evidence designed to enhance our understanding about the impact of amicus curiae briefs on the Supreme Court and therefore also about the validity of different models of judging. . . .

Briefly, our principal findings are as follows. First, our study shows conclusively that the incidence of amicus curiae participation in the Supreme Court has increased dramatically over the last fifty years. . . . [T]he number of amicus filings has increased by more than 800%.

In terms of the influence of amicus briefs on outcomes, our study uncovers a number of interesting patterns. We find that amicus briefs supporting respondents enjoy higher success rates than do amicus briefs supporting petitioners; that small disparities of one or two briefs for one side with no briefs on the other side may translate into higher success rates but larger disparities do not; that amicus briefs cited by the Court appear to be no more likely to be associated with the winning side than briefs not cited by the Court; and that amicus briefs filed by more experienced lawyers may be more successful than briefs filed by less experienced lawyers. Among institutional litigants that appear frequently before the Court, we confirm the finding of other researchers that the Solicitor General, who represents the United States before the Supreme Court, enjoys great success as an amicus filer. . . .

We cautiously interpret these results as providing more support for the legal model than for either the attitudinal or interest group models. Contrary to what the attitudinal model would predict, amicus briefs do appear to affect success rates in a variety of contexts. And contrary to what the interest group model would predict, we find no evidence to support the proposition that large disparities of amicus support for one side relative to the other result in a greater likelihood of success for the supported party. In fact, it appears that amicus briefs filed by institutional litigants and by experienced lawyers—filers that have a better idea of what kind of information is useful to the Court—are generally more successful than are briefs filed by irregular litigants and less experienced lawyers. This is consistent with the legal model's prediction that amicus briefs have an influence to the extent they import valuable new information. Moreover, the greater success associated with amicus briefs supporting respondents can be explained by the supposition that respondents are more likely than petitioners to be represented by inexperienced lawyers in the Supreme Court and hence are more likely to benefit from supporting amici, which can supply the Court with additional legal arguments and facts overlooked by the respondents' lawyers.

Discussion Questions

1. Professor Ehrenberg compares the English and U.S. systems' reliance on writing and maintains that more reliance on writing improves the quality of the legal result. In a large section of the article not reprinted here, she carefully shows us more about how a writing-centered legal system produces better reasoned results. If you have time, you might want to read the full version of the article, but if you don't have time, you might be able to make some guesses about why a writing-centered system might be more reliably good. Why do you think that might be so?
2. Is it surprising to learn that the components of today's appellate brief were created nearly 2,500 years ago, with the same purposes and strategies in mind? Why might so little have changed?
3. Professors Kearney and Merrill describe three views of judicial decision making: (1) the conventional "legal" model, in which judges try to resolve cases according to legal requirements as understood by professionals in the legal community; (2) the "attitudinal" model, in which judges resolve cases according to their own ideological preferences; and (3) the

"interest group" theory, in which judges decide cases at least in part based on the outcomes supported by the most influential groups in society. The results of the study by Kearney and Merrill (explained in the full version of the article) seem to support the first model. What do you think?

4. What role should an amicus brief play in Supreme Court decision making? Should they be prohibited? Significantly limited? If so, what should be the criteria for receiving permission to file an amicus brief? Do you see how deciding the criteria requires us to decide what we think about a judge's role?

Endnotes

1. Only [since the mid-1990s] have English appellate courts required written submissions of any type to be lodged in advance of the hearing, and these submissions provide only a summary of the arguments to be made in court.

2. Julius J. Goebel, Jr., *Antecedents and Beginnings to 1801*, in *The Oliver Wendell Holmes Devise, History of the Supreme Court of the United States* 1 (Cambridge U. Press 1971).

3. Sup. Ct. R. 8, *established in* 3 U.S. (3 Dall.) 120 (1795).

4. Sup. Ct. R. 30, *established in* 19 U.S. (6 Wheat.) xiii (1817).

5. *See Schooner Catherine v. United States*, 11 U.S. (7 Cranch) 99 (1812) (dismissing case for failure by appellant to furnish statement, and then reinstating with consent of the parties); *Peyton v. Brooke*, 7 U.S. (3 Cranch) 92, 92 (1805) (warning counsel that future cases will be dismissed or continued unless written statements were furnished to the court).

6. Sup. Ct. R. 40, *established in* 32 U.S. (7 Pet.) iv (1833).

7. *Id.* The practice of submitting cases on written argument most likely predates this rule. R. Kirkland Cozine, *The Emergence of Written Appellate Briefs in the Nineteenth-Century United States*, 38 Am. J. Legal Hist. 487 n.28 (1994). Indeed, the fact that attorneys initiated the rule suggests that they had some knowledge of the practice and recognized its advantages.

8. Sup. Ct. R. 44, *established in* 36 U.S. (11 Pet.) xvi (1837).

9. Sup. Ct. R. 53, *established in* 48 U.S. (11 Pet.) xvi (1837).

10. *Id.*

11. Sup. Ct. R. 21, *established in* 62 U.S. (21 How.) xii-xiii (1858).

12. Sup. Ct. R. 21, *established in* 78 U.S. (11 Wall.) ix (1870).

13. Sup. Ct. R. 21, sec. 2(3), *established in* 108 U.S. 584 (1884).

14. Cozine, *supra* note 7, at 482.

15. *Id.*

16. *Id.* at 523.

17. *See* Sup. Ct. R. 28(3). . . .

18. *See* Sup. Ct. R. 45, *established in* 346 U.S. 951, 997 (1954).

19. Fed. R. App. P. 34(a)(2).

20. For a short time, in the nation's early years, the Supreme Court justices rendered their opinions orally, like their English counterparts. Eventually, however, the justices began to write out their opinions before reading them in court. And ultimately, the Court adopted the practice of having one judge write the opinion for the majority, without presenting it orally. Robert J. Martineau, *Appellate Justice in England and the United States* (William S. Hein & Co. 1990), 110.

21. *Id.* at 117-118.

22. Sup. Ct. R. 15; Sup. Ct. R. 34.

23. E. Corbett, *Classical Rhetoric for the Modern Student* 595 (2d ed., Oxford U. Press 1971).

24. *Id.* at 595.

25. Aristotle, *The Rhetoric of Aristotle* (L. Cooper trans., Appleton, Century, Crofts 1932).

26. *Rhetorica ad Herennium* 9 (H. Caplan trans., Harvard U. Press 1954).

27. [The authors are careful to say that they] do not mean to suggest that Judge Posner . . . or Justice Scalia . . . is necessarily committed to the explanatory models of judging [the authors] associate with their remarks.

28. *See* Jeffrey A. Segal & Harold J. Spaeth, *The Supreme Court and the Attitudinal Model* 65-73 (Cambridge U. Press 1993) (describing the rationale and historical antecedents of the attitudinal model).

5. *The Court*

The briefs introduced in the second part of this book were all filed in the United States Supreme Court. The Court itself and the traditions it still maintains have their roots in the very beginning of our legal system. We'll need at least a cursory understanding of those traditions and that rhetorical setting in order to evaluate the briefs filed there. To help us, we turn to Professor Elizabeth Beske, who clerked for Justice Sandra Day O'Connor and now teaches legal writing at American University's Washington College of Law.

Elizabeth Beske, *Perspectives of a (Fleeting) Insider*

On a sweltering July day in the nation's capital, someone takes John Q. Law Clerk's picture and hands him keys and an ID card. In that instant, he is transformed from consumer of Supreme Court work product into "person with some role in production." His first week is a blur of paperwork, computer classes, tours, and special training on the process of handling capital cases. He grabs the baton from confident, relaxed, collegial clerks who have finished up their year on the Court and exchanges nervous glances with fellow newbies. He is one of four law clerks in the chambers of an Associate Justice of the United States Supreme Court.

His Justice has had a say in the decoration of chambers, and one of the first things John notices as he makes his way through the building is that all chambers bear that unique imprint. Wall colors in various chambers range from soft peach to dark hunter green. Every Justice is allowed to pick a few paintings from the storage of the National Gallery, and these give all chambers a radically different look—from rococo to abstract, neoclassical to southwestern. It is hard to say whether there's any relationship between judicial philosophy and décor, but John suspects it is a possibility. His work station is either an alcove or big shared room in chambers, or a smaller, more private room up the stairs. John figures out how to log on to his computer, and he's off and running.

With his key and card, he quickly learns to maneuver the building, cruising the red and gold carpeted halls, surveying the interior courtyards, trying his layup on the "highest court in the land" (the Supreme Court's basketball court), and locating other spots that will feature prominently in tours he gives his visiting grandparents. He develops a particular fondness for a ridiculously high white marble spiral staircase that is in the shape of an oval, and henceforth makes a passing glance down it each time he heads to the gym on the top floor. Someone tells him that oval-shaped spiral staircases are exceedingly rare, and he files that fact away under possibly useful miscellany.

He has lunch each day in one of two places—either in the law clerks' dining room off of the cafeteria, which someone has carefully cordoned off from the nearby reporters having their lunch—or in chambers with his boss. In either event, he traipses daily through the Supreme Court Cafeteria to select his meat loaf, potatoes, and cooked zucchini (fish on Fridays).

Although he is not specifically aware of it, with every day John passes through the grand entrance to the building, it becomes a little less surreal. A feeling of near-normalcy starts to creep in.

Diving into the Cert Pool

Each year, the Supreme Court gets several thousand "petitions for certiorari" asking that the Court hear a case. With some exceptions—involving suits between states over water rights and such—the Court has unfettered discretion to choose its cases, and from these thousands of petitions, it typically selects fewer than a hundred cases per term.

Because of its unique objectives, a cert petition is very different from other kinds of legal writing. The purpose of an appellate brief is to urge the correction of some defect in the lower court's order or opinion. Unlike an appellate brief, a successful cert petition does not merely claim that the lower court made a mistake. To be sure, most petitions *do* contend that the lower court got it all entirely wrong; however, the Supreme Court rarely steps into the fray simply to correct an error. A good cert petition focuses less on why "client A" should win, and more on why the Court should look at the issue itself, irrespective of the winner or loser. Successful petitions come in all shapes and sizes, but typically they persuasively demonstrate that the issue itself has broader significance than the instant case; that the question has vexed a lot of smart people; or that the question has life-or-death significance, sometimes literally.

Eight Justices—all but Justice Alito—currently participate in the "cert pool." The Chief's office divides the incoming petitions at random amongst these eight chambers, and each clerk within chambers takes a ¼ share. A law clerk has a fixed deadline by which to submit work product known as a "pool memo" to the other chambers with a recommended disposition. Justice Alito's separation from the process, like that of Justice Stevens before him, operates as a useful check and balance on the system.

Our law clerk John cuts his teeth on these cert petitions, and the stack is monumental and very daunting during the months of July and August as he tackles petitions on the "Summer List." He is insecure in the knowledge that he is doing it not just for his boss, but for seven other bosses, as well. He has to figure out by trial and error what it is that makes a case worth the Court's time, energy, and resources. Initially, each petition looks like a diamond-in-the-rough. He learns a lot by muttering with fellow clerks, and he spends a chunk of late August revisiting those recommendations he made in mid-July.

The format of the pool memo he is charged with producing is fairly straightforward. The first page identifies the parties, the docket number, the court and judges below, and the basis for federal jurisdiction. The memo begins with a one- or two-sentence description of the issue, followed by a couple of sentences summarizing the writer's recommendation—such as "this case is fact-bound" or "the issue is not squarely presented." This is followed by the recommendation itself, typically DENY, but occasionally GRANT or CVSG (call for the views of the Solicitor General). All this is on the first page. After that, the writer summarizes the facts and procedural history below and the contentions of the parties and amici, then proceeds to analysis of "certworthiness." Pool memos can range from two or three pages to twenty or more, depending on the importance of the issue.[1]

The biggest nail-biter of a recommendation by far is a grant, because the consequences of error are enormous. After John gets the format down, the potential grants take up all his time. He will develop tremendous fondness for his grants. In fact, it is like a practice-run on parenthood. Like any new parent, the moment a grant memo goes out, he may fret—did the lower court enter a final order/ was the claim cleanly raised/ is there standing/ is it ripe? Did the Court already answer this in a case he missed? To have the Court take a case on his recommendation and then "DIG" it—dismiss it as improvidently granted—would be to plumb the depths of despair, where he does not want to go. Each year the Court DIGs two or three cases for one reason or another. John will live with a low level of background stress until final issuance of a published opinion on his grant months later—the first moment that his grant is truly out of harm's way.

Many observers have noted the dwindling number of cases on the Court's docket in recent years. Undoubtedly, the lessening number is due to a confluence of several different factors, among them fewer statutes to interpret, fewer habeas cases, strategic voting on the part of justices uneasy granting a case they may not win, and greater unanimity amongst the lower courts. Linda Greenhouse laid these possible reasons out a few years ago in an insightful article entitled, "Dwindling Docket Mystifies Supreme Court," N.Y. Times (Dec. 7, 2006). She also flagged what she called "institutional conservatism" born of the cert pool process and suggested that law clerks might be conservatively recommending "deny" for fear that they might look too credulous (or, possibly, wet-behind-the-ears).

Is there anything to this fear of the grant? To a significant degree, any law clerk will prefer that a petition be marked with obvious jurisdictional defects. "DENY" is the path of least resistance; it means you can grab that beer after work after all. When a weighty petition comes, and they do, John's number is up. He has to buckle down and do a ton of work until he reaches absolute certainty that the case is worth the Court's time and energy. The cert pool may intensify his sense of the stakes—he must be *right*!—but in the generality of cases, it does not change his sense of the Court's standards. Certainly, there are hot button issues that come up, and he may or may not count noses and have an opinion as to whether it's a propitious time to make law on a given issue. But his credibility is at stake, and the year is long. Moreover, that obvious hot-button petition presenting enormously significant issues will certainly garner attention in every chambers. John is not likely to monkey around.

At the end of the summer, the Justices sit for a very long conference at which they discuss the Summer List. Prior to that point, the Chief will circulate a memo identifying cases of particular interest for discussion. Each Justice may add to the list, but no one seems to strike anything from it. The list itself makes sense. Generally, it includes every grant recommendation and many intriguing close-but-no-cigar deny recommendations. If a petition vexed John and kept him up at night, his pool memo probably reflected that, and it makes the list.

The conference itself takes place in the conference room off of the Chief's chambers, and it is a Justices-only affair. One assumes that the Chief sits at the head of the long conference table and manages the discussion, overlooked by a couple of large oil paintings of legal luminaries and shelves of case reporters. With respect to the summer list, John may get a sense of anticlimax, because the Court might relist a couple of cases for additional consideration or call for the views of the Solicitor General. Still, within a week or two, the spring "semester" starts to take shape. There are cases about which everyone is thrilled—a great year, totally different from that awful, mundane year last year!—and, well, other cases.

U.S. Supreme Court, 2004

Merits Briefs

By September, the whole cert pool thing is starting to feel almost manageable, which clearly means John is overdue for a new and daunting responsibility. Enter the stack of merits briefs. Merits briefs are long and involved. If cert petitions were the chips and salsa, merits briefs are clearly the big burrito.

Every chambers has its own spin on dividing up the merits cases for each sitting, but most probably have a system of rotating first picks. "Sexy," high-profile cases tend to go first, but sexiness is frequently in the eye of the beholder, and it is not unknown to have co-clerks behaving strategically to land that at-first-blush unglamorous dormant commerce clause case. John might also give passing thought to whether his Justice is likely to write in the case—either because he or she may get assigned the majority opinion or because he or she feels strongly about an issue and will write something regardless of the senior Justice's assignment. John leaves the divvying process with two to three assigned cases, which usually means two to three bench memos on his plate.

Nowadays, virtually every case comes in accompanied by briefs of amicus curiae, or "friends of the Court," reflecting a steep upward trend in the proliferation of amicus briefs over the past several decades. Amici can file briefs either on consent of the parties or by seeking leave from the Court. Supreme Court Rule 37 indicates that amicus briefs should address "relevant matter not already brought to [the Court's] attention by the parties." John will learn in short order that when amicus briefs are good, they are very, very good. Occasionally, they introduce a brilliant new way to conceptualize the problem or highlight a consequence of ruling one way that might otherwise escape the Court's notice. When they are bad . . . well, hmm. They might be a poorly-written rehash of a party's brief, a collection of non sequiturs, or (worse) a mail-it-in effort on the part of an organization that wishes to claim participation in a key case to drum up member support.

Two kinds of cases seem to bring with them stacks of colorful amicus briefs that reach John's shoulders. First, the really juicy, front-page-of-the-paper cases. Literally everyone wants to weigh in on these cases, and John will likely recognize some of his professors from law school on the caption pages, as well as many collections of people, like "states attorneys general" or "real estate brokers of America." The second type of case that commands a flotilla of amici is one he probably did not think much about in law school—the seemingly humdrum case with lots of money at stake. These aren't sexy, really. But the bottom-line of many different companies nationwide may hang in the balance. Companies with big legal budgets.

John reads the parties' briefs first to get a sense for the issue as presented to the Court. Then, he scans the towering stack of amicus briefs to see which lawyers have rung in, and on whose behalf. He might separate the stack into Petitioner and Respondent piles. If he has a profound sense one way or the other as to how the case should be decided, he hopes (sometimes in vain) that its stack is taller or weightier.

Lawyers in the established Supreme Court Bar command high billing rates, and John will probably decide during his tenure as a law clerk that they earn their keep.[2] Given the awesome significance of the issues and the going-by-the-seat-of-your-pants feeling that many 27-year-old law clerks nurse intermittently during their tenure on the Court, it can be reassuring to see repeat players.

John learns pretty quickly, though, that a significant number of advocates get the tone wrong in approaching the Court. They are lofty, formal, unequivocal, and bombastic precisely when he wants calm, grounded, balanced, and unvarnished. Suggesting you have a slam dunk, or that any human with a brain will naturally find total victory on your behalf, does not inspire confidence. The cases that come before the Supreme Court are generally fairly hard. Even the garden-variety circuit split has divided some of the nation's top jurists. Reasonable, often brilliant people, guided by the same precedents and statutes, have written pages and pages drawing utterly different conclusions. Thus, if a brief boldly proclaims victory without lingering over nuances, John will have the urge to toss it aside and look at what the amici have to say.

High-minded rhetoric is similarly unappealing. John finds it a lot in petitions for certiorari—assertions like, "[i]n the history of Anglo-Roman law, this case stands alone." (I kid you not.) Familiar with the oft-told adage about pounding the law when you have no facts and pounding the facts when you have no law, the reader can easily discern when lawyers are simply pounding the table. To keep the reader's confidence, the best brief writer sneaks advocacy into an overall mien of restraint.

In reading a brief, in truth, John sort of wants a little Chuck Yeager. Tom Wolfe aptly describes in *The Right Stuff* how generations of pilots after the legendary speed-of-sound-breaking Chuck Yeager adopted his folksy-West-Virginian manner of speaking to passengers. A Yeager-speaking pilot acknowledges the problem (some bumps) but calmly talks you out of any concern (we had a little chat with the air traffic folks, and they say we should follow that little ol' indicator and climb a bit higher). At once, you know that they are on the case and have calmly and unflappably figured out a solution to your discomfort. The veteran Supreme Court hands approach the Court in the same fashion. Absolutely, there's a problem, and we appreciate that the solution is not clear cut. The result we think is correct is a little tricky to square with the Smith case, but you can do it, given what was said in the Jones case. Moreover, it makes sense, and it will resolve more than it stirs up. Now-Chief, then-advocate John Roberts had god-like abilities in this regard.[3]

Our law clerk John will follow the chambers guidelines for preparing a bench memo. Typically, he will read every case cited by the parties and, additionally, conduct his own research. More than anything else, he is looking for the answer that seems correct, but he has a few constraints. First, he is obviously constrained by the Court's precedents and practicalities. He may fervently believe that the Constitution does not permit issuance of paper money, but two centuries of practice has foreclosed this avenue of innovation, at least as a practical matter. He will not *lightly* recommend overruling any of the Court's decisions, because—irrespective of politics—he will be mindful of institutional cost and settled expectations.

In addition, for obvious reasons, he is constrained by positions his boss has taken in prior cases. No matter who his boss is, he or she will likely value consistency, virtually above all else. There is both an obvious and a much subtler set of considerations at play here. First, and most obviously, if his boss has said X in the past, John certainly cannot recommend "not X." Second, and equally important, he must have consistency in *approach*. If his boss approaches a question from a strict constructionist, or a pragmatic, or a law-and-economics perspective, he will want to bring that perspective to bear in each case and ensure that snippets his boss has written in seemingly unrelated cases do not suggest internal inconsistencies. This ends up being quite tricky; he will learn that an approach to statutory interpretation suggested in an ERISA case may well have significance in his approach to the Telecommunications Act. Thus, in his research, he may have to cast a pretty wide net, and this can take a long time.

Before oral argument, John will probably switch bench memos with his co-clerks and have some sort of formal discussion with his boss. This exchange undoubtedly has as many formats as there are justices, but justices and clerks typically vet the issues in anticipation of oral argument very thoroughly. The best vettings, of course, involve food.

Courtroom of the U.S. Supreme Court

Oral Argument

After the pre-game discussion of cases, it is exciting to go to oral argument. For starters, although most chambers are on the same floor as the courtroom, John spends a lot of time working at the

Supreme Court without running into tourists and the public. On a daily basis, John has learned to negotiate a series of little corridors and back doors that get him from Point A to Point B by means of nonpublic spaces. On "game day," though, he walks into the court-room and sees nearly 400 people assembling to watch the Court's business. Some look like pros; some like law students; some like Hollywood extras in a big budget tourist flick. Their presence lends a hustle and bustle to the proceedings that makes even the most arcane argument a bit thrilling.

The courtroom, too, is awe-inspiring. The Justices sit at a long, finely sculpted wooden desk, backed by an extremely tall red curtain with gold trim, several white marble columns with ionic pedestals, and a gold clock. Through the red curtains, a back entrance for the Justices feeds into their robe room. The Justices have black leather chairs, embossed with their names on the back, which rock and swivel. Traditionally, on a Justice's retirement, his or her colleagues purchase the chair for the retiree as a parting gift. Sometimes, the Justices rock their chairs like a bunch of fidgety nine-year-olds when they get bored or excited.

Law clerks do not get primo seats at oral argument. While attorneys, parties, and visitors get churchlike pews and good views, law clerks get metal folding chairs that are placed in between large marble pillars at one side of the courtroom. From these seats, it can be difficult to see the Justices. After the first couple of sittings, though, John recognizes (virtually) every Justice's voice, so he can take effective notes without craning to see who is talking. Unless it is a glamorous, high-profile case, typically only the law clerk assigned to a case from each chambers will be sitting between the pillars for argument.

Justice Alito recently told an audience that "[o]ral argument is a relatively small and, truth be told, relatively unimportant part of what we do." *Alito Says Preparation, Briefs Play Bigger Role in Supreme Court Decisions than Oral Arguments*, Wash. Post, May 16, 2011. He noted that prior to argument, the Justices will have read hundreds, if not thousands, of pages of material on each case. Argument lasts only an hour, and 40% of the words spoken in argument are spoken by the Justices themselves. Justice Alito suggested that the Justices already knew their inclinations by that point, and they did not, in any event, allow the lawyers to do much talking.

While Justice Alito's personal, comparative assessment about the value of briefs vs. oral argument offers a valuable insider's view-point, it might be hasty to dismiss oral argument as a quaint artifact of a different era. For starters, the Justices generally go into oral argument personally well-prepared, but with no sense of how their colleagues are leaning on a particular issue. Even Justice Alito admitted that, although Justices frequently have lunch together, they make it a rule never to talk about cases. Oral argument thus serves as *the* point at which the Justices can get information on which way their colleagues are leaning, or what issues are giving them trouble. These insights can sharpen their own thinking and can occasionally lead to some strategic behavior from the bench. A savvy listener can discern in the verbal sparring of the Justices efforts to resolve their colleagues' concerns and to themselves advocate for certain positions or principles. Clearly, briefs are the most important input *from the lawyers* in any given case. The principal value of oral argument may lie not in lawyer input at all, but in subtle, Justice-to-Justice communication, using lawyers as foils.[4]

For John's part, he will be hanging in between the pillars, frantically taking notes. One handy perk of his job is that he will quickly learn all the Justices' middle initials, and he will be bandying about "AMK" and "SGB" like a pro in short order.

The Opinion

Chief Justice
John Roberts

After oral argument, the Justices go into conference. In his 2006 interview, Chief Justice Roberts indicated that conference follows argument by two to three days. The Chief begins the discussion on a case by giving his decision and sketching out his reasoning. The next-senior Justice, now Justice Scalia, goes next, and so on down through Justice Kagan. No Justice is allowed to speak twice until every Justice has spoken once, and—in a move that will be recognizable to parents everywhere—Chief Justice Roberts has ruled that facial expressions, like eye-rolling, count as "speech." *Interview with Chief Justice John Roberts* (ABC Nightline television broadcast Nov. 28, 2006) (transcript available at http://abcnews.go .com/Nightline/story?id=2661589).

The senior-most Justice in the majority on a case traditionally has the privilege of assigning the opinion, whether to him/herself or a colleague. Justices leave conference with their assignments in pocket. The law clerk's role at that point varies considerably depending upon the chambers. John and his co-clerks will certainly have a role of substance, as of course will the Justice, but just *how* intensive the intra-chambers back-and-forth becomes depends on each Justice's unique working style and defies the handy generalization.

The opinion-production task is not easy. If the Court simply had to give a thumbs-up or thumbs-down to rule on a case, it might be fairly straightforward. But the task of justifying each logical step—like a geometry proof, only with lots more theorems—can be extremely, mind-wrenchingly difficult. As his chambers works on an opinion, John may have frequent "brick wall" moments. John, his boss, and fellow clerks may spend hours on a single sentence, dickering over the wording of a standard or a principled line.

When the draft opinion is complete, the Justice will circulate it to his or her colleagues for feedback. In a 9-0 case, this process is not a nail-biter. Waiting for word from other chambers in a sharply divided decision, though, is definitely no picnic. There's always a bit of a delay, and John will expend lots of energy pondering the significance of each additional minute. When word comes, John finds that Justices will sometimes join an opinion outright. More frequently, however, they will send comments and initiate a back-and-forth process.

When John knows a dissent is coming, he will anxiously await it. Sometimes dissents can be quite charged.[5] When it comes, it usually will expose some kind of flaw in the draft majority opinion, which will set his chambers back a bit and necessitate deep thinking and additional research. Majority authors differ in how they respond to dissents. Some Justices will commence the battle of the footnotes and attempt to refute every last statement made in dissent. Others will forgo response altogether, perhaps on the theory that statements in the dissent are just that.

At the end of the day, the decision is announced at oral argument. The Justice who has authored the majority opinion delivers a brief summary of the facts, result, and reasoning from the bench. Rarely, when a Justice feels very strongly about an issue, he or she will deliver a dissent from the bench, too. This practice is on the rise. *See* Adam Liptak, *In a Polarized Court, Getting the Last Word*, N.Y. Times, March 9, 2010, at A12. In his 34-year tenure on the Court, Justice William Brennan authored 404 dissents, only *one* of which he read from the bench. (It was *Regents of the University of California v. Bakke*). At the other extreme, as of the end of the 2007-2008 term, Justice Ruth Bader Ginsburg had authored 75 dissents and read 8 of them from the bench. On average, a dissent is read from the bench about three or four times per term, and, with the insider's privilege of advanced notice, John will definitely show up for the rare spectacle.

The final opinions begin at the little pamphlet stage and make their journey to the Supreme Court Reporter, then on to U.S. Reports. As the cases John worked on go to binding, his year on the Court begins to wrap up. His workload during the year was fugue-like. He started with the simple task of writing pool memos, onto which he added the rhythm of bench memos, then the melody of opinions. Now, the layers of sound start to fade. As the Court completes its last oral argument of the year in April, his bench memo days are behind him. When that final opinion comes out in early July, his chambers is done with its official output of the term. John finds himself right back where he started, with a thick stack of pool memos from the new Summer List.

Somehow, this task that seemed so difficult and daunting last July he now handles with ease. Nervous new clerks arrive one by one in successive weeks, as each chambers staggers their arrival to make use of outgoing clerks for training. John and his colleagues, the veterans, give them perfunctory instruction but spend most of their time looking beyond the Court to what comes next. All too soon, John bids farewell to the Justice and staff, the Supreme Court police, and his fellow clerks. One afternoon, he surrenders his ID and hands over the keys.

As abruptly as it started it ends, and John Q. Law Clerk is now on the other side of the door, once again a Supreme Court consumer. He will remember his year in the rosiest of terms. He will leave with a profound sense of confidence that the Justices take their work very seriously and that we are all in good hands. His experience with the good and bad in legal writing will give him instincts about rhetoric that cause him to prefer candor and balance over bombast and white-wash. He will probably feel a profound sense that *his* term was the most important term since OT 1803, when Chief Justice John Marshall penned *Marbury v. Madison.* Moreover—and this is clearly a significant plus—he will have an uncanny ability to quote from arcane FERC decisions that came down his term as a law clerk forever after.

Discussion Questions

1. What surprised you about Professor Beske's description of her year at the Court? What did you learn that you had not realized before reading this piece?
2. Looking back at the process a case goes through, what are the critical points where persuasion is necessary? Who are the possible advocates other than the lawyers, and who are the critical audiences?
3. In Chapter 4, we briefly considered the role of amicus briefs. What additional information did we learn here about how an amicus brief might be received and used? What role did Professor Beske seem to think they should play?
4. From the perspective of the clerk, what makes a brief good? What might be particularly irritating?

Endnotes

1. The papers of Justice Blackmun, released to the public on March 4, 2004, contain pool memos from his tenure on the Rehnquist Court (1986-1993) and offer a fascinating glimpse into behind-the-scenes machinations in key cases. *See* Lee Epstein, Jeffrey A. Segal & Harold J. Spaeth, *The Digital Archive of the Papers of Justice Harry A. Blackmun* (2007), available at: http://epstein.law.northwestern.edu/blackmun.php?p=0.

2. Interestingly, Justice Scalia recently recounted a moment on the D.C. Circuit when he found a brief in a stack that captured his attention, because it was "felicitously put," "elegant," and "crisp." He turned to the cover page, and "it made me so happy to see that it was one of the best lawyers in Washington, and it made me very happy to know that you could tell the difference." *Interview with Justice Antonin Scalia*, 13 Scribes J. Legal Writing 52 (2010).

3. Justice Kennedy said in an interview that "[t]he good lawyer is one who says, 'The proposition that we wish this Court to adopt is X. We think that that is the correct rule for this case because justice will be served. . . . We recognize that there are authorities against us on this point. We recognize, in fact, Your Honor, that this is an uphill battle, but we are here to tell you why we think this rule should be adopted.'" *Interview with Justice Anthony Kennedy*, 13 Scribes J. Legal Writing 90 (2010).

4. *See Interview with Chief Justice John Roberts* (ABC Nightline television broadcast Nov. 28, 2006) (transcript available at http://abcnews.go.com/Nightline/story?id=2661589) ("[Y]ou know, it's no secret we're communicating with each other through the lawyers").

5. *See Interview with Justice Antonin Scalia, supra* note 2, at 64 ("You don't have to get permission from somebody else to put in a vivid metaphor or something like that.").

SECTION III

Our Art Form

This section considers three key characteristics of our genre: beauty in language, effective tone, and the tension between freedom and form. In an introductory legal writing course, the objectives in these areas are less ambitious. Serviceable language (clear, grammatical, error-free, and accurate) is the goal. A generic professional tone will do the trick. And we do not stray from the "rules" about what sections to write, what each section should include, and how to speak the message. But now it's time for some more ambitious goals and maybe even a little risk-taking.

6. Language

Of course, everything in this book is about language. But in this chapter, we'll look at the beauty of language and the impact it can have on persuasion. Up to this point, the topics have been part of the background material for our project, but now we begin learning some specific terms and concepts. Therefore, we'll begin adding a summary of terms and concepts at the end of each relevant chapter. These terms and concepts will become the criteria you'll use to analyze the briefs introduced in this book and to work on your own writing.

Our first reading is an excerpt from Professor Stephen Smith's exploration of some principles of poetry (imagery, figures of speech, word choice, and stylistic variety) and how they relate to brief-writing. This excerpt provides a few examples of the kinds of small language choices that can make such a difference in persuasion.

Excerpt from

Stephen E. Smith, *The Poetry of Persuasion: Early Literary Theory and Its Advice to Legal Writers*

6 J. ALWD 55 (Fall 2009)

Why is [aesthetic pleasure] important? . . . There is, unsurprisingly, unanimous agreement among critics that to bring a reader pleasure is the goal of poet and persuader alike. . . .

The Elements of Good Writing

Through the ages, critics have tried to provide roadmaps to, or perhaps cookbooks for, good [beautiful] writing. They have been unwilling to simply throw up their hands, and leave good writing to the muses. . . . There are a few categories in which the voices of many critics, over many centuries, have had much to say. By attending to these elements, writers should be able to increase the aesthetic appeal of their writing. The sections below discuss the use of imagery, word choice, figures of speech, variety, and tone.

Visual Imagery

Early on, Aristotle champions the use of visual imagery. . . . Longinus, too, emphasizes the use of imagery. . . . Ezra Pound, an originator of literary Modernism, if not *the* originator, describes the power of imagery—"An 'Image' is that which presents an intellectual and emotional complex in an instant of time."[1] He, and the writers before him, identify a singular power in the vivid presentation of an idea or action.

To this day, it is standard advice to legal writers to use visual images. This advice is supported not only by intuitive appeal, but also by experimental evidence. A 1980 study by three Stanford psychologists concluded that "flashy, dramatic facts can flood the mind of the decision-maker, outweighing by their insistence alone the more pallid truths of the case."[2] The writers first reviewed existing literature, noting that "[w]ords and phrases that are concrete and evoke vivid imagery are better remembered than abstract, pallid words in practically all verbal learning experiments."[3] They then set forth their hypothesis: that vivid imagery is more memorable and therefore available to the hearer/reader, and as a result the material is used disproportionately by the hearer/reader in making judgments.[4]

Here is an example of the sort of "vividness adjustment" made in the study. The posited case was a trial on a drunk driving charge. The subjects were to determine whether the defendant had, indeed, been drunk. The pallid version of the driver's condition before arrest described this scene: "On his way out the door, Sanders [the defendant] staggered against a serving table, knocking a bowl to the floor."[5] The vivid version, on the other hand, revealed that: "On his way out the door, Sanders staggered against a serving table, knocking a bowl of guacamole dip to the floor and splattering guacamole on the white shag carpet."[6]

The study confirmed that "subjects disproportionately recalled the vivid arguments."[7] More important, they were not only easily recalled, but provided the "disproportionate impact on evaluative judgments" the authors hypothesized.[8]

This experiment confirms what literary theorists have long said. It also makes clear the connection between the literary and the legal. The same tools that provide the "liveliness" prescribed by Aristotle and the "raptness" sought by Longinus may also lead to a measurable effect on the decision made by a judge reviewing a brief.

hopeandmegans flickr photostream

**"Bong Hits 4 Jesus," taken at a parade on
July 4, 2007, Columbus, Ohio**

Petitioners' opening brief in *Morse v. Frederick*[9] provides an example of vivid presentation. *Morse* is the notorious "Bong Hits 4 Jesus" case, in which a high school student claimed his speech rights were violated when he was suspended for displaying a banner containing those words at a civic event in Juneau, Alaska. The petitioners did not merely mention a vague "civic event," however. In an effort to emphasize the importance of the event disrupted by the student's banner, great detail is provided:

> January 24, 2002 marked the first time in Olympic history that the Olympic Torch Relay visited Alaska. In preparation, a local task force of approximately two dozen local civic leaders planned for Juneau's participation in the international event—a ten-mile relay through Juneau. Members of the city government, including the mayor's office and the Juneau Department of Parks and Recreation, lent their support. Local businesses, as well as national sponsors of the torch relay, supported the event. The torch ceremony involved a week of community festivities. Upon its arrival in Juneau, the Olympic flame was welcomed by Tlingit Clan dancers, transported in a native canoe around Gastineau Channel, and carried through several miles of Juneau's streets, including past the State Capitol and the Juneau-Douglas High School.[10]

This passage walks the reader through the labor-intensive efforts to organize the relay, notes the comprehensive scope of community involvement, and makes clear the momentousness of the occasion.

It reads as though the Olympics themselves were taking place in Juneau. Providing this vivid description of the circumstances makes the student's prank all the more disruptive and far-reaching—the entire city suffered for his acts. Perhaps unsurprisingly, the Supreme Court ruled in favor of the school district, and against the student. While no calculations can assess the effectiveness of vividness in this or other particular cases, the persuasive power of detailed description cannot easily be dismissed.

Figures of Speech

... It may seem as though there is little place for colorful figures in the matter-of-fact world of legal writing, but their use can be engaging and emphatic, without being distracting. An example is provided by a recent amicus brief to the United States Supreme Court.[11] Here, the authors use two familiar devices, isocolon [a sequence of clauses of identical length][12] and antithesis [a method of contrasting ideas sharpened by the use of opposite meanings][13] to emphasize policy concerns arising in patent law. The authors note that "[a]s a practical matter, objective standards such as those defined by the TSM requirement promote the goals of certainty over uncertainty, and predictability over unpredictability."[14] Antithesis, of course, is found in the adjective opposites of certainty and uncertainty, and of predictability and unpredictability. Isocolon is found in the parallel form of "X over Y, and X1 over Y2."

Shortly thereafter, the authors use the same devices again: "The patent system rewards those who can *and do,* not those who can but don't."[15] Using these figures draws the reader's attention to the policy benefits the authors suggest. They do this by essentially doubling the idea, and, perhaps, by creating a rhythmic pleasure in the words. The figures provide persuasive assistance and readability, without becoming overwrought. ...

Word Choice—*Le Mot Juste*

In poetry criticism, there is a long history of attention to word choice. Longinus proclaimed that "we may say with strict truth that beautiful words are the very light of thought."[16] And Flaubert is famous for his search for *le mot juste—the* one right or apt word.[17] The attention to word choice in poetry is suited to the legal writer, as well.

Aristotle addressed the orator's choice of words in ways particularly pertinent to the legal writer. ... [It] is an issue of reasoning, in a concrete sense—a reason for every word. ... [W]hat do the cases really say, and how does the matter one is working on find support in or distinction from those cases? Every word counts, every modifier, every verb, every denotation.

Another important aspect of word choice is achieving clarity. ...

Library of Congress (photo by Harris & Ewing)

Justice Benjamin Cardozo, 1937

But these are substantive issues, again, the right word for the right reason. What about aesthetic word choice? What about choices that *need* not be made, but perhaps *should*? . . . [T]here are almost always choices to be made in the selection of words, and some of the alternatives may be more engaging than others.

Justice Cardozo provides an example. In this passage, it is plain that choices were made. Many different sentences, and many different words, could have conveyed the same meaning. But these sentences, and these words, engage the reader in a way the other choices might not have:

> In the presence of this urgent need for some remedial expedient, the question is to be answered whether the expedient adopted has over-lept the bounds of power. The assailants of the statute say that its dominant end and aim is to drive the state Legislatures under the whip of economic pressure into the enactment of unemployment compensation laws at the bidding of the central government. Supporters of the statute say that its operation is not constraint, but the

Library of Congress

"Make-up artist," 1961

creation of a larger freedom, the states and the nation joining in a co-operative endeavor to avert a common evil.[18]

From the interior rhyme of "remedial expedient," to the unusual usage of "overlept," through the frightening vision of "assailants," and the metaphoric "whip," culminating in the selection of the quasi-alliterative words "constraint," "creation," "co-operative" and "common," this is unmistakably aesthetically motivated—an effort not only to report, but to provide pleasure.

Evocative word choice need not be limited to judicial writing. The briefs in *Jespersen v. Harrah's*[19] bear witness to the possibilities available to the legal writer. The *Jespersen* plaintiff sued her employer after she was terminated for refusing to wear makeup on the job. In one of plaintiff's briefs to the Ninth Circuit, she asserted that "notwithstanding her twenty-one years of loyal, 'outstanding' service, Harrah's terminated Jespersen's employment. Nothing else mattered if she declined to paint her face."[20] The choice of "paint her face," rather than, say, "wear makeup" suggests something almost grotesque and cartoonish—hardly something an employer should want, let alone require, from an employee. It also sounds singularly unrelated to the performance of work duties.

An amicus brief counters that an employer should be able to maintain appearance standards of its choosing, lest it find itself represented by "employees who sport jewelry like Mr. T, wear makeup like Gene Simmons of Kiss, dress like Dennis Rodman, have hair like Fabio or beards like a member of ZZ Top."[21] Here, rather than a coolly rational explanation of makeup and its benefits to the employer, a parade of comic horribles sets forth and drives home the dangers of unregulated employee appearance.

Other examples of word choice in the *Jespersen* briefs are less dramatic but equally important. The defendant characterizes plaintiff's interpretation of Title VII as an "all-encompassing law that eradicates sex-based stereotypes, and, thus, prohibits all gender-based appearance standards."[22] There is drama to the scope of the proposed interpretation described by the defendant. "All-encompassing" sounds dangerously broad and lacks subtle, considerate responsiveness from the law. "Eradicate," as well, has a draconian, severe tone. This presentation of extremity may raise the hackles of a moderate reader. Perhaps sensing this, the plaintiff replies with a dismissive, hyperbolic restatement of defendant's characterization, calling it "a hypothetical mandate of universal androgyny."[23] Something "hypothetical," of course, is nonexistent. And it is hard to imagine anyone positing something so inconceivable to us as a "mandate of universal androgyny." Through careful word choice, defendant makes plaintiff's argument sound unreasonable and ham-fisted. Plaintiff then undermines that strategy by making defendant sound shrill.

Not every writer can be Justice Cardozo. Not every writer should invoke Mr. T in a brief. But because "the choice of appropriate and striking words has a marvellous power and an enthralling charm for the reader," the fitting word choice should be an ongoing challenge addressed by the legal writer, both for substantive reasons, and for the degree to which words can provide aesthetic pleasure and engage the reader.

Stylistic Variety

To keep a judge's attention through the course of a long brief, the tools used and strategies employed must be varied. No one wants to read a brief in which every sentence is structured as dependent clause followed by independent clause. Nor should every sentence be the same number of words. Just as in music, where a song typically has verses, choruses, and a bridge to add a twist, a new element, legal writing and poetry must carefully mix the elements available to them. . . .

Although good legal writing should not have to compete with the work of Shakespeare, it should take to heart this lesson of these theorists and employ a style with varied elements. A good recent example of such variety—within a very few words—is contained in Justice Breyer's partial dissent in *Exxon v. Baker*.[24] He writes:

> In my view, a limited exception to the Court's 1:1 ratio is warranted here. As the facts set forth in Part I of the Court's opinion make clear, this was no mine-run case of reckless behavior. The jury could reasonably have believed that Exxon knowingly allowed a relapsed alcoholic repeatedly to pilot a vessel filled with millions of gallons of oil through waters that provided the livelihood for the many plaintiffs in this case. Given that conduct, it was only a matter of time before a crash and spill like this occurred. And as Justice Ginsburg points out, the damage easily could have been much worse. The jury thought that the facts here justified punitive damages of $5 billion. The District Court agreed.[25]

Justice Breyer begins with a reasonably short declarative sentence. He then writes a somewhat longer two-clause sentence, containing a metaphor ("mine-run," a variant of "run of the mine," or the more common "run of the mill"). The next sentence not only provides a vivid description of the scene and its attendant risks, but uses subtle initial alliteration ("reasonably," "relapsed," "repeatedly"). The passage ends with two short declarative sentences, each buttressing the other.

This short paragraph does not, of course, provide a blueprint for legal writing. But it does demonstrate the ways in which attention to variety can create an interesting, and perhaps pleasing experience for the reader. . . .

Conclusion

Legal writing that attends to issues of aesthetic pleasure may be more persuasive. While no one will ever suggest that clarity and sense should be sacrificed in favor of clever artifice, the proper use of art should nonetheless be part of the writer's toolbox. To keep writing interesting and enjoyable can only help a client's case.

When writing, it is difficult to remember to use various stylistic elements that can elevate and energize prose. But by paying attention to the dictates of poetry critics throughout the ages, it may be possible to pay that little bit of extra attention to style—to use a vivid image, to think that extra moment about word choice. There is no formula. An asyndeton a day does not keep the unfavorable judgment away. It can never hurt, however, to be attentive to the many possibilities, and to try to take advantage of every opportunity to persuade our readers.

Next, a short excerpt from Professor Bruce Ching exploring the almost magical power of "things in threes."

Excerpt from

Bruce Ching, *Things in Threes—Utilizing Tricolons—a Linguistic Look*
The Law Teacher 18 (Fall 2008)

Classical rhetoric, the art of persuasion, taught the practitioner to present items and actions in groups of three. A well-known example is Julius Caesar's summary of his military campaign in Gaul: "I came, I saw, I conquered." Another is the assertion of abiding qualities of "Faith, hope, and love" in the Christian new testament. Still another is the slogan of "liberty, equality, fraternity" from the French Revolution.

Such tricolons also occur in judicial opinions. For example, in a Title VII sexual harassment case, an appellate judge excoriated the employer by stating that "[i]ts efforts at investigation were lackluster, its disciplinary efforts nonexistent, its remedial efforts perfunctory."[26] Recognizing the judicial opinion's rhetorical technique, one commentator declared that the judge's statement "expresses indignation in a tricolon of ascending condemnation. . . ."[27] . . .

The effectiveness of the tricolon technique is enhanced by parallel linguistic structure among components. One legal writing textbook notes that "[b]y making phrases or clauses syntactically similar, you are emphasizing that each element in a series is expressing a relation similar to that of the other elements in the series. Such coordination promotes clarity and continuity."[28] . . .

Grouping items into threes emphasizes parallel structure—once is an occurrence, twice could be a coincidence, but three times appears to be a pattern. Of course, results tend to be better when content and structure are mutually reinforcing. . . .

The article then reports on class discussions of two famous examples of tricolons. We will look at only one here: "our lives, our fortunes and our sacred honor."

At the end of the Declaration of Independence, Jefferson states that "for the support of this declaration, with a firm reliance on the protection of Divine Providence, we mutually pledge to each other our lives, our fortunes and our sacred honor." First, we observe that the repetition of the word "our"—in classical terms, an anaphora—at the beginning of each tricolon component helped to facilitate transition between components. We then considered why Jefferson would have used the particular sequence of "our lives, our fortunes, and our sacred honor"—rather than, e.g., "our lives, our sacred honor, and our fortunes." One student said that finishing the phrase with "our fortunes" would run the risk of "sounding sort of greedy." Other students observed that "our sacred honor" was the highest and noblest of the tricolon components and placing it at the end gave it a position of emphasis. I noted this was an example of the principle of recency—placing something last gives it the most emphasis. I then pointed out that placing "lives" at the beginning of the tricolon also gave it a position of emphasis, under the principle of primacy. Jefferson's sequence therefore gave some emphasis to the Continental Congress delegates' pledge of their lives, mentioned but deemphasized the pledge of their property, and gave the strongest emphasis to the pledge of their "sacred honor."

We also looked at the meter of the tricolon components—lives (one syllable), fortunes (one stressed syllable followed by one unstressed syllable), sacred honor (one stressed syllable followed by one unstressed syllable, then again one stressed syllable followed by one unstressed syllable). We concluded that the metrical arrangement could subtly suggest an increasing importance as the phrase reached its finish. . . .

Conclusion

As noted above, the presentation of tricolons can use sequencing— such as metrical considerations and progressive shifts in theme—to link content to structure with varying degrees of subtlety. Although students commented favorably on our discussion of tricolons, they seemed rather relieved when I said they did not *have* to use them in their papers. But I was unexpectedly moved when one of my students later came back with excitement to tell me about her experience in a moot court competition, and how she concluded her argument by saying "There are three reasons my client should win: law, policy, and equity."

In this next excerpt, Professor Bret Rappaport shows us the musical quality of rhythm, a writing quality notoriously difficult to explain.

Excerpt from

Bret Rappaport, *Using the Elements of Rhythm, Flow, and Tone to Create a More Effective and Persuasive Acoustic Experience in Legal Writing*
16 J. Legal Writing 65 (2010)

As recent scholarship reveals, there is a scientific basis for why rhythm, flow, and tone attract and keep readers' interests—the innate connection between language and music. . . . This article . . . summarizes research establishing how music and language co-evolved. The neurological mechanisms that operate to perceive and be influenced by music are the same ones (or many of the same ones) that operate in the brain for language—first spoken and then written. We hear what we read. . . .

Part II [of the article] offers background on evolutionary psychology and explores how human and proto-human brains evolved through natural selection to house information processing traits that we moderns call "human nature." It examines the scholarship of biomusicology and explains the neurological overlap of music and language—musilanguage. . . .

Incorporating musical elements into written text enhances . . . comprehension. . . . Research by University of Massachusetts Professor Emeritus Peter Elbow demonstrates that including musical elements in writing accomplishes enhanced comprehension by pulling the reader in and pulling the reader along. Musical elements of rhythm, and to a lesser degree melody (flow), create energy to "bind written words together so as to pull us along from one part to the next and to make us feel that all parts are held together into a magnetic or centripetal whole."[29]

Dr. Elbow, author of the landmark *Writing Without Teachers*,[30] was a pioneer of the process revolution in the teaching of writing. He helped free students from formal rules during the drafting stages of writing and helped them learn to explore themselves through creative uses of English. He points out how academics (and by analogy lawyers) fail to recognize that readers hear what they read. These writers ignore the organizational lessons of music "to bind time." Dr. Elbow cites to the evolutionary concepts explained earlier to conclude that "hearing—the modality that works in time—reaches an older, deeper, and more instinctual part of the brain than sight. Rhythm and movement reach inside us."[31] Those writers who "lead us on a journey to satisfaction by way of expectations" recognize that "[s]entences are little pieces of energy or music—they have rhythm and melody—even on the page. . . ."[32]

Dr. Elbow's notion of incorporating musical elements into writing to pull the reader in and along is also used by speech makers who implicitly recognize the musilanguage. Thus, from the steps of the Lincoln Memorial, Martin Luther King resorted to musical elements to pull the multitudes in and along. His *I Have a Dream* speech is punctuated by musical elements of rhythm and repetition (italicized), with its call-and-response cadences:

> *I have a dream* that one day on the red hills of Georgia the sons of former slaves and the sons of former slave owners will be able to sit down together at the table of brotherhood.
>
> *I have a dream* that one day even the state of Mississippi, a state sweltering with the heat of injustice, sweltering with the heat of oppression, will be transformed into an oasis of freedom and justice.

> *I have a dream* that my four little children will one day live in a nation where they will not be judged by the color of their skin but by the content of their character.
>
> *I have a dream* today.
>
> *I have a dream* that one day, down in Alabama, with its vicious racists, with its governor having his lips dripping with the words of interposition and nullification; one day right there in Alabama, little black boys and black girls will be able to join hands with little white boys and white girls as sisters and brothers.
>
> *I have a dream* today. . . .[33]

. . . Great speeches are not unique examples of how musical elements can be used to enhance memory, comprehension, and persuasiveness of words. . . . "Nature, [Cicero] tells us, has placed in the ears a register which tells us if rhythm is good or bad" and everyone has rhythm.[34] Here is how lawyers should use it. . . .

A. Rhythm in Writing

. . . Rhythm is recurrence, and recurrence captivates because recurrence is innate. Recurrence is seen in Nature's rolling waves, patterns in leaves, and in the "noise of the wind." In music, recurrence is heard as the background beat that holds the piece together. In text, recurrence is heard in the mind's ear as it serves to move the piece along from word-to-word, sentence-to-sentence, paragraph-to-paragraph, and section-to-section, binding together a comprehensive whole. The essential elements of rhythm are balance, cycles of sounds, and sentence structure and variety.

1. Balance

Balance in music (once a button on a stereo equalizer but now an iPod setting) moderates the acoustic relationship of sound sources to one another. Balance in writing is the relationship between, or repetition of, words or sounds within a sentence, as well as the variation of sentence length within a paragraph.

Literature offers . . . example[s]. . . . Just as Hemingway and Wolfe did in their novels, legal writers like Judges Learned Hand and Benjamin Cardozo employed balance in their opinions. A good example of this effective use of balance in persuasive legal writing is *Palsgraf v. Long Island Railroad*, in which Judge Cardozo opened his opinion this way:

> Plaintiff was standing on a platform of defendant's railroad after buying a ticket to go to Rockaway Beach. A train stopped at the station, bound for another place. Two men ran forward to catch it. One of the men reached the platform of the car without mishap, though the train was already moving. The other man, carrying a package, jumped aboard the car, but seemed unsteady as if about

to fall. A guard on the car, who had held the door open, reached forward to help him in, and another guard on the platform pushed him from behind. In this act, the package was dislodged, and fell upon the rails. It was a package of small size, about fifteen inches long, and was covered by a newspaper. In fact it contained fireworks, but there was nothing in its appearance to give notice of its contents. The fireworks when they fell exploded. The shock of the explosion threw down some scales at the other end of the platform, many feet away. The scales struck the plaintiff, causing injuries for which she sues.[35]

As pointed out by others, notice how Cardozo varies the length of the sentences and how after the word "moving" the choppiness of the sentences mirrors the chaos happening on the railroad platform.[36] It is the length of the sentences, individually and in connection with those that precede and come after, that creates rhythm.

2. Cycles of Sound - repetition of sound.

The term "cycles of sound"[37] refers to repetition of a sound, syllable, word, phrase, line, stanza, or metrical pattern in a written work. It is the basic unifying device in all poetry, which itself owes much to music. Repetition can operate on many levels within a written work. For example, alliteration is when repetition of letters, syllables, or sound is found in the same sound at the beginning of two or more stressed syllables. The repetition of similar vowel sounds is called assonance. . . .

These lessons . . . are not lost on some judges. Justice William O. Douglas used repetition (bold and underscored) and alliteration (italicized) to illustrate that Jacksonville's vagrancy ordinance was not only unconstitutional but bad for our well being. He wrote of the right to wander, stroll, and loaf and that:

> These unwritten *amenities* have been in part responsible for giving our people the feeling of independence and self-*confidence*, the feeling of *creativity*. These *amenities* have *dignified* the **right** of *dissent* and have honored the **right** to be non-conformists and the **right** to *defy* submissiveness. They have encouraged lives of high *spirit* rather than hushed, *suffocating silence.*[38]

Justice Douglas deliberately chose words with similar front end sounds, like "self-confidence" and "creatively," "dignified" and "dissent" and "defy," and "spirit" and "suffocating silence," to create that cycle of sound that strolls through this passage, like the plaintiff whose constitutional right to wander was being adjudicated.

Finally, the repetition of ideas is perhaps the most important repetition device for a legal brief. Repetition of the main terms of an argument is known as *epanodos* and can be used effectively by lawyers. A *traductio* is a more subtle means of repeating the same main terms of an argument by settling on a key term and repeating that term throughout the work.

In the majority opinion in *Texas v. Johnson*,[39] Justice William Brennan used a *traductio* (that the flag is "cherished"), several alliterations (italicized), and an anaphora (underscored) to create a masterful piece of legal writing that illustrates the importance of upholding a person's right to burn the American flag.

> We are tempted to say, in fact, that the flag's deservedly **cherished** place in our community will be strengthened, not weakened, by our holding today. Our decision is a reaffirmation of the principles of freedom and inclusiveness that the flag best reflects, and of the conviction that our toleration of criticism such as Johnson's is a *sign* and *source* of our strength. Indeed, one of the proudest images of our flag, the one immortalized in our own national anthem, is of the bombardment it survived at Fort McHenry. It is the Nation's *resilience*, not its *rigidity*, that Texas sees *reflected* in the flag—and it is that *resilience* [italics added] that we *reassert* today. . . .
>
> The way to preserve the flag's special role is not to *punish* those who feel differently about these matters. It is to *persuade* them that they are wrong. . . . We can imagine *no more* appropriate response to burning a flag than waving one's own, *no better* way to counter a flag burner's message than by saluting the flag that burns, *no surer* means of preserving the dignity even of the flag that burned than by—as one witness here did—according its remains a respectful burial. We do not consecrate the flag by punishing its *desecration*, for in *doing* so we *dilute* the freedom that this **cherished** emblem represents.[40]

Returning to the crossroads of music and persuasive writing, lawyer and writer Bill Long noted one easy way to remember the power and importance of cycles of sound like an *epanodos*. On his website, he writes: "'Epi' is 'upon,' 'ana' is 'again,' and 'odos' is 'road.'" I always hear Willie Nelson singing 'On the Road Again,' whenever I think of the word epanodos."[41]

Later in the article we just sampled, Professor Rappaport gives some sage advice about how to find the inner rhythm that can produce such beautiful writing:

Excerpt from

Bret Rappaport, *Using the Elements of Rhythm, Flow, and Tone to Create a More Effective and Persuasive Acoustic Experience in Legal Writing*
16 J. Legal Writing 65, 108 (2010)

[A] writer must write in silence—real silence: the total absence of distraction in any form. Purge the noise from the room and with it the clutter from your mind. The ears on the side of your head must sit idle for the mind's ear to truly hear. A recent study of college students proves the point.[42] Twenty-somethings often listen to music while they use a computer. Forty-five psychology undergraduates wrote brief expository essays with music playing. Others did so in silence. The results were clear that background music significantly disrupted writing fluency . . . even though no response to the music was required. The researchers concluded that even unattended music places heavy demands on working memory and disrupts writing. UCLA Professor Susan K. Perry writes that rhythm must come from within and "[a]ctual musical rhythms coming from outside your mind may interfere with the inner voices and cadence you're listening so intently for."[43]

Write in silence.

Finally, a suggestion: Part Four of Ross Guberman's excellent book, *Point Made: How to Write Like the Nation's Top Advocates* (Oxford U. Press 2011) (buy it if you don't already have it) provides additional strategies for strikingly beautiful and effective writing choices. Among them are examples of using colorful verbs ("plunged" rather than "fell"); effective figures of speech ("cooking the books"); short pithy sentences balanced with longer sentences ("Substituting one decisionmaker for another may yield a different result, but not in any sense a more 'correct' one. So too here.");[44] parallel constructions; and even rhetorical questions.

Key Concepts

Visual imagery
Figures of speech
Word choice
Stylistic variety
Tricolons
Rhythm (balance and cycles of sound)

Discussion Questions

1. Professor Rappaport strongly suggests writing in silence. How do you write? What kinds of distractions surround you? Would it work for you to write in silence? What would that be like?
2. What other examples of tricolons can you think of? If none come to mind immediately, start listening for them.
3. Bring to class an example of beautiful or striking legal language you have seen. Share it with your classmates or your small group, seeing if, together, you can identify some of the qualities that make it effective. Don't limit your analysis to the ideas mentioned in this chapter.
4. Do you think that beautiful and striking language (like the examples in these articles) increase persuasiveness?
5. Do you think you might be able to create language as beautiful as some of these examples? Can you do it now? Might you learn to do it with practice? What other strategies can you think of for learning to write more beautifully?
6. If you have time, read Ruth Anne Robbins, *Painting with Print: Incorporating Concepts of Typographic and Layout Design into the Text of Legal Writing Documents*, 2 J. ALWD 108 (2004), an excellent article that explains the importance of a document's visual layout and shows us how to do a better job with those formatting decisions.

Endnotes

1. Ezra Pound, *A Few Don'ts by an Imagiste*, in *Modernism, an Anthology* 95 (Lawrence Rainey ed., Blackwell Publg. 2005) (originally published 1912).
2. Robert M. Reyes, William C. Thompson & Gordon H. Bower, *Judgmental Biases Resulting from Differing Availabilities of Arguments*, 39 J. Pers. Soc. Psychol. 2, 11 (1980).
3. *Id.* at 3.
4. *Id.*
5. *Id.* at 4.
6. *Id.*
7. *Id.* at 5. The authors noted that "vivid information might be better recalled because it is better learned initially or forgotten less rapidly." *Id.* at 8 n.2.
8. *Id.* at 8.
9. *Morse v. Frederick*, 551 U.S. 393 (2007).
10. Br. for Petr. At 2-3, *Morse v. Frederick*, 551 U.S. 393 (2007) (citations omitted).
11. Br. of the Intell. Prop. L. Assn. of Chi. As Amicus Curiae in Support of Tespt., *KSR Intern. Co. v. Teleflex Inc.*, 550 U.S. 398 (2007).

12. Isocolon is "[a] sequence of clauses or sentences of identical length." J.A. Cuddon, *The Penguin Dictionary of Literary Terms and Literary Theory* 432 (4th ed., Penguin Books 1999).

13. Antithesis is a method of "contrasting ideas sharpened by the use of opposite or noticeably different meanings." *Id.* at 46.

14. Br. of the Intell. Prop. L. Assn. of Chi. At 4, *KSR Intern. Co.*, 550 U.S. 395.

15. *Id.* at 11.

16. Longinus, *On the Sublime* 57 (H.L. Havell trans., Macmillan & Co. 1890) (originally published third century).

17. *See e.g.*, Charles Carlut, *La Correspondance de Flaubert* 173 (Ohio State U. Press 1968) (quoting Flaubert correspondence with George Sand). . . .

18. *Charles C. Steward Mach. Co. v. Davis*, 301 U.S. 548, 587 (1937).

19. *Jespersen v. Harrah's Operating Co., Inc.*, 444 F.3d 1104 (9th Cir. 2006).

20. Reply Br. of Appellant Darlene Jespersen, *Jespersen*, 444 F.3d 1104 (no pagination available).

21. Br. of amici curiae Council for Empl. Law Eq. et al., *Jespersen*, 444 F.3d 1104 (no pagination available).

22. Appellee's Answering Br. at 8, *Jespersen*, 444 F.3d 1104.

23. Reply Br. of Appellant Darlene Jespersen, *Jespersen*, 444 F.3d 1104.

24. *Exxon Shipping Co. v. Baker*, 128 S. Ct. 2605, 2640 (2008) (Breyer, J., concurring in part and dissenting in part).

25. *Id.* at 2640 (citations omitted).

26. *Carr v. Allison Gas Turbine Division, General Motors Corp.*, 32 F.3d 1007, 1012 (7th Cir. 1994).

27. Martha Nussbaum, *Poets as Judges: Judicial Rhetoric and the Literary Imagination*, 62 U. Chi. L. Rev. 1477, 1508 (1995).

28. Helene S. Shapo, Marilyn R. Walter & Elizabeth Fajans, *Writing and Analysis in the Law* 174 (4th ed., Foundation Press 1999).

29. Peter Elbow, *The Music of Form: Rethinking Organization in Writing*, 57 College Composition & Commun. 620, 625 (June 2006).

30. Peter Elbow, *Writing Without Teachers* (2d ed., Oxford U. Press 1998).

31. Elbow, *supra* note 29, at 626.

32. *Id.*

33. The full text of the speech is available on line at http://www.usconstitution.net /dream.html. . . . [You can listen to the full speech at http://www.americanrhetoric.com /speeches/mlkihaveadream.htm.]

34. Albert C. Clark, *Prose Rhyme in English* 3 (Oxford at Clarendon Press 1913).

35. 248 N.Y. 339 (1928).

36. Stephen V. Armstrong & Timothy P. Terrell, *The Subtlety of Rhythm*, 12 Perspectives 174 (Spring 2004).

37. Jack Hart, *The Writer's Coach: An Editor's Guide to Words that Work* 134 (Pantheon Bks. 2006).

38. *Papachristou v. City of Jacksonville*, 405 U.S. 156, 164 (1972) (emphasis added). . . .

39. 491 U.S. 397 (1989).

40. *Id.* at 419-420 (emphasis added).

41. Bill Long, *Similar but Different*, http://www.drbilllong.com/Words/Similar.html (2004).

42. Sarah Ransdell & Lee Gilroy, *The Effects of Background Music on Word Processed Writing*, 17 Computers in Human Behavior 141-148 (Mar. 2001).

43. Susan K. Perry, *Writing in Flow: Keys to Enhanced Creativity* 171 (Writer's Dig. Bk. 1999).

44. John Roberts et al., *Brief for Petitioner, Alaska v. EPA*, 2003 U.S. Sup. Ct. Briefs, LEXIS 482, 44-45.

7. Tone

Chapter 2 gave us a pair of definitions: "Voice" is what your writing says about *who you are*. Closely related, "tone" is what your writing says about your *attitudes*—attitudes toward your audience, your topic, and the parties about whom you are writing.

How does our language communicate those attitudes? We begin with some sage advice from Justice Scalia and Bryan Garner about how a lawyer should envision her relationship to the Court.

Excerpt from
Antonin Scalia & Bryan A. Garner, *Making Your Case: The Art of Persuading Judges*
33-35 (Thomson/West 2008)

Assume a posture of respectful intellectual equality with the bench.

Scalia and Garner first give high praise to the rhetorical posture assumed by the Solicitor General of the United States. The Solicitor General is sometimes referred to as the "tenth justice." This description refers, in part, to the relationship the Solicitor General assumes—a relationship of "respectful intellectual equality":

Intellectual equality requires you to know your stuff, to stand your ground, and to do so with equanimity. When you write your brief, . . . have clearly in mind this relationship. . . . It is *not* the relationship of teacher to student—and if the judges get the impression that this is your view of things, you will have antagonized them. Nor is it the relationship of supplicant to benefactor. You are not there to cajole a favor out of the judges but to help them understand what justice demands, on the basis of your intimate knowledge of the facts and law. Perhaps the best image of the relationship you should be striving to establish is that of an experienced junior partner in your firm explaining a case to a highly intelligent senior partner.

Next, Professor McArdle helps us begin to look at how tone can be heard in a text, as she examines the differing judicial tones of two Supreme Court justices, Justice Breyer and Justice Scalia.

Excerpt from

Andrea McArdle, *Teaching Writing in Clinical, Lawyering, and Legal Writing Courses: Negotiating Professional and Personal Voice*

12 Clinical L. Rev. 501, 510-514 (2005-2006)

Justice Breyer's concurrence in *Chicago v. Morales*,[1] a case decided in 1999, is marked by its brevity and directness. In that case, the Supreme Court invalidated a Chicago ordinance that gave local police discretion to arrest suspected street gang members standing with one or more persons in a public place when they refused to obey an order to disperse. Concurring in the judgment and concurring in the opinion in part, Justice Breyer wrote:

> The ordinance is unconstitutional, not because a policeman applied this discretion wisely or poorly in a particular case, but rather because the policeman enjoys too much discretion in *every case*. And if every application of the ordinance represents an exercise of unlimited discretion, then the ordinance is invalid in all its applications.[2]

The quoted language is straightforward and succinct. Its balanced, parallel structure (not because/but rather because, in a particular case/ in every case) and the repetition of language (discretion, application) give it its cadence. Note also the use of an if/then rule structure, which suggests the writer's lawyerly vocation: if every application . . . then the ordinance is invalid. . . . Examined in isolation, this passage may not have the stamp of the writer's individual, idiosyncratic personality, but it has a notable clarity and assertiveness—[a] declarative tone—and it exudes confidence. . . . [T]he salient qualities are . . . the clarity and confidence of his point. . . . He achieves this effect by . . . resorting to a kind of rhythmic repetition.

[Justice Breyer's dissent in *Bush v. Gore*[3] is similar.] In the opening he repeats the straightforward declarative statement that the Court was "wrong": "The Court was wrong to take this case. It was wrong to grant a stay. It should now vacate that stay and permit the Florida Supreme Court to decide whether the recount should resume."[4] In the concluding passage, he uses variations of the verb form "to do" (do/doing/does/done) and the adjective formed from the verb (undone) to underline the fact that refraining from acting in response to limits on the judicial role is itself judicial action:

I fear that in order to bring this agonizingly long election process to a definitive conclusion, we have not adequately attended to that necessary "check upon our own exercise of power," "our own sense of self-restraint," (citation omitted). Justice Brandeis once said of the Court, "The most important thing we do is not doing." (citation omitted). What it does today, the Court should have left undone. I would repair the damage done as best we now can, by permitting the Florida recount to continue under uniform standards. I respectfully dissent.[5]

This passage . . . [invokes an] authoritative judicial voice, the use of the collective "we" and "our" of the Court. And the language at times has a professional formality to it (definitive conclusion/adequately attended/uniform standards). But Breyer inserts his own personality by juxtaposing the institutional "we" with the use of the first person, and by communicating that he shares with the larger American public the experience of enduring the "agonizingly long" process of verifying how the Florida electorate actually voted. That confession of a personal response, and the candid acknowledging that the Court itself is subject to limits, and bears institutional responsibility for failing to observe them, speaks to a range of readers, professional and non-legally-trained.

Contrast these selections with Antonin Scalia's dissent in *Troxel v. Granville*.[6] There, a plurality of the Court invalidated as applied a state statute permitting grandparents and other third parties to petition for child visitation even over a parent's objection, on a showing of "best interests" of the child. The fractionated court produced six opinions, including this excerpt from Scalia's dissent:

In my view, a right of parents to direct the upbringing of their children is among the "unalienable rights" with which the Declaration of Independence proclaims "all men . . . are endowed by their Creator." And in my view that right is also among "other rights retained by the people" which the Ninth Amendment says the Constitution's enumeration of rights "shall not be construed to deny or disparage." The Declaration of Independence, however, is not a legal prescription conferring powers upon the courts; and the Constitution's refusal to "deny or disparage" other rights is far removed from affirming any one of them, and even further removed from authorizing judges to identify what they might be, and to enforce the judges' lists against laws duly enacted by the people. . . . If we embrace this unenumerated right, I think . . . that we will be ushering in a new regime of judicially prescribed, and federally prescribed, family law. I have no reason to believe that federal judges will be better at this than state legislatures; and state legislatures have the great advantage of doing harm in a more circumscribed area, of being able to correct their mistakes in a flash, and of being removable by the people.[7]

Note here how the writer announces his authorial presence in the text by the extent of the self-referencing, starting with the repetition of the somewhat formal phrase "in my view" in the first two sentences. The placement of this phrase at the beginning of the sentence foregrounds it, communicating to readers that the writer's view is indeed noteworthy. The repetition of the phrase reinforces it, conveying that it is the writer's view . . . that, in the end, matters.

The passage bears the earmarks of professional writing in its textual quotations and use of lawyerly language (duly enacted/ unenumerated right/judicially prescribed/removable), and by including an if/then rule-like sentence: if we embrace/we will be ushering in. It has an assertive quality, again reinforced by repetition of phrasing (is far removed from affirming/and even further removed from authorizing). The quotation from the Declaration of Independence, suggesting that parental rights are God-given ("endowed by their Creator"), is a smart rhetorical ploy; although the Justice finds no affirmative legal authority to override the state law granting third parties visitation rights, by associating his views with the originary status and sanctity of the Declaration and the Founding Fathers, he projects onto his own language some of that same patriarchal authority. The effect of the passage is unrelenting, and to some stalwart readers, haranguing. But it is nothing if not confident. At the same time, Scalia smuggles in an informal phrase ("in a flash"), hinting that he has a more accessible side. If the overall impression is hardly [that of a "man in the street"], the combination of "emotional response and legal argument" seems calculated . . . to align the writer with the reader against the majority's view.[8]

Should legal writers emulate these judicial writing voices? The extensive self-referencing and the assertive-bordering-on-combative tone . . . would be out of place in most of the contexts in which lawyers typically write. Yet the vigor of [the] language, . . . the momentum . . . , [and the cadence, clarity, and directness construct a powerful voice and demand the reader's engagement. Surely these are crucial qualities in any lawyer's brief to a court.]

Now we return to Professor Rappaport for more helpful examples and analysis of how a text can generate tone. This excerpt analyzes text from such diverse writers as Judge Cardozo, Judge Learned Hand, Charles Dickens, and Chief Justice Roberts.

Excerpt from

Bret Rappaport, *Using the Elements of Rhythm, Flow, and Tone to Create a More Effective and Persuasive Acoustic Experience in Legal Writing*

16 J. Legal Writing 65, 99-107 (2010)

In music, tone is simply the quality of musical sounds. Tone in writing . . . is the connection between the reader and the writer. Tone can be detached or personal. Tone is set by the author's attitude toward his characters or subjects and conveyed by the words and the literary techniques employed. Tone modifies objective meaning and helps establish the writer's credibility with the reader—classically called "ethos."

Generally, tone is either subjective or objective. The writer adopts the first when trying to affect the reader in some way. He adopts the second when he wants to provide the reader with authoritative information. Legal writing is a tonal sleight of hand—or sleight of ear. The purpose is to affect the reader—persuade him or her to agree with the proposition, and yet the surface presentation must be objective.

We all remember Lucy, Lady Duff Gordon—from the first day of law school. What do we remember about her? Why? In *Wood v. Lucy, Lady Duff Gordon*,[9] Judge Cardozo crafted the perfect example of tone. He opened with the following:

> The defendant styles herself a "creator of fashion." Her favor helps a sale. Manufacturers of dresses, millinery, and like articles are glad to pay for a certificate of her approval. The things which she designs, fabrics, parasols, and what not, have a new value in the public mind when issued in her name. She employed the plaintiff to help her turn this vogue into money.[10]

Cardozo's statements are objective fact, but his tone resonates from every sentence. The reader is guided to the only possible outcome by the words; their placement—the tone. Lady lost.

Tone in legal prose should be "measured rationality."[11] Too strident a tone and the reader will feel bludgeoned and may become angry; too colloquial and the reader will not believe the writer or take the matter seriously. So between these poles, the writer must find the use of words and phrases that fosters the reader's trust in the writer. Such tone is achieved by a constant level of discourse and atmosphere that emerges from the entirety of the written work. This consistent level of tone is controlled by three levers: punctuation, descriptors, and the selection and presentation of the information included.

Library of Congress

Justice Benjamin Cardozo, circa 1932

After a revealing section on how punctuation creates intonation in written text, Professor Rappaport discusses descriptors:

Descriptors

Tone is helped by punctuation but set mostly by word choice—those left in and those left out. Nouns and verbs are the powerhouses of prose and in the editing process must remain so. Descriptors—adjectives and adverbs—often fall victim to brevity's modern scissors—the delete key. But stop. Although descriptors are unnecessary to convey essential information, in some cases like Cardozo's Lady Duff case discussed above, adjectives and adverbs are important because they often carry the load in setting tone; they add color and texture to otherwise naked text.

[Gentleman Jockey] Crawford Burton sold his testimonial and picture for use in a 1934 ad for Camel cigarettes. The photograph, with the legend beneath it that read, "When you feel all in—get a lift with a Camel," was plastered on the pages of magazines across the country. It showed Mr. Burton holding his saddle and girth "reproduced in such a manner that to a prurient or imaginative eye it appeared to show Mr. Burton indecently exposed as only a man could be."[12] He sued [because of] the penis picture. The district

Library of Congress

Learned Hand, circa 1900-1915

court dismissed the defamation action because there was no falsity. Judge Learned Hand wrote an economical but powerful opinion reversing that dismissal. His judicious use of descriptors adds to the persuasive readability of this defamation decision where truth was not a defense:

> We dismiss at once so much of the complaint as alleged that the advertisement might be read to say that the plaintiff was deformed, or that he had indecently exposed himself, or was making obscene jokes by means of the legends. Nobody could be fatuous enough to believe any of these things; everybody would at once see that it was the camera, and the camera alone, that had made the unfortunate mistake. If the advertisement is a libel, it is such in spite of the fact that it asserts nothing whatever about the plaintiff, even by the remotest implications. It does not profess to depict him as he is; it does not exaggerate any part of his person so as to suggest that he is deformed; it is patently an optical illusion, and carries its correction on its face as much as though it were a verbal utterance which expressly declared that it was false. It would be hard for words so guarded to carry any sting, but the same is not true of caricatures, and this is an example; for, notwithstanding all we have just said, it exposed the plaintiff to overwhelming ridicule. The contrast between the drawn and serious face and the accompanying fantastic and lewd deformity was so extravagant that though

utterly unfair, it in fact made of the plaintiff a preposterously ridic-
ulous spectacle; and the obvious mistake only added to the amuse-
ment. Had such a picture been deliberately produced, surely every
right-minded person would agree that he would have had a genuine
grievance; and the effect is the same whether it is deliberate or not.
Such a caricature affects a man's reputation, if by that is meant his
position in the minds of others; the association so established may
be beyond repair; he may become known indefinitely as the absurd
victim of this unhappy mischance. Literally, therefore, the injury
falls within the accepted rubric; it exposes the sufferer to "ridicule"
and "contempt."[13]

This passage includes more than twenty descriptors including
the adjective/adverb laden decisive statement "the contrast
between the **drawn** and **serious** face and the accompanying
fantastic and **lewd** deformity was so extravagant that, though
utterly unfair, it in fact made of the plaintiff a **preposterously ridic-
ulous** spectacle; and the **obvious** mistake only added to the amuse-
ment." Without those descriptors, the power and effect of the
paragraph would be lost. Seeing the actual photograph is unnecessary to come to agreement with Judge Hand.

In literature, descriptors are often associated with old-fashioned
writing, but "there is much to be said of the sentences of Dickens."[14]
For example, in the third paragraph of *Great Expectations*, Pip
describes the land where he grew up:

> This bleak place overgrown with nettles was the church yard . . . the
> dark flat wilderness beyond the church yard, intersected with dykes
> [a]nd mounds and gates, with scattered cattle feeding on it, was the
> marshes; . . . the low leaden line beyond was the river; and . . . the
> distant savage lair from which the wind was rushing, was the sea.[15]

Extract "bleak," "dark," "leaden," or "savage" and tone vanishes.

Descriptors must be chosen carefully to be effective. In legal
writing, avoid adjectives that tell the reader how the writer feels
such as "nice" or "great." Descriptors must be chosen carefully to
paint a picture to convey the proper tone. "Mammoth," for
example, conveys a tone distinct from the word "big."[16]

From the English moor let us go to the streets of North Philadel-
phia to see how the absence of descriptors can create tone.
In *Pennsylvania v. Dunlap*,[17] a Fourth Amendment probable cause
case, Chief Justice Roberts employed a clear type of voice (*noir fiction*) and started his dissent from a denial of certiorari as follows:

> North Philly, May 4, 2001. Officer Sean Devlin, Narcotics Strike
> Force, was working the morning shift. Undercover surveillance.
> The neighborhood? Tough as a three dollar steak. Devlin knew.
> Five years on the beat, nine months with the Strike Force. He'd
> made fifteen, twenty drug busts in the neighborhood.

> Devlin spotted him: a lone man on the corner. Another approached. Quick exchange of words. Cash handed over; small objects handed back. Each man then quickly on this own way. Devlin know the guy wasn't buying bus tokens. He radioed a description and Officer Stein picked up the buyer. Sure enough: three bags of crack in the guy's pocket. Head downtown and book him. Just another day at the office.[18]

In this opinion, the voice is set by the absence of adjectives and adverbs coupled with choppy short sentences and use of terms and metaphors, they convey a gritty hard-bitten image, like "tough as a three dollar steak." Purists can argue that such writing has no place in the writings of the Supreme Court of the United States, but it is hard to argue with the fact that the two paragraphs that start this opinion co[n]vey a message and meaning that the reader will remember. That is the first step in persuasion.

Now a short excerpt from Justice Scalia and Bryan Garner, raising and answering the crucial, ubiquitous question of what tone to adopt toward opposing counsel and parties:

Excerpt from

Antonin Scalia & Bryan A. Garner, *Making Your Case: The Art of Persuading Judges*
34-35 (Thomson/West 2008)

Restrain your emotions. And don't accuse.

Scalia and Garner begin this section by cautioning lawyers not to show indignation, either on behalf of their client or against opposing lawyers. They advise that a calm and dispassionate description will be more effective than introducing a tone of antagonism. They agree with the old adage, "Show, don't tell." Then they describe the desired tone of advocacy:

Cultivate a tone of civility, showing that you are not blinded by passion. Don't accuse opposing counsel of chicanery or bad faith, even if there is some evidence of it. Your poker-faced public presumption must always be that an adversary has misspoken or has inadvertently erred—not that the adversary has deliberately tried to mislead the court. It's imperative. [Attacking opposing lawyers] undercuts the persuasive force of any legal argument. The practice is uncalled for, unpleasant, and ineffective.

Finally, continuing our examination of civil tone, Professors Fajans and Falk compare and critique the voice and tone of several Supreme Court briefs and opinions. These authors raise ethical questions about the proliferation of "bad rhetoric" in today's advocacy.

Excerpt from

Elizabeth Fajans & Mary R. Falk, *Shooting from the Lip:* United States v. Dickerson, *Role [Im]morality, and the Ethics of Legal Rhetoric*

23 U. Haw. L. Rev. 1 (2000-2001)

Lawyers engage in distinctive language behavior, brandishing a specialized rhetoric of advocacy. Like some other "role-differentiated" lawyer behavior,[19] this rhetoric has features that are undesirable from a "universalist" moral perspective. Legal rhetoric is often overbearing, even hostile. It employs misdirection and omission, distorts opposing views, ridicules or vilifies opponents, and uses these and other verbal strategies to make arguments that are not convincing even to the speaker. This aggressive and deceptive behavior is plainly inconsistent with the universal moral imperative of respect for all persons.

Yet, the matter is more complicated: like other forms of . . . behavior in which lawyers engage, their wild-west rhetoric is susceptible of strong moral justification as well as condemnation. Justifications for otherwise morally criticizable behavior by lawyers traditionally rely on the lawyer's role in the adversary system, maintaining that justice (if not always truth) is best served by a high-noon duel of well-matched opponents shooting from the lip. Thus, condemnation and justification of legal rhetoric seem equally tenable positions.

Yet, the matter is more complicated still. The adversary-system justification of otherwise morally criticizable role-differentiated lawyer behavior presupposes the prototype advocacy situation in which life, liberty or some other invaluable good depends on zealous representation. Role-differentiated legal rhetoric seems most justified, therefore, in a summation in a capital or other major felony trial, or in a trial memorandum or appellate brief in some similar matter of real consequence. But lawyers are not just litigators: they are counselors, mediators, judges, scholars, and teachers as well. Yet, despite these "role-differentiations," the rhetorical strategies of advocacy are used in letters, judicial opinions, law reviews, and classrooms: no matter what the context, lawyers often talk the same talk.

In this article, we look at the ways judges, advocates, and scholars employ the "disrespectful" rhetorical strategies of advocacy. After sketching some background theory on role-differentiated morality and the ethics of advocacy in Part IA, we describe in part IB some features of legal rhetoric that seem to offend universalist notions of morality—*e.g.*, abuse of classical rhetoric's strategies of *logos, ethos,* and *pathos,* as exhibited in *ipse dixit* argument [an assertion without proof], misuse of precedent, use of "false implicature" to mislead,[20] arguing what one does not believe, misreading opposing views, and belittling those who hold such views. In Part II, we examine a microcosm of legal rhetoric—the judicial, advocacy, and scholarly prose that has been engendered by one issue in criminal procedure. Finally we examine the possible moral, institutional, and practical justifications for the law's disrespectful rhetoric and consider whether a radical change in language behavior is, realistic or not, the only solution consistent with the duty of respect.

We conclude that the negative potential of the law's rhetoric of disrespect is troubling enough to require radical change. The deceit, insincerity, hyperbole, and scorn that characterize much legal rhetoric are especially problematic because of the law's rhetoricity—the law is in large part affirmation and declamation.[21] Thus, if the law's dishonest and disrespectful rhetoric causes it to fall into disrepute, it has no other practice with which to redeem itself. Moreover, the rhetorical excesses of judges are especially dangerous, because judicial rhetoric is consequential—disposing of life, liberty, property, and reputation—and almost always immutable. Dissenters and commentators may expose the weak arguments and mean spirits of a judicial opinion, but short of reversal the court's words will not only stand but resonate in future controversies. . . . [R]ole-differentiated rhetoric of advocacy is also undesirable because legal rhetoric encourages oversimplification and over-certainty in complex situations and promises exemption from moral agency. . . .

We come to these conclusions after a look at the rhetoric that has arisen around an issue that was pending in the Supreme Court as we wrote this article: the status of the Supreme Court's decision in *Miranda v. Arizona.*[22] We chose this issue because it generated legal rhetoric at its disrespectful worst and its respectful best in the judicial, advocacy, and scholarly contexts. Indeed, the writing of this article was prompted by the roughness with which readers were treated by the Fourth Circuit's decision in *United States v. Dickerson,*[23] on which certiorari had been granted, and which the Supreme Court eventually reversed. Although the fate of *Dickerson,* and thus of *Miranda,* was unresolved during most of the writing of this article, as rhetoricians we were less interested in the outcome of the debate than in the verbal wars waged over *Miranda* by judges, advocates, and scholars. Our purpose was not to second-guess the Supreme Court but rather to articulate ethical norms by which the rhetoric of the profession—including that of the Court in *Dickerson*—can be measured. In this respect, we are pleased to note that Justice Rehnquist's majority opinion is measured and respectful in tone and relatively candid in argument. The worst excesses of the Fourth Circuit's opinion have been removed to the dissent, surely a safer place for such conduct so long as it continues to be a part of the legal culture. . . .

Our critique of legal rhetoric is informed in substantial part by Richard Wasserstrom's critique of the "role-differentiated" conduct of lawyers and the work of Robert Audi on the use of reasons in advocacy. Between them, Wasserstrom and Audi call into question two conventional ideas about the ethics of advocacy. First, Wasserstrom challenges the view that the lawyer's role as her client's zealous representative permits the lawyer to be indifferent to the morality of the client's goals and to the means used to effectuate those goals. Second, Audi criticizes the view that advocates may with moral justification adduce weak reasons made to seem strong by rhetorical skill and adduce reasons, weak or strong, that do not motivate their own belief. Like Wasserstrom, Audi approaches the ethics of lawyers from a universalist and foundationalist perspective.

The work of Richard Wasserstrom and Robert Audi on roles and advocacy raises difficult questions about the morality of traditional legal rhetoric. Both writers suggest that any exemption from universal moral obligation conferred by the lawyer's role is both narrow and problematic. Indeed, Wasserstrom and Audi seem inclined to believe that only where the stakes are life or liberty may the demands of a lawyer's role override those of universal moral agency.

Applying this critique of the practice of law (Wasserstrom) and of advocacy (Audi) to the rhetorical practices of lawyers, one might conclude that this characteristically aggressive and deceptive role-differentiated language behavior is acceptable only in persuasive writing for the court, and only in situations of great consequence. Regardless of one's position on this issue, however, it is not hard to conclude that disrespectful rhetoric is as frequent as it is inappropriate in judicial opinions and legal scholarship.

The article continues, first summarizing Wasserstrom's and Audi's ideas on the ethics of roles and advocacy and providing a background on logos, ethos, and pathos. The authors then critique the voice and tone of the Dickerson opinions and the parties' briefs as well as the early legal scholarship the case generated. The article concludes as follows:

The solution to the problem of disrespectful legal rhetoric is as clear as it is next to impossible: We have to change the way we talk and write, an enterprise that begins with a profession-wide commitment to avoid rhetorical practices that, by their nature, violate Audi's threshold[24] and desirability[25] principles.

Like all solutions to complicated questions, this solution raises more questions. To what extent, if at all, should there be different rules for different roles? Should litigators be exempted from the duty of respectful rhetoric? Should any such exemption be made only for criminal defense? Would a defendant whose counsel conceded the weaknesses of an argument have her rights to counsel and due process compromised? Before we make any exemptions, should we conduct empirical research to determine whether traditional advocacy rhetoric is in fact a more effective method of persuasion than forthrightness and balance? Should judges be held to the highest ethical standards because their words are so consequential? Although nothing justifies aggression and nastiness in judicial rhetoric, might there nonetheless be circumstances that justify violating the motivational and evidential principles—to get a majority, to spare the feelings of the court below, or to avoid hierarchical conflict, for example? Are there institutional arguments sufficiently strong to override the constraints on otherwise undesirable behavior? These are hard questions.

What seems certain, however, is that scholars should be held to the highest ethical-rhetorical standard, because truth-seeking is a scholar's primary goal. There are strong reasons for holding judges to the same high standard. Equally certain is that reform will not come from wishful thinking or from rules of professional conduct but from a commitment to an ethic of universal respect that is reflected in our use of language. The distinctions between persuading and silencing and between putting something in its best light and putting it in a false light are too important for mere lip service.

Discussion Questions

1. What do you think of Justice Scalia's advice to assume a posture of respectful intellectual equality with the Court? Does that seem potentially arrogant or at least intimidating? What are the other options for the kind of relationship you might envision? Have you seen lawyers who assumed Justice Scalia's suggested posture in court? How did it seem to work?

2. Look again at the examples in the excerpt from Professor McArdle's article (from Justices Breyer and Scalia). Using just those quotes, how would you describe the personality and character of each of those Justices? What attitudes do they seem to hold? Do you pick up any emotion? Remember that emotions include far more than sympathy or anger. How do the quotes communicate those personal characteristics and attitudes?

3. Look again at the Rappaport excerpt's detailed analysis of Cardozo's language. That exegesis (an interpretation or explanation of a text) is an

example of the kind of analysis your professor might ask you to undertake in evaluating some of the briefs covered in this book. What do you notice about how one does that kind of rhetorical analysis?

4. Professors Fajans and Falk raise ethical and moral questions about the use of a disrespectful tone. Do you agree? Is there ever a time when a disrespectful tone is appropriate? What consequences to the legal system may result from increased use of a combative tone?

5. If you have time, read the omitted parts of the Fajans and Falk article, where the authors explore the limits of what tone would meet a "threshold" standard (barely ethical) and what tone a lawyer should aspire to achieve. Do you agree with the authors' assessments? If you do not have time to read the entire article, attempt to answer those questions for yourself, and ask yourself why you draw the lines where you do.

Endnotes

1. 527 U.S. 41 (1999).
2. *Id*. at 71 (Breyer, J., concurring in part and concurring in judgment) (emphasis in original).
3. 531 U.S. 98, 144 (2000).
4. *Id*.
5. *Id*. at 158.
6. 530 U.S. 57 (2000) (plurality opinion).
7. *Id*. at 91-93 (Scalia, J., dissenting).
8. Laura Krugman Ray, *Judicial Personality: Rhetoric and Emotion in Supreme Court Opinions*, 59 Wash. & Lee L. Rev. 193, 227-229 (2002).
9. 118 N.E. 214 (N.Y. 1917).
10. *Id*. at 214 [language slightly edited to match opinion].
11. Pamela Samuelson, *Good Legal Writing: Of Orwell and Window Panes*, 46 U. Pitt. L. Rev. 149, 156 (1984).
12. *Camel Jockey*, Time (Jan. 18, 1937). . . .
13. *Burton v. Crowell Publg. Co.*, 82 F.2d 154 (2d Cir. 1936).
14. Robin Kacel, *They Have Their Place: Adjectives and Adverbs*, 22 Writing 14 (Apr./May 2000).
15. Charles Dickens, *Great Expectations* ch. 1 (1861) (cited *id*. at 14).
16. Kacel, *supra* note 14, at 15.
17. 129 S. Ct. 448 (2008).
18. *Id*. at 448.
19. "Role-differentiated" behavior is the result of reasoning that "places weight upon the role that the person occupies and locates concerns about how one ought to behave within a context of what is required, expected, or otherwise appropriate of persons occupying that role." Richard Wassertrom, *Roles and Morality*, in *The Good Lawyer: Lawyer's Roles and Lawyer's Ethics* 25, 25-26 (David Luban ed., Rowman & Allanheld 1984).
20. The term "implicature" is borrowed from linguistic pragmatics. Implicature is the mechanism by which participants in a conversation understand that which is not stated. For example, when Speaker A asks, "Would you like some coffee?" and speaker B replies, "Does the Pope say Mass?" implicature allows Speaker A to understand Speaker B's response as "yes." False implicature is the intentional exploitation of implicature by a speaker or writer to suggest a proposition that is not true. . . .
21. Richard Wasserstrom, *Lawyers as Professionals: Some Moral Issues*, in *The Ethics of Lawyers 3, 16 (David Luban ed., New York U. Press 1993)*.
22. *Miranda v. Arizona*, 384 U.S. 436 (1966) (holding that unless the legislature devises other fully effective means to inform defendants in criminal cases about their Fifth Amendment right to silence and to assure the continuous opportunity to exercise it, defendants must be advised, before any custodial interrogation can begin, of the right to remain

silent, the fact that any statement may be used in evidence against them, and the right to the presence of an attorney, retained or appointed).

23. 166 F.3d 667 (4th Cir. 1999) *rev'd*, *Dickerson v. United States*, 120 S. Ct. 2326 (2000) [hereinafter *Dickerson II*]. . . .

24. [Audi's "threshold" principles set out minimal standards that establish a floor beneath which a moral advocate may not go. Robert Audi, *The Ethics of Advocacy*, 1 Legal Theory 251, 257 (1995).]

25. [Audi's "desirability" principles establish a higher, more aspirational standard than the minimal threshold. Advocates can inhabit the gray area between the two, but they risk legitimate criticism for doing so. *Id.*]

8. *Freedom and Form*

"Freedom is feeling comfortable in your harness."

—Robert Frost

"We cannot learn to fly by following the tracks left by birds in the sand. We must find our own wings and soar. . . . An insatiable appetite and energy for learning and a fresh inquiring mind are among life's greatest assets. This is why the concept of beginner's mind has been emphasized in the East. When we come to learning as a beginner, we are open, questioning, looking. When we approach a subject as an expert, we are more closed and fixed in the accumulated information we have gathered, in the past experiences we have had. When we're an expert, or experienced, when we know something, even a yoga posture, we tend to approach it mechanically, from the past. We lose the freedom of discovery, the freedom of being fresh and new."

—Ganga White[1]

These two quotations place us squarely in the tension we face head-on in this chapter—the tension between liberty and restraint, between creativity and the norms and structures of the profession. First, an excerpt from Professor Stanley Fish, one of the most influential scholars in the legal academy in the last 50 years, extols the virtues of writing within a prescribed form. Like Robert Frost, he tells us that the constraints of form actually free us to be creative.

Excerpt from
Stanley Fish, *How to Write a Sentence*
32-33 (HarperCollins 2011)

A famous sonnet by William Wordsworth begins, "Nuns fret not at their convent's narrow room; / And hermits are contented with their cells; / and students with their pensive citadels." Wordsworth's point is that what nuns, hermits, and students do is facilitated rather than hindered by the confines of the formal structures they inhabit; because those structures constrain freedom (they remove, says Wordsworth, "the weight of too much liberty"), they enable movements in a defined space. If the moves you can perform are prescribed and limited—if, for example, every line in your poem must have ten syllables and rhyme according to a predetermined pattern—each move can carry a precise significance. . . . That is why Wordsworth reports himself happy "to be bound/Within the Sonnet's scanty plot of ground." It is a scanty plot because it is bounded, and because it is bounded, it can be the generator of boundless meanings.

This, then, is my theology: *You shall tie yourself to forms and the forms shall set you free.* I call this the Karate Kid method of learning how to write. In the 1984 cult movie (recently remade), the title figure is being trained to perform in a match, but rather than being instructed in a match's rhythms and demands, he is asked by his teacher to practice polishing cars ("wax on, wax off") and painting fences. Although the kid thinks he isn't learning anything, he is learning everything; he is learning the formal motions that, when actual combat occurs, will come to him naturally. Like the verbal forms that enable thought and meaning, these physical forms enable action in a sequence, even though they are essentially static and abstract.

Our next two excerpts are part of a conversation. Professor Jim Elkins thinks that first-year legal writing courses overemphasize the teaching of form. In portions of his article omitted here, he critiques that form, in part by finding it lacking in stories, which he describes as "an antidote to a flat, de-energized world."[2] He critiques the method of teaching writing by taking apart an accepted format for a brief and then learning to reproduce each section. In her reply, Professor Teresa Godwin Phelps agrees that the goal is to become a "strong poet" but, like Professor Fish, she rejects the idea that tradition and discipline are inconsistent with creativity, seeing all three as fundamental to the art of strong legal writing.

Excerpt from

James R. Elkins, *What Kind of Story Is Legal Writing?*
20 Legal Studies Forum 95-135 (1996)

We worry about the loss of soul in writing because we can never let ourselves be ruled by Necessity alone. Necessity may claim a good part of our day but it can never go unquestioned.

We worry about the soul of legal writing shaped by Necessity. The fruits of that false god are in ready view—bad, notoriously bad, writing. Soul-less writing has consequences: "It erodes self-respect. Hurried careless writing weakens the imagination, saps intelligence, and ultimately diminishes self-esteem and professionalism."[3] . . .

When we mimic a conventional style (whether of legal writing or [any other genre]), we twist ourselves into knots and play with soul-fire.[4] Bad writing subjects us to ridicule . . . and creates problems for clients. There are social costs when legal writing makes the law more inaccessible and the parties to a dispute more prone to litigation. Legal writing leads to public disdain for lawyers and the work we do, as well as self-denigration.

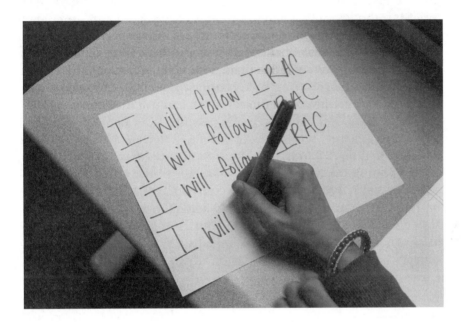

If legal writing cannot escape the "technical" fix it is in, it will forever be a desert story—flat, remote, barren. When legal writing is imagined as Technical Writing, writing by rule and formula, there is a story in place, but one no [one] truly wants to live or tell or pass on to a future generation. . . . To conceive legal writing as a technical skill flattens it. In psychology, we identify those who make human interactions into a technical project, by their flat affect. Flat affect is prevalent in those who suffer from a restricted emotional register, range, and depth of speech and feeling. The flat affect of the neurotic and the narrow range of human experience/emotion/life/soul found in legal writing suggest a danger for legal writing, that its pathologies will be associated with a dampening and pervasive erosion of human spirit—depression, anxiety, and denial.

Legal writing is neurotic in its flatness; neurotic in its denial of the life of language. Legal writing is neurotic when it sets up a professional barrier and provides a psychological defense against life, passion, care, competence, imagination, creativity, and wildness. "[B]ecause it aspires to objectivity, legal language may refuse to recognize troublesome concepts such as hope, candor, or even love."[5] . . .

We try to teach and learn writing by a kind of reductive functionalism. Following this approach, legal brief writing is taught by taking the brief apart, learning to write by learning to reproduce the various structural parts of the brief and then putting the brief back together much like a bicycle. In this industrial or manufacturing approach to writing the focus is on parts, reproduction, replication. There may indeed be a level of skill and technique involved in writing a legal brief but the learning is more a matter of exposure and experience than a highly developed, complex art. The most straight-forward way to learn how to write an appellate brief is to write one. It helps to do the writing in a context in which the final result matters, the writing takes place in a community of fellow learners, and is done under the tutelage of one who has had the experience of writing such texts. The "form" of a legal brief is straight-forward and easy to replicate. Writing briefs is the kind of activity you get good at by doing, by repetition, familiarity, and habit. Legal writing, like gardening and sailing, is not learned from instructional manuals. To profit from reading about gardening and sailing you need to put out a garden and have ready access to a sail boat.

Legal writing ultimately depends upon the quality of legal education. The instruction in the technical skills associated with writing can never replace the education that makes good writing possible.

Here is part of Professor Phelps's reply to Professor Elkins. Like several of the authors in Chapters 1 and 2, Professor Phelps reflects on her long experience as a legal writing teacher and writer.

Excerpt from

Teresa Godwin Phelps, *Tradition, Discipline, and Creativity: Developing "Strong Poets" in Legal Writing*
20 Legal Stud. Forum 89 (1996)

Consider the poor legal writing teacher: caught between a Scylla composed of the American Bar Association, law school deans, and law firms, all demanding disciplined writing from law school graduates and the Charybdis of having to require soulless, repetitive, formulaic writing from students. Can legal writing teachers do their jobs—i.e., turn out competent legal writers—without becoming the vampires of the first year, draining their students of the lifeblood of creativity and storytelling?

I find myself caught in . . . such a paradox. For years I have devoted much of my scholarly output to arguing the importance of narrative. A look at my own writing reveals a near addiction to the notion that narrative is requisite to the law . . . ; that "[l]aw divorced from narrative impoverishes us and our students; rules without stories result in bad law and bad lawyers."[6]

Yet late each August I meet with my Teaching Assistants and then with my 180 first year legal writing students and argue the importance of discipline, of forms, of uniformity. I ask the students to be, in Jim Elkins' words, "formulaic, dispassionate, objective." Am I a hopeless hypocrite, speaking one thing to my students and another to my peers and colleagues, privately embracing narrative, yet publicly advocating formulas? Is disciplined writing opposite to narrative writing?

[handwritten margin note] - Advocating formula. - legal writing is formulaic, dispassion- ate & objective.

At many turning points in my life, I have accepted such false dualisms. In doing so, I created for myself a rigid either/or structure and assumed I was forced to choose one or the other. I embraced the theme of Robert Frost's poem, "The Road Not Taken":

> And both that morning equally lay
> In leaves no step had trodden black.
> Oh, I kept the first for another day!
> Yet knowing how way leads on to way
> I doubted if I should ever come back.

Frost suggests that our lives are comprised of forks in the road, and that choosing one thing means *not* choosing the other: a rigid dualistic structure, A or not/A. So, do I, as a law teacher, scholar, writer encourage my students to indulge in narrative or do I do the job that seems to be demanded by the profession and the firms for which my students will work, by my colleagues and my dean—that is, teach these students to turn out well-crafted, readable, useful memos and briefs? My professional choices lie like two roads in a New England wood.

Or do they? Perhaps this too is a false dualism: perhaps I do not have to choose between (A) insisting on discipline and formulas *or* (B) allowing my students to find their own unique narrative legal voices. Perhaps disciplined competence and creativity can happily coexist. . . .

Yet if this is right, if this coexistence is possible, then the story that I have heard and told myself about legal writing is somehow inaccurate and Jim Elkins is right: legal writing is in need of a new story, a story that does away with the forced and false dualism of discipline *or* creativity. Jim is certainly right that any absence of storytelling is a sign of bankruptcy and soullessness. In his book of essays written in 1987, *The Content of Form,* Hayden White observed that "so natural is the impulse to narrate, so inevitable is the form of narrative for any report of the ways things really happen, that narrativity could appear problematic *only* in a culture in which it was absent."[7] If narrativity is absent from the way we [learn] legal writing, we . . . do have a problem. . . . If *this* is our story, then indeed we are in need of a new one. Yet what is our new story and where can we find it?

First, let me begin by deconstructing the old story, the either/or nature of narrative and "real" legal writing. What is the source of this dualism? Why does it feel so either/or to us? When I begin to teach persuasive writing . . . , I try to rehabilitate the notion of "persuasion," of rhetoric, by revealing what I perceive to be a false split between truth-telling (scientific writing) and rhetoric (persuasive writing). Philosophers from the time of Plato, Aristotle, Locke and Bacon have insisted on the division, and . . . lawyers contributed to the dualism by using persuasive language in a manipulative way. [Instead,] I present . . . the post-modernist position that all language is at best referential, no particular mode has a stronghold on the "truth." Hence, there is no dualism, there is only language to be used well or not so well.

Similar to the devaluation of rhetoric, narrative became undervalued in academic disciplines. . . . It is only recently that legal scholars have begun to use narrative (and get published). Narrative is (or at least was until very recently) perceived as not quite as objective, not as truthful, as other sorts of writing. If we want to do away with that story—the story that good legal writing eschews narratives, the story that tells us that disciplined writing discourages and drowns out creative writing—what can we put in its place? . . . Let me suggest a few building blocks.

Stories are told in language, and with language no choices are neutral. What words have I chosen to present the dilemma? I have, in this case, made *discipline* the enemy of creativity.

The word *discipline* has some interesting meanings, according to the OED: 1. the instruction of disciples. Etiologically, the OED says, discipline, as pertaining to the disciple or scholar, is antithetical to doctrine, the property of the doctor or teacher; hence, in the history of words, *doctrine* is more concerned with abstract theory and *discipline* with practice or exercise; 2. gradually teaching the mysteries of the Christian faith to neophytes; 3. a branch of instruction or education; 4. instruction having for its aim to form the pupil to proper conduct and action; mental and moral training; 5. the orderly conduct and action which results from training, a trained condition; 6. a system or method for the maintenance of order; 7. correction, chastisement, punishment.[8] Thus the meaning of *discipline* slides down a slippery slope from a beneficent idea of learning as a disciple or a neophyte to punishment, and we tend to focus primarily on the latter meaning. If we readjust our focus and consider the importance of the instructions of novices in the mysteries of a new discipline, we can regard ourselves in a more kindly fashion as introducing [new lawyers], as disciples, into the tradition of legal writing.

In fact, the necessity of tradition has long been honored by creative artists. In his 1920 essay "Tradition and the Individual Talent," T.S. Eliot attempted to rehabilitate the notion of tradition, which he noted was usually a "phrase of censure"—i.e., so-and-so is "too traditional." Eliot writes of the importance of a poet having the "historical sense" which

> involves a perception, not only of the pastness of the past, but of its presence; the historical sense compels a man to write not merely with his own generation in his bones, but with a feeling that the whole of the literature of Europe from Homer and within it the whole of the literature of his own country has a simultaneous existence and composes a simultaneous order. This historical sense, which is a sense of the timeless as well as of the temporal and of the timeless and the temporal together, is what makes a writer traditional. . . . In a peculiar sense he will be aware that he must inevitably be judged by the standards of the past.[9]

In another place, Eliot writes about "free" verse, which he finds as anything but free. Free verse, he argues, is the conscious *breaking* of the iambic pentameter: "[T]he ghost of some simple metre should lurk behind the arras in even the 'freest' verse. . . . Or, freedom is only freedom when it appears against the background of an artificial limitation."[10] Without the pentameter, free verse is mere babbling.

Now this, it seems to me, is precisely the condition of the fledgling legal writer. She, while searching for her own unique legal voice, must be cognizant of where that voice fits into the simultaneous order that comprises the law. A disembodied voice with no recognition of the discipline (the system or method for the maintenance of order) in which it speaks can become mere babbling.

A more recent example of this theory may be found in Harold Bloom's *The Anxiety of Influence.* Bloom differentiates between strong poets and weak poets. Weak poets "lack the strength to overcome the anxiety of influence," that is the influence of their precursors, their teachers, their models. Strong poets, on the other hand, are figures of "capable imagination" who can "appropriate for themselves immense anxieties of indebtedness."[11] Bloom makes a fascinating comparison to Milton's *Paradise Lost,* the substance of which is immaterial here, but for one point—he describes Adam in that poem as a "strong poet at his weakest moment, when he has yet to find his own voice."[12] Adam has not yet entered the necessary phase if one is to become a strong poet, a stage Bloom calls *kenosis,* a movement toward discontinuity with the precursor, in this case Satan. To further his point about the requisite connection between past and present, Bloom quotes two of his own precursors: Nietzsche and Kierkegaard. Nietzsche, one of our most original thinkers, wrote "There is all this talk about originality, but what does it amount to? As soon as we are born the world begins to influence us. . . ."[13] And Kierkegaard: "If the young man believed in repetition, of what might he not have been capable?"[14] Discipline, in the sense of introduction into a tradition, is not the enemy of creativity, but its necessary ally, the requisite foundation without which fruitful creativity is not possible.

Finally, a last building block from composition theory: the notion of discourse communities. A discourse community is the world of language that a group occupies. [In law, we] share language, jargon, conventions, forms. We can talk to each other in a shorthand of our own, a kind of language that outsiders might not understand. Legal writing, like all other writing, is a social construct, involving readers and writers, as well as a particular subject matter.

[When first-year students begin law study], they are outsiders in the legal discourse community. Our primary task is to initiate them, as disciples, into the discipline of legal writing. This requires a knowledge of and a practice of forms and conventions. It also requires a knowledge of what legal documents do, what they are, and what audiences they serve. Once this knowledge is attained, the novice legal writer can find and develop her unique legal voice and enter the ongoing conversation that comprises the law.

Here is a start toward a new story. . . . [New law] students are like disciples [learning] the tradition of legal writing. To do this, they must discipline themselves in the forms, just as novice poets discipline themselves by writing sonnets and villanelles. This done they can move toward becoming strong legal writers, in Bloom's sense of strong poets. . . . They will write, in Eliot's terms, with a sense of the history and tradition of legal writing in their bones. We do not bind our students to form. Instead, we, in introducing them to the discipline of legal writing, free them to find and use their own legal voices. And, inevitably, these will be, at least in part, their storytelling voices.

Discussion Questions

1. Do you think that the first-year legal writing course should teach the professionally accepted forms for the components of a brief? Do you think that you could write more persuasive briefs if you did not have to comply with such forms?
2. Even if forms are necessary, it is undeniable that there is a tension between compliance with professional norms and unbridled creativity. How can you negotiate that tension?
3. Do experienced legal writers, even the best of them, comply with all the norms you learned in your first year? If not, why not? Might they have already learned what the forms were there to teach them, bringing them now to a place where they can leave the forms (at least some of them) behind? Is that part of what Professor Phelps is saying?
4. Look at the briefs this book introduces, and ask yourself how many of them followed the forms you learned in your first-year legal writing class. To the extent they did not, there were probably many reasons for the variances. Ask yourself whether and why those briefs were effective without following all of the forms you learned.

Endnotes

1. Ganga White, *Yoga Beyond Belief*, 6-7 (North Atlantic Books 2007).
2. James R. Elkins, *What Kind of Story Is Legal Writing?* 20 Leg. Stud. F. 95, 119 (1996).
3. Tom Goldstein & Jethro K. Lieberman, *The Lawyer's Guide to Writing Well* 5 (Berkeley: U. Calif. Press 1989).
4. Genre writing is efficient and safe. How can anyone be critical of your writing if it follows the *form* that other such writing has taken? Genre writing is requirement writing, hoop-jumping, an eyeing of the bottom-line. In Genre writing the thinking and worrying is transferred from what we do to what we make, a shift away from process to product. In Genre Writing we absolve our creative impulses by reference to form, to filling an empty container. Fill-in the form, follow the form, stay out of trouble. We let the *pro forma*, prosaic nature of the task—filling the form, satisfying the requirement, doing what we think is expected—shape not only the product but the process of writing. It is hard to argue against such writing. It gets the job done. It is writing that takes out insurance against critique. The problem with Genre Writing is that we grow stale and lazy and it shows in the writing. The writing becomes cluttered with easy thinking, group thinking, and clichés. And then we over compensate. We try to "fix" writing, to spruce it up with jargon and high-flying phrases. There is nothing more noticeable and glaring in a piece of flat writing than a discordant effort to boost the writing with fancy sounding words.
5. Steven Stark, *Why Lawyers Can't Write*, 97 Harv. L. Rev. 1389, 1391-1392 (1984). . . .

6. Teresa Godwin Phelps, *Review of Wayne Booth's* The Company We Keep, 39 J. Legal Educ. 463, 367 (1989).

7. Hayden White, *The Content of Form: Narrative Discourse and Historical Representation* 1 (The Johns Hopkins U. Press 1987).

8. J.A. Simpson & E.S.C. Warner, 4 *Oxford English Dictionary* 734-735 (2d ed., Oxford U. Press 1989).

9. T.S. Eliot, "Tradition and the Individual Talent," in *Selected Essays* 3, 4 (Harcourt, Brace, and Company 1932).

10. T.S. Eliot, "Reflections on Vers Libre" (1917), in *To Criticize the Critic and Other Writings* 187 (Farrar, Straus & Giroux 1965).

11. Harold Bloom, *The Anxiety of Influence: A Theory of Poetry* 6 (Oxford U. Press 1973).

12. *Id.* at 5.

13. *Id.* at 52.

14. *Id.* at 76.

Our Readers

Now we look at our readers, the key decision-makers for our clients' cases. In this section, the study of cognitive science will teach us much about how readers respond to the ordering of arguments, their own involvement in the questions to be decided, and their own emotions; and the ways we deal with opposing arguments. Few introductory courses can cover this material, and few first-year writing students would be able to master it. But you are well beyond that first-year course now, and it is time for a deeper exploration into what we can know about our readers.

9. *Order*

With this chapter, we begin our study of readers. One of the most important recent developments in the understanding of lawyering has been the realization that we should pay attention to cognitive psychology (the study of how people perceive, think, remember, and decide) and other social science disciplines. And one of the best scholars applying cognitive psychology to brief-writing is Professor Kathryn Stanchi. We will be relying on excerpts from her work throughout the next several chapters as we study our audience, legal readers. In this chapter, Professor Stanchi invites us to consider what cognitive psychology can teach us about deciding how to order arguments.

This article begins by observing that the received conventions and practices about brief-writing, handed down from lawyer to lawyer, have been the result of a sort of "armchair psychology" developed mostly from instinct and speculation. Instead of accepting these unquestioned assumptions, Professor Stanchi argues, we should look to the growing body of work in the social sciences for evidence about whether these conventions are accurate assessments of effective persuasion. The article then discusses data in two key topics important to brief-writing. In this chapter, we look at the first of these: deciding how to order the main points in a brief. The conventional answer we often hear is that the advocate should begin with her strongest points. But is that always the best strategy? Professor Stanchi helps us begin to answer that question. The social science terms for this topic are "sequential request strategies" and "chaining." To help you become familiar with the social science vocabulary, these and other key terms are sometimes italicized below.

Excerpt from

Kathryn M. Stanchi, *The Science of Persuasion: An Initial Exploration*

2006 Mich. St. L. Rev. 411

Sequential Request Strategies and the Chaining of Legal Arguments

Sequential request strategies test how message recipients react to a series of persuasive messages that are presented in a certain order.

In the two most well-known sequential request strategies, the *"critical"* request (the one the persuader is most interested in the recipient's reaction to) follows some other request.[1] The idea is to determine whether it is possible to influence the recipient's decision about the critical request by *"priming"* the recipient with a certain kind of prior request.

[M]uch of the conventional wisdom of legal writing incorporates the concept [of priming]. Persuasive writers are told to begin their briefs with the strongest arguments, to lead paragraphs with strong thesis sentences, and to precede legal text and rules with strong argumentative statements. In the most artful briefs, the advocate has devised an organization that carefully *primes* the reader by leading her, step-by-step, toward acceptance of the final thesis that is the winning proposition for the advocate.

This *organizational priming* means that the advocate has consciously constructed a series of overlapping propositions together in a *chain*, so that the acceptance of one proposition leads inexorably to the next. The most interesting and effective argument chains link points or premises that the reader might not have necessarily connected together. In legal writing, *chaining* is not only a way of structuring an argument but also of moving the argument forward. A useful metaphor for this tactic is the series of steps up to the high diving board: as the persuader gets the *target* [the decision-maker] up each step closer to the edge of the board, it becomes that much easier to decide to jump and that much harder to decide to go back down.[2]

Chaining is a successful persuasive tactic in part because of the nature of arguments. Arguments are "goal-directed" conversations that revolve around an issue about which the parties have conflicting opinions. Each party is trying to move the conversation toward acceptance of her opinion, using an array of persuasive strategies, sometimes called *"moves."* An argument strategy or "move" is successful if it "extrapolates forward" toward the goal of the conversation. A move that "extrapolates forward" helps resolve the conflict by showing one or the other proposition to be more or less likely.[3] Put another way, the goal of persuasion is to move the target audience forward along the *"action decision sequence"* away from the human propensity for inaction or habitual action and toward the advocate's desired action.[4] This decisional momentum is one of the primary purposes of chaining.

In persuasive legal writing, argument chaining is a longstanding and fairly typical strategy, though not all lawyers use it well. The strategy harkens back to the *syllogism*, the quintessential form of deductive reasoning in classical rhetoric. Unlike the classical syllogism, however, the forward chain in legal writing almost always has points of weak connection between the premises and conclusion.

The artful advocate can make the chain look ironclad, even when it is not.

In contrast to the formally valid syllogism, the forward chain in legal writing is usually a form of *"quasi-logical argumentation,"* in which the advocate presents elements or premises in such a way as to give the target audience the impression that the elements or premises are logically connected. In quasi-logical argumentation, the advocate creates the illusion that the link between the premises and ultimate conclusion is as unassailable as a formal syllogism, but the logic may not actually be provably valid in the formal sense. Rather, the advocate seeks to influence the audience by making the argument look like a mathematical or logical proof. To make the chain appear strong and solid, advocates manipulate language to make the premises look homogenous, congruent, and unambiguous to the audience.[5]

The First Link: How to Start an Argument

Chaining arguments is a kind of *sequential request strategy*. As with any sequential request strategy, a key decision is how to begin the forward chain—with what premise(s) should the writer *"prime"* the audience to influence acceptance of the *"critical"* request. The entire chain, and therefore the structure of the argument, will be determined by the premises that begin it. In persuasive legal writing, the conventional wisdom often suggests that the advocate begin the chain with relatively uncontroversial premises, on the theory that if the reader agrees with the first few premises, she is more likely to accept the ultimate thesis. Using the diving board metaphor, this tactic begins by attempting to convince the message recipient to get on the first step of the high dive.

Sometimes the argument chain will be preceded by the ultimate conclusion—the assertion, however controversial or bold, that the advocate is trying to get the court to accept. This is typical of legal reasoning, and represents a form of *"anti-climax"* order. Preceding the chain with the conclusion, as opposed to starting with a less controversial premise, is a common approach in legal writing. In the high-dive metaphor, this tactic would begin by urging the message recipient to jump off the high dive, and would follow with an argument chain detailing why this is a good idea. Since the conclusion is often followed by argument chains that begin with a less controversial premise (at some point the persuader must try to convince the message recipient to get on that first step), the two tactics are less dissimilar than they may first appear.

The focus here is less on whether to begin with the conclusion or not, but in what way to begin the chain of reasons supporting the conclusion. In many cases, the persuader will have a choice among arguments, some of which may be "safe"—i.e., likely acceptable—and those that may be riskier. The theories about human decisionmaking that follow tell the persuader a bit about how the message recipient might react to the different approaches. An understanding of these theories gives the legal advocate a deeper knowledge with which to make strategic decisions about the construction of the chains.

The following sections of the article introduce and analyze two seemingly inconsistent chaining strategies: "foot in the door" (which resembles the conventional wisdom of starting with strong arguments) and "door in the face" (in which the most controversial argument is presented first).

"Foot in the Door": Starting with Premises Likely to Be Accepted

Empirical research on human behavior and decisionmaking provides some evidence that argument chains are more likely to persuade readers if the first links of the chain are well-settled or widely accepted premises. In one experiment, researchers tested the so-called *"foot in the door"* strategy by studying how test targets reacted to a large and difficult request if the targets had previously agreed to perform a small and easy request.[6] The foot-in-the-door strategy posits that [past compliance is strongly and positively linked to future compliance]. The results demonstrated that people are more likely to accede to large requests if they had previously agreed to smaller ones, even if there is a significant time delay,

and even if there is no obvious relationship between the two demands.[7] It is almost a "bobble-head" effect: once the message recipient starts nodding "yes," it is likely that she will continue to nod "yes." The foot-in-the-door response is so strong that it creates a "halo effect": when people agreed to the initial commitment, future agreement was likely even for requests that were only remotely related to the initial one.[8]

Researchers attribute the success of foot-in-the-door to a change in self-perception that occurs when people perform—or agree to perform—the initial request.[9] That is, once a person accedes to the initial request, she begins to see herself differently; her attitude changes and in her own mind she becomes the sort of person who agrees to certain kinds of requests.[10] This is a fairly common psychological observation about human beings: they derive their current attitudes and decisions from observing their own past behavior. People asked to make a decision do a *"self-observation"* and then use their own past behavior as a way of gauging their attitudes and beliefs. They then use what they have observed about their belief system to reach a decision about a current problem. In other words, much like legal reasoning, people have a cache of personal decisional "precedent" which they use to decide current problems. . . .

The persuader who uses the foot-in-the-door technique manipulates the "self-observation" process of the message recipient. The persuader influences the recipient's assessment of her belief system by purposefully adding a particular decision to the cache that the recipient will use to determine her beliefs and make the future decision. Foot-in-the-door is a way of creating precedent for a message recipient to use in deciding a problem. . . . By carefully choosing that first request, the persuader can alter the course of the recipient's decision-making.

The success of foot-in-the-door depends not only on the process of human decisionmaking, but also on certain aspects of human nature. Foot-in-the-door is particularly effective in people who have a strong preference for consistency in behavior.[11] But, overall, most people tend to seek *"self-consistency,"* which is why foot-in-the-door has such broad success as a compliance strategy. People tend to make decisions that decrease feelings of inconsistency and increase feelings of consistency when compared with their prior behaviors.[12] So, when they engage in the decisionmaking process, they are scanning their prior decisions so they can make consistent future decisions. If they make a decision that seems inconsistent with prior behavior or with their perception of their belief system, they experience *"cognitive dissonance"* and will resolve that dissonance by changing their belief system to conform to the decision made, or changing their decision. Foot-in-the-door works when the persuader creates a scenario that leads the recipient to make a certain decision that is consistent with the decision the persuader ultimately wants from the recipient.

The second reason for the consistent success of foot-in-the-door is that people seek *"self-affirmation."* A person will therefore seek to make a decision that confirms her belief that she is a person of integrity and morality. People have attitudes or beliefs in part to serve their self-image. Thus, attitudes are said to be ego-defensive; that is, people will not espouse attitudes or beliefs that force them to admit negative information about themselves. Attitudes are also *"value-expressive,"* as they allow us to present ourselves as having certain core traits such as competence, knowledge, and sensitivity.[13] People will make decisions that protect and affirm their positive images of themselves. The foot-in-the-door strategy taps into the self-image part of human decisionmaking because the recipient's agreement to the first request leads her to a certain generalization about what kind of person she is. The recipient will then make future decisions in a way that affirms this generalization.

What does all of this have to do with persuasive legal writing? On the most concrete level, advocates can interpret the foot-in-the-door data to strongly suggest that argument chains should begin with premises that the reader will readily accept. In part, a successful argument chain breaks down the ultimate thesis of the argument into a series of linked premises that lead to the thesis. Foot-in-the-door suggests that the audience is more likely to accept the ultimate thesis if the earlier premises leading up to it are phrased in a way that induces compliance in the reader. The persuasive writer wants to create an argument chain that leads the judge to start nodding "yes" to her arguments.

Most judges also share the common human desire to affirm their positive self-image. They want to see themselves as fair, compassionate, logical, and moral people. A well-constructed argument chain can create the impression that the ultimate decision is the fairest, most compassionate, most logical, and so on. This is also a confirmation of the common strategy in which the advocate struggles for the high moral or policy ground, attempting to convince the judge that a decision for the advocate's client is the fairest, most compassionate decision.

But, on a theoretical level, the premise underlying the foot-in-the-door technique gives persuasive writers much information about how to sway judges. The knowledge that most human beings perform a *"self-observation"* of past behavior to determine their beliefs and then will use those beliefs to make the current decision is especially useful. The strong pull toward self-consistency is also useful information. In law, there is an even greater value placed on consistency and order. This means that even though judges are skeptical readers trained to ferret out any dubious premises or tenuous connections, they are susceptible to a strong human drive to behave consistently with their own prior decisions. Of course, lawyers already know that judges will seek to make future decisions that are consistent with prior ones. Indeed, the whole foundation of the legal decision-making process—stare decisis—presupposes a high level of consistency in decisionmaking This is not necessarily news to the persuasive writer, though it is certainly helpful to have empirical confirmation of the conventional wisdom.

However, the newer and more powerful implication of foot-in-the-door for persuasive writers is the knowledge that the *"self-observation"* process of message recipients does not always involve a "set" cache of beliefs and decisions; rather, the process is susceptible to influence by the advocate. The advocate can organize her argument in such a way as to add to the cache of prior decisions that the reader will use to perform her self-observation. In that way, the advocate can influence the message recipient's determination—or perception—of the beliefs that will drive the ultimate decision. By crafting argument chains that add to the body of prior decisions that the reader will use to determine "what kind of person" she is, the advocate can demonstrate to the reader that she is the "kind of person" who agrees with the advocate's ultimate position. The impact on the reader's decision-making process can be especially significant when the argument chain leads with premises that the reader is likely to accept, but that the reader may not have independently connected to the advocate's thesis.

Foot-in-the-door also has the advantage of subtlety. It affects the reader's desire for consistency and self-affirmation, but does so in a somewhat indirect and non-obvious way. Affecting the "self-observation" process of the reader preserves the reader's impression that she has independently arrived at the decision, when in fact the decision has been influenced by the advocate. Preserving the appearance of audience autonomy lessens the likelihood that the audience will feel coerced and angry, feelings which can lead to the so-called *"boomerang effect"* in which the message recipient responds to the persuasive message by rejecting it or making a decision opposite to the one advocated.[14]

This is not to say that a well-crafted argument chain will convince a reader that she is a completely different "kind of person," or that it effectively convinces judges to make decisions they are otherwise firmly against. But, for example, in close cases where judges do not have a firm predisposition, or where the argument chain demonstrates non-obvious links between prior favorable decisions or premises and the decision sought, foot-in-the-door suggests that the momentum of agreement is difficult to resist.

The momentum created by a series of agreeable premises is important in the creation of legal argument chains because the chains are rarely ironclad or formally valid. The *"halo"* effect of the foot-in-the-door strategy that occurs because people tend to generalize about their beliefs from prior decisions implies that the persuasive writer has some flexibility in crafting a chain. The advocate is not necessarily bound rigidly to premises with obvious connections; though, of course, the degree to which the argument chain deviates from acceptable norms correlates to the risk that the reader will reject one or more of its premises, destroying the foot-in-the-door effect.

The foot-in-the-door research suggests a number of strategies for argument chaining. First, the initial request must be attractive and induce compliance, but it also must be [large enough] to trigger the self-scanning process. The request must "prompt" the message recipient to "infer attitudes from behaviors."[15] So, the first few links in the argument chain must be carefully chosen to be small enough to ensure a positive reaction from the legal audience, but large enough to trigger a self-consistency and self-affirmation process. Moreover, in terms of stare decisis and choice of authority, foot-in-the-door suggests that prior decisions by the same judge will be especially persuasive, and can be forged into the chain to stimulate an even stronger self-consistency reaction. However, this is not necessary to the principle; essentially, the chaining process works by formulating legal arguments with which the judge will agree at the time she reads the brief, creating a flow of agreement leading to the advocated premise.

Examples of the "Foot in the Door" Principle

The vast majority of well-written, persuasive appellate briefs contain multiple examples of argument chains that begin with a series of linked premises that the court is likely to accept and that lead the court to agree with the more controversial premise—the critical request. In *Davis v. Monroe County Board of Education*,[16] for example, the petitioner's brief used a number of argument chains that began with widely accepted premises that set the reader on the path to acceptance of the advocate's ultimate thesis.[17] In two basic argument chains designed to convince the Supreme Court that Title IX covers student-to-student sexual harassment, the petitioner's argument followed this complex path:

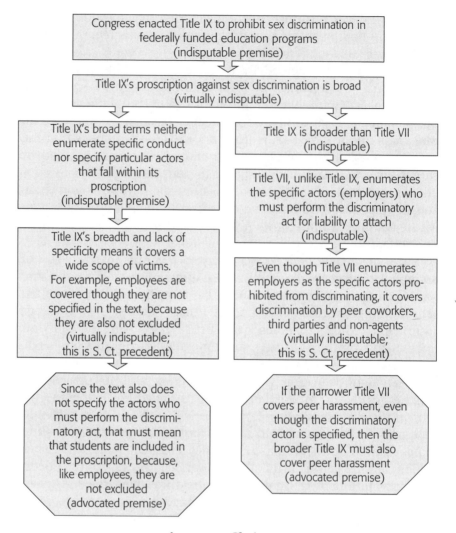

Argument Chain

In both chains, the advocated premise is preceded by several premises that either must be agreed with or are virtually indisputable. The reader is set early on a path of acquiescence. Moreover, the argument premises are linked so that the premise of one forms the foundation or reason for the next one, so that agreement with the prior premise leads to agreement with the subsequent. The form of the chain is: if A, then B; if B, then C; etc. The premises that lead up to the advocated premise are not only individually difficult for the reader to disagree with (A, B, and C are all uncontroversial), but also interconnected so that it is difficult to agree with one and disagree with the next (if you agree with A, you must agree with B, because the form of the chain is that if A, then B).

The two chains work on the same principle as the foot-in-the-door in that they play on the reader's preference for consistency.

The chains create for the reader a cache of prior consistent decisions linked to the advocated premise, so that the reader will be likely to experience dissonance if she rejects the advocated premise. It is, of course, still possible for the reader to disagree with the advocated premise, because the logic here only looks ironclad. But the chain makes acquiescence easier mentally, because it makes acquiescence seem more consistent with the reader's beliefs. If the reader rejects the advocated premise, she will have to work to resolve the apparent inconsistency created by her rejection.

The foot-in-the-door phenomenon can be especially useful to the advocate who must make comparisons that are both unconventional and push the boundaries of law and social norms. In the *Davis* example, an inevitable consequence of petitioner's argument is that an elementary school child can be a sexual harasser, a position that is socially and culturally problematic. Yet, petitioner's argument chains are constructed in a way that makes the comparison appear simple and conventional. For example, in the chain comparing Title VII to Title IX, the reasoning is a simple syllogism that is difficult to dispute: if X is broader than Y, and X covers B, Y must cover B also. The chain encourages the reader to focus on this simple transitive instead of the more problematic comparison between peers who are office coworkers and peers who are elementary school students.

But, foot-in-the-door can also help in cases where the advocate decides to—or must—confront a difficult legal or social norm directly. In these cases, foot-in-the-door chaining can help by convincing the reader that a particular decision is properly included in the prior cache the reader will use to make the decision. For example, in the case of *Rosa v. Park West Bank and Trust Co.,*[18] plaintiff-appellant Rosa, a biological male, was denied a loan by the defendant bank because he appeared for his loan request dressed in "traditionally female" clothing.[19] The audience might not have readily made the comparison between *Rosa* and *Price-Waterhouse v. Hopkins,*[20] in which a woman was denied partnership in part because of her abrasive, aggressive demeanor. The argument chain crafted by appellant Rosa, however, makes this non-obvious connection seem self-evident:

> Actions based on sexual stereotypes are acts of impermissible sex discrimination (virtually indisputable, S. Ct. precedent).
>
> When a firm denies a woman partnership because the woman did not meet the firm's stereotype of femininity, the firm has impermissibly discriminated against her (virtually indisputable, S. Ct. precedent).
>
> When a woman is told that she should walk, talk and dress more femininely, she is the victim of impermissible sex stereotyping because she did not conform to notions of what a "real woman" should look like (virtually indisputable, S. Ct. precedent).

When a man is told to dress in a more masculine fashion, he is the victim of sex stereotyping because he has not conformed to what a "real man" should look like (advocated premise).

When a man is the victim of sex stereotyping, he has been subject to an act of impermissible sex discrimination (advocated premise).

The chain works, in part, because of the foot-in-the-door principle. It is constructed in such a way that the reader is led to believe that if she agrees with the prior premises, she must find for appellant Rosa. In other words, if the reader believes sex stereotyping is illegal, she must agree that the bank's behavior was also illegal. A decision against appellant Rosa would be inconsistent and dissonant.

"Door in the Face": Creating a Scenario of Initial Rejection

Seemingly contrary to foot-in-the-door, there is some research that compliance is enhanced by making a large request first. The strategy of beginning a persuasive message with a more contentious proposition that the reader is likely to reject is called the "*door in the face*" strategy.[21] The research shows that the recipient, having rejected the first larger request, is thereafter somewhat more inclined to acquiesce to a second, smaller request.[22] Door-in-the-face is not as consistently successful as foot-in-the-door, however, and can depend on context.

For example, door-in-the-face is effective mostly if there is little or no time delay between requests, if there is no change in the identity of the requester, and if the request relates to the public interest or other humanitarian cause.[23] Although these limitations suggest that the door-in-the-face is a somewhat unpredictable persuasive tactic, many of them (time delay, identity of requester) will not affect the application of the strategy to persuasive legal writing. However, in considering door-in-the-face in the advocacy-writing context, it is important to be clear that door-in-the-face persuades the target to acquiesce to the *smaller* request; the result is not that the audience eventually acquiesces to the larger request.

Nevertheless, the door-in-the-face phenomenon, and particularly the explanations for why door-in-the-face works, should be of interest to the persuasive legal writer. At first glance, door-in-the-face seems to be of greatest relevance to legal negotiators in that it confirms the longstanding negotiating practice of posing an initial request that overshoots the desired outcome. But the principles that underlie door-in-the-face can bear on advocacy techniques as well, and have the potential to change the way advocates think about forward chaining in certain contexts.

One primary explanation for the effectiveness of door-in-the-face is that it works because the sequence of the requests can reestablish the interaction between persuader and target as a bargaining or negotiation interchange, as opposed to a situation where the persuader is "acting upon" a passive message recipient.[24] Once the situation is reestablished as a negotiation, the social "rules" of negotiation apply, one of which is that concession by one side should be reciprocated by concession on the other. Thus, the persuader's concession in asking for the smaller request leads to concession in the message recipient, and the recipient is led to accede to the smaller request.

Relatedly, some researchers attribute the door-in-the-face effect to the message recipient's feelings of obligation, responsibility, or duty to someone who has made a concession or done the recipient "a favor."[25] For this reason, the effect is likely to be stronger in cultures in which "tit-for-tat" reciprocity is the norm. Others attribute the door-in-the-face effect to guilt: refusal to accept the initial request induces guilt and agreeing to the smaller request reduces it.[26] Another explanation posits that the contrast between the two requests increases the likelihood of agreement to the smaller, because the message recipient perceives the smaller request as less burdensome because she will compare it to the larger request.[27]

A number of things about these explanations bear closer examination in the persuasive-legal-writing context. First, the implication that door-in-the-face works by changing the nature of the interaction between persuader and recipient is something that should pique the interest of any advocate. Persuasion is, at its core, a coercive process. Yet, no one likes to feel as though she is being coerced. In fact, a danger of pushing too hard with any persuasive message is a phenomenon called *"psychological reactance,"* in which the message recipient perceives the persuasive message as a threat to her autonomous decisionmaking. The message recipient will seek to reestablish her autonomy through various means, which can result in a boomerang effect.[28]

The explanations for door-in-the-face suggest that this strategy changes the appearance of the persuasive process so that it looks less coercive and more like a dialogue, which in turn may reduce the risk of a boomerang effect. Altering the process of audience decisionmaking is one of the primary ways for a persuader to gain compliance (the other being altering the content of the message).[29] In typical advocacy situations, the persuader uses certain techniques to gain something from the recipient, whose role is to "receive" the message and make a decision; the persuader is "working on" the recipient. Door-in-the-face seems to work by changing the recipient's perception of her role in the dialogue from the more coercive "worked on" to the more cooperative "worked with."

Instead of someone who "receives" the message and makes a decision, the recipient becomes someone who is actively engaged with the persuader in finding a solution to the problem (as with two negotiating parties).[30] This role makes the persuader look less like a coercer, which reduces the threat to the recipient's feelings of autonomy and reduces the possibility of psychological reactance. Instead, persuader and recipient look like partners in the quest for mutual agreement. In addition to encouraging compliance, this perception can also increase the recipient's motivation, a psychological state that is favorable to the persuader. . . .

The other facet of door-in-the-face that should be of interest to the legal advocate is that, as with foot-in-the-door, audience self-concept plays a central role in the persuasive process. Whereas with foot-in-the-door the recipient is moved to comply so that she behaves consistently with her (possibly idealized) self-concept, with door-in-the-face the initial rejection can create a conflict with the recipient's self-concept. Rejecting an initial foray can elicit feelings of guilt or hypocrisy and make the recipient question whether she is—or wants to be—the kind of person who says "no" to certain requests.[31] The persuasive message has created a subtle threat to the recipient's self-image that the recipient will be motivated to resolve. The persuasive message that elicits rejection can work to compromise the recipient's feelings of integrity—for example, her feelings that she is a moral, ethical, fair person. The recipient seeks to reduce this threat (or "*cognitive dissonance*") by complying with the second request, thereby reaffirming her self-image.[32]

Compliance that is the result of a threat to the recipient's self-concept and the resulting feelings of guilt is called "*transgression compliance*," because it is the recipient's perceived or actual "transgression" that drives the compliance.[33] Transgressions have a "powerful" and "dependable" effect on subsequent compliance. Although powerful, transgression compliance is a persuasive strategy with significant risks. The primary risk is that most people do not like to have their self-concept threatened, and may react with anger or resentment, neither of which are conducive to persuasion. However, this negative effect is more pronounced when the persuader explicitly points out the recipient's inconsistency, and is less likely when the persuader simply creates a scenario in which the message recipient independently realizes it, which is what happens with door-in-the-face.[34]

The complex psychological processes that make up the decision-making process during door-in-the-face encounters can be useful information for the persuasive legal writer. First of all, door-in-the-face implies some support for preceding an argument chain with the conclusion, however controversial, because initial reader skepticism can prime the reader for future compliance. Relatedly, and perhaps more surprisingly, the door-in-the-face phenomenon contradicts one of the most widely held pieces of conventional wisdom in advocacy: advocates should never ask for anything more than they need to get the desired result for the client, and they certainly should not start a brief with an argument that is likely to elicit rejection. Consistent with foot-in-the-door, the conventional wisdom is that the narrowest and least controversial request represents the surest route to persuading a judge, and the advocate should always start the brief with the strongest (surest) argument.

The door-in-the-face phenomenon suggests that, in some instances, it may be worthwhile for the advocate to rethink or reject this piece of conventional wisdom, and that it may be less risky to do so than legal advocates think. While I am not suggesting that advocates start briefs with high-risk arguments of dubious validity, the data does suggest that the rigid conservatism of legal writing might be worth rethinking in some cases. The data offers some support for advocates to take greater risks and use more creativity in legal argumentation, and to do so earlier in the brief. For example, an advocate might consider an argument chain that employs door-in-the-face principles in contexts such as "impact" litigation, where a big request may be worth the risk, or when a client can get a favorable result with a safer argument but would ultimately be better served by a riskier one. Beginning the chain with the riskier proposal may elicit rejection (or it may not), but it can also prime the audience for compliance with smaller assertions. The door-in-the-face phenomenon implies that the advocate does not lose much by making the big request—and actually may gain ground, particularly if a smaller request is also a part of the chain, and is still ultimately a "winner" for the client.

Finally, the success of door-in-the-face challenges the idea that arguing in the alternative, or offering a number of different routes to the desired outcome, is evidence of a weak argument. Door-in-the-face, like starting an argument chain with a bigger premise and then proposing a smaller one, is a kind of *"argument in the alternative."* Although arguing in the alternative is a familiar strategy, it is one that advocates disagree about. While some commentators see argument in the alternative as a valid persuasive strategy, others caution that the strategy can make both arguments appear weak. Echoing the explanations for door-in-the-face, the concerns about "argument in the alternative" are that the strategy makes the advocate look like she is negotiating, and therefore that she herself is not fully persuaded by or committed to the bigger argument. However, the data about door-in-the-face suggests that the advocate's shift to a stance that looks more like negotiation can be a position of strength rather than weakness, precisely because it looks less like a power play, and encourages the recipient to react as if she were negotiating.

On the other hand, the legal culture is not one in which "tit-for-tat" reciprocity is the norm between judges and lawyers. Judges know that they are the decisionmakers and most are not disposed to "negotiate" with counsel about a decision; they are less likely to feel the sense of guilt or obligation that leads to the door-in-the-face reaction. Nevertheless, reciprocity is the norm in American society, and judges are undoubtedly at least somewhat susceptible to the "social rules" of discourse, particularly when the issue is one—or the persuader presents an argument—that induces feelings of guilt or hypocrisy that the audience is moved to resolve. The door-in-the-face data suggests that this strategy might be especially useful in cases that raise important or compelling policies related to the public interest.

In designing legal argument chains, door-in-the-face suggests great care in the crafting of those first links. The first premises must be large enough to induce rejection, but not so large that rejection is reasonable and the recipient believes that the rejection is appropriately a reflection of her attitudes and beliefs.[35] Unlike foot-in-the-door, it is important for door-in-the-face messages *not* to trigger the self-scan process in such a way as to confirm for the audience that continuous rejection would be the most consistent (and affirming) approach. Moreover, the initial premise(s) must not be absurd or likely to stimulate a hostile response; they need only be of sufficiently greater magnitude to incur rejection—just a few steps away from the critical request with which compliance is sought.[36]

Argument Chains that "Work on" the "Door in the Face" Principle

Because the door-in-the-face principle conflicts with a longstanding tradition of appellate advocacy writing, briefs that begin with an aggressive, controversial premise are rarer than those that begin with benign, agreeable premises. There are, however, some examples that demonstrate the tactic. In the plaintiff-respondent's brief in *Meritor Savings Bank v. Vinson*,[37] for example, the respondent began her merits brief before the United States Supreme Court by arguing that certiorari was improvidently granted, and made arguments about the record that she did not make in her brief responding to the petition for certiorari.[38]

Although beginning the merits brief with this argument had its strategic and logical advantages, the argument had many of the hallmarks of a door-in-the-face initial request. First, it was risky. It was highly unlikely that the Supreme Court would accede to an argument that raised something new in the merits brief that was not argued in the response to the petition for certiorari, which, as petitioner pointed out, was the more appropriate place for the argument procedurally.[39] Moreover, there was nothing to indicate that there was disagreement among the members of the Court about granting the petition for certiorari, which means that, at a minimum, four Justices voted to grant certiorari and the others did not feel strongly enough to dissent.[40] Second, the attack on certiorari was a "big" request. It asked the Court to reverse its initial decision and publicly admit that it had mistakenly granted the original cert petition. Finally, the request asked for a "big" win; were respondent to convince the Court to reverse its initial grant of certiorari, that decision would let stand as precedent a court of appeals opinion highly favorable to the respondent on a number of cutting-edge issues. For all of these reasons, the Court was likely to reject the argument, and, indeed, it did. Neither the majority opinion nor the two separate concurring opinions even mention the argument.

On the other hand, the request was neither unreasonable nor absurd, and there is evidence that the Court found aspects of it persuasive. Aspects of the respondent's arguments about certiorari, particularly the abstract and ambiguous quality of key facts in the record, are echoed in the Court's discussion of respondeat superior liability.[41] A request that involves a high risk of rejection but is reasonable is critical to the door-in-the-face response. Moreover, the respondent achieves a number of significant victories with the arguments that follow the "big" request, including an overall win on result (the Court affirmed the favorable decision below). But, respondent also achieves victories on a smaller scale. For example, the Court somewhat surprisingly accepts respondent's argument about how "voluntary" sexual conduct can be the result of "unwelcome" sexual advances. It also accepts the validity of her analogy to racial harassment cases.[42]

The context of *Meritor* is also consistent with the door-in-the-face phenomenon. The Court characterized the behavior in the case as "pervasive harassment" as well as "criminal conduct of the most serious nature."[43] Moreover, the Court notes that because the petitioner's grievance procedure required respondent to complain first to her supervisor, who was also the perpetrator, it was "not altogether surprising that respondent failed to invoke the procedure."[44] The allegations make the case one in which an initial rejection might very well induce a guilt or dissonance reaction, making even Supreme Court Justices wonder whether they are the "kind of people" who decide that this conduct is without federal remedy. Consistent with the door-in-the-face strategy, respondent's brief first lays the groundwork for a dissonance reaction, and then offers multiple ways to resolve it, several of which the Court takes.

While it is impossible to say with certainty whether the result in *Meritor is* a function of the door-in-the-face phenomenon, the case gives an excellent example of how the strategy might translate in an appellate writing context, and demonstrates a result that is consistent with a door-in-the-face response. At the very least, the example should give advocates pause about the conventional wisdom of appellate writing that advocates should always make the least controversial request first. It seems clear that the respondent did not *lose* anything by leading with a "big" request, and there is some evidence that she may have gained some ground. *Meritor,* along with the social-science data, demonstrates that the safe route is not the only route, and gives creative advocates yet another tool for persuasion.

Key Concepts

Priming
Chaining
Argument chain
Ego-defensive
"Foot in the door" strategy
"Door in the face" strategy
Self-observation; self-consistency; self-affirmation
Transgression compliance

Discussion Questions

1. Priming is placing something ahead of the main thesis in order to prepare the reader to be more receptive to the main thesis. Priming is one of the most important concepts in this excerpt, in part because it applies to many topics other than deciding the order of arguments. Can you think of other ways a good brief writer prepares the reader to be more receptive to her argument?

2. What did you learn in your first-year legal writing course about how to decide the order of your arguments? This excerpt from Professor Stanchi's article presents two different strategies. How do they compare with what you learned in your introductory course? Which of the two strategies from the excerpt do you think is generally more effective? Why?

3. The ideas in this excerpt apply to more than deciding the order of major point headings. Potentially, they might apply to how you organize the discussion under each heading. Usually, discussions proceed according to some variety of IRAC (Issue, Rule, Application, Conclusion). Might the ideas in this excerpt mean that sometimes a strict IRAC format might not be the best choice?

4. Notice that the reasons these strategies work have to do with a set of characteristics about people as readers. Look back through the reading

and make a list of all the characteristics you find there (e.g., a person wants to be and be seen as a good person or people are pulled toward consistency). Do these observations about people seem consistent with your experience of others and of yourself?

5. Lawyers and scholars have only recently begun to pay attention to principles of psychology and other social science disciplines. What do you think might account for the delay in recognizing the important connections between these disciplines and the work of lawyers?

Endnotes

1. Daniel O'Keefe, *Persuasion: Theory and Research* 169 (Sage Publications 1990).

2. G. Ray Funkhouser, *The Power of Persuasion: A Guide to Moving Ahead in Business and Life* (Crown Publishers 1986).

3. Douglas N. Walton, *A Pragmatic Model of Legal Disputation*, 73 Notre Dame L. Rev. 711, 724 (1998).

4. Funkhouser, *supra* note 2, at 70-72.

5. Frans H. Van Eemeren et al., *Fundamentals of Argumentation Theory: A Handbook of Historical Backgrounds and Contemporary Developments* (Routledge 1996).

6. O'Keefe, *supra* note 1, at 169. . . .

7. *Id.* at 169-170.

8. Kelton V.L. Rhoads & Robert Cialdini, *The Business of Influence: Principles that Lead to Success in Commercial Settings*, in *The Persuasion Handbook: Developments in Theory and Practice* 513, 526 (James Price Dillard & Michael Pfau eds., Sage Publications 2002).

9. Rhoads & Cialdini, *supra* note 8, at 526; O'Keefe, *supra* note 1, at 170-171.

10. Michael Burgoon & Erwin P. Bettinghaus, *Persuasive Message Strategies*, in *Persuasion: New Directions in Theory and Research* 141, 156 (Michael E. Roloff & Gerald R. Miller eds., Sage Publications 1980).

11. Rhoads & Cialdini, *supra* note 8, at 526. . . .

12. Eddie Harmon-Jones, *A Cognitive Dissonance Theory Perspective on Persuasion*, in *The Persuasion Handbook: Developments in Theory and Practice* 99, 102; Kathleen Kelley Reardon, *Persuasion: Theory and Context* 68-69 (Sage Publications 1981).

13. Reardon, *supra* note 12, at 67.

14. Michael Burgoon et al., *Revisiting the Theory of Psychological Reactance: Communicating Threats to Attitudinal Freedom*, in *The Persuasion Handbook: Developments in Theory and Practice* 213, 215-216.

15. Burgoon & Bettinghaus, *supra* note 10, at 158-159.

16. 525 U.S. 1065 (1999).

17. *See* Brief of Petitioner, *Davis*, 525 U.S. 1065 (No. 97-843).

18. 214 F.3d 213 (1st Cir. 2000).

19. Jennifer L. Levi & Mary L. Bonauto, *Brief of Plaintiff-Appellant Lucas Rosa in the United States Court of Appeals for the First Circuit*, 7 Mich. J. Gender & L. 147, 149 (2001) (reprinting the brief in full with minor changes).

20. 490 U.S. 228 (1989).

21. O'Keefe, *supra* note 1, at 171-173.

22. *See id.* at 171-172. . . .

23. *See id.* at 172-173.

24. *See id.* at 172.

25. *See* Rhoads & Cialdini, *supra* note 8, at 516.

26. *See* O'Keefe, *Guilt as a Mechanism of Persuasion*, in *The Persuasion Handbook: Developments in Theory and Practice* 333, 333-334.

27. *See* O'Keefe, *supra* note 1, at 172.

28. Burgoon et al., *supra* note 14, at 215-216.

29. Funkhouser, *supra* note 2 at 101.

30. Rhoads & Cialdini, *supra* note 8, at 516. . . .

31. O'Keefe, *supra* note 26, at 331-335. . . .

32. Harmon-Jones, *supra* note 12, at 100-102.

33. O'Keefe, *supra* note 26, at 332.

34. *Id.* at 332-339.

35. Burgoon & Bettinghaus, *supra* note 10, at 159.

36. *Id.*

37. 477 U.S. 57 (1986).

38. Brief of Respondent Michelle Vinson at 1, 15-23, *Meritor Savings Bank v. Vinson*, 477 U.S. 57 (1986) (No. 84-1979), 1986 WL 728234, at 1, 8-11 [hereinafter *Meritor* Respondent's Brief]; *see also* Reply Brief of Petitioner, *Meritor*, 477 U.S. 57 (No. 84-1979), 1986 WL 728303 [hereinafter *Meritor* Petitioner's Reply Brief].

39. *Meritor* Petitioner's Reply Brief, *supra* note 38, at 2-3.

40. *PSFS Savings Bank v. Vinson*, 474 U.S. 815 (1985) (petition for certiorari granted; no dissenting opinions).

41. *Compare Meritor* Respondent's Brief, *supra* note 38, at 16-18 (record is "cloud[ed]" and "ambigu[ous]" because a key finding of fact is "wholly hypothetical" and makes "any consideration of notice, knowledge, policy or procedure . . . wholly abstract"), *with Meritor*, 477 U.S. at 72 (question of employer liability has "rather abstract quality" because of "state of record" and makes determination of notice standard premature).

42. . . . *Compare Meritor* Respondent's Brief, *supra* note 38, at 35-36 (court of appeals was correct in finding the "sexual intercourse may appear voluntary even though the advances that initiated it were entirely unwelcome"), *with Meritor*, 477 U.S. at 68 ("correct inquiry is whether respondent . . . indicated that the alleged sexual advances were unwelcome, not whether her actual participation in sexual intercourse was voluntary"). The race analogy is less difficult, but could easily have been rejected, given a history of some divergence between sex and race cases and petitioner's heavy reliance in its brief on the distinction between sex and race. *Compare Meritor* Respondent's Brief, *supra* note 38, at 44-45, *with Meritor*, 477 U.S. at 66 (same principle used for racial harassment cases should be used in sexual harassment cases).

43. *Meritor*, 477 U.S. at 67.

44. *Id.* at 73. . . .

10. *Involvement*

In this chapter, we return to another part of Professor Stanchi's article from Chapter 9. Here, Professor Stanchi explores the crucial importance of involving the reader in the issue and the argument. Once again, some of the new terminology will be highlighted to help you become familiar with it.

Excerpt from

Kathryn M. Stanchi, *The Science of Persuasion: An Initial Exploration*

2006 Mich. St. L. Rev. 411

A critical variable affecting the impact of a persuasive message is the level of involvement of the target audience with the issue and the message. "*Involvement*" . . . generally refers to the level of personal relevance to the issue felt by the audience. It is what allows the audience to connect the content of the persuasive message to personal experience, or to personal beliefs or values.

Defined this way, audience involvement is not a new concept for persuasive legal writers. However, while legal writers have long sought to influence the level of audience connection with a legal issue, the conventional wisdom of persuasive legal writing can treat the relationship between emotional or motivating arguments and their result as a kind of linear equation. The thinking often runs along these lines: if an advocate makes the "right" motivating argument, the judge will "want" to make a decision consistent with the policy or value raised by the argument and will be more inclined to make a decision in the advocate's favor.

While this is undoubtedly part of the story, the social-science data shows that when an advocate makes a convincing motivating argument, something else—something a bit more complex—

happens to the audience other than picking from among competing values. While there is no question that most people, judges included, will respond to arguments directed at values, the question is why, and how? A look at the data and theories about audience involvement—and there is a great deal of it—reveals that involvement or motivation is a significantly more complex and multi-faceted concept that deserves more thoughtful treatment by legal advocates.

Skepticism

A. How Involvement Affects the Decisionmaking Process

One of the most interesting things about audience involvement is that it affects not only the ultimate decision, but also the process by which a person thinks about a persuasive message. In other words, involvement plays such a central role in *what* the ultimate decision or result is because it affects *how* the decision is made. A motivating argument can affect how the judge reads the briefs, how she approaches the arguments made, what kinds of arguments will sway her, and whether her decision will be strong and long-lasting or weak and easily shakable. To truly understand what she is doing when she makes arguments directed toward audience motivation, therefore, the advocate must understand involvement and how it affects the process by which decisions are made.

The relationship between audience involvement and the decisionmaking process is described by a theory called the *Elaboration Likelihood Model (ELM)*. The ELM posits that evaluation of persuasive arguments takes place on a continuum; at one end of the continuum is *central route processing* and at the other is *peripheral route processing.*[2] Central and peripheral processing of persuasive messages differ in the depth of audience consideration of the issue and the message. Central route processing is characterized by careful, critical evaluation of the merits of arguments, or *"high elaboration."* During central route processing, the message recipient actively engages with the persuasive message, generating her own thoughts and arguments in response to the information she has received. Peripheral route processing, on the other hand, is less thoughtful and engaged, and is often based on heuristics or short-cuts unrelated to the substantive merits of the message.[3] For example, when a judge considers whether the facts of a precedent case are applicable or distinguishable from the case before her, she is actively engaged with the merits of the arguments before her, and processes more centrally. When a judge decides to reject an argument because the advocate lacks credibility, the process is more peripheral.

One of the tenets of the ELM is that, generally, as audience involvement increases, the audience moves toward central processing of the persuasive message; as it decreases, the audience moves toward peripheral processing.[4] A typical experiment testing audience involvement studied the decisionmaking processes of college undergraduate students. The students heard identical persuasive messages advocating that senior comprehensive examinations be required as a condition of graduation. The only variable was that one group of students was told that the policy was to be adopted at their institution (high-involvement condition) and another group was told that the policy was to be adopted at a different, far away institution (lower involvement). In contrast to the low-involvement group, the high-involvement group exhibited decisionmaking processes associated with the central route—that is, more thoughtful consideration of the arguments.[5] The students who felt more personally connected to the issue were more careful and critical in their evaluation of the merits.

In terms of persuasive legal writing, this data confirms something relatively unsurprising: the decision in a case will be affected by how much the audience cares about the issue. More specifically, the ELM suggests that the degree of attention that the judicial audience gives to a case or an advocate's argument will vary with the judges' level of involvement in the issue. While the description of central route processing sounds like the process in which most judges engage when evaluating briefs, it is unlikely that judges process all messages with the same degree of elaboration. Judges are busy, and likely prioritize both the cases and the arguments and give different levels of attention to different cases, issues, and arguments.

The ELM also suggests that advocates can influence the level of attention given to their persuasive messages by influencing the level of involvement the reader feels. The advocate can move the audience closer to central processing and more elaboration or push her away from central processing to a more peripheral consideration. While most persuasive legal writers are aware of the importance of influencing how much their audience cares about an issue, what they may not know is that involvement has a significant effect on the ultimate decision because it affects the process of audience decisionmaking.

So, why should legal writers care about *how* the audience processes the message? Why would they want to influence the decision-making process? After all, the ELM does not purport to direct the substance of persuasive messages. Advocates can achieve a "good" (or "bad") result through either central or peripheral processing. Moreover, advocates already use a number of strategies to influence involvement—even if they do not know the social-science term of art. Policy arguments, analogies or examples, precedent choice, and factual narratives all play on audience involvement, in different ways and to different degrees. Is it really necessary for legal advocates to understand the intricacies of how involvement affects result?

The answer is yes. Legal advocates should care about how the audience processes the message. They will be better and more effective writers if they understand and have greater control over their handling of involvement. A main reason that legal writers should care about the decisionmaking process is that, in the context of persuasion (as with many areas of law), process is inextricably entangled with result. It is an axiom of legal practice that if you influence the process, you influence the result, and advocacy is no exception. With involvement, the ways in which the decision-making process can affect result [are] illuminated by the differences between the central and peripheral processes of decisionmaking.

There are two primary differences between the decisionmaking processes that will interest the persuasive legal writer seeking to influence involvement: the different decisionmaking routes (1) call for different argument strategies and (2) produce different kinds of decisions. In terms of argument strategy, different kinds of persuasive messages will influence the message recipient who processes centrally versus the recipient who processes peripherally. For example, substantive argument merits are quite important to central processing, and less important to messages processed peripherally. When recipients process centrally, strong merits arguments will elicit favorable results and weak arguments will elicit unfavorable results.[6] Things like typographical errors and advocate credibility become less important as a person moves closer to central processing of a message. The opposite is true for messages processed peripherally.[7] In peripheral route processing, argument merits exercise less influence on the message recipient. Strong merits arguments will not necessarily yield favorable results, and weak arguments will do less damage. Rather, things like advocate likability or credibility will loom larger in the decision.[8]

Uninvolved

Photo by Aidan Whiteley, Oct. 12, 2009

Central and peripheral processing also differ in the strength of the result they produce. The decision that results from central processing—because it is based on an elaborative, critical process of argument evaluation—is likely to be stronger and more persistent than decisions reached through peripheral processing. Because during central processing the message recipient, often independently, has generated, evaluated, and answered counterarguments to the arguments presented, the resulting decision is less vulnerable to counterarguments raised by opponents.[9] Decisions resulting from peripheral processing, on the other hand, are more vulnerable and held with less confidence.

At the very least, this data suggests that legal advocates approach involvement and motivation carefully, with an understanding that motivating arguments will affect the audience decisionmaking process, and with an eye toward what kind of process might favor the client's position. This disrupts some of the linearity with which lawyers have approached audience motivation. Audience involvement does not simply lead the decisionmaker in a straight line to a particular decision.

Moreover, the persuasive legal writer needs to know that involvement will affect how much influence strong (and weak) merits arguments will have on the reader, and how critically the reader will assess them. She should also know that when she makes a motivating argument, she is not merely giving the judge a reason to find for her client; she is ensuring that the audience will give close, critical consideration to the merits of the arguments, testing the argument with self-generated counterarguments and examples. It is also important for her to know how certain decisions she makes will affect the impact of other rhetorical features of the argument, such as her own credibility or likability, or grammatical or typographical errors.

This is important news; it can mean the difference between winning and losing. Legal advocates are well-aware that argument merits are not the only influence on judicial decisionmaking; they know that credibility, how a brief looks, and other things unrelated to substance can affect the decision. But, they may not have known that they can assert some control over how much influence these criteria have. There will certainly be times when an advocate wants scrutiny that is more careful and considered. But there are also times—for example, if she wants a summary affirmance or a denial of review or certiorari, or if her position has a strong surface appeal but will weaken under critical scrutiny—that she might prefer a less central process or a process that is more influenced by peripheral cues. In either case, she should have control over the tools that affect these processes. In addition, the advocate should also know what she risks when courting a favorable decision through a more peripheral process. The decision might be favorable, but also vulnerable to her opponent's arguments and subject to change. This may be a risk that the advocate wants to or must take, but she should do so consciously.

Finally, advocates should understand the intricacies of how involvement works, because otherwise they risk using it ineffectively. Advocates already use strategies to affect involvement, but may not know the nuances of how particular motivating strategies affect the decisionmaking process. So, they may be using strategies in ways that are ineffective or, worse, harmful to their cases. As the following section demonstrates, involvement is as complex as human motivation, and different advocacy goals call for different involvement strategies.

B. The Nuances of Audience Involvement

If the first step for the advocate in the use of motivating arguments is whether and under what circumstances to stimulate audience involvement, the second question is how to stimulate involvement effectively and knowledgeably. Like the decision whether to push judges toward greater involvement, how to do so is a more complex question than legal advocates might think. It is a bit more complicated than figuring out what beliefs or values the judges hold in the greatest esteem and finding a way to connect those values to the issue in the case. First of all, there are different kinds of involvement a message recipient can feel, and the recipient will process the message differently depending on what kind of involvement is experienced.[10] Second, the different kinds of involvement mean that a message can be pitched to trigger a certain kind of involvement, depending on how the advocate wants the recipient to process the message.

1. The Different Kinds of Audience Involvement

In terms of a message recipient's intrinsic beliefs, social scientists draw a distinction between *"outcome-relevant"* involvement and *"value-relevant"* involvement.[11] *Outcome-relevant involvement* refers to a direct personal stake in the outcome of the issue; the college students in the ELM study who believed that the graduation requirements at their own institution were going to change had high outcome-relevant involvement. On the other hand, *value-relevant involvement* refers to issues that impact important personal values or beliefs.[12] Message recipients also can experience another type of involvement called *"response involvement."* When a decision is in some way public, as are judicial opinions, message recipients may be motivated to exhibit the "correct" attitude or response, which may be different from their actual personal belief.[13] In a given case, a message recipient can experience some or all of these different kinds of involvement, to different degrees for different issues.

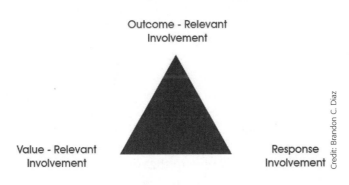

Outcome - Relevant
Involvement

Value - Relevant
Involvement

Response
Involvement

Credit: Brandon C. Diaz

Value and outcome involvement, in particular, have very different (and somewhat surprising) effects on message processing. High outcome involvement is, as with the graduation requirements study, associated with central processing. Those recipients with high outcome involvement showed a high degree of attention to argument merits; they had a favorable response when confronted with strong arguments and an unfavorable one when confronted with weak arguments. High value-relevant involvement, however, was *not* associated with the same degree of argument attention as high outcome involvement.[14] Message recipients whose strongly held values were at issue in a case did not show high elaboration and were not influenced favorably by strong arguments (or unfavorably by weak ones).

In terms of message framing, the data suggests that a message crafted to induce a feeling of personal outcome involvement in the recipient is more likely to be processed centrally, with great elaboration, and with increased attention to argument merits.[15] If the message is reframed in terms of more abstract values, the result is a decreased elaboration, a more peripheral mode of processing, and minimal impact of argument strength—closer to what we might call a "knee-jerk" response.[16] As one commentator explained, this means that an appeal to values could be a way to "short-circuit intelligent debate."[17] Think of how politicians use appeals to "family values" to stimulate a certain response, one that can be quite impervious to logical arguments.

Another wrinkle is that a value-involved message recipient will experience a different reaction depending on whether the message conflicts with or confirms her values. If a message conflicts with the recipient's values, the recipient is motivated to "protect" her beliefs ("*value-protective processing*").[18] To protect her beliefs, the message recipient will respond to any substantive arguments that conflict with her beliefs by generating counterarguments. This means that in value-protective situations, stronger arguments in the persuasive message will not lead to attitude change, and may make the belief of the message recipient more entrenched. Rather, to induce attitude change in someone who has strongly held beliefs, the peripheral—not central—route is the more effective means, particularly "if values are held with any real commitment."[19] In other words, if a person has strong values and the advocate's desired result conflicts with those values, merits arguments are not likely to wield great influence, regardless of their strength. The opposite occurs for a value-involved message recipient when the message confirms her beliefs ("value-affirmative processing"). In that situation, strong merits arguments will influence the message recipient by making more secure the beliefs consistent with the message.[20]

[The article here describes a study showing that] "statistical evidence is superior for reinforcing beliefs of those already inclined

to believe the message, and anecdotal evidence is superior for influencing a much more difficult audience—those who disagree with the message."[21]

2. How the Data About Involvement Informs Persuasion in Law

The data about involvement . . . confirms the persuasive strength and effectiveness of narrative, and adds a couple of intriguing details. It gives legal writers a glimpse of *how* narrative works—by a largely peripheral process that discourages counter-arguing—but also *on whom* it is most effective. While it is unlikely to have any influence on people who agree with the message, anecdotal or narrative messages are the *only* likely path to attitude change in an audience whose beliefs or values conflict with the message. By contrast, substantive merits arguments induce greater entrenchment in the value-protective audience. Not only does this data give renewed validity to the place of good storytelling in legal argumentation, but it also may bestow some greater respect for the effectiveness of nontraditional narrative briefs such as that filed by amici in *Webster v. Reproductive Health Services.*[22] Persuasive legal writers should use this information to decide not only the structure but the emphasis of their persuasive documents. Deciding how much narrative to include in the brief and whether to structurally highlight it can affect the outcome, particularly in cases where the advocate is in a difficult position with a skeptical or hostile audience.

The other intriguing part of the data is the distinct effects on audience decisionmaking induced by the different kinds of involvement. These distinct effects suggest that advocates should make conscious, deliberate decisions about crafting their persuasive messages to encourage different types of audience involvement, depending on what kind of involvement is likely to serve the client's interests. If the audience experiences response involvement, argument merits will matter less than what the message recipient thinks the "correct" public response should be. If the message triggers outcome-relevant involvement, the audience will process centrally, arguments will be evaluated carefully and critically with a high degree of counter-arguing, and argument strength will be influential. If the message induces value-relevant involvement, the audience is likely to process more peripherally, which means argument merits will not be highly influential, and instead the audience will use heuristics or "shortcuts" to make a decision.

The critical piece of information is that legal writers may not know that when they ratchet up value involvement, they are not necessarily increasing the level of care and attention to their message. Nor are they pushing the reader toward deeper

> "Statistical evidence is superior for reinforcing beliefs of those already inclined to believe the message, and anecdotal evidence is superior for influencing a much more difficult audience—those who disagree with the message."
> —*Michael Slater*

consideration of the merits of the arguments; in fact, just the opposite is occurring. Advocates ratcheting up value involvement may be "short-circuiting" the elaborative process. They may get a decision in their favor, but they also risk that the decision might be weak and vulnerable to counterargument. It is outcome involvement that is the key to greater depth of message processing, a process in which argument strength will be a decisive factor.

3. Drafting Legal Arguments to Affect Involvement

. . . [I]n *Oncale v. Sundowner Offshore Services, Inc.*, the question before the Supreme Court was whether sexual harassment perpetrated by men against men is actionable under Title VII.[23] In his brief, the petitioner attempted to persuade the Justices that the harassment of him by a group of his male colleagues occurred because of his sex, even though there was no evidence that his colleagues' treatment of him stemmed from either sexual desire or from hostility to males.[24] Petitioner had to prove that the harassers treated him the way they did because of his maleness. In particular, petitioner had to contend with respondents' suggestion that the conduct, while it might be considered uncivil and even offensive in the "outside" world, was typical day-to-day life on an isolated all-male oil rig, where the male employees routinely engaged in aggressive rough-housing when establishing the male pecking order.

Library of Congress (photo by Carol M. Highsmith, 1980)

Oil rigs, Galveston, Texas

In their briefs, respondents tried to establish distance—i.e., lack of connection—between the judicial audience and the experience of oil rig employees. Respondents sought to push the judges away from personal involvement in a case where the behavior was egregious and shocking; essentially, respondents argued "this could never happen to you."[25] So, a repeated "theme" in respondents' briefs is that an oil rig is different from law offices or judicial chambers, and different norms and behavior govern the different places, and the Justices should not draw conclusions about what is appropriate for an oil rig by imagining the same behavior in a law office or their own chambers.[26]

Petitioner, on the other hand, tried to emphasize the common ground between the Justices and the harassed employee. One of petitioner's themes was the common ground of manhood (Justices O'Connor and Ginsburg notwithstanding), and what behavior is acceptable (or not) within male norms. To do so, petitioner's brief— twice within a span of ten pages or so—comes very close to asking the Justices directly to imagine themselves in the shoes of the petitioner. In the first reference, petitioner argued:

> The gender of Mr. Oncale's harasser neither defines nor detracts from the sexually harassing nature of the defendants' conduct. To the contrary, one can assert with some confidence that there is no type of conduct more repulsive to the non-consenting heterosexual male and more certain to drive him from the work place than that engaged in by the defendants in this case. Why is this conduct so degrading and humiliating? Because Joseph Oncale is a man.[27]

The second reference is also quite direct:

> Can there be any treatment more demeaning and objectively harassing to a married, heterosexual male with two children than to be subjected to sexual taunts, sexual touching and physical, sexual assault by other men with whom he must work in a closely confined work space . . . ?[28]

These two passages . . . clearly are meant to induce greater personal involvement with the issue. By inviting the Justices to imagine how they would feel if they were required to endure similar harassment, the rhetoric moves the audience from an abstract level of involvement to a greater personal one. Although direct, the rhetoric is carefully tempered in a number of ways. First, neither passage appears in a position of emphasis in the brief. Rather, one is buried in the middle section and the other appears toward the end. In terms of language, both examples use a generalized third-person term ("heterosexual male") instead of speaking in the second person or about petitioner specifically. This syntax invites connection while simultaneously keeping a respectful distance. There is also considerable qualification and weakening language and syntax in both examples.[29] All of these maneuvers serve the important function of making a direct appeal to judicial personal involvement appear less aggressive and direct, to the end of making the target audience more likely to process it centrally, and be less likely to boomerang.

Another interesting example of a subtle appeal to involvement appears in *Harris v. Forklift Systems, Inc.*, which, like *Oncale*, was a Title VII sexual harassment case.[30] The primary issue in the case was whether a sexual harassment plaintiff must prove severe psychological injury to prevail in a hostile work environment case.[31] At the heart of the case was the definition of what is "abusive" in a work environment, and what a "reasonable person" might find offensive. Twice in the plaintiff-petitioner's (Harris's) brief, she notes that both the perpetrator of the harassment and an employee of Forklift (the defendant-respondent) stated that they would be angered and offended if men spoke to their wives or daughters the way the perpetrator spoke to her.[32] As in the *Oncale* petitioner's brief, the point is not structurally highlighted, although it is mentioned twice; it is first raised in the middle of the "Statement of the Case," and then again in a footnote in the "Argument" section.[33]

The argument seems directly pitched toward those men on the Supreme Court who have close familial relationships with women. For example, the footnote in the Argument section reads, "neither [defendant nor the Forklift employee] *would allow* their wives to be subjected to the behavior that [the defendant] imposed on [petitioner] at Forklift."[34] Although the testimony is of some relevance to the point that reasonable people can agree about the offensiveness of the conduct in the case (even the perpetrator agrees!), the relevance is tangential at best and was probably included for its emotional power. But the argument also has the added benefit of ratcheting up the level of outcome involvement of the Justices at whom it is directed (married and/or fathers of daughters), moving them from a more abstract value involvement toward a greater personal investment in the outcome of the case. . . .

The purpose of exploring the persuasive potential of involvement is not to convince lawyers to make openly personalized arguments to appellate judges, a strategy which would undoubtedly backfire. Rather, the purpose of learning about involvement is to help advocates do more effectively what they are already doing with motivational arguments. Lawyers attempt to influence involvement all the time. They may not, however, always know that the technique that seems "right" to them is really about involvement. More important, they are not always using it in the most effective way. A greater understanding of involvement and the ways to influence it are the keys to using the techniques most effectively and skillfully. This means understanding the different kinds of involvement and the persuasive power of involvement, and understanding how to influence reader involvement in ways that are powerful, yet ethical and acceptable to the audience.

Conclusion

In persuasive legal writing, audience is paramount. There is simply no such thing as "too much information" about the audience to whom a persuasive message is directed. Yet the concept of the legal audience has remained somewhat two-dimensional in the conventional wisdom. This two-dimensionality is neither necessary nor advisable. There is a wealth of data and theory outside law that can help flesh out the identity of the legal audience beyond the amorphous figure of the busy judge who is unfamiliar with the facts and law of the case.

[I]nformation about the psychology of human decisionmaking is one path to greater knowledge about the legal audience. . . . Every small piece of information helps to fill in another part of the picture of who that elusive legal audience is and what makes her react.

[This] is not to say that the audience can be defined exactly and accurately. Persuasive legal writing is, and remains, an art, not a science. Nevertheless, science can be a part of art. The best persuasive legal writers already try to predict how their audiences will react to certain arguments, syntax, analogies, or vocabulary. On the simplest level, this Article argues that if you are going to do it, you should do it right. The data about human decisionmaking will not give lawyers all the answers, but it can show us strategies that we might never have known about or considered, and it can put a fresh spin on other, more familiar strategies.

Key Concepts

High elaboration vs. low elaboration
Central vs. peripheral processing
Motivating arguments
Outcome-relevant involvement vs. value-relevant involvement vs. response involvement
Value-protective processing

Discussion Questions

1. Presumably, the rules of judicial conduct will prohibit a judge from having a direct personal stake in the outcome of a case; at the least, involvement like owning shares in the corporate defendant or being personally related

to one of the parties. But judges might *feel* a personal stake if they strongly identify with possible future situations in which the legal issue might arise. For instance, try as she might to avoid it, the judge might identify with an employer, since the judge employs a staff. Or the judge might identify with a parent in a custody dispute if a family member of the judge has experienced a similar situation. Is this idea troubling? Or is it simply inevitable and thus fair game for persuasion?

2. The reading quotes a commentator as saying that an appeal to values could be a way to "short-circuit intelligent debate." The cognitive science seems to indicate that this is the case. We should be able to find a way to have intelligent debate about our values, yet it seems difficult to do. How can we do a better job of talking about values, both in legal argument and as a nation?

3. You are probably used to using techniques to increase emphasis. Does it surprise you that sometimes you might want to decrease the attention a judge might pay to a part of your argument (move from central to peripheral processing), and perhaps for reasons other than the weakness of the argument?

Additional Suggested Reading

Lucille A. Jewel, *Through a Glass Darkly: Using Brain Science and Visual Rhetoric to Gain a Professional Perspective on Visual Advocacy*, 19 So. Cal. Interdisc. L.J. 237 (2010).

Kathryn M. Stanchi, *The Power of Priming in Legal Advocacy: Using the Science of First Impressions to Persuade the Reader*, 89 Or. L. Rev. 305 (2010).

Endnotes

1. Ian Gallacher, *Thinking Like Non-Lawyers: Why Empathy Is a Core Lawyering Skill and Why Legal Education Should Change to Reflect Its Importance*, 8 LC&R: JALWD 109 (2011).

2. Steve Booth-Butterfield & Jennifer Welbourne, *The Elaboration Likelihood Model: Its Impact on Persuasion Theory and Research*, in *The Persuasion Handbook: Developments in Theory & Practice* 155, 157 (James Price Dillard & Michael Pfau eds., Sage Publications 2002); Daniel O'Keefe, *Persuasion: Theory and Research* 98 (Sage Publications 1990).

3. Booth-Butterfield & Welbourne, *supra* note 2, at 156-157.

4. *Id.* at 159-160.

5. O'Keefe, *supra* note 2, at 99-100.

6. *Id.* at 110.

7. *Id.* at 97-98, 110.

8. *Id.* at 98.

9. Booth-Butterfield & Welbourne, *supra* note 2, at 157-158.

10. *Id.* at 161-162.

11. *Id.*

12. Michael D. Slater, *Involvement as Goal-Directed Strategic Processing: Extending the Elaboration Likelihood Model*, in *The Persuasion Handbook: Developments in Theory and Practice* 175, 177; O'Keefe, *supra* note 2, at 99 . . . ; Andrew J. Cook, Kevin Moore & Gary D. Steel, *The Taking of a Position: A Reinterpretation of the Elaboration Likelihood Model*, 34 J. Theory Soc. Behav. 315, 316 (2004).

13. O'Keefe, *supra* note 2, at 115-116.

14. *Id*. at 177, 179.

15. Slater, *supra* note 12, at 180.

16. *Id*.

17. *Id*.

18. *Id*. at 179-180.

19. *Id*. at 180.

20. *Id*.

21. *Id*. at 185.

22. Brief for Women Who Have Had Abortions et al. as Amici Curiae Supporting Appel-lees, *Webster v. Reproductive Health Servs.*, 492 U.S. 490 (1989) (No. 88-605), 1989 WL 1115239.

23. *Oncale v. Sundowner Offshore Servs., Inc.*, 523 U.S. 75, 76 (1998).

24. *See generally* Brief of Petitioner, *Oncale*, 523 U.S. 75 (No. 96-568), 1997 WL 458826 [hereinafter *Oncale* Petitioner's Brief].

25. Brief of Respondent at 33-40, *Oncale*, 523 U.S. 75 (No. 96-568), 1997 WL 634147 [hereinafter *Oncale* Respondent's Brief].

26. *Id*. at 20.

27. *Oncale* Petitioner's Brief, *supra* note 24, at 18-19.

28. *Id*. at 27-28.

29. For example, the key sentence of the first example uses the qualifying filler "one can assert with some confidence," a piece of linguistic flab that would ordinarily be cut to increase the strength of the substantive statement. *Id*. at 18-19. The second reference is phrased as a rhetorical question, a form less direct and confrontational than a bald statement. It is also a form that increases the reader's interaction with the text, since most readers will be inclined to answer the question.

30. *Harris v. Forklift Systems, Inc.*, 510 U.S. 17, 17 (1993).

31. *Id*. at 20.

32. Brief of Petitioner at 6, 40 n.21, *Harris*, 510 U.S. 17 (No. 92-1168), 1993 WL 302216.

33. *Id*.

34. *Id*. at 40 n.21 (emphasis added). . . .

11. *Emotion*

> *"[Judges] do not stand aloof on these chill and distant heights; and we shall not help the cause of truth by acting and speaking as if they do. The great tides and currents which engulf the rest of men, do not turn aside in their course, and pass the judges by."*
>
> —Benjamin J. Cardozo[1]

The matter of whether judges are affected by emotion has been debated by scholars for some years, but most experienced lawyers know the answer. In this chapter we will consider the question for ourselves and think more specifically about how those emotions work and what lawyers might do (or not do) in light of those psychological realities. We begin again with advice from Justice Scalia and Bryan Garner. Read this short excerpt carefully. At first it may seem inconsistent with Justice Cardozo's statement above. But if you look carefully, you may notice that it is not. It does, however, provide us with a crucial addendum to Justice Cardozo's comment. More about this later.

Excerpt from

Antonin Scalia & Bryan A. Garner, *Making Your Case: The Art of Persuading Judges*

31-32 (Thomson West 2008)

It is often said that a "jury argument" will not play well to a judge. Indeed, it almost never will. The reason is rooted in the nature of what we typically think of as "jury argument"—a blatant appeal to sympathy or other emotions, as opposed to a logical application of the law to the facts. Before judges, such an appeal should be avoided. . . .

Appealing to judges' emotions is misguided because it fundamentally mistakes their motivation. Good judges pride themselves on the rationality of their rulings and the suppression of their personal proclivities, including most especially their emotions. And bad judges want to be good judges. So either way, overt appeal to emotion is likely to be regarded as an insult. ("What does this lawyer think I am, an impressionable juror?")

COMMONWEALTH OF KENTUCKY
KENTON CIRCUIT COURT
FIRST DIVISION
CASE NO. 09-CI-00165

ENTERED
KENTON CIRCUIT/DISTRICT COURT
JUL 19 2011
JOHN C. MIDDLETON
BY _____ D.C.

BARBARA KISSEL   PLAINTIFF

vs.

SCHWARTZ & MAINES & RUBY CO., LPA, et al.   DEFENDANTS

ORDER

The herein matter having been scheduled for a trial by jury commencing July 13, 2011, and numerous pre-trial motions having yet to be decided and remaining under submission;

And the parties having informed the Court that the herein matter has been settled amicably[1] and that there is no need for a Court ruling on the remaining motions and also that there is no need for a trial;

And such news of an amicable settlement having made this Court happier than a tick on a fat dog because it is otherwise busier than a one legged cat in a sand box and, quite frankly, would have rather jumped naked off of a twelve foot step ladder into a five gallon bucket of porcupines than have presided over a two week trial of the herein dispute, a trial which, no doubt, would have made the jury more confused than a hungry baby in a topless bar and made the parties and their attorneys madder than mosquitoes in a mannequin factory;

IT IS THEREFORE ORDERED AND ADJUDGED by the court as follows:

1. The jury trial scheduled herein for July 13, 2011 is hereby CANCELED.

_____

[1] The Court uses the word "amicably" loosely.

There is a distinction between appeal to emotion and appeal to the judge's sense of justice—which, as we have said, is essential. *Of course* you should argue that your proposed rule of law produces a more just result, both in the present case and in the generality of cases. And there is also a distinction between an overt appeal to emotion and the setting forth of facts that may engage the judge's emotions uninvited. You may safely work into your statement of facts that your client is an elderly widow seeking to retain her life-long home. But don't make an overt, passionate attempt to play upon the judicial heartstring. It can have a nasty backlash.

_____

Notice that Scalia and Garner distinguish "emotion" and "a sense of justice." Is that distinction viable? Next, we read an excerpt from Professor

2. Any and all pending motions will remain under submission pending the filing of an Agreed Judgment, Agreed Entry of Dismissal, or other pleadings consistent with the parties' settlement.

3. The copies of various correspondence submitted for in camera review by the Defendant, SMRS, shall be sealed by the Clerk until further orders of the Court.

4. The Clerk shall engage the services of a structural engineer to ascertain if the return of this file to the Clerk's office will exceed the maximum structural load of the floors of said office.

Dated this _19_ day of _____ July _____, 2011.

_____
MARTIN J. SHEEHAN
Kenton Circuit Judge

Distribution:
Original   -   Kenton Circuit Clerk
One Copy   -   Hon. Paul Vesper
One Copy   -   Hon. Mark Arnzen
One Copy   -   Hon. Sean Ragland
                Hon. John Phillips
One Copy   -   Hon. Robert Block
One Copy   -   Hon. James Kruer

Susan Bandes's introduction to her book on the myriad relationships between law (including justice) and emotion. These two paragraphs make at least three crucial points about emotion in law. Look for them as you read it.

Excerpt from
Susan A. Bandes, *Introduction,* in *The Passions of Law*
2, 11 (Susan A. Bandes ed., New York U. Press 1999)

The law . . . is imbued with emotion. Not just the obvious emotions like mercy and the desire for vengeance but disgust, romantic love, bitterness, uneasiness, fear, resentment, cowardice, vindictiveness, forgiveness, contempt, remorse, sympathy, hatred, spite, malice, shame, respect, moral fervor, and the passion for justice. Emotion pervades not just the criminal courts, . . . but the civil courtrooms, the appellate courtrooms, the legislatures. It propels judges and lawyers, as well as jurors, litigants, and the lay public. Indeed, the emotions that pervade law are often so ancient and deeply ingrained that they are largely invisible. . . .

Most important, . . . is to avoid the trap of calling "emotional" that which is different, or that which law wishes to marginalize. It is important to keep the functional, strategic, and political consequences of defining *emotion* in sight. Emotion tends to seem like part of the landscape when it's familiar, and to become more visible when it's unexpected. The law perpetuates the illusion of emotionless lawyering and judging by portraying certain "hard" emotions or emotional stances as objective and inevitable. Even a legal process devoid of such "soft" emotions as compassion or mercy is not emotionless; it is simply driven by other passions. But the passion for predictability, the zeal to prosecute, and mechanisms like distancing, repressing, and isolating one's feelings from one's thought processes are the emotional stances that have always driven mainstream legal thought. As a result, they avoid the stigma of emotionalism. That derogatory term is reserved for the "soft emotions": compassion, caring, mercy. One of the most important functions of these essays is to challenge the notion of a neutral, emotionless baseline and to identify such invisible emotions. When emotions remain invisible, they remain impervious to evaluation or change.

Finally, we read an excerpt from Professor Terry Maroney, who helps us deconstruct the false cultural script that judges must or even that they can put aside emotion and decide cases based only on cool rationality. Once we realize that emotion is inevitably and perhaps appropriately a part of judicial decision making, we can turn freely to the implications of emotion for lawyers in the practice of law.

Excerpt from

Terry A. Maroney, *The Persistent Cultural Script of Judicial Dispassion*
99 Cal. L. Rev. 629 (2011)

Is it ever appropriate for emotions—anger, love, hatred, sadness, disgust, fear, joy—to affect judicial decision making? In contemporary Western jurisprudence, there is only one accepted answer: no. A good judge should feel no emotions; if she does, she should put them aside and insulate the decision-making process from their influence.

Insistence on emotionless judging—that is, on judicial dispassion—is a cultural script of unusual longevity and potency. Thomas Hobbes declared in the mid-1600s that the ideal judge is divested "of all fear[], anger, hatred, love, and compassion."[2] In 2009, more than three centuries later, then-Judge Sonia Sotomayor testified at her Supreme Court confirmation hearing that judges "apply law to facts. We don't apply feelings to facts."[3] . . . Then and now, to call a judge emotional is a stinging insult, signifying a failure of discipline, impartiality, and reason.

Not only is the script wrong as a matter of human nature—emotion does not, in fact, invariably tend toward sloppiness, bias, and irrationality—but it is not quite so monolithic as it appears. It has been met with periodic dissent. . . . But none of these dissents has meaningfully eroded the script's power. Nor has any blossomed into a robust theory of how emotion might coexist with, or even contribute to, competent judicial decision making.

An exploration of this hidden intellectual history of dissent reveals the fundamental cause of this stunted evolution: Scholars and judges consistently have stumbled over foundational questions about emotion's nature and value. . . . Judges often feel emotions when hearing and deciding cases, and they sometimes express those emotions despite strong cultural incentives not to do so.

The script has retained power despite its tension with reality because it is anchored to an entrenched view of emotion. This traditional view holds that emotion is by its nature irrational, undisciplined, and idiosyncratic. But as Part II reveals, this view has shifted dramatically over the last century. Part II synthesizes the core tenets of contemporary emotion research, which has undermined the theory of emotion on which the script of judicial dispassion depends. Emotion reflects reasons, motivates action, enables reason, and is educable. This evolved view of human emotion provides a new baseline from which evaluation of judicial emotion may proceed. . . .

Supreme Court then-nominee Sonia Sotomayor, 2009

Talk Radio News Service's flickr photostream

I. The Cultural Script of Judicial Dispassion: Its Origins and Persistence (and Apparent Futility).

The script of judicial dispassion is so entrenched in Western jurisprudence as to seem beyond dispute. This is surprising, for on a moment's reflection it is obvious that litigation is "an intensely emotional process" for jurors, parties, witnesses, and lawyers;[4] further reflection suggests the same likely holds true for judges. And yet the script persists.... It draws much of its power from its deep roots in Enlightenment ideals. Indeed, judicial dispassion has come to be regarded as a core requirement of the rule of law, a key to moving beyond the perceived irrationality and partiality of our collective past. The strength of that belief is still apparent: it was vividly displayed during the Sotomayor hearings and the debates they sparked, debates that continue to this day. This Part traces that history. It then shows that the script is in tension with reality. Despite rhetorical devotion to the contrary, the legal system does not (and likely cannot) suppress all (or even most) of judges' emotions.

A. Judicial Dispassion: An Origin Story

The script of judicial dispassion reflects Western jurisprudence's longstanding insistence on a dichotomy between emotion and reason, and therefore between emotion and law. Devotion to the dichotomy is traceable to the influence of European Enlightenment ideals, which—sharply simplified—centered on rational inquiry, science, secularization, and intellectual and political equality. In this era, emotion came to be associated with those forces from which Enlightenment figures sought to be freed—religious fervor, ignorance, prejudice, and reliance on epistemological sources such as tradition and revelation.[5]

This negative conception of emotion was in no small tension with the Enlightenment's commitment to individual worth. "Reason," once the exclusive province of elites, was thought to be the natural faculty of all, a belief that justified a move away from monarchy and other nonmerit-based forms of hierarchy. To the extent that emotion already was associated with the natural faculty of ordinary persons, it might have come to be regarded as an element of, or as not in necessary conflict with, their rational faculty. Instead, the natural state was conceptually subdivided. Within it, emotion was thought to be both more primitive and at war with rationality, which—though within the reach of all persons—needed active cultivation. Common people could achieve the reason formerly reserved for elites, but only by conquering emotion, and this they often failed to do. Emotion thus came to be associated with anti-Enlightenment views and continued to be associated

Emotion & rationality at war.

with the irrational beliefs and unrestrained impulses of common people.[6]

Indeed, the very tripartite structure of American government was conceptualized as a mechanism for ensuring the triumph of reason over emotion.[7] As Madison famously declared in *The Federalist No. 49*, "It is the reason, alone, of the public, that ought to control and regulate the government. The passions ought to be controlled and regulated by the government."[8] Law too, not just the structure of government, was thought to be a bulwark against popular emotion. The judge came to be seen as the primary figure guarding this realm of rationality, by taming the emotions of litigants, ignoring the emotions of the public, and divesting herself of her own.[9] . . .

The growth of legal scientism cemented the script. Exemplified by Christopher Langdell's concept of "law as science," legal scientism encouraged a view of judges as clinically detached, objective, and unmoved by irrelevant particularities. Drawing on those concepts, Karl Wurzel classified "dispassionateness of the judge" as a fundamental tenet of Western jurisprudence.[10] Indeed, he wrote, lawyers were "the first and the most emphatic in insisting on the absence of emotional bias," because "absence of emotion is a prerequisite of all scientific thinking," and judges, more so than other scientific thinkers, regularly are "exposed . . . to emotional influences."[11]

Thus, in pre-twentieth-century American legal theory the perceived need for judicial dispassion was well-established. By protecting the judiciary from direct political control (at least in the federal system), government freed judges to prevent popular emotion from affecting the rational development of law. Partiality, in this theory, was the essence of politics, but the antithesis of judging. Some quantum of emotion therefore was to be expected from legislative and executive officials. Their political commitments to issues and constituencies naturally would give rise to emotions of their own; further, they were expected to be at least somewhat responsive to popular emotion, even while checking its excesses. The expected quantum of judicial emotion, in contrast, was zero, because the judge was to bring to bear no commitments or loyalties of his own. Moreover, because emotion was thought to be an undisciplined and idiosyncratic force, it threatened the judge's ability to maintain his scientific stance. By walling off his own emotions, not just those of the people and their political proxies, the judge freed himself to correctly discern the law using reason alone. Thus, the judge in a democratic system was commanded to reflect the twin meanings of dispassion: he was to be both *emotionless* and *impartial*, qualities seen as necessarily linked.

B. The Sotomayor Confirmation Hearings: Evidence of the Script's Persistence

If there were any doubts as to the script's contemporary potency, debates over judicial "empathy" in the context of the 2009 Sotomayor confirmation laid them to rest. Those debates demonstrated just how alive the script is and just how flat the dialogue remains.

President Obama sparked the controversy by declaring that he would nominate a candidate with empathy, and by listing among Sotomayor's qualifications her "sense of compassion."[12] Though the reaction played out largely as a political story, ... there was in fact a common enemy against which virtually all rallied—judicial emotion.

This convergence is visible in competing constructs of empathy, the concept around which the controversy swirled. Empathy is an inherently ambiguous term. Empathy can be defined not as an emotion but rather a capacity to imagine the world from the perspective of another. However, it sometimes is defined to include both that perspective-taking element and a subjective experience of emotion, usually (though not necessarily) the same emotion one perceives the other to be feeling.[13] Those who criticized the empathy standard adopted the latter view, which contemplates an emotional component, and invoked the ostensibly pernicious effects of emotion as evidence of empathy's flaws. Those who praised the empathy standard adopted the former view and argued that empathy's severability from emotion demonstrated its value.

Those attacking empathy repeatedly linked it to emotion's purportedly undisciplined nature and anti-democratic impact.... In contrast, those defending the empathy standard stressed empathy's nonemotional attributes. They cast empathy as an essential tool through which accurately to perceive and value the human realities at stake.... By pursuing this approach, they tacitly accepted the premise that emotion is a pernicious force....

Thus, while it may have appeared that warring political forces were adopting sharply dichotomous views, they were largely in agreement on one critical assertion: judicial emotion is negative. Sotomayor dealt the final stroke herself. "Judges can't rely on what's in their heart[s]," she testified before the Senate Judiciary Committee, because "[i]t's not the heart that compels conclusions in cases, it's the law." Though judges are "not robots [who] listen to evidence and don't have feelings," the only acceptable response is "to recognize those feelings and put them aside."[14] Sotomayor clearly understood precisely what script was required of her, and she delivered it....

C. The Apparent Futility of the Script of Judicial Dispassion

The cultural script of judicial dispassion thus has both a long pedigree and considerable contemporary purchase. But despite the promise suggested by its credentials, the script has not actually eliminated judicial emotion. Indeed, from time to time judges admit as much. Chief Justice Hughes, for example, reportedly told Justice Douglas that, at "the constitutional level where we work, ninety percent of any decision is emotional."[15] Justice Scalia frequently displays anger, even contempt.[16] . . . Legion are the sentencing judges who voice disgust with a defendant's actions and the trial judges who express sadness at feeling bound to rule in a particular way. In a recent survey, Australian magistrate judges identified managing their emotional responses to cases as a key element of their work; these judges reported a range of emotions including sympathy, revulsion, disgust, and sadness, the experience of which can be "emotionally . . . wearing."[17]

"At the constitutional level, ninety percent of any decision is emotional."
—Chief Justice Charles Evan Hughes

The script's adherents, of course, would regard the persistence of judicial emotion as a sign of failure on the part of individual judges. . . . [J]udicial image maintenance requires ritual homage to dispassion. Thus, the script of judicial dispassion not only fails to reflect a recurrent aspect of judges' reality, it also encourages judges to distance themselves from—and even deny—that reality when it surfaces.

As this Part has shown, then, the cultural script of judicial dispassion is alive and well. It stands in tension, however, with the everyday reality of judging. In evaluating whether the script nonetheless embodies something of sufficient value as to justify its maintenance, it is critical to determine whether emotion actually poses the contemplated danger to judging. Under the entrenched view of emotion historically underlying law, the answer appeared obvious. However, as the next Part shows, this view has been seriously undermined by contemporary emotion research. As the new view applies to all human emotion, it provides a baseline from which to reevaluate judicial emotion.

II. Emotion and Legal Reason

That the script of judicial dispassion is deeply ingrained does not make it correct, either as an account of human nature or as an ideal toward which judges should aspire. This has become increasingly clear through two recent developments: the greater receptivity of law to insights from other disciplines, and the enormous growth of research on emotion in those other disciplines, particularly psychology. A vibrant literature on law and emotion has begun to flourish at that intersection. This Part demonstrates how these recent developments have begun to erode the stark division between reason and emotion in law, the division on which the script depends. Two critical insights of the literature on law and emotion are relevant here. First, emotions are ubiquitous in law. Second, and more importantly, emotion is not necessarily—or even usually—a pernicious influence. Emotion reveals reasons, motivates action in service of reasons, enables reason, and is educable.

First, law is infused with emotion and ideas about emotion. Examples range from the excited utterance exception to the hearsay rule (reflecting the idea that statements made while in an intense emotional state are likely to be truthful), to heightened protection of homes (because of presumed emotional attachment to them), to awards of damages for emotional suffering (which assumes pain can be monetized), to victim impact statements (thought to provide emotional "closure").[18] Judges therefore regularly encounter emotion in their work. They must construe legal rules that implicate emotion; they must manage the emotions of litigants and attorneys; and—as the prior Part demonstrated—they experience emotional reactions of their own.

Judges are Managers of emotion

Of course, just as the persistence of judicial emotion could signify individual failure, the reality that emotion runs through law could signify not its value but, rather, our failure adequately to root it out. But this is not the case. Though emotion does not invariably deserve legal respect, the following core tenets of contemporary emotion research teach that its destructiveness ought not be presumed and that its value ought be considered. These tenets rightly guide our evaluation of judges' emotions, not just the emotions of other legal actors, for judges are—like them—human. Judges' emotions must be differently engaged and trained so as to respond to their unique professional demands, but such training builds on core human capacities rather than supplanting them.

Consider, first, the assertion that *emotion reveals reasons*. This is so because emotion relies on thoughts and on evaluation of thoughts. This critical point is often called the "cognitive theory" of emotion. If the traditional legal view is that emotions are "unthinking, opposed to reason in some very strong and primitive way," just "mindless surges of affect," the cognitive theory responds that emotions embody beliefs about its objects.[19] [T]his is the dominant theory—one might call it a bedrock theory—within modern affective psychology and philosophy. To illustrate, an angry person is angry for a reason: she perceives that an intentional wrong has been committed, of which she disapproves.[20] Every emotion contains such an underlying belief structure. For example, fear reflects perception of "an immediate, concrete, and overwhelming physical danger"; guilt attends self-evaluation of having "transgressed a moral imperative"; sadness indicates a belief that one has "experienced an irrevocable loss"; and so on for every

Cognitive theory— Emotion reveals reason.

emotion.[21] Thus, emotion embodies thought, often complex thought, and those thoughts can be evaluated just like any others. The appropriateness of the angry person's emotion can be evaluated by reference to the accuracy of the perception of the triggering event, as well as by a social judgment of her evaluation. That is, we may judge both whether the event really occurred as she believes it did, and whether it constitutes a wrong of which one rightfully should disapprove.

Consider, too, the assertion that *emotion motivates action in service of reasons.* Emotions do not simply reflect passive assessment of stimuli; they prompt us to respond. This, too, is a point of relative consensus, rooted in the theory that emotions are evolved mechanisms for maximizing survival chances.[22] To illustrate, if a human perceives that a bear is approaching, her perceptions and resulting thoughts will spur fear. Fear will both focus her attention on the dangerous stimulus and prompt her to evaluate its relevance to her goals—for example, the desire not to be mauled or killed. Fear then motivates and enables appropriate responsive action . . . . Thus, emotion not only reflects thoughts, but also serves as an adaptive signal that something of import . . . is at stake and activates a program of responsive action. . . . Just as every emotion involves a particular thought pattern, every motivated response attaches to both that thought pattern and to one's particular goals.

Next, consider the assertion that *emotion enables reason* . . . . Contemporary scientific research is moving strongly in the direction of concluding that emotion is necessary to rationality. Such

investigations typically involve the study of persons with known impairments to emotional function—for example, because of focal brain abnormalities or injury. In such persons, the research demonstrates that emotional capacity and substantive rationality experience a mutual decline.[23] Persons without access to minimally normal emotional reactions generally cannot engage in vital forms of practical reasoning.... While capable of "reasoning" in some literal fashion, these emotionally incompetent persons generally are unable to act rationally.... [This research] suggests, at a minimum, a high degree of interdependence between emotion and reason. It further suggests that emotional competence is necessary to substantive rationality....

Scientific research also lends strong support to the conclusion that emotion plays a critical role in moral judgment.[24] ... [M]odern theorists increasingly assert that emotion, at least sometimes, is integral to moral judgment, not merely incidental to it.[25]

This evidence, taken together, represents a dramatic shift in how emotion and reason are thought to interact. In contrast to the Enlightenment view that emotion and reason are at war, contemporary theorists are forging a new consensus that emotion is a necessary element of much of the practical and moral reasoning on which law depends.

Carrying the analysis one step further, these three intertwined assertions—emotion reveals reasons, motivates action in service of reason, and enables reason—illustrate that, absent pathology, *emotion is educable.* As emotions rest on thoughts and are shaped by one's goals, emotions can be altered by changing one's thoughts and goals.[26] This flexibility also accounts for emotional diversity. Humans display significant cross-cultural convergence around a core set of emotions (like fear and joy) with similar physical manifestations; that is, when humans are afraid or happy, they tend to embody those emotions in strikingly similar ways. But what makes any given person afraid or happy varies enormously. Implicit and explicit social and cultural learning supplies many of the critical goals and beliefs, meaning that emotional response is extraordinarily diverse. For example, in the case of anger, what constitutes a "demeaning offense" will vary; who counts as being part of the group "me and mine" will vary; even the proper goal to be advanced—for example, vindicating honor or restoring community harmony—will vary.

Further, such flexibility exists not just between groups of persons with a shared social or cultural heritage but also within individuals. People generally are motivated to regulate their emotions, as well as those emotions' overt expression, in service of cultural, social, and professional norms. We learn to suppress behaviors (like laughing) in service of superseding goals (such as observing etiquette or not hurting someone's feelings). We also can train ourselves to think differently about stimuli. For example, a trauma surgeon cannot afford to feel disgust when cutting into human flesh or handling bodily fluids, nor can she afford constantly to expend energy suppressing disgust. Her professional goals require her to think differently about those stimuli than she did before—for example, conceptualizing them as diagnostically relevant, or as opportunities to demonstrate skill—and that cognitive recasting creates a different emotional response.

Thus, the traditional legal story casting emotion as stubbornly irrational is simply not true. Emotion's critical role in reflecting and enabling reason coexists with an ability to shape our experience and expression of it in accordance with a hierarchy of reasons.

It is critical here to note that nothing in the above account suggests that emotion is not sometimes associated with irrationality and disadvantageous action. As the above account demonstrates, emotion can rest on factually wrong or morally reprehensible beliefs—for example, hatred fueled by racism. But in the case of emotions based on problematic beliefs, those beliefs, not the emotions, are the proper targets, for changing the former is the most direct route by which to change the latter. Further, this account accepts that emotion—even if *not* based on undesirable beliefs—can feel uncontrollable, distorting, and resistant to change.... But to the extent that non-pathological emotion *sometimes* is associated with error, as law presumes it *usually* to be, that relationship is the same as between cognition and its associated heuristics and biases. Errors result from processes that are adaptive when taken as a whole but maladaptive in particular situations.[27]

The approaching-bear scenario provides an example. One function of emotion is to quickly narrow attention to sources of threat and opportunity—in this instance, the bear and possible escape routes, respectively—to the exclusion of other stimuli. That narrowing is vital, but it has costs: the person is less able to perceive and remember less emotionally vivid aspects of the situation.[28] The intensity of the attentional funnel might cause her to not notice indications that the "bear" is actually someone in a bear suit, not see the ditch standing between her and the escape route, or not remember important information she was told immediately before seeing the "bear."

Similarly, different emotionally infused mood states tend to dispose one to different decisional styles, which might be disadvantageous in particular situations.[29] For example, persons in sad moods tend to scrutinize evidence more carefully than do happy or angry persons, meaning that those emotional states sometimes contribute to blind spots.[30] Emotion, therefore, does not invariably lead to normatively positive processes and outcomes.

But such a concession is necessary for every other core human capacity, each of which entails the possibility of disadvantageous outcomes. Eyewitness testimony is far less reliable than we once thought, but we do not, on that basis, dismiss the importance of eyesight.[31] . . . Only with emotion are the necessary costs of functionality thought to evidence the irrationality of the entire function, and only with emotion are its pathological manifestations thought to characterize the entire enterprise. The correct attitude, instead, . . . [is] to [identify the situations in which particular] cognitive tools lead to suboptimal outcomes. Such an approach . . . would seek to isolate and control the decisional contexts in which emotion, too, predictably leads to suboptimal outcomes, knowing that those outcomes are the exception rather than the rule.

As this Part has shown, the theoretical foundation from which the script of judicial dispassion derives has been meaningfully eroded. Emotion is not antithetical to legal reason. Legal scholars can no longer rely upon the traditional supposition to the contrary to conclude that emotion is antithetical to judicial reason. The role of emotion in judges' professional lives clearly will differ from its role in judges' personal lives, for the professional and democratic demands of judging require unique beliefs, goals, and hierarchies of reasons. But under no plausible theory could those demands be met by literal absence of emotion.

———————————

The readings in this chapter have shown that judicial emotion is both inevitable and, sometimes, appropriate. Emotion reveals reasons and motivates action in service to those reasons. More fundamentally, emotion actually enables reason. Modern cognitive neuroscience has clearly shown this to be the case. (If you still doubt it, read Antonio Damasio's tiny, fascinating book *Descartes' Error: Emotion, Reason, and the Human Brain,* mentioned in the bibliography below.) We can think *because* we can feel.

Given that emotion is both inevitable and necessary to judicial decision making, consider Professor Mahoney's last point: Emotion is educable. In other words, we can affect a judge's emotional reaction to a dispute or a legal issue. How best can we do that? Here is where Justice Scalia's advice must be our bedrock. Notice how resistant he is to the perception that a lawyer is making a "blatant appeal to sympathy or other emotions." The cultural script is well engrained.

But notice what Scalia and Garner say next: "There is a distinction between overt appeal to emotion and the setting forth of facts that may engage the judge's emotions uninvited." In other words, the lesson here is to "show, not tell." Set out the facts in a seemingly neutral way, but designed subtly to arouse emotions in the judge *without seeming to do so*. As Scalia and Garner's advice shows us, a judge will resist any overt attempt to cause an emotional response. The necessary skill is to let the facts themselves do the emotional work. Avoid descriptors (too fast, huge, violent); intensifiers (very); minimizers (only, a small amount). Instead, use the actual facts (97 mph, 6 foot 6 inches and 240 pounds, broke Smith's nose, knifed Smith in the ribs, two tenths of a milligram). So evoke, don't exhort; show, don't tell. This is one of the hardest lessons to learn on the way toward expertise.

Discussion Questions

1. The introduction to this chapter said that the two paragraphs from Professor Bandes make three important points. What are they?
2. What is the difference between emotion and empathy?
3. What surprised you most about the readings in this chapter?
4. What emotions might a judge have? Make a list, checking it against the lists in the Bandes and Maroney readings. Notice that the list includes far more than sympathy. Why is it that assertions that judicial emotions are bad often seem to focus only on judicial "sympathy" or even "empathy"?
5. Are there gender implications to this topic? As part of thinking about this question, you might be interested to know that cognitive scientists have shown that men and women have the same quantity and quality of emotions.
6. An interesting example of subtly evoking emotions is Marc Antony's funeral oration in Shakespeare's "Julius Caesar." Read it again (just

enter the words in your search engine). Can you identify how the oration evokes emotions without doing so expressly?

Additional Suggested Reading

Books

Susan Bandes, *The Passions of Law* (New York University Press 1992).

Antonio Damasio, *Descartes' Error: Emotion, Reason, and the Human Brain* (Penguin Books 1994).

Martha C. Nussbaum, *Hiding from Humanity: Disgust, Shame, and the Law* (Princeton University Press 2006).

Michael R. Smith, *Advanced Legal Writing: Theories and Strategies in Persuasive Writing* (2d ed., Wolters Kluwer Law & Business 2008).

Symposia

Law, Psychology, and the Emotions, 74 Chi.-Kent L. Rev. 1423 (2000).

Articles

Peter Bayer, *Not Interaction but Melding—The "Russian Dressing" Theory of Emotions: An Explanation of the Phenomenology of Emotions and Rationality with Suggested Related Maxims for Judges and Other Legal Decision Makers*, 52 Mercer L. Rev. 1033 (2001).

Justin D'Arms, *Empathy and Evaluative Inquiry*, 74 Chi.-Kent L. Rev. 1468 (2000).

Michael Frost, *Ethos, Pathos & Legal Audience*, 99 Dick. L. Rev. 85 (1994-1995).

Michael Frost, *With* Amici *Like These: Cicero, Quintilian and the Importance of Stylistic Demeanor*, 3 J. ALWD 5 (2006).

Ian Gallacher, *Thinking Like Non-Lawyers: Why Empathy Is a Core Lawyering Skill and Why Legal Education Should Change to Reflect Its Importance*, 8 Legal Comm. & Rhetoric: J. AWLD 109 (2011).

Lynne N. Henderson, *Legality and Empathy*, 85 Mich. L. Rev. 1574 (1987).

Peter H. Huang & Christopher J. Anderson, *A Psychology of Emotional Legal Decision Making: Revulsion and Saving Face in Legal Theory and Practice*, 90 Minn. L. Rev. 1045 (2005-2006).

Lucille A. Jewel, *Through a Glass Darkly: Using Brain Science and Visual Rhetoric to Gain a Professional Perspective on Visual Advocacy*, 19 S. Cal. Interdisc. L.J. 237 (2009-2010).

Mary Kate Kearney, *Justice Thomas in* Grutter v. Bollinger*: Can Passion Play a Role in a Jurist's Reasoning?* 78 St. John's L. Rev. 15 (2004).

Laura E. Little, *Negotiating the Tangle of Law and Emotion*, 86 Cornell L. Rev. 974 (2000-2001).

Linda C. McClain, *Supreme Court Justices, Empathy, and Social Change: A Comment on Lani Guinier's Demosprudence Through Dissent*, 89 B.U. L. Rev. 589 (2009).

Eric A. Posner, *Law and the Emotions*, 89 Geo. L.J. 1977 (2000-2001).

Jeffrey M. Shaman, *The Impartial Judge: Detachment or Passion?* 45 Depaul L. Rev. 605 (1995-1996).

Kathryn M. Stanchi, *Feminist Legal Writing*, 39 San Diego L. Rev. 387 (2002).

Endnotes

1. Benjamin J. Cardozo, *The Nature of the Judicial Process* 168 (1921), quoted in Shaman, *The Impartial Judge: Detachment or Passion?*

2. Thomas Hobbes, *Leviathan* 203 (A.R. Walter ed., Cambridge U. Press 1904) (1651) (emphasis omitted).

3. *Confirmation Hearing on the Nomination of Hon. Sonia Sotomayor, to Be an Assoc. Justice of the Supreme Court of the United States: Hearing Before the S. Comm. on the Judiciary*, 111 Cong. 121 (2009) [hereinafter *Sotomayor Confirmation Hearing*] http://frwebgate.access.gpo.gov/cgi-bin/getdoc.cgi?dbname=111_senate_hearings&docid =f:56940.pdf.

4. Richard A. Posner, *Frontiers of Legal Theory* 226 (Harvard U. Press 2001).

5. Henry F. May, *The Enlightenment in America* xiv, 42 (Oxford U. Press 1976). . . .

6. *Id.* at 337. . . .

7. *Id.* at 97. . . .

8. *The Federalist* No. 49, at 317 (James Madison) (Clinton Rossiter ed., New American Library 1961). . . .

9. William J. Brennan, Jr., *Reason, Passion, and "The Progress of the Law,"* 10 Cardozo L. Rev. 3 (1988). . . .

10. Karl Georg Wurzel, *Methods of Juridical Thinking* in *Science of Legal Method: Select Essays* 298 (Ernest Bruncken & Layton B. Register trans., New York, Macmillan 1921).

11. *Id.* at 298-299.

12. John Hasnas, *The "Unseen" Deserve Empathy Too*, Wall St. J., May 29, 2009, at A15, *available at* http://online.wsj.com/article/SB124355502499664627.html. . . .

13. Jean Decety, *Empathy (Neuroscience Perspectives)*, in *The Oxford Companion to Emotion and the Affective Sciences* 151-153 (David Sander & Klaus R. Scherer eds., Oxford U. Press 2009). . . .

14. Amanda Terkel, *Sotomayor: "We're Not Robots,"* Think Progress (July 14, 2009, 11:28 A.M.), http://thinkprogress.org/2009/07/14/sotomayor-robots.

15. Lawrence S. Wrightsman, *Judicial Decision Making: Is Psychology Relevant?* 47 (Springer 1999).

16. *Id.* at 20-21.

17. Sharyn Roach Anleu & Kathy Mack, *Magistrates' Everyday Work and Emotional Labour*, 32 J. L. & Society 590 (2005). . . .

18. Susan A. Bandes, *Introduction*, in *The Passions of Law* 1-2 (Susan A. Bandes ed., New York U. Press 1999) [hereinafter Bandes, *Introduction*]. . . .

19. Martha C. Nussbaum, *Emotion in the Language of Judging*, 70 St. John's L. Rev. 23, 24-25 (1996) [hereinafter Nussbaum, *Emotion in Language*]. . . .

20. Richard S. Lazarus, *Universal Antecedents of the Emotions*, in *The Nature of Emotion* 163, 164-165 (Paul Ekman & Richard J. Davidson eds., Oxford U. Press 1994). . . .

21. *Id.*

22. Joseph LeDoux, *The Emotional Brain: The Mysterious Underpinnings of Emotional Life* 37-72 (Touchstone/Simon and Schuster 1996); Leda Cosmides & John Tooby, *Evolutionary Psychology and the Emotions*, in *Handbook of Emotions* 91, 93 (2d ed., Michael Lewis & Jeannette M. Haviland-Jones eds., The Guilford Press 2000).

23. The best known of these studies (which continue to proliferate) are by Antonio Damasio, Antoine Bechara, and their collaborators. *See generally* Antonio R. Damasio, *Descartes' Error: Emotion, Reason, and the Human Brain* (1994) . . . ; Antonio R. Damasio, *The Feeling of What Happens: Body and Emotion in the Making of Consciousness* (Mariner

Books 1999) . . . ; Antoine Bechara et al., *Characterization of the Decision-Making Deficits of Patients with Ventromedial Prefrontal Cortex Lesions*, 123 Brain 2189 (2000).

24. Dacher Keltner et al., *Emotions as Moral Intuitions*, in *Affect in Social Thinking and Behavior* 162-175 (Joseph P. Forgas ed., Cambridge U. Press 2006); Jesse Prinz, *The Emotional Basis of Moral Judgments*, 9 Phil. Explorations 29 (2006). . . .

25. Keltner et al., *supra* note 24, at 166-167. . . .

26. James J. Gross & Roos A. Thompson, *Emotional Regulation: Conceptual Foundations*, in *Handbook of Emotion Regulation* 3, 13-15 (James J. Gross ed., The Guilford Press 2007). . . .

27. Stephanie H.M. van Goozen et al., *Preface, Emotions: Essays on Emotion Theory* x (Stephanie J.M. van Goozen et al. eds., Lawrence Erlbaum Assoc. Inc. 1994) . . . .

28. Patrik Vuilleumier, *Attention and Emotion*, in *The Oxford Companion to Emotion and the Affective Sciences* 54-58 (David Sander & Klaus R. Scherer eds., Oxford U. Press 2009).

29. Gerald C. Clore, *Why Emotions Are Felt*, in *The Nature of Emotion* 109-110 (Paul Ekman & Richard J. Davidson eds., Oxford U. Press 1994); Daniel C. Molden & E. Tory Higgins, *Motivated Thinking*, in *The Cambridge Handbook of Thinking and Reasoning* 295, 311 (Keith J. Holyoak & Robert G. Morrison eds., Cambridge U. Press 2005).

30. For a review, see Jennifer S. Lerner & Larissa Z. Tiedens, *Portrait of the Angry Decision Maker*, 19 J. Behav. Decision Making 115 (2006).

31. Elizabeth F. Loftus, *Eyewitness Testimony: Psychological Research and Legal Thought* 3 Crime & Just. 105, 107-108 (1981). . . .

12. *Disagreeing*

The Model Rules of Professional Responsibility require lawyers to disclose to the court legal authority that is both controlling and directly adverse to the client's position.[1] The Rules also prohibit the misstatement of law or facts.[2] In this section, we will assume that lawyers will comply with these modest rules about dealing with adverse authority. We will deal instead with the more common and more vexing question of whether and how to disclose information or arguments when disclosure is not required by disciplinary rules. We begin with a short excerpt from Professors McElroy and Coughlin, giving us a glimpse into why it is difficult even to anticipate opposing arguments.

Excerpt from

Lisa T. McElroy & Christine N. Coughlin, *The Other Side of the Story: Using Graphic Organizers To Counter the Counter-Analysis Quandary*

39 U. of Balt. L. Rev. 227 (2010)

[As important as it is, recognizing and accurately assessing the strength of opposing arguments can be quite difficult. Several of the reasons that make this recognition difficult for writers also provide insight into a reader's resistance to arguments inconsistent with the beliefs the reader already holds:]

While this process may sound relatively straight-forward, it is anything but easy. Social scientists have studied the theory of conceptual change, the corollary to counter-analysis in a non-legal context, and have recognized that this task involves the following steps: (1) thinking deeply about the alternative conception, (2) juxtaposing [the] argument against the alternative, (3) explaining anomalous pieces of data, and (4) weighing issues and arguments.[3] . . .

The mental process of *coherence-based reasoning* may help to explain why [readers and writers] become invested in their conclusions to the point of having difficulty making effective counter-conclusions. According to this theory, because difficult decisions are intimidating in many ways, a legal decision-maker will unconsciously transform that decision into a "seemingly straightforward choice between a compelling alternative and a weak one."[4] In other words, in order to make a supportable and defensible decision, a legal decision-maker will transform "[a]mbiguous, equivocal, and conflicting variables ... into coherent models, that is, lopsided and exaggerated mental representations in which the variables that support the emerging decision are strongly accepted while those that support the losing decision are dismissed, rejected, or ignored."[5]

Similarly, *cognitive dissonance theory*, a popular psychological theory on decision-making ... , explains that "[w]hen a person with a strong belief is challenged by contradictory evidence, he is less likely to discard the belief than to 'show a new fervor about convincing and converting other people to his view.'"[6] ...

Assuming that we can bring ourselves to recognize counterarguments, how do we decide whether and how to confront that adverse material? We return to Professor Stanchi one last time for help with cognitive science principles that can guide our choices.

Excerpt from

Kathryn M. Stanchi, *Playing with Fire: The Science of Confronting Adverse Material in Legal Advocacy*
60 Rutgers L. Rev. 381 (2008)

Although much of the attention on persuasion in law has focused on how to frame supporting arguments, persuasion is not only about how to present favorable information. Confronting and defusing negative information is a critical aspect of the art of persuasion. But disclosure of negative information raises substantial and thorny questions about advocacy and persuasion because [the information] is, by definition, not helpful to the client's position. Lawyers have depicted the dilemma of what to do with negative information in vividly unpleasant terms, likening disclosure to a "self-inflicted wound" and describing the decision to disclose as "agonizing" and "painful."[7]

Given these descriptions, it is not surprising that there is considerable controversy among both appellate practitioners and trial lawyers regarding when and how to address information that potentially undermines the position they are advocating. Although the rules of professional responsibility require some disclosure of negative information, the rules leave much discretion to lawyers, and so the decision is, in most instances, a strategic one.[8] The vehemence of the disagreement among lawyers about the appropriate strategy, as well as the pain of the dilemma, is a testament to the high stakes of the question. If the advocate makes a strategic decision to disclose negative information and that decision turns out to be a mistake, the advocate has not only weakened her own case, but has taken affirmative steps that will strengthen the other side's case. . . .

A careful study of the science reveals that, overall, it is advantageous for the advocate to volunteer negative information and rebut it early, and that a direct and in depth confrontation of negative information is generally more effective than an indirect and cursory treatment. A close look at the finer points of the data, however, reveals that the question of disclosure is a complicated one. . . .

The article then summarizes commonly articulated rationales for disclosing and not disclosing, as well as common advice about where and how to disclose. The next sections test those rationales by examining the social science research on the subject:

There is a substantial body of social science research on the treatment of negative information, and this research can start lawyers on the path to resolving the wide divergence of opinion regarding the treatment of negative information. . . .

In the nonlegal context, there are two significant bodies of social science research implicated in the question of how to deal with negative information in a persuasive message. One, the research into *one-sided versus two-sided messages*, tests both the persuasive value of the message as well as whether the message made the recipient resistant to attacks from opponents. The other body of research, *inoculation theory*, focuses on making message recipients resistant to attacks on a persuasive message. Inoculation does not make an argument more persuasive, but rather seeks to make sure that the audience does not accept an opponent's arguments. This aspect of persuasion—convincing an audience to resist arguments that contravene an opposing position—is a bit different from developing and communicating a set of positive justifications for one's own position.

There is also a small but growing subset of social science research devoted to the handling of negative information in legal advocacy. . . . Taken together, the research supports the general proposition that, in many situations, there is a strategic advantage to preemptively raising negative information.

A. Message Sidedness [One-Sided or Two-Sided]

. . . One-sided messages simply offer only positive or bolstering information—only support of the advocated position without any acknowledgment of the existence of opposing arguments.[9] . . . Two-sided messages offer support for the advocated position as well as an acknowledgment of the opposing view.[10] But two-sided messages come in a variety of forms. . . . Researchers have attempted to classify two-sided messages into two categories: *refutational* and *nonrefutational*. Two-sided *nonrefutational messages* offer only an acknowledgment of opposing views, with no direct refutation of those views.[11] [E.g., "On the one hand, excluding statements made without Miranda warnings might prevent prosecution of some guilty offenders. On the other hand, without that sanction, police would have little incentive to safeguard the rights of the accused." Notice that the second sentence does not refute the first sentence, that is, does not argue that all guilty offenders could still be prosecuted.] . . .

Two-sided *refutational messages* offer not only an acknowledgment of opposing views, but also a refutation of opposing arguments.[12] . . . These messages attempt to "remove" the negative information either by denying the truth of the opposing claims or by arguing that the negative information is irrelevant. Examples of refutational two-sided messages are: "[s]ome people say this economic policy will increase unemployment, but that isn't so because" (*direct refutation*) or "[i]t's true that my client was convicted of robberies in the past, but past convictions are not evidence of guilt in the current case" (*arguing irrelevance*).[13]

1. Two-Sided Refutational Messages Are the Most Effective

As a general matter, the results of the research are quite consistent. Two-sided refutational messages are more effective because they cause sustained attitude change that is less vulnerable to opposing arguments. In other words, when message recipients are exposed to two-sided refutation arguments, they are more likely to be persuaded by the message and less likely to change their minds when confronted with an opposing viewpoint. On the other hand, two-sided refutational messages are the least persuasive, significantly less effective than one-sided messages that ignored opposing viewpoints entirely. In other words, the data suggest that if a persuader is not going to refute the arguments, it is better to ignore them entirely.[14] . . .

The advantages of two-sided messages can be explained in a number of ways. Like lawyers, social scientists theorize that the credibility of the message source is at the heart of the power of two-sided messages, but there are other important reasons as well.[15]

The boost that two-sided messages offer to the credibility of the message source stems from the audience's expectations. Most people expect issues to have two sides and expect persuaders to address both sides.[16] This theory is borne out in the studies, which find overall that both refutational and nonrefutational two-sided messages lead the audience to perceive the message source as more credible and knowledgeable than one-sided messages.[17]

Credibility also explains the advantage of refutational two-sided messages over nonrefutational. The theory is that if the persuader raises, but does not rebut, opposing arguments, message recipients tend to discount the persuader's credibility and expertise.[18] In other words, message recipients confronted with an unrebutted opposing view will assume that the persuader, while perhaps more knowledgeable than someone who seems to know only the supporting view, does not have the requisite expertise to adequately address the opposing view. The audience may view the speaker who raises opposing views without rebuttal as less knowledgeable, less fair, and less honest than one who has addressed opposing viewpoints.[19] . . .

Another widely embraced theory supporting the superiority of two-sided messages focuses on the depth of thought stimulated by two-sided messages. People are more motivated to think about the content of messages when the message is more stimulating and the source of the message is perceived as more credible.[20] A two-sided message appears well-informed and balanced.[21] This leads people to think more favorably about the ultimate message and makes them more likely to change their minds to agree with the message.[22]

Finally, one of the primary theories explaining the effectiveness of two-sided messages is called inoculation. Inoculation posits that two-sided messages work because they make the message recipient able to resist and reject attacks on the message.[23] . . .

B. Inoculation Theory

. . . The theory of inoculation is based on the idea that advocates can make the recipient of a persuasive message *"resistant"* to opposing arguments, much like a vaccination makes a patient resistant to disease.[24] In an inoculation message, the message recipient is exposed to a weakened version of arguments against the persuasive message, coupled with appropriate refutation of those opposing arguments.[25] The theory is that introducing a "small dose" of a message contrary to the persuader's position makes the message recipient immune to attacks from the opposing side.[26] Inoculation works because the introduction of a small dose of the opposing argument induces the message recipient to generate arguments that refute the opposing argument, the intellectual equivalent of producing antibodies.[27] Once the message recipient generates refutational arguments, she will be less likely to accept the opposing argument when it is presented to her by the opposing side because she will already have a cache of ammunition with which to resist the opposing argument.[28]

Inoculation does not focus on the persuasive value of the message; rather, the focus of inoculation is in making the recipient resistant to attack. In other words, unlike most persuasive message strategies, inoculation strategy is not designed to change one's beliefs, but to stop a recipient from changing a belief based on a competing message.[29] . . .

In addition to creating a shield around a message recipient, inoculation also has another positive persuasive effect. . . . Message recipients are often skeptical of a one-sided persuasive message and will react to wholly positive advocacy by generating counter-arguments to the positive message. This is particularly true if the message recipient is somehow forewarned that a persuasive message or argument is coming her way, such as "You will soon hear a message advocating that quitting smoking will improve your health."[30] This type of forewarning tends to lead most people to generate arguments against the message. Inoculation appears to stop this process, which means it also has some strengthening effect on the original persuasive message. . . .

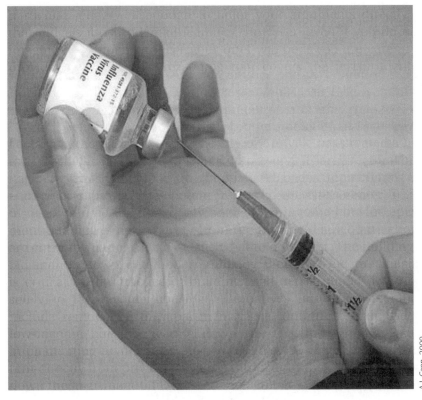

A.J. Cann, 2009

Influenza vaccination

The key to inoculation is the warning of the impending attack, or "threat," combined with the refutation of the attack.[31] Refutation alone is not sufficient to produce the inoculation response.[32] The two components work in tandem—for the inoculation response to occur, challenges must be explicitly raised and then answered.

[Since] the key to the inoculation response is "threat," the . . . process is primarily emotional, and only secondarily cognitive.[33] The threat creates the motivation: the raising of a weak counter-argument to the position advocated produces an implied challenge or threat to the position.[34] This threat stimulates the recipient to generate arguments that refute the counter-arguments; the recipient becomes motivated to counter the threat.[35] In other words, when people read a set of supporting arguments, they experience a "threat" or "dissonance" when presented with an opposing viewpoint. This threat motivates them to develop or seek out refutational arguments; people want to resolve dissonance and will gravitate toward a path that allows them to alleviate the threat to the position advocated. . . .

The refutation portion of the inoculation message serves a more cognitive, as opposed to emotional, purpose. The refutation gives the message recipient an example of how to resist the attack. Often, the refutation explicitly reiterates the attacks. . . . Cognitively, the refutational argument gives the message recipient the *capability* (as opposed to motivation) to refute the counter-argument; it gives the message recipient a partial "script" for refutation of counter-arguments. The preemptive quality of inoculation also gives the persuader the opportunity to reframe the attack arguments before the opposition has an opportunity to present them.[36] . . .

In sum, the inoculation effect occurs when an advocate preemptively raises a negative issue within a persuasive message. Inoculation puts a "shield" over the message recipient, making her resistant to attacks on the persuasive message. Consistent with the two-sided message research, inoculation creates the strongest shield when accompanied by refutation of the negative information. While the inoculation shield is strongest with message recipients who already agree with the persuasive message, it is nevertheless present even with message recipients who are undecided. Overall, when an advocate for a controversial position makes even a weak refutational argument in addition to supporting arguments, the audience is more resistant to multiple counter-arguments by the other side. . . .

The article here describes several studies of disclosures in law practice. In the first, Professor James Stratman showed that one-sided argument was not effective, in part because readers were skeptical of one-sided arguments. They considered the one-sided arguments unfair and less valuable and tended to reject the precedent as irrelevant or inapplicable. Other studies in the trial context found that preemptive disclosure of negative information ("stealing thunder") was strategically advantageous.

Although the success of the "stealing thunder" strategy [preemptive disclosure] can be attributed in part to the inoculation effect and to credibility boosts, researchers have looked beyond these reasons to determine why "stealing thunder" works so consistently....

One explanation that researchers offer is "framing," a concept that is familiar to most legal advocates. The theory is that because "stealing thunder" permits the advocate to "frame" the negative information in the best possible light, jurors mentally process and accept the more positive spin before they are exposed to the attack.[37] ...

[Another possible explanation is] the "change of meaning" hypothesis and the "old news is no news" hypothesis. The "change of meaning" hypothesis suggests that preemptively disclosing negative information actually motivated message recipients to change the meaning of the information to be less damaging to the side offering it.[38] In other words, ... jurors expect lawyers to offer information that is positive for their side, and so jurors experience some "dissonance" when lawyers offer negative information.... [S]ocial scientists theorize that jurors will resolve the dissonance by reinterpreting the information to be more positive to the side that is offering it.[39]

The "old news is no news" hypothesis posits that if negative information is preemptively disclosed, then its later use by opposing counsel is perceived by the jury as "old news" and therefore will carry less weight.[40] This is the concept for which "stealing thunder" is the core metaphor: once the jury has heard the "thunder," hearing it again will have less impact.... The results [of a study] showed support for the "change of meaning" hypothesis as a reason for the success of "stealing thunder."[41] Jurors hearing the "stolen thunder" scenario were more likely to consider negative evidence to be weaker and less damaging than those hearing the "thunder" scenario.[42] ...

The article concludes with a list of possible implications for persuasion in law:

1. As a general principle, lawyers should usually be open about negative information, but the following caveats may apply.
2. Volunteer negative information only if attack is certain.
3. Consider that post-hoc refutation may sometimes be better than preemptive refutation.
4. Volunteer negative information only if you can refute it.
5. A more balanced approach may enhance credibility.

6. A time lapse between reading and deciding may reduce the effectiveness of preemptive disclosure.

7. The benefits of preemptive disclosure may be reduced if the reader thinks carefully about the arguments presented (high elaboration).

Despite the possible caveats, the research seems to show that, where attack is likely, preemptive disclosure is the best default rule.

In our last excerpt, Professor Mark DeForrest gives us a classic example of effectively refuting opposing arguments in Dr. Martin Luther King's "Letter from a Birmingham City Jail."

Excerpt from

Mark DeForrest, *Introducing Persuasive Legal Argument via the Letter from a Birmingham City Jail*
15 J. Legal Writing 109 (2009)

. . . One of the qualities that makes the *Letter from a Birmingham City Jail* an effective introduction to persuasive legal argumentation is its quality as a rebuttal document. . . . [T]he letter can be analogized to a reply brief, written to convince King's readers that the position set forth by his opponents was mistaken. . . .

Martin Luther King, Jr.

Readers approaching the letter for the first time are often surprised to find that King wrote it in response to a detailed, public statement attacking the work of the Civil Rights Movement in Birmingham, Alabama. While in jail after being arrested for participating in a march . . . King received word that an interdenominational group of clergymen had issued a statement calling on the community to refrain from demonstrations against the regime of segregation then unlawfully in effect in Alabama. . . . [T]he clergy stated that demonstrations protesting segregation were "unwise and untimely," and that the civil rights marches in the city, "however technically peaceful," had "incite[d] to hatred and violence."[43] Characterizing the marches as "extreme measures," the clergy denied that such direct action was "justified," and called on the local African-American community to "withdraw support from these demonstrations."[44]

The clergymen's statement began with a moderate tone, noting that the authors had previously issued an appeal calling for obedience to judicial decisions mandating desegregation.[45] The statement went on to urge reconciliation and negotiations among local leaders regarding racial issues, declaring the "recent public events"—a reference that included the civil rights protests that King had helped organize—"have given indication that we will have opportunity for a new constructive and realistic approach to racial problems."[46]

Library of Congress (Thomas J. O'Halloran, 1963)

This moderate and even hopeful tone, however, soon fades from the statement as it begins to deal more directly with the demonstrations in which King was involved. The clergy praised the law enforcement tactics of Bull Connor's Birmingham police department, commending the "calm manner" of the police, and called on law enforcement to continue their "calm" efforts to "protect our city from violence."[47] The clergy voiced concern that "outsiders"—a not-so-veiled reference to King—were at least "in part" responsible for the demonstrations, and called on local

members of the community, whites and African-Americans, to work for "honest and open negotiation of racial issues" using their knowledge and experience of the local situation."[48]

The clergymen minimized the African-American community's legitimate grievances in Birmingham by referring to the ongoing civil rights protests as the result of "impatience" and emotionalism, understandable to be sure, but ultimately a product of "people who feel that their hopes are slow in being realized."[49] The statement closed with an appeal to the African-American community to cease its support for the protests, for disputes regarding civil rights and equal treatment to be settled in the courts and via "negotiations among local leaders," and for whites and African-Americans to "observe the principles of law and order and common sense." Any steps involving demonstrations or nonviolent civil disobedience were to be avoided, according to the clergymen, in preference for efforts not through "the streets" but through proper channels.[50]

In his reply, King methodically countered the arguments set forth by the clergymen, and defended the direct action program that the Civil Rights Movement was then undertaking in the city.[51] The text he produced has become famous world-over for its defense of civil disobedience, human dignity, and non-violence. Beleaguered as King was, his rebuttal was not an effort to preach to the choir. King was writing not only to bolster the morale of those involved in protests in Birmingham or elsewhere across the South; he hoped to convince his readers and Southern white Christians in particular, of the legitimacy of the Civil Rights Movement. Many of those Southern whites were not necessarily opposed to the Civil Rights Movement, but neither were they necessarily supportive; they often sought to maintain a kind of neutrality between those who supported segregation and those who sought reform for equality.[52] King was seeking, at least in part, to persuade this host of individual decision-makers, those who had to decide in their consciences and in their public actions, whether they would work for a more racially just civic polity.

Library of Congress, 1968

... For those of us who have come of age after the 1950s and 1960s, it is sometimes difficult to imagine that any person of good faith—the kind of person open to the moral persuasion that King brought to bear in his letter—would need much convincing regarding the legitimacy of non-violent protest to bring attention to civil rights abuses. During the time, however, for people faced with the challenge of moving through and beyond segregation, the situation was often less than clear.... [W]hile a good deal of the opposition was due to overt racism, not all of it was.... In the middle of the conflict and controversy over civil rights often stood Southern white clergy and the churches they pastored.[53] Many of these clergy sought to maintain a neutral position regarding the civil rights struggle and were often attacked by both civil rights activists and segregationists.[54] The clergy who issued the statement calling for an end to the demonstrations in Birmingham generally fit within this group, considered moderate or even liberal in their sympathies.[55] King hoped that his letter would at least in part have the effect of moving moderate Southern white Christians from a position of neutrality to one of support for the civil rights struggle.[56]

The article then goes on to identify several key strategies that contribute to the power of King's letter as a rebuttal document. These include the use of (a) logos, pathos, and ethos; (b) classical rhetorical methods and structures; (c) appeals to the Platonic commitment to truth and justice; (d) rhetorical patterns most familiar to the letter's audience; (e) theory to maintain a theme; (f) organizational priming of its readers; (g) appeals to persuasive authority; and (h) plain (but not boring) language.

Read the Letter and look for these strategies. Then, if your professor assigns it, read the rest of this excerpted article to see what Professor DeForrest finds in the Letter.

Key Concepts

One-sided vs. two-sided messages
Inoculation effect
Audience motivation
Dissonance
Direct negation
Indirect negation

Discussion Questions

1. What in these readings surprised you?
2. Is it difficult to decide to concede? Why?
3. Think back to the briefs you have written, including the brief you wrote in your introductory legal writing class. Did you notice that the more you

worked on the brief, the more convinced you became that your side was right? Did you notice that your classmates who were writing for the other side had the same experience, becoming more convinced of the merits of their own side? Why? One of the lessons you can take from this experience is that once you've worked on a case, even a little, you cannot trust your own assessment of the strength of your arguments. What can you do to counteract your loss of perspective?

4. What is the main point to take from the Stanchi reading? Or perhaps more than one?

Additional Suggested Reading

Beverly J. Blair, *Ethical Considerations in Advocacy: What First-Year Legal Writing Students Need to Know*, 4 J. Legal Writing 109 (1998).

Judith D. Fischer, *Pleasing the Court: Writing Ethical and Effective Briefs* (Carolina Academic Press 2005).

Judith D. Fischer, *Bareheaded and Barefaced Counsel: Courts React to Unprofessionalism in Lawyers' Papers*, XXXI Suffolk U. L. Rev. 1 (1997).

Judith D. Fischer, *The Role of Ethics in Legal Writing: The Forensic Embroiderer, The Minimalist Wizard, and Other Stories*, 2003-2004 Scribes J. Legal Writing 77.

Michael J. Higdon, *Something Judicious This Way Comes . . . The Use of Foreshadowing as a Persuasive Device in Judicial Narrative*, 44 U. Rich. L. Rev. 1213 (2009-2010). . . . [A portion of the article discusses inoculation theory as a means of anticipating and defusing resistance to a particular message.]

Michael R. Smith, *Advanced Legal Writing: Theories and Strategies in Persuasive Writing* ch. 16 (2d ed., Aspen 2008).

Melissa H. Weresh, *Legal Writing: Ethical and Professional Considerations* (LexisNexis 2006).

Endnotes

1. Model R. Prof. Conduct 3.3(a)(3).
2. Model R. Prof. Conduct 3.3(a)(1) & (2).
3. E. Michael Nussbaum & Gale M. Sinatra, *Argument and Conceptual Change*, 28 Cont. Educ. Psychol. 384, 384 (2003) (citing J.S. Dole & Gale M. Sinatra, *Reconceptualizing Change in the Cognitive Construction of Knowledge*, 33 Educ. Psychologist 109, 121 (1998)).
4. Dan Simon, *A Third View of the Black Box: Cognitive Coherence in Legal Decision Making*, 71 U. Chi. L. Rev. 511, 513 (2004). . . .
5. *Id.* at 545.
6. Julie A. Seaman, *Cognitive Dissonance in the Classroom: Rationale and Rationalization in the Law of Evidence*, 50 St. Louis U. L.J. 1097, 1112 (2005-2006).
7. Angela Gilmore, *Self-Inflicted Wounds: The Duty to Disclose Damaging Legal Authority*, 43 Clev. St. L. Rev. 303 (1995); Kay Nord Hunt & Eric J. Magnuson, *Ethical Issues on Appeal*, 19 Wm. Mitchell L. Rev. 659, 672 (1993); Risa B. Lischkoff, *Recent Decisions on Citing Authorities to Courts: Model Rule 3.3(a)(3) of the Model Rules of Professional Conduct*, 19 J. Legal Prof. 315, 315 (1995).
8. Model R. Prof. Conduct 3.3 (2007). . . .

9. James B. Stiff & Paul A. Mongeau, *Persuasive Communication* 140 (2d ed., The Guilford Press 2003).

10. *Id.* at 140.

11. *Id.* at 141. . . .

12. *Id.* at 140-141. . . .

13. Daniel J. O'Keefe, *How to Handle Opposing Arguments in Persuasive Messages: A Meta-Analytic Review of the Effects of One-Sided and Two-Sided Messages*, 22 Comm. Y.B. 209, 215 (1999).

14. Stiff & Mongeau, *supra* note 9, at 141-142.

15. Michael R. Smith, *Advanced Legal Writing* 101-102 (2002). . . . Stiff & Mongeau, *supra* note 9, at 140-141.

16. Stiff & Mongeau, *supra* note 9, at 139-141.

17. O'Keefe, *supra* note 13, at 226.

18. Stiff & Mongeau, *supra* note 9, at 141.

19. Mike Allen, *Meta-Analysis Comparing the Persuasiveness of One-Sided and Two-Sided Messages*, 55 West. J. Speech Comm. 390, 392 (1991).

20. Mike Allen, *Comparing the Persuasive Effectiveness of One- and Two-Sided Messages*, in *Persuasion: Advances Through Meta-Analysis* 87, 87-88 (Mike Allen & Raymond W. Preiss eds., Hampton Press 1998).

21. *Id.*

22. Stiff & Mongeau, *supra* note 9, at 142.

23. *See generally* Quentin Brogdon, *Innoculating Against Bad Facts: Brilliant Trial Strategy or Misguided Dogma?* 63 Tex. B.J. 443, 447 (2000); Michael J. Saks, *Flying Blind in the Courtroom: Trying Cases Without Knowing What Works or Why*, 101 Yale L.J. 1177, 1187-1188 (1992).

24. Richard M. Perloff, *The Dynamics of Persuasion: Communication and Attitudes in the 21st Century* 125 (2d ed., Routledge 2003).

25. *Id.*

26. *Id.*; O'Keefe, *supra* note 13, at 179; Alison Szabo & Michael Pfau, *Nuances in Inoculation: Theory and Applications*, in *The Persuasion Handbook: Developments in Theory and Practice* 234 (James P. Dillard & Michael Pfau eds., Sage Publications, Inc 2002).

27. Perloff, *supra* note 24, at 125.

28. *Id.* . . .

29. Michael Pfau, Steve Van Bockern & Jong Geun Kang, *Use of Inoculation to Promote Resistance to Smoking Initiation Among Adolescents*, 59 Comm. Monographs 213, 214, 218 (1992); Michael Pfau & Michael Burgoon, *Inoculation in Political Campaign Communication*, 15 Human Comm. Res. 91, 92 (1988). . . .

30. Perloff, *supra* note 24, at 123. . . .

31. Michael Pfau, Henry C. Kenski, Michael Nitz & John Sorenson, *Efficacy of Inoculation Strategies in Promoting Resistance to Political Attack Message: Application to Direct Mail*, 57 Comm. Monographs 25, 28 (1990).

32. *Id.*

33. Szabo & Pfau, *supra* note 26, at 235-237.

34. *Id.* at 235.

35. O'Keefe, *supra* note 13, at 182. . . .

36. Perloff, *supra* note 24, at 126.

37. Lara Dolnik et al., *Stealing Thunder as a Courtroom Tactic Revisited: Processes and Boundaries*, 27 Law & Hum. Behav. 267, 267-269 (2003).

38. *Id.* at 275-279.

39. *Id.* at 269-270.

40. *Id.* at 269.

41. *Id.* at 283.

42. *Id.*

43. *Statement by Alabama Clergymen*, www.stanford.edu/group/King/frequentdocs/clergy.pdf (Apr. 12, 1963).

44. *Id.*

45. *Id.*

46. *Id.*

47. *Id.*

48. *Id.*

49. *Id.*

50. *Id.*

51. Martin Luther King, Jr., *Letter from a Birmingham City Jail*, 26 U.C. Davis L. Rev. 835 (1993) (reprinted with permission).

52. *See* David L. Chappell, *A Stone of Hope: Prophetic Religion and the Death of Jim Crow* 150-151 (U. of North Carolina Press 2004). . . .

53. *Id.* at 6.

54. *Id.*

55. Wendell L. Griffen, *Race, Law, and Culture: A Call to New Thinking, Leadership, and Action*, 21 U. Ark. Little Rock L. Rev. 901, 909 (1999). . . .

56. Chappell, *supra* note 52, at 151.

Our Reasons

In this section and the next, we will look at the substance of a brief's arguments. This section covers arguments made expressly and traditionally recognized as legal reasoning. You are already quite familiar with the workhorses of legal reasoning and persuasion: rules, analogies, policies, principles, and stories, so we will not return to those here. Instead, in this section, we'll look at legal theory (jurisprudence) and the methods of interpreting a constitution. Both of these topics will help you find, make, and refute legal arguments.

13. *Legal Theory*

> "Man's mind, once stretched by a new idea, never regains its original dimensions."
>
> —Oliver Wendell Holmes, Jr.

This chapter covers legal theory (often called "jurisprudence"). Recall that in Chapter 3, Professor Linda Berger proposed a rhetorical view of the law as "a place to stand" between formalism and realism. This chapter will give you a better sense of what she means. Even more important, though, it will give you another strategy for finding, using, and refuting legal arguments in an appellate brief.

Excerpt from

Linda H. Edwards, *Legal Writing and Analysis*
227-243 (3d ed., Aspen Publishers 2011)

Using Legal Theory to Sharpen Your Arguments

If we were to apply each of the major forms of reasoning and persuasion (rules, analogies, policies, principles, stories) to a particular case, these forms might easily lead to differing outcomes. The question then is which form or forms will trump the others in the adversarial process? Jurisprudence—the philosophy of law—provides part of the answer to that question.

Forms of reasoning draw their persuasive force from underlying assumptions about the nature and function of law—about how cases are and should be decided. These are the questions of jurisprudence. Jurisprudence ponders such topics as what law is; where it comes from; whether it is internally consistent; whether it is or can be neutral; how we should decide new or hard cases; and whether and how law relates to morality, social values, economics, or politics.

The more you know about jurisprudence, the more it will show you practical arguments and lawyering strategies. Your own grasp of the jurisprudential basis of a form of argument and your sensitivity to the jurisprudential approach of the judge will strengthen your ability to use these forms of argument to represent your clients well. This section introduces some of the major schools of American jurisprudence and explores how these jurisprudential schools relate to the forms of legal reasoning described above.[1]

A caveat is in order. One cannot draw lines tightly defining jurisprudential schools of thought because the categories overlap and because different strains have developed within each school. Nonetheless, a broad and general description is helpful to introduce the field. With that goal in mind, here is the story of the development of American jurisprudence with particular reference to three of its most vexing questions: (1) the relationship between law and morality; (2) the degree to which law is predictable; and (3) the degree to which law is, can, or should be neutral—that is, not inherently favoring any particular segment of society.

Aaron Mayes, 2009

I. Natural Law

American jurisprudence began with natural law, the predominant jurisprudential school the American colonies inherited from English law. Natural law holds that law is a product of "natural reason." This natural reason has often been associated with religious thought, but natural law is actually much broader. It relies on the deepest moral instincts of humanity and attempts to justify these instincts rationally. According to natural law theory, law and morality (our beliefs about right and wrong, justice and injustice) are both grounded in natural reason and so are inevitably intertwined. An acceptable legal system must also be an acceptable moral system; that is, law should comply with standards of justice, fairness, and reasonableness. Therefore, laws can be defended or challenged on the basis of whether they are reasonable and moral.

Natural law theory favors the common law (case law) over statutes. The common law is more apt to reflect natural reason, whereas statutes, resulting from the political process, are thought to preempt the natural reason on which the common law was based. We see natural law theory in action, for instance, in the canon of construction asserting that statutes "in derogation of the common law" should be narrowly construed.

A judge with a natural law bent might therefore be willing to take more liberties when interpreting a statute or more willing to hold it unconstitutional than would a judge of another jurisprudential persuasion. The natural law judge might use some of the canons of construction to justify a result consistent with her sense of natural reason and morality, for example, the canon that presumes that a legislature usually does not intend to enact a statute that impairs fundamental and commonly held societal values.

A natural law judge also would be more willing to consider disregarding old or flawed precedent, justifying the decision by citing to the age of the precedent and to more recent moral development or the evolution of human understanding. By such a decision, this judge might be inviting the higher court to reconsider its earlier decision.

Forms of Legal Reasoning. Principle-based arguments are most persuasive to judges with natural law leanings. Principles of justice, fairness, reasonableness, and equity can be used to interpret rules or to challenge the strict application of legal rules. Principle-based reasoning represents a direct appeal to natural law.

Narrative reasoning is a less direct but sometimes more effective way to appeal to the values of natural law. Stories contain themes, encode principles, and espouse values. The effective use of narrative, especially the narrative of the client's case, can appeal to a decision-maker's sense of justice and morality. Custom-based reasoning can also be effective, because natural law is assumed to be consistent with generally accepted practices. Aberrations from the norm are suspect.

Although it is almost always good to organize an argument according to the structure of the rule, a natural law judge will not be overly constrained by the precise language of legal rules. Rule-based reasoning will not be strong here unless the advocate can show that the rule is a reasonable expression of a fair principle. One must not only demonstrate what the rule is but also that the rule is right.

Few judges today would be so solidly in the natural law camp that they would blatantly disregard a clear statutory mandate or a binding precedent. But if the judge has any leeway to interpret ambiguities in the rule or if the rule asks the judge to apply a flexible legal standard, our natural law judge will interpret and apply the rule in ways consistent with her understanding of natural law's abiding truths.

Strengths and Weaknesses. Natural law is attractive because it ties law to standards of justice, fairness, and reason, but it has disadvantages as well. Its two most problematic characteristics are its unpredictability and its inherent subjectivity. "Natural reason" is difficult to define or predict. And decisions resting on natural law theory historically have looked a lot like the moral perspectives of that generation's power structure. For instance, a natural law perspective might be more willing to condemn the morality of a homeless person stealing bread than the morality of the landowner who had evicted the person or the business owner who had fired him for no cause.

EXERCISE 1

What natural law influences do you see in the following excerpts from court opinions?

1. "[Requiring an adverse possessor to have known that he did not have record title to the land] rewards . . . the intentional wrong-doer and disfavors an honest, mistaken entrant." *Mannillo v. Gorski*, 255 A.2d 258, 261 (N.J. 1969).
2. "It cannot be expected that every purchaser will or should engage a surveyor to ascertain that the beach home he is purchasing lies within the boundaries described in his deed. Such a practice is neither reasonable nor customary.... [T]he squatter should not be able to profit by his trespass." *Howard v. Kunto*, 477 P.2d 210, 214 (Wash. 1970).
3. "We therefore hold that antiquated real property concepts which served as the basis for the pre-existing rule shall no longer be controlling where there is a claim for damages under a residential lease. Such claims must be governed by more modern notions of fairness and equity. A landlord has a duty to mitigate damages where he seeks to recover rents due from a defaulting tenant." *Sommer v. Kridel*, 378 A.2d 767, 772-773 (N.J. 1977).
4. "Where fairness and common sense dictate that an exception should be created, the evolution of the law should not be stifled by rigid application of a legal maxim." *Stambovsky v. Ackley*, 572 N.Y.S.2d 672, 676 (1991).

II. Formalism

In the last third of the nineteenth century, the Civil War had left American intellectuals disillusioned and skeptical. Further, the cultural infatuation with Darwinism and the scientific method was in full swing.[2] In that climate, the idea of "natural reason" began to seem like unprovable superstition.

Meanwhile, on the other side of the Atlantic, leading English scholars were espousing positivism, a blatant rejection of natural law in favor of the idea that law is simply whatever the sovereign decrees and is willing to enforce. Positivists are unimpressed with the common law and with the role of judges. According to positivists, statutes—through which the sovereign speaks—are the most legitimate form of law.

Positivism seemed to dethrone law from its natural law pedestal, and Darwinism seemed to call for a "scientific" approach to everything. In 1870, when Christopher Columbus Langdell became the Dean of the Harvard Law School, he set out to establish law as a science too. He created the case method of law teaching—the method you probably are experiencing now in most of your classes—in the hope of showing the scientific nature of law. Langdell often is described as the father of legal formalism.

For formalists, law is drawn from a set of rules ("first principles") governing recurring situations,[3] not from a set of timeless moral standards. According to some strains of formalism, these first principles resemble the laws of science, like gravity or photosynthesis. They preexist any particular articulation of them, and they can be discovered and organized according to legal categories, much like the scientific categories of animal species.

According to formalism, the judge's job is simple. He is to select the appropriate legal rule from the appropriate legal category and apply it to the facts at hand. Formalists thought that this should be a straightforward, easy process. Granted, not every case would be clear, but the more difficult cases simply signal that we legal "scientists" have more work to do. As soon as we have discovered and articulated all the first principles, all cases will be simple and clear.

Law study and legal practice still reflect the influence of formalism. We still have the West key numbering system. Legal encyclopedias and other research sources are still organized according to categories that resemble Langdell's vision. The first-year curriculum still reflects formalist legal categories, and law school pedagogy still employs the Socratic method. The classic paradigm for organizing a legal discussion begins by stating and explaining a rule and then applying that rule to the client's facts. As we saw when we studied the paradigm more closely, however, the process it requires is usually far more complex and unpredictable than Langdell envisioned.

Forms of Legal Reasoning.   For the formalist, rule-based reasoning is the heart and soul of legal rhetoric. To persuade a formalist judge, the advocate must carefully and precisely articulate the rule, offer strong authority to prove that the rule is as she has articulated it, and then carefully apply the rule to the facts of the case. But what if the literal application of the language of the rule leads to an unfavorable conclusion? All is not lost. Remember that formalism is the jurisprudential cousin of positivism. What matters is the will of the sovereign, that is, the intent of the legislature or the court that established the binding precedent. You can engage in rule-based reasoning, arguing not from the literal language of the rule but from the intent of the rule-maker.

Analogical reasoning can be persuasive to a formalist judge because it demonstrates that the judge has accurately identified the legal issue and therefore the appropriate governing legal rule. Because formalist judges believe that they should avoid decisions based on moral principles or public policy, they are not as receptive to principle-based or policy-based reasoning as such. However, you can use principle and policy arguments couched as the intent of the rule-maker. Pure formalists would be unimpressed by custom-based reasoning, considering it the weakest possible basis for a decision.

Strengths and Weaknesses.   Assuming that formalism accurately describes law, it scores high on both predictability and objectivity, the two major weaknesses of natural law. Formalism recognizes that statutes and binding case law exist and that sometimes a judge is constrained to follow a clear binding rule. In such a case, the result does not depend on what the judge thinks of the litigants or on whether the judge agrees with the rule.

Formalism carries major weaknesses, however, and the most serious is inaccuracy. Simply put, legal principles cannot remove subjectivity from judging. Judges do not decide cases just by looking up rules. And even if they were willing to limit their decision-making to that mechanical exercise, rules cannot be articulated in ways that account for all human situations. Human situations are infinitely varied, and a legal system that ignores these variations would not be desirable. Rules are made of words, and words must be interpreted by human beings.

Further, formalism enshrines the articulated rule as the real decision-maker, and articulated rules, whether statutory or common law, tend to reflect and entrench the values and perspectives of the economically and socially powerful. On this score, then, formalism was no improvement over natural law. In fact, it might have been a step backward because it leaves little room for escape. Because it disallows external standards like justice and reasonableness, it provides no basis for challenging a bad or outmoded law.

EXERCISE 2

What formalist influences do you see in the following excerpts from court opinions?

1. "[The parties are co-owners of the property. The Defendant has taken possession of the property and is using it for a warehouse. The Plaintiff seeks payment from the Defendant of one-half the fair rental value of the property. The rule on occupancy by a co-owner permits each co-owner the right to possess the premises.] Thus, before an occupying cotenant can be liable for rent . . . , he must have denied his cotenant the right to enter. It is axiomatic that there can be no denial of the right to enter unless there is a demand or an attempt to enter. [Therefore, if the Plaintiff had first sought to enter into possession herself and been denied by the Defendant, she could then demand that the Defendant pay rent.]" *Spiller v. Mackereth*, 334 So. 2d 859, 862 (Ala. 1976).

2. "[It seems to us that] this doctrine of causa mortis [gifts given by a donor on his death bed] is in direct conflict with the spirit and purpose of [the statute requiring wills to be in writing and properly witnessed. The purpose of that statute is] the prevention of fraud. . . . We were at first disposed to confine [gifts causa mortis] to cases of actual manual delivery, and are only prevented from doing so by our loyalty to our own [prior rulings] . . . ." *Newman v. Bost*, 29 S.E. 848, 849 (N.C. 1898).

III. Legal Realism

Ironically, Langdell's case method, which he had hoped would demonstrate the scientific nature of law, might have provided the most powerful evidence against his own thesis. As students and professors systematically studied cases, they began to see that the deductive application of legal rules did not account for the results they observed. What, then, did?

Oliver Wendell Holmes, Jr., a contemporary of Langdell's, began the shift toward a set of ideas that later developed into legal realism, perhaps the preeminent American contribution to jurisprudence. Holmes's famous statement is often cited as an early description of legal realism:

> The life of the law has not been logic; it has been experience. The felt necessities of the time, the prevalent moral and political theories, intuitions of public policy, avowed or unconscious, even the prejudices which judges share with their fellow-men, have a good deal more to do than the syllogism in determining the rules by which men should be governed.[4]

Legal realists believe, as Holmes suggested, that law is made by people as the need arises. Law is not a manifestation of preexisting

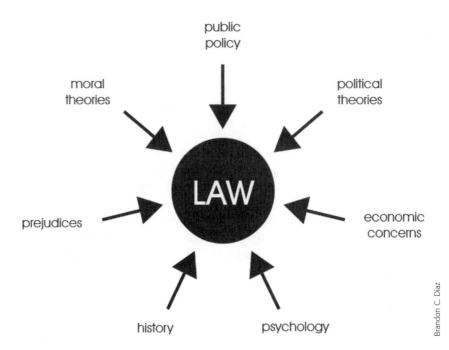

natural law or an objective application of rules. Our legal language still reflects this realist idea. We say that a judge "finds" facts, but we avoid saying that a judge "finds" a legal conclusion.[5] Thus, realists are willing to live with much less predictability than are formalists.

Realists also reject the assumption that law is or ever could be objective. Realism acknowledges subjectivity and could even be said to embrace it, describing law as reflecting historical, social, political, anthropological, psychological, and economic influences. Realists admit that outcomes will vary according to the identity of the decision-makers and the cultural influences bearing upon them.

This reliance on the real world of place and time for law creation leads realists to believe that law should accurately reflect and effectively participate in that real world. Prior to the realist revolution, the law had become insular, largely indifferent to other disciplines. Realism called law back into dialogue with the social sciences. Therefore, realists encourage lawyers and judges to consult interdisciplinary materials such as sociology, psychology, and economics to help them decide cases.

Louis Brandeis, a legal realist who later sat on the United States Supreme Court, filed a brief in *Muller v. Oregon*,[6] relying on social science research to argue the propriety of a law limiting working hours for women. To this day, we call a brief that provides the court with social science or other interdisciplinary information a "Brandeis brief." The plaintiff's brief in *Brown v. Board of Education*[7] was just such a brief.

Library of Congress (Harris & Ewing, circa 1905)

Justice Louis Brandeis

Legal realism forever unmasked the humanity, complexity, and malleability of the law. Realism's critique of formalism "cut so deeply into the premises of American legal thought that no amount of enlightened policy making and informed situation sense could ever really put Humpty Dumpty together again."[8] Every subsequent jurisprudential school is either an attempt to escape the implications of legal realism or to embrace them.

Forms of Legal Reasoning. Policy arguments are the life blood of realist rhetoric, especially at the appellate level. As in the natural law context, the realist court does not feel overly constrained by the words of a rule. In the natural law context, one asked the court to interpret the rule, or even reject the rule, based on external standards of justice and reason. Here one asks the court to interpret the rule, or even reject the rule, based on sound social policy. Such an argument should be supported, not by subjective speculation, but rather by solid data from interdisciplinary sources. In his classic, *The Nature of the Judicial Process*, Justice Cardozo called for more and better "Brandeis briefs."[9]

Realist judges also find analogical reasoning more persuasive than rule-based reasoning because factual comparisons contain within them the coded cultural influences that realists believe actually account for legal results. Custom-based reasoning is consistent with the realist admission of subjectivity and the impact of cultural norms.

Narrative, especially at the trial-court level, is also well-suited to legal realism. Narrative is the broadest, most flexible, and most inclusive form of persuasion. It can, therefore, do the most comprehensive job of touching all the subjective factors that, in the realist's view, actually govern the outcome of cases.

However, a realist judge, at least one with Holmes's distrust of grand principle, might be uncomfortable with principle-based reasoning, preferring a more concrete analysis of how the proposed result actually would work in the world.

Strengths and Weaknesses.   Realism acknowledges that law is a human institution, with a limited capacity for objectivity and predictability. It honestly admits the inevitable influence of the dominant culture and of powerful economic interests. For the advocate, realism sets us free from formalism's insistence on rigid, mechanical application of formulaic rules. Realism legitimates broader, more flexible approaches to legal argument.

Still, realism sometimes suffers from its own excesses. It has a conflicted relationship with external criteria such as reason, justice, and morality as standards for interpreting or applying law. True, realism grants that current notions of morality have a role to play, because current cultural norms inevitably influence law. But realism is hesitant to ask whether those cultural norms are objectively right or true. Thus, realism undermines an advocate's arguments that law should be tested by external standards. In place of these standards, realism offers an advocate the criteria of sound social policy, which can be supported by evidence that is more substantive than the abstract claims and subjective values of natural law.

Finally, realism seems to leave us without a stable ground on which to stand. Early realism often was summed up as asserting that the law depended less on precedent than on "what the judge ate for breakfast."[10] If that describes our legal system, can we have confidence in its results? And how can individual and corporate citizens plan their lives and fortunes? A purely realist analysis leaves the law without consistency, apt to shift with the wind at any moment. Realism left us in need of a stabilizing movement. To meet that need, the legal process school developed.

EXERCISE 3

What realist influences do you see in the following excerpts from court opinions?

1. "It has long been the policy of our law to discourage landlords from taking the law into their own hands, and our decisions ... have looked with disfavor upon any use of self-help to dispossess a tenant in circumstances which are likely to result in breaches of the peace.... To approve this lockout ... merely because [the tenant was absent and so no] actual violence erupted while the locks were being changed would be to encourage all future tenants ... to be vigilant and thereby set the stage for the very kind of public disturbance which it must be our policy to discourage...." *Berg v. Wiley*, 264 N.W.2d 145, 149-150 (Minn. 1978).
2. "[T]he requirement of delivery [to prove a valid gift] is not rigid or inflexible, but is to be applied in light of its purpose to avoid mistakes by donors and fraudulent claims by donees." *Gruen v. Gruen*, 496 N.E.2d 869, 874 (N.Y. 1986).
3. "[A joint tenant has long been able to sever the joint tenancy by conveying his interest in the property to a straw person and then having that straw person convey the interest back to the former joint tenant. We now hold that the joint tenant can sever by conveying directly to himself.] Common sense as well as legal efficiency dictate that a joint tenant should be able to accomplish directly what he or she could otherwise achieve indirectly by use of elaborate legal fictions." *Riddle v. Harmon*, 162 Cal. Rptr. 530, 534 (Ct. App. Calif. 1980).
4. "There is no sound policy reason to deny plaintiff relief for failing to discover a state of affairs which the most prudent purchaser would not be expected to even contemplate." *Stambovsky v. Ackley*, 572 N.Y.S.2d 672, 676 (1991).

IV. Legal Process

As we have seen, formalists said that a judge could and should follow legal rules, assumed to be neutral, regardless of the preferences of the judge. Realists said that judges did not and could not do this because judges are human and because legal rules are not really neutral. The legal process school tried to find a middle ground that would recognize the realists' critique of formalism but still would curb the unpredictability of realism.

The hope lay in turning our attention to the legal process itself, especially to judicial decision-making. Perhaps careful study and development of judicial roles and systemic controls would restore some sense of predictability and objectivity in law. If the *content* of the law was not objective, perhaps we could articulate neutral standards for *how* decisions were to be made. Legal process adherents look to institutional controls (division of governmental authority, adherence to fair procedure, judicial restraint, and mandated reasoned elaboration) to constrain arbitrary judging.[11]

According to the legal process school, judges are to restrain their personal preferences in favor of neutral procedures and standards of judging. For instance, a trial judge cannot overturn a jury's verdict simply because the judge would have decided the case otherwise. The judge can overturn the verdict only if there was no reasonable evidentiary basis for the jury's decision.

Similarly, on questions of fact, an appellate judge cannot reverse a trial judge's decision merely because the appellate judge would have decided the case differently. The appellate judge can reverse the trial judge only if no reasonable consideration of the evidence in the record would support the trial judge's decision. Legal process adherents hope that neutral standards like these will restore a sense of stability and predictability and provide protection against abuse of the judicial role.

Forms of Legal Reasoning. A judge with a legal process bent is persuaded by rule-based reasoning when the rule is binding on her court and has a clear meaning directly applicable to the pending case. In that instance, the legal process judge will feel constrained to follow the rule and will monitor carefully her personal preferences to keep them from interfering subtly with her judicial duty. Similarly, analogical reasoning is persuasive to a legal process judge because she is concerned about procedural fairness. After all, when the facts are similar, the results should not vary from court to court.

When no clear binding rule applies or when the rule allows discretion, a legal process judge is willing to consider policy-based reasoning because it seems reliable and objective. But a legal process judge will be uncomfortable with pure custom-based reasoning because it seems too close to subjective personal preference. Principle-based reasoning will be persuasive when the principles relate to procedural fairness. Other principles might seem too abstract to be applied without subjectivity. Direct reliance on narrative is the most subjective of all, and a legal process judge will try to resist her personal reaction to the client's stories.

Strengths and Weaknesses. The legal process school succeeds in restoring some stability for the legal system. Undoubtedly, its success is limited by its necessary reliance on imperfect human beings to achieve its goals. Most judges have been thoroughly encultured with the legal process school's description of the judicial role, however, and they try to conform to that role as best they can.

But the legal process school still does not help us find a way to explore whether the *content* of our law is consistent with fundamental principles of justice and commonly shared principles of morality. Lon Fuller, himself a natural law advocate, tried to provide a link by suggesting that a fair process with public, reasoned decision-making was itself moral,[12] but the legal process movement itself did not rush to make this connection. A movement in that direction came with the development of the fundamental rights school.

EXERCISE 4

What legal process influences do you see in the following excerpts from court opinions?

1. "Even if we were to feel that the referee was mistaken in so weighing the evidence, we would be powerless to change the determination where, as we have seen, there is some evidence in the record to support his conclusion." *Van Valkenburgh v. Lutz*, 106 N.E.2d 28, 32 (N.Y. 1952) (dissenting opinion).

2. "[The goal of our law is] to prevent those claiming a right of . . . possession of land from redressing their own wrongs by entering into possession in a . . . forcible manner. . . . The law does not permit the owner of land, be his title ever so good, to be the judge of his own rights with respect to possession . . . , but puts him to his remedy under the statutes." *Lobdell v. Keene*, 88 N.W. 426, 430 (Minn. 1901).

Library of Congress

Chief Justice Earl Warren

V. Fundamental Rights

By now we were entering the 1950s, and the Supreme Court, under the leadership of Earl Warren, was in a period of judicial activism. *Brown v. Board of Education*[13] and other landmark decisions were establishing principles of human rights and opening doors to political and economic power.

But where was the jurisprudential justification for this kind of judicial activism? Natural law did not provide it because the old view of natural law seemed tied to the perspectives of the established power structure, and these decisions ran counter to that power structure. Formalism did not provide it because formalism enshrines the status quo. The legal process school could help on procedural issues like due process and access to courts. But on non-procedural issues, legal process is uncomfortable with decisions that seem based on personal political preferences. We had to return to the vexing question of how law relates to broad principles like justice and human dignity. From this renewed struggle emerged the fundamental rights school.

The fundamental rights school argued that promoting justice and human welfare outweighs the need for predictability and stability.[14] Judges should be ready to apply overarching principles inherent in the law, especially if the principle has been given greater certainty through judicial interpretation. For fundamental rights proponents, the results of this decision-making process are objectively correct, not merely the subjective product of political preferences.[15]

Forms of Legal Reasoning.   Principle-based reasoning is primary in fundamental rights jurisprudence, as it is in natural law. However, the principles here are not the principles that preserve the status quo, but rather the principles of liberal political philosophy that assert the rights of poor and marginalized people. Fundamental rights judges are readily guided by such principles, especially when the principle is enshrined in the Constitution or other forms of law.

Rule-based reasoning remains valuable here, but in this context it is helpful to look for the principle that the law serves. A fundamental rights judge will prefer to interpret the rule in accordance with the principle. She will overturn the rule in favor of a principle only as a last resort.

Narrative reasoning works in the fundamental rights context much as it did in the natural law context. It is an indirect but highly effective way to communicate the principles and values that should guide the decision-maker. The principles comprising "fundamental rights" are persuasive when stated directly; but they gain affective force when conveyed through the warm, human medium of story, especially the client's story.

Policy-based reasoning has its place in fundamental rights jurisprudence, but it is a narrower place. The fundamental rights judge does not see herself as a free-form social engineer, but fundamental rights are meaningless unless they are grounded in social reality. So interdisciplinary sources might be needed to show how an application of the law will play out in society to either advance or undermine fundamental rights. Custom-based reasoning will generally not be very persuasive to a fundamental rights judge unless it shows that a certain right is widely recognized as fundamental.

Strengths and Weaknesses.   The fundamental rights school resurrects a place for something resembling morality, reclaiming an aspirational and even a pedagogical function for law. It defines a ground of decision-making that can connect us to our past and help us mold our future. But like natural law, it suffers from the difficulty and inherent subjectivity of defining the principles to be enforced. It is vulnerable to the charge of preferencing one person's politics over another's. To the extent that the fundamental rights school seemed synonymous with liberal politics, the conservatives were ready with an alternative: law and economics.

EXERCISE 5

What fundamental rights influences do you see in the following excerpts from court opinions?

1. "This pattern of land use regulation has been adopted for the same purpose in developing municipality after municipality. Almost every one acts solely in its own selfish and parochial interest and in effect builds a wall around itself to keep out those people or entities not adding favorably to the tax base, despite the location of the municipality or the demand for varied kinds of housing. . . . One incongruous result is the picture of developing municipalities rendering it impossible for lower paid employees of industries they have eagerly sought and welcomed with open arms . . . to live in the community where they work." *Southern Burlington Co. NAACP v. Township of Mount Laurel,* 336 A.2d 713, 723 (1975).

2. "One should not be able to stand behind the impervious shield of caveat emptor [buyer beware] and take advantage of another's ignorance. . . ." *Johnson v. Davis,* 480 So. 2d 625, 628 (Fla. 1985).

3. "Confronted with a recognized shortage of safe, decent housing, today's tenant is in an inferior bargaining position compared to that of the landlord. *Park West Management Corp. v. Mitchell,* 391 N.E.2d 1288, 1292 (N.Y. 1979). Tenants vying for this limited housing are 'virtually powerless to compel the performance of essential services.' *Id.* at 1292. . . . In light of these changes in the relationship between tenants and landlords, it would be wrong for the law to continue to [hold that landlords have no duty to provide a habitable dwelling]. . . . Therefore, we now hold expressly that in the rental of any residential dwelling unit an implied warranty exists in the lease . . . that the landlord will deliver over and maintain . . . premises that are safe, clean and fit for human habitation." *Hilder v. St. Peter,* 478 A.2d 202, 207 (Vt. 1984).

VI. Law and Economics

Law and economics assesses legal doctrine on the basis of economic principles such as market dynamics, pricing, supply, and demand. Economics has been a part of legal analysis since the realists, but in recent years, economic analysis has become important enough to support a powerful jurisprudential movement of its own.

Proponents argue that, unlike the abstract values of fundamental rights, economic principles are concrete and objective. Some proponents would claim that economic analysis is apolitical. Law and economics emphasizes efficiency, market maximization, and the reduction of governmental controls. Early law and economics theorists argued that the law's goal should be maximizing social wealth, even at the expense of harm for individuals.[16]

The law and economics school includes a broad spectrum of approaches. For instance, some adherents still believe that law's primary goal should be wealth maximization, whereas more moderate proponents consider economic analysis only a component in law-making, albeit an important one. Some assume that individual actors will act rationally to advance their own economic positions, whereas others recognize the perversities of human psychology. This breadth of exploration coupled with the badly needed economic expertise the movement encouraged has made law and economics a valuable jurisprudential movement.

Money

Forms of Legal Reasoning.   A judge with law and economics leanings would be persuaded particularly by policy-based reasoning,
especially economic policy. Such a judge would be willing to
interpret and apply legal rules in ways that would advance economic growth and would be ready to find seemingly analogous
cases distinguishable because of differences in economic implications. Principle-based reasoning and custom-based reasoning
would seem too amorphous to be of reliable help, and the narratives of the individual litigants might seem almost irrelevant
unless they implicate the economic issues in the case. For a
law and economics judge, rule-based reasoning should focus
not on literal application of the rule's words, but on an interpretation of the rule on the assumption that its purpose is to increase
social wealth.

Strengths and Weaknesses.   Law and economics has offered a
helpful and grounding counterweight to the fundamental rights
school's abstraction and subjectivity. It has improved the economic
sophistication of law and made important corrections to inaccurate
economic assumptions. Its less extreme proponents have worked to
improve the ways economic considerations can interact with other
important considerations for the welfare of the society. In that
sense, it has continued the work of the realists.

Law and economics has suffered primarily from three weaknesses: It sometimes has been too willing to credit economic conclusions not backed by sufficient research; it has been susceptible to
unrealistic applications; and it sometimes has been unwilling to
admit the inherent political bias of its own perspective.

EXERCISE 6

What law and economics influences do you see in the following
excerpts from court opinions?

1. "[According to the applicable statute, a court can order the sale
   of co-owned property if one owner seeks partition and if division of the property cannot be made without great prejudice to
   the owners.] The language of this statute means that a sale may
   be ordered if it appears to the satisfaction of the court that the
   value of the share of each cotenant, in case of partition, would
   be materially less than his share of the money equivalent that
   could probably be obtained for the whole. [We give no weight
   to the fact that several of the cotenants have made the property
   their home for nearly forty years or to their interest in remaining on the family homestead.]" *Johnson v. Hendrickson,* 24
   N.W.2d 914, 916 (S.D. 1946).

2. "[When the markets of the nation are furnished by a business], there is great reason to give encouragement [to that business] ... [T]he people who are so instrumental by their skill and industry so to furnish the markets should reap the benefit...." *Keeble v. Hickeringill*, 3 Salk. 9 (Queen's Bench 1707).

3. "Economic policies influence our decision as well. '[B]y virtue of superior knowledge, skill, and experience in the construction of houses, a builder-vendor is generally better positioned than the purchaser to ... evaluate and guard against [and insure against] the financial risk posed by a [latent defect in the construction]." *Lempke v. Dagenais*, 547 A.2d 290, 295 (N.H. 1988) (internal citations omitted).

4. "The safety of real estate titles is considered more important than the unfortunate results which may follow the application of the rule in a few individual instances." *Sweeney, Administratrix v. Sweeney*, 11 A.2d 806, 808 (Conn. 1940).

VII. Critical Legal Theory

One could never accuse the proponents of critical legal theory of denying its political bias. Critical legal theory admits that its own movement is all about politics, and it maintains that everyone else's is as well. For the sake of brevity and simplicity, we will include a number of diverse jurisprudential movements under the umbrella of critical legal theory, most notably critical legal studies, critical race theory, and feminist legal theory. Most of this description will focus on critical legal studies because much of its thinking is consistent with that of the other critical schools.

Critical Legal Studies (CLS) is perhaps the most direct heir of the Legal Realist School. CLS proponents consider law to be entirely subjective and political. They believe that purportedly objective legal rules actually reflect value choices that privilege politically powerful segments of society. CLS asserts that all legal reasoning is simply a post hoc rationalization rather than a description of a method of decision-making. Therefore, instead of articulated rules, CLS scholars trust narratives about the experiences of oppressed groups.

Ironically, CLS is willing to use a form of economic analysis, too, one that asks directly about the distributional consequences for politically marginalized groups.[17] CLS supports the idea of an activist judiciary to empower such segments of society. Part of this political empowerment should be the demystification of legal processes so lay people can participate more effectively.

Critical race theory and feminist jurisprudence largely agree with CLS approaches but from an explicitly racial or gendered perspective.

Forms of Legal Reasoning.   Because CLS has been largely a critique of the legal system from the outside, few CLS proponents have become judges. A judge with CLS sympathies, however, would pay particular attention to the narratives presented by the litigants and would be especially willing to explore the differing perspectives of the "outsiders." The judge also would be willing to listen to policy- and principle-based reasoning to support a result that opens legal and political process and increases self-determination for marginalized groups. A CLS judge would be less persuaded by rule-based and custom-based reasoning, as each is embedded in the political and social power structure.

In comparison to the other schools of jurisprudence, CLS is less helpful as a guide to rule interpretation and application. It is most effectively used to challenge rule-based, natural law, and custom-based arguments by showing that they are masked assertions of oppressive power. It is not so much a form of argument in itself as a tool for deconstructing arguments for the status quo.

Strengths and Weaknesses.   CLS has provided helpful deconstructions of law and law's origins, and it has reminded us that law must hear and represent all segments of society. It has, however, been heavy on critique and light on cure, and like law and economics, it has been vulnerable to extreme views. In the case of CLS, some of these views have advocated refusal to participate in a tainted process, but boycotting a process significantly limits one's ability to change it.

EXERCISE 7

What critical legal theory influences do you see in the following excerpt from a court opinion?

1. "The plain truth is that the true object of the ordinance in question is to . . . regulate the mode of living of persons who may hereafter inhabit it. In the last analysis, the result to be accomplished is to classify the population and segregate them according to their income or situation in life. The true reason why some persons live in a mansion and others in a shack, why some live in a single-family dwelling and others in a double-family dwelling, why some live in a two-family dwelling and others in an apartment, or why some live in a well-kept apartment and others in a tenement, is primarily economic. . . . [The ordinance furthers] these . . . class tendencies. . . ." *Amber Realty Co. v. Village of Euclid,* 297 F. 307, 316 (N.D. Ohio 1924).

VIII. The Jurisprudence of Brief Writing

We have seen a wide diversity of legal thought, just in this brief overview of some of the major jurisprudential schools, but they all have been vulnerable to one major weakness: the temptation of exclusivity. Each school has been a little too willing to think that it alone has discovered the truth. Each school has been a little too ready to reject the observations of the others.

Practicing lawyers and legal writers, however, know that exclusivity is folly. Every one of these jurisprudential schools teaches us something important about law. Each has perceived something real and true about how our legal system does and should function. And each of them needs the others' perspectives to support or temper its own.

More important for our purposes, each of these jurisprudential schools provides lawyers with important lessons about predicting what a judge might decide and about persuading a particular judge to rule in favor of a client. Sometimes you will know a particular judge well enough to tailor your arguments directly to that judge's jurisprudential leanings. However, even if you do not, imagine how much stronger your brief will be if you are careful to provide the judge with reasoning that covers the jurisprudential bases.

EXERCISE 8

Facts. In the past few years, the city of Annville has created a historic district in an effort to restore and preserve its architectural heritage. Several municipal programs have been implemented to encourage suburban residents to return to the city's center to live in restored older homes. A city-owned low-income housing apartment building is not far away from the historic district, and efforts are currently under way to decide what to do with it. The building is old and run down, and modern thinking about low-income housing is critical of the practice of building high-density units dedicated solely to low-income housing. Alternatives under consideration include remodeling the apartments and continuing their use as low-income housing; tearing down the apartment building and implementing a voucher system to enable low-income families to rent directly from private landlords throughout the city; and tearing down the apartment building and replacing it with city-owned low-income duplexes interspersed among private homes meant for moderate-income families.

A drug treatment clinic recently purchased property adjacent to the historic district, intending to open a drug treatment facility there. The location would be ideal because many of the clinic's present and potential patients live in the low-income apartments.

At the time of the purchase, the zoning classification for that property permitted a treatment facility. Upon learning of the clinic's plans, however, residents of the historic district became fearful of the facility's effect on their neighborhood. These residents petitioned the zoning board to rezone the block that includes the clinic's newly purchased property. In response to the residents' petition, the zoning board has rezoned that block to prohibit the clinic. The board notified the clinic's directors of the petition and allowed them to file a written response, but the board did not take testimony at a hearing, make any factual findings, or write an opinion that explained the reasons for the change. The following is the relevant statute pertaining to zoning changes:

> At any time after the adoption of a zoning ordinance, the zoning board may . . . amend the ordinance by a two-thirds vote of its members.

The clinic has appealed the zoning board's decision to the appropriate court, arguing both that the decision was wrong and that the procedure was faulty. Consider how the major jurisprudential perspectives might view this situation. What arguments could you use to support the clinic? What arguments would support the zoning change?

Endnotes

1. Much of the material in this chapter is explained more fully in Chapter 6 of an excellent book by Professors Bailey Kuklin & Jeffrey W. Stempel, *Foundations of the Law: An Interdisciplinary and Jurisprudential Primer* (West 1994).

2. Louis Menand, *The Metaphysical Club: A Story of Ideas in America* (Farrar, Straus & Giroux 2001).

3. Kuklin & Stempel, *supra* note 1, at 149.

4. Oliver Wendell Holmes, *The Common Law* 1 (Little, Brown & Co. 1881).

5. We say instead that a judge "holds" a legal conclusion.

6. 208 U.S. 412 (1908).

7. 347 U.S. 483 (1954).

8. Elizabeth Mensch, *The History of Mainstream Legal Thought*, in *The Politics of Law* 27 (David Kairys ed., Pantheon 1982).

9. Benjamin N. Cardozo, *The Nature of the Judicial Process* (Yale U. Press 1921).

10. Kuklin & Stempel, *supra* note 1, at 155.

11. *Id.* at 159.

12. Lon Fuller, *The Morality of Law* (Yale U. Press 1964).

13. 347 U.S. 483 (1954).

14. Kuklin & Stempel, *supra* note 1, at 165.

15. *Id.* at 166; Ronald Dworkin, *Law's Empire* (Belknap Press 1986); Ronald Dworkin, *A Matter of Principle* (Harv. U. Press 1985).

16. Kuklin & Stempel, *supra* note 1, at 169.

17. *Id.* at 175.

14. *Constitutions*

Since the briefs we analyze in this book are all constitutional cases, it will be important to understand the main schools of constitutional interpretation. This understanding will be important to your own brief-writing as well. In this chapter, Professor Ian Bartrum gives us an excellent and accessible overview of some of the key methods of constitutional interpretation along with illustrative examples of each method at work.

Then Professor Ian Gallacher gives us a fresh and effective look at three such methods by showing us how they might apply in a different context—the conducting of a symphony. Perhaps surprisingly, taking the predictable constitutional debate out of law and placing it in an unexpected arena can help us think about these important questions in fresh ways.

Ian C. Bartrum, *The Modalities of Constitutional Argument: A Primer*

The Constitution is the subject of seemingly endless debate in courtrooms, committee rooms, classrooms, boardrooms, and living rooms across the United States and around the world. We argue about the meaning, or more precisely the application, of constitutional phrases and principles in an ever-changing world of human endeavors and policies. And, in our current system, lawyers and judges enjoy a place of privilege in the constitutional forum. This is so because it is lawyers (through argument) and judges (through decision) that have the most direct influence on the interpretive norms that give rise to constitutional meaning in disputed cases. It is by understanding and shaping these norms that lawyers and judges help determine how the Constitution will guide politics and statecraft in the face of unprecedented challenges. Thus, it is profoundly important for the young constitutional lawyer to understand the conventions that govern the practice of constitutional argument.

Interpretive norms have their roots in an unavoidable tension between the indeterminate nature of language and the desire for a determinate rule of law. This tension always exists, but it is necessarily more acute when we use language in deliberately vague or underdetermined ways, as is the case with many of our most significant constitutional provisions. The "vagueness" problem is well known and much debated among language philosophers,[1] but the basic difficulty is easily summarized: Propositions that rely on vague terms cannot be verified (or falsified) empirically.[2] In our everyday lives, vague language does not present much of a problem, because there is rarely a pressing need to understand each other in precisely determined ways. When it comes to constitutional argument, however, the question of what exactly the "equal protection of the laws" (for example) means is often quite important. Because the term "equal protection" is deliberately vague, lawyers and judges must often "interpret" its meaning—that is, they must decide what *counts* as "equal protection" in various contexts. This need for interpretation presents a real problem for those who want the Constitution to have "objective" or verifiable kinds of meanings; meanings that can place clear normative constraints on judges. Put in current political parlance, if "equal protection" had a verifiable meaning, it would be quite easy to know when a judge was "making," as opposed to "applying," the law.

> Interpretive norms have their roots in an unavoidable tension between the indeterminate nature of language and the desire for a determinate rule of law.

Words, though, often do not have verifiable "objective" or "foundational" meanings that can provide this kind of normative constraint. This is because words often do not refer to something "in the world" that we can see or touch; something we might use as a kind of measuring stick to assess the truth of particular statements.[3] Of course, this does not mean that words cannot provide *any* normative constraints; it just means that the source of those constraints cannot be something "objective" in the sense of being independent of the practical conventions of language.[4] For this reason, we can only justify a normative judgment about a judicial interpretation in terms of that interpretation's consonance with conventional practice—not by reference to some "factual" or verifiable state of affairs in our world, or, as some suggest, in the Founders' world.[5] More importantly, these conventions—what I have called interpretive norms—can derive only from the *practice of interpretation itself.* That is, these norms develop out of our actual arguments, as we learn by trial and error what others will or will not accept as legitimate interpretations of a particular word or phrase. Thus, the only way we can understand what "equal protection" means is by understanding the norms that govern its acceptable use, and, these norms necessarily evolve as the practice confronts new contexts and communicative problems.

Phew. At this point, you may be wondering what all this esoteric theory can possibly mean to a practicing constitutional lawyer. What it means, in short, is that those who want to succeed in constitutional argument must be fully versed in the norms that govern its practice. Put another way, a good constitutional lawyer must completely master the language—the grammar—of constitutional argument. Fortunately, these norms have been the subject of some study, and Professor Philip Bobbitt has given a particularly helpful account of the basic rules. Bobbitt has identified and described six fundamental "modalities" (or forms) of argument that are accepted by convention as legitimate in constitutional practice.[6]

The forms of argument Bobbitt has identified are:

> [1] the ***historical*** (relying on the intentions of the framers or ratifiers of the Constitution); [2] ***textual*** (looking to the meaning of the words of the Constitution alone, as they would be interpreted by the average contemporary "man on the street"); [3] ***structural*** (inferring rules from the relationships that the Constitution mandates from the structure it sets up); [4] ***doctrinal*** (applying rules generated by precedent); [5] ***ethical*** (deriving rules from the moral commitments of the American ethos that are reflected in the Constitution); [6] ***prudential*** (seeking to balance the costs and benefits of a particular rule).[7]

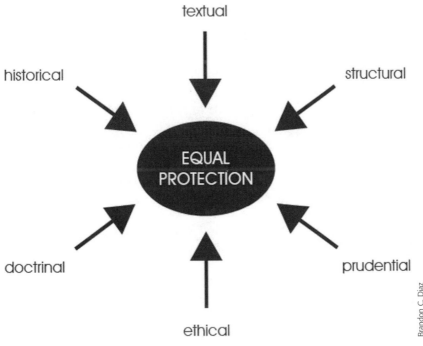

Brandon C. Diaz

Bobbitt's modalities

According to Bobbitt, an assertion of constitutional meaning based in one of these six modalities is legitimate, while an assertion based in something else—i.e., Hammurabi's Code, the teachings of the Quran, or the principles of astrology—is not. Just because an assertion of meaning is *legitimate* does not mean it is compelling or persuasive. If a lawyer makes a weak historical argument about the meaning of "equal protection," for example, she may never convince anyone—much less a judge—to adopt her assertion. But at least she is playing the game by the appropriate rules; she is, in effect, speaking the language of constitutional law.

Because the modalities arise out of the real-life practice of constitutional argument, the best way to understand them is to examine how they are used to make actual constitutional assertions. With that in mind, the rest of this essay illustrates each argumentative modality in action. And, in an effort to demonstrate the central place the modalities have occupied in the practice over time, I have selected examples from various points in American history, and I have tried to choose some of the best-known decisions and briefs in the constitutional catalogue.

A. Textual Argument in *Youngstown Sheet & Tube Co. v. Sawyer*

In 1951, in the midst of the Korean War, an untimely labor dispute arose in the American steel industry.[8] After a long series of failed negotiations, the steelworkers' union gave final notice of its intention to strike in April of 1952.[9] Recognizing the industry's critical importance to the war effort, President Harry Truman issued an Executive Order directing the Secretary of Commerce to seize many of the steel mills and keep production flowing.[10] The Secretary then informed the mill managers that they worked for the United States government, and told them to carry on their business at his direction.[11] President Truman reported his action to Congress the next morning, and the steel companies promptly brought suit in District Court claiming that the President had exceeded his constitutional authority.[12] Just over a month later, after a string of expedited hearings, the Supreme Court heard oral arguments in the case.[13]

The government conceded that the President lacked express constitutional or statutory authority to seize the steel mills, but argued that Truman was "acting within the aggregate of his constitutional powers as the Nation's Chief Executive and the Commander in Chief of the Armed Forces."[14] In other words, even without explicit constitutional language, the authority to seize the mills in an emergency was inherently a part of the "Executive power" vested in the President. That argument did not persuade Justice Hugo Black, however, who wrote the Court's majority opinion.[15] Justice Black was a dyed in the wool textualist—he once caustically reminded an interviewer, "You see, you have laws written out. That's the object in law, to have it written out"—and he began his *Youngstown* opinion in typical form.[16] National emergency or not, "[t]he president's power, if any, to issue the [seizure] order must stem either from an act of Congress or from the Constitution itself."[17] He searched the provisions the government relied on—those providing that "the executive Power shall be vested in a President"; that "he shall take Care that the Laws be faithfully executed"; and that he "shall be the Commander in Chief"—and, of course, found no mention of seizing steel mills.[18]

Without an express constitutional grant, Black had little trouble concluding that Truman's order amounted to an exercise of Legislative, rather than Executive, power. And he did so in paradigmatically textualist terms:

> In the framework of our Constitution, the President's power to see that the laws are faithfully executed refutes the idea that he is to be a lawmaker. The Constitution limits his functions in the lawmaking process to the recommending of laws he thinks wise and the vetoing of laws he thinks bad. And the Constitution is neither silent nor equivocal about who shall make the laws that the President is to execute. The first section of the first article says that "All legislative Power herein granted shall be vested in a Congress of the United States."[19]

Black's conclusion was thus as uncompromising as it was straightforward. Unlike his colleague Robert Jackson, who argued for some kind of contextual sliding scale or spectrum of implicit or inherent Executive power, Black entirely rejected anything not "written out."[20] He made no attempt to discern what, if anything, the constitutional Framers might have thought about emergency or wartime powers, even though the undefined concept of executive authority might seem to call for such an inquiry. Instead, he took a straightforward textualist approach: all that matters is what the words might mean to an average person on the street.

B. Historical Argument in *District of Columbia v. Heller*

In early February of 2003, Dick Heller and five other plaintiffs filed suit against the District of Columbia challenging city code provisions that, in effect, banned the home ownership of handguns.[21] Heller was a Special Police Officer at the Thurgood Marshall Judicial Center and he carried a handgun while at work.[22] The code, however, did not allow city residents to possess unregistered guns at home, and, beginning in 1974, the city had refused to issue new registrations for handguns. On relatively rare occasions, the city would grant special licenses for handguns, but Heller's application had been rejected.[23] Convinced that this handgun policy violated his Second Amendment right to "keep and bear arms," Heller asked the Federal District Court to permanently enjoin enforcement of the city code provisions.[24] The District Court dismissed Heller's complaint, but the D.C. Circuit reversed, and the case eventually made it to the Supreme Court.[25]

In the Supreme Court, the city argued that the text of the Second Amendment contemplates a right to bear arms rooted firmly in the context of militia or military service.[26] The text seems to make this contextual understanding explicit by prefacing the right with an explanatory phrase: "A well-regulated militia, being necessary to the security of a free State, the right of the people to keep and bear Arms, shall not be infringed."[27] Thus, the city argued, the right to bear arms must be understood as a *collective* right—one held by "well-regulated" militias—not as the kind of *individual* right a citizen like Heller could claim against the government. Heller disagreed and argued that the prefatory clause specifies just one of many possible justifications for the right to bear arms, and that the Amendment's operative clause also protects gun ownership for the purpose of individual self-defense. Although there was some relevant doctrine, the Supreme Court opinions turned largely on historical arguments—that is, the Court looked not to what a modern reader would think the text means, but rather to what someone reading the text in 1791 would have thought.

Writing for the majority, Justice Antonin Scalia turned to a variety of historical sources in an effort to demonstrate that the founding generation understood the right to "keep and bear arms" as serving an individual right of self-defense.[28] In a notable passage, he offered his interpretation of the English common law rights he claimed the Second Amendment codified:

> By the time of the founding, the right to have arms had become fundamental for English subjects. Blackstone, whose works, we have said, "constituted the preeminent authority on English law for the founding generation," cited the Arms provision of the Bill of Rights as one of the fundamental rights of Englishmen. His description of it cannot possibly be thought to tie it to militia or military service. It was, he said, the "natural right of resistance and self-preservation," and "the right of having and using arms for self-preservation and defence." Other contemporary authorities concurred.[29]

For Scalia, then, the reason we should interpret the Second Amendment as protecting the right to possess handguns in the home is *historical*: it is part of the right the framers and the ratifiers thought they were protecting when they adopted the text in question.

Writing in dissent, Justice John Paul Stevens made different historical arguments. Instead of looking to English common law, he focused on the particular problems motivating the Second Amendment's inclusion in the Bill of Rights. In particular, he focused on the states' fear of consolidated federal military power.

> [T]he original Constitution's retention of the militia and its creation of a divided [state and federal] authority over that body did not

prove sufficient to allay fears about the dangers posed by a standing [federal] army. For it was perceived by some that Article I contained a significant gap: While it empowered Congress to organize, arm, and discipline the militia, it did not prevent Congress from providing for the militia's *dis*armament. . . . This sentiment was echoed at a number of state ratifying conventions; indeed, it was one of the primary objections to the original Constitution voiced by its opponents.[30]

According to Stevens, it was this fear of a federal power grab that led the framers to protect the militia explicitly in the Second Amendment—the English right of self-defense simply did not enter into the conversation.

Regardless of who is right on this question, the larger point is that both sides accepted the legitimacy and significance of historical arguments about constitutional meaning. That the sides could disagree so forcefully about history's lesson in this case only illustrates the point that history cannot provide the kind of objective measuring stick that can effectively constrain judges. It is still just one modality of argument, which may be utilized more or less persuasively in particular cases.

> Regardless of who is right on this question, the larger point is that both sides accepted the legitimacy and significance of historical arguments about constitutional meaning.

Justin Valas, 2010

"No taxation without representation," ITIN march

C. Structural Argument in *McCulloch v. Maryland*

Perhaps the most important opinion in the constitutional canon is Chief Justice John Marshall's powerful argument in *McCulloch v. Maryland*. There the Court confronted fundamental questions about the relative scope of state and federal power under the

Constitution. The case arose out of a controversy over the creation of a National Bank, which had begun almost as soon as the Constitution was ratified. At Alexander Hamilton's urging, the First Congress established such a bank in 1791, with the proviso that its charter would expire in twenty years.[31] As it turned out, James Madison—who opposed the original bank—was President in 1811, and he successfully campaigned against renewing the charter.[32] But, after the War of 1812 left the new nation in serious financial trouble, Madison changed his mind and got behind the movement for a Second National Bank.[33] Unhappy with this development, the state of Maryland decided to impose an annual tax of $15,000 on the bank's Baltimore branch.[34] When cashier James McCulloch refused to pay, Maryland took him to court arguing that Congress had no constitutional authority to create the bank.[35] Not surprisingly, Maryland won in its state courts, but an appeal to the Supreme Court quickly followed.[36]

The Court addressed two distinct questions: (1) whether Congress had the power to create the bank; and (2) if so, whether Maryland could tax it. Marshall's opinion utilized the full array of constitutional modalities, but in answering the first question he leaned most heavily on prudentialism, arguing that Congress must have the means to establish public credit and pay troops in far-flung locales.[37] In addressing the second question, however, Marshall turned decisively to structural argument in defining the relative scope of state and federal taxing powers:[38]

> The only security against the abuse of [the taxing] power, is found in the structure of the government itself. In imposing a tax, the legislature acts upon its constituents. . . . The people of a state, therefore, give to their government a right of taxing themselves and their property . . . resting confidently on the interest of the legislator . . . to guard them against its abuse. But the means employed by the government of the Union have no such security, nor is the right of a state to tax them sustained by the same theory. Those means are not given by the people of a particular state, not given by the constituents of the legislature, which claim the right to tax them, but by the people of all the states.[39]

Marshall's structural argument here recalls the famous Revolutionary War slogan, "No taxation without representation!" A state government may tax its own citizens because they are represented in the state legislature. But the federal government—the government of *all* Americans—is not represented in the Maryland legislature. And, Marshall concludes, Maryland cannot impose a tax on the unrepresented citizens of other states.

This is a straightforward and powerful structural argument. It infers constitutional meaning from the institutional relationships the document establishes.[40] It relies on no specific text, nor on any particular history or doctrine, but instead points us to the simple necessities—the laws of constitutional physics, perhaps—that govern our political architecture.

D. Doctrinal Argument in *United States v. Morrison*

In the fall of 1994 a woman at Virginia Tech alleged that two members of the varsity football team raped her and bragged about it around campus.[41] After a series of mismanaged internal disciplinary proceedings—which resulted in only nominal punishment—the woman withdrew from school.[42] She then filed suit against both the football players and the college under the Violence Against Women Act of 1994 (VAWA), which provided federal civil remedies for victims of gender motivated violence.[43] The District Court dismissed the claims against the college, and concluded that Congress had no constitutional authority to enact civil remedies contemplated in VAWA.[44] After a hearing en banc, the Fourth Circuit agreed that VAWA was unconstitutional, and the case went up to the Supreme Court.[45]

Chief Justice William Rehnquist's majority opinion first considered VAWA within the doctrinal framework the Court had adopted to evaluate exercises of Congressional power under the Commerce Clause.[46] For almost six decades, that doctrine had been very deferential to Congressional prerogatives, but in 1995 the Court added some new teeth to the old tests. In *United States v. Lopez*, the Court struck down a federal law banning guns in school zones because the connection to interstate commerce was too attenuated.[47] In *Morrison*, Rehnquist worked his way methodically through the new doctrine, which he said had identified four important factors: (1) whether a law regulated "economic activity"; (2) whether a law contains an express "jurisdictional element" limiting its scope to interstate commerce; (3) whether the legislative history "contains express congressional findings" connecting the regulated activity to interstate commerce; and (4) whether the link between the regulated activity and interstate commerce was too attenuated.[48] He then concluded, "With these principles underlying our Commerce Clause jurisprudence as reference points, the proper resolution of [this case] is clear."[49] Violence against women is not economic activity, VAWA contained no jurisdictional element, and the congressional findings were insufficient to establish an unattenuated connection to interstate commerce.[50] Thus, the law exceeded Congress's power under the Commerce Clause.[51]

Rehnquist's opinion is a clear-cut example of doctrinal argument, which aims to derive and apply what Professor Herbert Wechsler has called "neutral principles" to solve constitutional

The skilled doctrinalist must have deft facility with the many tests, categories, formulas, and factors that the Court has created over time and passed down as precedent.

problems.[52] The doctrinal approach, which is the focus of much of the first year law school curriculum, aims to give stability, credibility, and coherence to the common law. The skilled doctrinalist must have deft facility with the many tests, categories, formulas, and factors that the Court has created over time and passed down as precedent. She well understands that arguments which seem to fit within the existing doctrine enjoy a substantial argumentative advantage, one that even has a Latin name: *stare decisis*. This is not to suggest, of course, that doctrine exists as some kind of constitutional algorithm—just plug in the facts and get the "neutral" legal answer. But a good doctrinalist can often make it seem that way, and that is the power of doctrinal argument.

Noaman Ali, 2006

"One person, one vote, one state"

E. Ethical Argument in *Reynolds v. Sims*

In 1961 a group of Alabama voters brought suit in federal District Court alleging that the apportionment of the state legislature violated the Equal Protection Clause of the Fourteenth Amendment.[53] Despite a provision in the state constitution requiring decennial reapportionment, the existing districting scheme still reflected the 1900 census.[54] In the intervening decades population shifts had created significant disparities in electoral influence, so that by 1961 Jefferson County's 600,000 residents had the same number of state Senators as did Lowndes County's 15,471 residents.[55] As a result, Lowndes County residents enjoyed a nearly 40 to 1 representative advantage in the Senate a dilution of voting power that the plaintiffs said amounted to a denial of the equal protection of law. The resulting Supreme Court decision is among the most controversial and important rendered in the second half of the 20th century.

Writing for the majority, Chief Justice Earl Warren repeated, and reemphasized, a powerful ethical argument Justice William Douglas had made just a year before in deciding a similar dispute over state primary elections.[56] In *Gray v. Sanders*, Douglas had written,

> The concept of "we the people" under the Constitution visualizes no preferred class of voters but equality among those who meet the basic qualifications. The idea that every voter is equal to every other voter in his State, when he casts his ballot in favor of one of several competing candidates, underlies many of our decisions. . . . The conception of political equality from the Declaration of Independence, to Lincoln's Gettysburg Address, to the Fifteenth, Seventeenth, and Nineteenth Amendments can mean only one thing—one person, one vote.[57]

Every first year law student learns that the Declaration of Independence, the Gettysburg Address, and even the Constitution's Preamble have no binding legal authority—so why do they appear in the center of an important constitutional argument? The answer is, in a word, *ethos*.[58] These texts are fundamental expressions of the American constitutional and democratic tradition, and it is to this tradition that the *ethical* modality of argument appeals.

It is important to note here that ethical arguments are not "moral" or "natural law" kinds of arguments. Rather, they look to our national traditions and founding commitments. In this sense, the word "ethical" as used here derives not from the Greek *ethike*, but from the Greek *ethos*. Thus, legitimate ethical arguments are rooted in broad and constitutive American values rather than in particularized claims of moral duty or right.[59] And for this reason, an ethical argument's persuasiveness ultimately depends upon how broadly the values it invokes are shared. In the case of *Reynolds v. Sims* (and by extension, *Gray v. Sanders*), the argument was very persuasive indeed, as "one person, one vote" has become the slogan of a generation of American election activists.[60]

Legitimate ethical arguments are rooted in broad and constitutive American values rather than in particularized claims of moral duty or right.

F. Prudential Argument in the "Brandeis Brief"

In 1903, the Oregon legislature limited the number of hours a day women could work at certain trades.[61] Two years later, Curt Muller, who owned a laundry in Portland, challenged the limitation as a violation of the constitutionally protected liberty of contract, and the case eventually made its way to the Supreme Court.[62] National

Consumer League lawyer Florence Kelley and her colleague Josephine Goldmark then hired the famous Boston Progressive lawyer Louis Brandeis to argue their case in Washington.[63] This turned out to be quite a momentous decision, one that Goldmark would later claim "gave a revolutionary new direction to judicial thinking; indeed to the judicial process itself."[64] Brandeis decided to present the Court with a new kind of written argument—a brief not limited to the traditional legal forms, but built instead upon facts and studies about the social conditions the Oregon law was meant to address.[65] The resulting 113-page argument ushered in a new era of appellate advocacy, and the phenomenon known as the "Brandeis Brief" was born.

Brandeis's argument exhibited almost none of the narrative structure that characterized briefs of the time. Instead, he assembled summaries of hundreds of studies and reports from many different states—and even from other democratic nations—regarding the health and safety dangers long hours presented to women workers.[66] Brandeis hoped the data would persuade the Court of the overwhelming rationality of Oregon's exercise of its police powers. In one notable passage under the heading "The General Benefits of Short Hours," he made the following prudential argument:

> History, which has illustrated the deterioration due to long hours, bears witness no less clearly to the regeneration due to the shorter working day. To the individual and to society alike, shorter hours have been a benefit wherever introduced. The married and unmarried working woman is enabled to obtain the decencies of life outside of working hours. With the improvement in home life, the tone of the entire community is raised. Wherever sufficient time has elapsed since the establishment of the shorter working day, the succeeding generation has shown extraordinary improvement in physique and morals.[67]

Brandeis followed up this brief narrative passage with abstracts of a dozen reports generated in Great Britain and various states on the "regenera[tive]" effects shorter hours tend to have on women and the community.[68] Brandeis's intention here—as is true of all of prudential arguments—was to convince the Justices that his position made good sense as a matter of sound constitutional policy.

Given the doctrinal climate, it is perhaps surprising that Brandeis won his case in *Muller*. Just a few years earlier the Court had struck down a maximum hours law for male bakers in the now-infamous *Lochner v. New York*.[69] In the formalistic jurisprudential culture of the time the Justices often held fast to theoretical legal ideals—such as the "liberty of contract"—even when faced with the stark reality of unequal bargaining power.[70] But the Brandeis Brief, with its avalanche of sociological data, seemed temporarily to overwhelm the formalist defenses and persuade the Court that, at least in the case of women laundry workers, state regulation of the workplace might be good policy. The years following *Muller* were a "golden age of Brandeis briefs," as lawyers tried to emulate the future Supreme Court Justice.[71] And, although the Brandeis model has evolved a great deal since 1908, prudential argument remains a vital and fundamental part of our constitutional practice.

Conclusion

My intention here has been to provide a brief primer on the interpretive norms—what Philip Bobbitt has called the "modalities"—that govern legitimate constitutional argument. Because these norms arise from actual arguments, I have chosen to illustrate them using examples drawn from the constitutional canon. While Bobbitt has argued, and I agree, that each of these modalities represents an independent and equal form of argument, there are those who would argue in favor of some kind of modal ranking—i.e. all things being equal, a textualist argument should trump a doctrinal argument.[72] While such a ranking might be possible if the *practice itself* resolutely adopted it, all of the efforts I have seen on this point simply reflect their authors' preferred forms of argument. But this observation itself raises a final, and I think very important, point. Judges, too, have modal preferences. There are those (such as Justice Antonin Scalia, perhaps) who respond to historical arguments; some (such as Chief Justice John Roberts) seem drawn to doctrinal arguments; while still others (such as Justice Steven Breyer) prefer prudential arguments. It is, I suggest, much more productive to understand judges' preconceptions along these lines than simply to classify them as "liberal" or "conservative." By this I mean that the lawyer who does a thorough modal assessment of both her case *and* the Court to whom she must present will always be better prepared for constitutional argument. And, as I have hinted in opening, the Constitution itself is really nothing more than this ongoing debate about the meaning of our founding commitments.

> The Constitution itself is really nothing more than this ongoing debate about the meaning of our founding commitments.

Now Professor Ian Gallacher shows us how three methods of interpretation might apply in a different context—the conducting of a symphony. "Hearing" the familiar arguments made in a new context can help us better understand their application in legal argument.

Excerpt from

Ian Gallacher, *Conducting the Constitution: Justice Scalia, Textualism, and the Eroica Symphony*
9 Vand. J. Entertainment & Tech. Law 301 (2006)

The more one studies the debate surrounding modes of Constitutional interpretation, the more dismaying the experience becomes. Lurking close to the surface of the coded discourse of Constitutional scholars is the aggressive tone and cultural dynamic of the playground. Reduced to its essence, the substance of the debate seems more akin to a Monty Python sketch than to the scholarly exchange of ideas one would hope for in this area.

Justice Scalia has adopted a particularly strident tone for those who disagree with him: at a recent meeting of the Federalist Society, Justice Scalia made a statement to the effect that one would have to be an idiot to believe in a "Living Constitution."[73] No clearer example of the recess rhetoric into which this important debate can so quickly slide is necessary, and there is no better illustration of why scholars need to step back from this *ad hominem* abyss and take a more dispassionate view of the interpretative techniques they employ to understand the Constitution.

One way to accomplish this is to look beyond the law to see how others tackle similar questions of interpretation. This perhaps allows for a less passionate inquiry into the interpretative process stripped of the life-changing outcomes of doctrinal orthodoxy. Without being so concerned about the end result, scholars might be able to make more reasoned conclusions about the means used to achieve that result. . . . [Music] offers a more neutral and potentially helpful forum. . . .

The goal of this article is a very modest one: to use one piece of music, the first movement of Beethoven's *Eroica* symphony, to consider how legal scholars, using the doctrinal principles they have developed to interpret the Constitution, would interpret the piece as conductors. . . . [The] article focuses most of its attention on Justice Scalia and his "textualist" approach to interpretation. Justice Scalia's relationship with the Constitution is analogous to that of a conductor of an orchestral score: he is the principal advocate for a single theory of Constitutional interpretation, and he is a Supreme Court Justice who has put his interpretative theory into practice. Both conductor and Justice must approach the text with an interpretative theory in mind and then apply that theory in a specific context that equates to a "performance." In particular, Justice Scalia's conviction that a textualist approach to Constitutional interpretation is the only coherent and legitimate approach . . . lends itself to examination by applying it to interpretation of a document from a different field. The benefits and problems of a textualist approach might stand out in clearer relief when projected against a musical rather than a legal background. . . .

Here the article introduces the three interpretive theories it will explore: the "textualist" approach; the "intentionalist" approach; and the "contextualist" approach. (Don't try to match these terms to Bobbitt's terms. They have slightly different meanings here.)

A. Textualism

In a sense, the name of this approach is its own description; textualism requires a devotion to the text above all other considerations. Justice Scalia [is] the most influential of textualists. . . . An unabashedly formalist approach to interpretation, textualism has several distinct features. It eschews the use of canons of construction and legislative history. Textualism also rejects the notion of a "flexible" Constitution in favor of restraining interpretation to the limited range of meanings associated with the words that comprise the text. Any interpretation going beyond the text's meaning is impermissible.

B. Intentionalism

I use this term to mean the familiar strategy wherein the interpreter seeks to glean the text's meaning as imparted by its creator or creators. Although the text in question might be the primary tool used to derive this meaning, the intentionalist interpreter can (and often does) go outside of the text, usually to look at the legislative history surrounding the text's creation, in order to fully understand the text's original meaning.

C. Contextualism

Contextualism is the term I use to describe the belief that a Constitution is a living document, and that its meaning must be derived, in part, from the context within which the text is being interpreted. For a contextualist, a text's meaning is derived from its content but is informed by the values of contemporary society. . . .

Musical Interpretation

Interpretative practices in the musical world are similar to methods of Constitutional interpretation, although the political labels one might attach to proponents of the various schools are reversed. The "conservatives" of the musical world are the contextualists, who believe that musical interpretation is an evolving issue and that music should be interpreted based on contemporary interpretative criteria. By contrast, the "radicals" of the musical world are the textualists who believe in devotion to the written note and to reproducing the written score as faithfully as possible.

A. Musical Contextualism

Musical contextualists are musicians who interpret music without regard to the performance practices or conventions of the time in which the music was written and instead offer an idiosyncratic response to the music. In essence, musical contextualists[74] encourage the audience to experience the musician's personal reaction to the musical text. This is not to say that the musical contextualist's performance is unthinking or anti-intellectual. To the contrary, a contextualist performance can be the subtly nuanced product of intense textual analysis and careful rehearsal designed to clarify the musician's intentions. But a contextualist performance is, at its heart, a performance of the musician's interpretation of the work, not a strict adherence to the soundworld[75] that the composer might have had in mind when the piece was written.

B. Musical Textualism

Standing in direct contrast to the contextualist approach is the musical textualist approach. Under this approach, the composer's soundworld is very much an element of the performance. Musical textualist performances are characterized by their attention to the performing styles and conditions that prevailed at the time that the musical text was written. Such performances usually use instruments of the time or modern recreations of those instruments.

Textualist performances are not identical, because musicians are almost always instrumentalists first and scholars second, and they will often disagree as to the meaning of the historical record. While musical textualist performances will differ in detail and sound, however, they are united in the attention they pay to the historical record and the sound made by instruments of the piece's composition period.

C. Musical Intentionalists

Located somewhere on the continuum between the polar opposites of musical contextualists and textualists are the intentionalists. These are musicians who take the printed score as their principal point of departure but who will countenance changes to the text to clarify what they believe to be the composer's intentions. I believe that musical intentionalists make up the majority of contemporary performers.

Perhaps the most concise statement of intentionalist principles comes from the conductor Erich Leinsdorf; "1. Great composers knew what they wanted. 2. The interpreter must have the means at his disposal to grasp the composers' intentions. 3. Music must be read with knowledge and imagination—without necessarily believing every note and word that is printed.[76] Intentionalist musicians will typically use contemporary instruments, but will be influenced, to some degree, by scholarship about performance practice.

Putting Theory into Practice

Having laid out the principal themes, the focus of this article will now shift to examinations of some interpretative problems presented by the first movement of the *Eroica* symphony and how Justice Scalia, as a textualist conductor, would employ his doctrinal philosophy to solve those problems.

This is not a simple process; conductors face an almost incalculable number of decisions over the course of a movement as long as this, and any attempt to discuss each of these possible decisions would bog this discussion down irretrievably. Rather than attempt this impossible task, this article will consider three principal interpretative elements—pitch, tempo, and textual error—as well as the particular problems raised by the *Eroica*'s first movement coda. Although this approach will leave numerous issues untouched, it should provide an insight into the way legal interpretative doctrines can produce both expected and unexpected results when applied to musical performance.

A. Pitch

The *Eroica* symphony is in E♭ major. It begins with a short but arresting introduction of two E♭ major chords, played *forte* [loud] by the entire orchestra, before the first subject begins with a *piano* [soft] theme played by the cellos that outlines an E♭ major triad:[77]

This is where the first problem arises: before the orchestra plays a single note, the conductor has to decide which E♭ the orchestra should play. This may, at first impression, appear to be a non-issue. Instrumentalists have a limited number of ways to play a note. While each way might produce a slightly different timbre and therefore might be the subject of discussion during rehearsal, an E♭ seems to be an E♭.

Which E♭ the orchestra should play, however, is a more nuanced question than this, and the answer depends on the A to which the orchestra has tuned. The current standard A was set by the International Standards Organization ("ISO") as 440 Herz [*sic*] ("Hz") in 1955.[78] Many contemporary orchestras, however, prefer the brighter sound given by an A of 441 Hz or even 442 Hz. The contextualist would likely be unperturbed by this, and would accept whatever A is on offer or, as is the case in some American orchestras, is contractually required.

But, the intentionalist and textualist would both have to consider the pitch problem more carefully. To accurately predict Justice Scalia's pitch choice, one must look at the original text and try to understand what a composer meant by E♭ in 1804 Vienna (the year and place in which *Eroica* was written). A collection of tuning forks from the early Nineteenth Century provides proof that in 1810 the London Philharmonic Society, as well as opera houses in Dresden, Berlin, and Paris, were all using an A that was "a significant portion of a semitone lower" than the contemporary 440 Hz standard. Although Vienna seems to have welcomed a brighter, higher sound than other cities, and while this was a period of rapid technological change which allowed a brighter tone and a sharper pitch, it is likely that the Viennese E♭ was still substantially flatter than the note recognized as E♭ today.

In selecting a pitch for his performance, Justice Scalia would likely look to what the text could reasonably be understood to mean, rather than what it was intended to mean. In other words, he would look to the "semantic intention" rather than the "original intention." To clarify this position, Justice Scalia has used as an example the meaning of the Eighth Amendment's "cruel and unusual" language.[79] In that context, he concluded that the words "cruel and unusual" abstract "the existing society's assessment of what is cruel" rather than "whatever may be considered cruel from one generation to the next."[80] Although this explains his disdain for the contextualist approach, the distinction between semantic and original intention is less clear. Also unclear is how a semantic intention can be determined without an inquiry, as here, into what may be called the legislative history of the meaning of E♭ to 1804 Viennese musical society.

Either way, we can safely conclude that Justice Scalia would conduct *Eroica* in what Nineteenth Century Vienna would assess E♭ major to mean, rather than what E♭ major has come to mean today. This result condemns Justice Scalia to having to evaluate the pitch information for every piece he conducts, just as he should consider every statute as meaning what the words meant when chosen by the legislators at the time of drafting. This is the only result consistent with a textualist philosophy.

B. Tempo

Now, the orchestra can play the *Eroica*'s first E♭ major chord, which sounds to contemporary ears like a slightly sharp D major chord. Before the orchestra plays the second chord, the conductor must decide at what tempo the movement will be played. This determination is somewhat more complicated than the pitch issue that was just resolved.

The text itself gives us three clues: 1) the time words "*Allegro con brio*," 2) the metronomic marking of the dotted half note = 60 (quarter note = 180), and 3) a theme that has a swinging, one beat to a measure feel, with some faster rhythmic figures later in the movement:

However, each of these clues presents additional problems. The words *"allegro con brio"* translate as "fast, with energy." This is not the most illuminating instruction, and it is one that, like much of the Constitution's text, is open to a substantial amount of interpretation. The concept of "fast" is as variable from person to person as the concept of how much process is "due," and "energy" is a term that is more helpful in determining expression than tempo.

The metronome marking is, on its face, more helpful. Unlike pitch, the number of beats per minute and the means of measuring them have not changed since the Nineteenth Century. A metronome marking appears to give us a scientific designation of tempo. However, Beethoven first published the metronome markings to his symphonies in 1817, thirteen years after *Eroica* was first performed. This makes the metronome markings akin to an amendment of the original text.

In fact, the metronome marking complicates rather than simplifies the tempo problem because it designates a very fast tempo, leading some to believe that Beethoven could not have intended the tempos suggested by the metronome markings that he supplied. Yet scholars who have studied the issue have concluded that the metronome markings for *Eroica* are consistent with the markings Beethoven gave for other music he wrote. Scholars have also established that Beethoven had a taste for very fast tempos that was shared by his contemporaries. . . .

The internal evidence, suggested by the speed of the written notes and an orchestra's actual ability to play them at or close to the speed indicated in the movement's passages, was the most important tempo clue for performers in Beethoven's time. And some of *Eroica*'s rapid rhythmic figures can sound rushed to our ears when taken close to Beethoven's designated metronome mark. In fact, very few performers—even those striving to make their performances as historically accurate as possible—actually reach and sustain a tempo of quarter note = 180. An analysis by Eric Grunin of nearly 350 recorded performances of *Eroica* shows only one performance, conducted by Hermann Scherchen in 1958, as having sustained a tempo anywhere close to that metronome mark, at quarter note = 174.6.[81]

For Justice Scalia, however, the internal evidence is likely unhelpful: he would reject as irrelevant any insight into the composer's "intent." Just as Beethoven amended his symphony by adding the metronome marking later, the framers of the Constitution amended their document as well. Once adopted, those amendments must receive the textualist treatment. Justice Scalia's *Eroica* would presumably be very fast.

C. Mistakes

It would be presumptuous to assert that Beethoven made "mistakes" in anything he wrote. But mistakes could and did occur in the copying of original holographic manuscripts. These errors can become deeply entrenched in a performance tradition once they are printed. One of a conductor's principal jobs is finding and correcting these mistakes when they occur. The *Eroica* score provides an interesting example of a potential misprint.

The article here provides an example of a possible mistake in the *Eroica* score.

Accepting [this possible mistake] for the purpose of argument, the path for the intentionalist and the contextualist conductor seems clear. The printed work fails to represent Beethoven's original intention and appears to be a misprint. Both the intentionalist and the contextualist would rewrite [it].

The textualist's position seems equally clear. A textualist would likely ignore the evidence of internal inconsistency from the exposition and disregard [the] subjective and contextualist contention that the note "can hardly be correct." In short, Justice Scalia and other textualists should play the bass E♭ as written in the text.

While Justice Scalia claims to be a textualist and a formalist, however, he denies that he is a literalist.[82] Therefore, he will accept the correction of "scrivener's errors."[83] Justice Scalia notes that "where on the very face of the statute it is clear to the reader that a mistake of expression (rather than of legislative wisdom) has been made[,] . . . it [is] not contrary to sound principles of interpretation . . . to give the totality of context precedence over a single word."[84]

This seems a strange position for a textualist to take. Either the text should be taken at face value or it should not. But Justice Scalia is willing to go even further by acknowledging that some words and phrases in a text should be given "expansive, rather than narrow, interpretation[s]."[85] For example, he argues that the First Amendment's "freedom of speech" and "freedom of the press" should include within them the concept of handwritten notes, even though these are neither spoken nor printed words, and the First Amendment makes no mention of them.[86] The concept of handwritten words, apparently, inheres in the limited range of meaning of the word "speech," even though the word's dictionary meanings suggest otherwise.

This interstitial textualism, where one must look in the gaps between definitions to ascertain a word's complete meaning, seems strangely at odds with a textualist philosophy. This has not gone unnoticed by Ronald Dworkin, who argues that a secret inten-tionalism must lie at the heart of Scalian textualism.[87] Putting aside any qualms, Justice Scalia would change the double bass part . . . , making it align musically with the bassoon line. Thus, in a rare moment of intellectual alignment, all three interpretative doctrines agree that this is the correct result.

But the strange results are not over. Justice Scalia's textualist phi-losophy has other troubling anomalies, exposed by the last conduct-ing problem I have picked from the many posed by *Eroica*'s first movement—one of the most celebrated and controversial conduct-ing problems in the symphonic canon—the coda.

D. Coda

By the time of the first movement coda [concluding section], every listener to the piece is familiar with the triadic principal theme of the movement, given again here for comparative purposes:

In the coda, Beethoven alters the contours of the theme to give it an appropriately peroratory [recapitulating the principal themes] effect:

The new form of the theme is first played *piano* [softly] by the horn, then by the first violins, and then again in the lower strings, this time with a *crescendo* [increased volume]. Next, it is played *forte* [loudly] in the winds and, most prominently, by the trumpets:

The problem is that the trumpets—the loudest of the instru-ments playing this version of the theme—do not actually play the entire theme. Rather, they only play two and two-thirds measures of the theme before joining the non-theme-playing instruments in a harmonizing [recurring fragment of melody]

The simple reason for this is that the trumpet for which Beethoven wrote could not comfortably reach the high B♭ above the staff, written as a G, that is necessary to play the new version of the theme. Faced with this technical problem, Beethoven probably had the trumpets play as much of the line as they could and then dropped them into the background.

Contemporary trumpets can play this high B♭ with little difficulty. . . . This change to the high B♭ transforms the trumpet line and the entire texture of the sound at this point in the coda:

[For over 100 years, the tradition has been to rewrite the trumpet part.] These are classic espousals of the contextualist's "living document" rationale: what once was impossible is now possible, and since it is better this way we should do it. It is possible to justify the rewrite on intentionalist grounds as well: Beethoven probably intended the line to go up, as suggested by the rest of the orchestration. The only thing preventing Beethoven from including the trumpet line with the other instruments playing the melody appears to have been the technical limitation placed on him by the trumpet's design. Under this rationale, contemporary technology allows conductors and performers to restore Beethoven's original intent, making the altered version more "original," in a way, than what Beethoven actually wrote. . . .

This presents an interesting problem for the doctrinal textualist like Justice Scalia. The written text itself is clear and unambiguous. The trumpet line literally goes down, not up. But Justice Scalia, as we have seen, is not a literalist—he will bend a little if a word or a phrase can be fairly interpreted as including a non-articulated meaning. Just as "speech" can, in his view, encompass handwritten words, the *Eroica* theme can be interpreted to encompass a note that only technology prevented Beethoven from writing. The First Amendment can be extended to encompass technologies that did not exist in the 1790s.[88] Perhaps this is no different.

Or perhaps this goes too far. Perhaps this is merely a justification for evolutionary interpretation, something a textualist like Justice Scalia cannot permit. The tradition of rewriting the trumpet line is well established, and Justice Scalia is willing to accept another "pragmatic exception" to his core textualist principles to allow for *stare decisis*.[89] While there is no direct doctrinal musical equivalent to the *stare decisis* doctrine, it does not seem too far a stretch to see Justice Scalia the conductor, perhaps grudgingly, accepting this rewrite as something that is well-founded "beyond doubt." This assumes, of course, that he has made a pitch decision that allows for the inclusion of trumpets of sufficiently recent vintage to allow them to play the high B♭.

What we are left with is the strange and slightly unsettling image of Justice Scalia, the radical conductor, thumbing his nose at the conservative musical establishment by leading a rendition of *Eroica* that is faster and flatter than we are used to hearing and is likely performed with period instruments. . . . This leads to a rendition with some puzzling textual deviations that are arguably more rooted in an intentionalist or even contextualist approach than a textualist should be willing to accept. . . . How Justice Scalia would respond to such a performance, were he to hear it, is an interesting question to ponder.

IV. Conclusion

What do we, as lawyers, learn from this brief excursion into a parallel interpretative universe? Perhaps we learn nothing more than the comforting knowledge that we are not alone. Other disciplines have interpretative problems with which they wrestle, and at least musicians have devised some strategies for resolving those problems that map directly onto the strategies lawyers and judges have adopted. A problem shared is, if nothing else, a problem shared.

Perhaps, though, looking at musical interpretation might allow a discussion about the appropriateness of different approaches to textual interpretation without a polarizing debate about social issues affected by these approaches' applications to Constitutional decisions. Being able to talk about the pitfalls and benefits of textualism, contextualism, and intentionalism without having to consider abortion, school prayer, or any of the other current controversies could be both constructive and refreshing. . . .

Key Concepts

Textual argument (Bobbitt's use of the term)
Historical argument (intentionalism) (Bobbitt's use of the term)

Structural argument (Bobbitt's use of the term)
Doctrinal argument (Bobbitt's use of the term)
Ethical argument (Bobbitt's use of the term)
Prudential argument (contextualism) (Bobbitt's use of the term)

Discussion Questions

1. Is there one "right" method of constitutional interpretation? If so, what is it and why? If not, why not? How can we use multiple and potentially conflicting methods in deciding a particular constitutional issue?
2. What are the main strengths and weaknesses of each method of interpretation?
3. What point(s) can we take from the exercise of looking at three of these methods in the context of deciding how to interpret a piece of classical music? What did you learn from Professor Gallacher's exploration?

Endnotes

1. *See, e.g.*, Bertrand Russell, *Vagueness*, 1 Australasian J. of Psych. & Phil. 84 (1923) (giving an introductory overview of the problem); Timothy Williamson, *Vagueness* (Routledge 1994) (surveying the subject).

2. Consider, for example, David Lewis's assessment of the complications that the vague kinds of language often used in ordinary conversation can present to the semantic logician:

> If Fred is a borderline case of baldness, the sentence "Fred is bald" may have no determinate truth-value. Whether it is true depends on where you draw the line. Relative to some perfectly reasonable ways of drawing a precise boundary between bald and not-bald, the sentence is true. Relative to other delineations, no less reasonable, it is false. Nothing in our use of language makes one of these delineations right and all others wrong. We cannot pick a delineation once and for all (not if we are interested in ordinary language), but must consider the entire range of reasonable delineations.

David Lewis, *Scorekeeping in a Language Game*, in *Philosophical Papers* v.1, 233, 244 (1983).

3. One might think, as a counterexample, of the word "kilogram," which refers to the mass of an actual metal cylinder in Paris. We could, in theory, verify uses of the word "kilogram" against the mass of that cylinder. There is, of course, no such empirical ideal for the phrase "equal protection."

4. For a thorough account of language in these terms, see Ludwig Wittgenstein, *Philosophical Investigations* 1-60 (3d ed., G.E.M. Anscombe trans., Wiley-Blackwell 1958).

5. For an account along these lines, see Lawrence Solum, *Semantic Originalism* . . .

6. Philip Bobbitt, *Constitutional Fate: Theory of the Constitution* (Oxford U. Press 1982).

7. Philip Bobbitt, *Constitutional Interpretation* 12-13 (Basil Blackwell 1991) (emphasis added).

8. *Youngstown Sheet & Tube Co. v. Sawyer*, 343 U.S. 579, 582 (1952).

9. *Id.* at 583.

10. *Id.*

11. *Id.*

12. *Id.*

13. Alan Westin, *The Anatomy of a Constitutional Law Case:* Youngstown Sheet & Tube Co. v. Sawyer 94 (Columbia U. Press 1990).

14. *Youngstown Sheet & Tube Co.*, 343 U.S at 584.

15. *Id.*

16. CBS News Special (Dec. 3, 1968), transcribed in *Justice Black and the Bill of Rights*, 9 S.W. L. Rev. 937, 940 (1977).

17. *Youngstown Sheet & Tube Co.*, 343 U.S. 585.

18. *Id*. at 586.

19. *Id*. at 587-588.

20. *See id*. at 635-640 (Jackson, J., concurring).

21. Complaint at 2-6, *Parker v. District of Columbia*, 311 F. Supp. 2d 103 (D.D.C. 2004) (No. 03-CV-0213-EGS, February 10, 2003).

22. *Id*. at 2-3.

23. *Id*. at 3.

24. *Id*. at 8.

25. *District of Columbia v. Heller*, 554 U.S. 570, 576 (2008).

26. *Id*.

27. U.S. Const. amend II (1791).

28. *Heller*, 554 U.S. at 581-610.

29. *Id*. at 593-594 (citations omitted).

30. *Id*. at 655 (Stevens, J., dissenting).

31. George Tindall & David Shi, *America: A Narrative History* 330-332 (4th ed., 1984).

32. *Id*. at 393.

33. *Id*.

34. *McCulloch v. Maryland*, 17 U.S. (4 Wheat.) 316, 319 (1819).

35. *Id*. at 318.

36. *Id*. at 317.

37. *Id*. at 408-409. The careful reader will recall that, contrary to modern mythology, Marshall did not rely on the text of the "necessary and proper clause"; he addressed that language only to refute Maryland's claim that the clause *limited* federal power. In so doing, he borrowed almost verbatim from Hamilton's defense of the original bank. Tindall & Shi, *supra* note 31, at 331-332.

38. *McCulloch*, 17 U.S. (Wheat.) at 428.

39. *Id*. at 428-429.

40. For the best treatment of structural argument, including an assessment of *McCulloch* in these terms, *see* Charles L. Black, Jr., *Structure and Relationship in Constitutional Law* 14-15 (La. St. U. Press 1969).

41. *United States v. Morrison*, 529 U.S. 598, 602-604 (2000).

42. *Id*. at 603-604.

43. *Id*. at 604.

44. *Id*.

45. *Id*. at 605.

46. *Id*. at 607.

47. *United States v. Lopez*, 514 U.S. 549, 551 (1995).

48. *Morrison*, 529 U.S. at 610-612.

49. *Id*. at 613.

50. *Id*. at 613-617.

51. *Id*. at 617.

52. Herbert Wechsler, *Toward Neutral Principles of Constitutional Law*, 73 Harv. L. Rev. 1 (1959).

53. *Reynolds v. Sims*, 377 U.S. 533, 536 (1964).

54. *Id*. at 540.

55. *Id*. at 546.

56. *Id*. at 557-558 (quoting *Gray v. Sanders*, 372 U.S. 368, 380-381 (1963)).

57. *Gray v. Sanders*, 372 U.S. 368, 380-381 (1963).

58. Some of these ideas first appeared in Ian Bartrum, *The Constitutional Canon as Argumentative Metonymy*, 18 Wm. & Mary Bill of Rts. J. 327, 368-369 (2009).

59. For a seminal discussion of this distinction in terms of "public" and "nonpublic" reasoning, see John Rawls, *Political Liberalism* 213-217 (1993).

60. In fairness, the slogan existed long before the Court adopted it. Indeed, the phrase's broad popularity helps explain its power in the ethical form of argument.

61. Nancy Woloch, Muller v. Oregon: *A Brief History with Documents* 21 (1996). Some of the material in this section first appeared in Ian Bartrum, *Metaphors and Modalities: Meditations on Bobbitt's Theory of the Constitution*, 17 Wm. & Mary Bill of Rts. J. 257 (2008).

62. *Muller v. Oregon*, 208 U.S. 412, 416 (1908).

63. Woloch, *supra* note 61, at 23.

64. *Id.*

65. *Id.*

66. Louis Brandeis, *Brief for the Defendant in Error in* Muller, *208 U.S. at 412, reprinted in* 16 *Landmark Briefs and Arguments of the Supreme Court of the United States* 63 (Philip B. Kurland & Gerhard Casper eds., University Publications of America 1975).

67. *Id.* at 120.

68. *Id.*

69. *Lochner v. New York*, 198 U.S. 45, 57 (1905).

70. Bartrum, *Metonymy, supra* note 58, at 358.

71. Woloch, *supra* note 61, at 41.

72. For a particularly thoughtful attempt at such a ranking, see Richard Fallon, *A Constructivist Coherence Theory of Constitutional Interpretation*, 100 Harv. L. Rev. 1189 (1987).

73. Justice Scalia made this comment at a meeting of the Federalist Society. . . . Associated Press, *Scalia Raps 'Living Constitution,'* Feb. 14, 2006, *available at* http://www.cbsnews.com/stories/2006/02/14/supremcourt/main1315619.shtml   (last visited March 8, 2006). . . .

74. I use this term here to balance my use of contextualism in a legal context. It is not a term that would be familiar to musicians.

75. I use the term "soundworld" here to capture a myriad of technical performance details, such as pitch, instrument choice, articulation, and so on, that collectively make up the sound of the music.

76. Erich Leinsdorf, *The Composer's Advocate: A Radical Orthodoxy for Musicians*, at viii (Yale U. Press 1981).

77. Ludwig Van Beethoven, *Symphony No. 3 in E Flat Major (Eroica)*, measures 1-7 (Max Unger ed., Ernst Eulenberg 1936 [hereinafter *Eroica*]. [Pinpoint citations to subsequent excerpts from the musical score will be omitted.]

78. Mark Lindley et al., *Pitch*, in 14 *The New Grove Dictionary of Music and Musicians* 779, 785 (Grove's Dictionaries of Music Inc. 1980).

79. Antonin Scalia, *A Matter of Interpretation: Federal Courts and the Law* 145 (Princeton U. Press 1997).

80. *Id.*

81. Eric   Grunin,   *An   Eroica   Project*,   http://www.grunin.com/eroica/index.htm ?page=credits.htm (last visited Dec. 15, 2006). . . .

82. *See* Scalia, *supra* note 79, at 38.

83. *Id.*

84. *Id.*

85. *Id.* at 37-38.

86. *Id.*

87. Ronald Dworkin, *Comment* in Scalia, *supra* note 79, at 16. . . .

88. *See* Scalia, *supra* note 79, at 45 (describing the Supreme Court's application of the First Amendment's "freedom of speech" guarantee "to new technologies that did not exist when the guarantee was created—to sound trucks, or to government-licensed over-the-air television" by following "the trajectory of the First Amendment, so to speak, to determine what it requires . . .").

89. *Id.* at 140.

Our Frames

The prior two chapters gave us summaries of the main schools of legal theory and methods of constitutional interpretation. But the debates among all these camps assume that we agree on *what* we're talking about—on what the issue is. As the chapters in this section on "frames" will show, however, the most important disagreement might not be about which school of jurisprudence or constitutional interpretation to use but rather on the foundational question, *What is the issue?* The chapters in this section (on categories, metaphor, and storytelling) will help us with that foundational question. When you finish reading these chapters, you may suspect that in legal argument, framing is more important than forms of reasoning, legal theories, methods of constitutional interpretation, or anything else.

15. *Categories*

When we talk about, study, and write about law, we are dealing with categories. Think about that idea a little. Probably one of the first things you learned in law school was the West Key numbering system. Among your courses, you took contracts, torts, and property. You probably covered the statute of frauds in both contracts and property, but you may have noticed some differences. You probably covered nuisance and trespass in both torts and property, but again, you may have noticed some differences. In your property course, you may have learned that a court decided which spectator owned a home run ball hit by Barry Bonds[1] by likening it to the wild fox in *Pierson v. Post*.[2] Consider the recent case of *Citizens United*.[3] We can probably all agree that the case is within the category of the law of free speech, but was the issue one of protecting the free speech rights of corporations and labor unions, or was it about protecting the free speech of human beings? Your answer to that question probably determines your opinion about how the case should have been decided.

These are just a few examples of the effects of categories in law. As the first reading shows, at least as long ago as 1930, one of the giants of American jurisprudence pointed out the critical importance of categories. Scholars were slow to continue the analysis, but good lawyers have innately known that changing the category can significantly change the results. In recent years, scholars like the author of our second reading have been doing a much better job of investigating how this works. That second reading introduces the topic of metaphor and its subset of study: categories.

Excerpt from
Karl N. Llewellyn, *A Realistic Jurisprudence— The Next Step*
30 Colum. L. Rev. 431, 453-454 (1930)

Like rules, concepts are not to be eliminated; it cannot be done. Behavior is too heterogeneous to be dealt with except after some artificial ordering. . . . Nor can thought go on without categories.

A realistic approach would, however, . . . [recognize] that to classify is to disturb. It is to build emphases, to create stresses, which obscure some of the data under observation and give fictitious value to others. . . . [A] realistic approach to any new problem would begin

by skepticism as to the adequacy of the *received* categories for ordering the phenomena effectively toward a solution of the new problem.
It is quite possible that the received categories as they already stand
are perfect for the purpose. It is, however, altogether unlikely....

... [A] realistic approach rests on the observation that
categories ... tend to take on an appearance of solidity, reality
and inherent value which has no foundation in experience. More
than this ... they tend, once they have entered into the organization
of thinking, both to suggest the presence of corresponding data
when these data are not in fact present, and to twist any fresh observation of data into conformity with the terms of the categories....
The [best approach would be to ask whether] the data are still present *in the form suggested by the category-name*. This slows up thinking. But it makes for results which mean[] something when one gets
them.

Excerpt from
Mark L. Johnson, *Mind, Metaphor, and Law*
58 Mercer L. Rev. 845 (2007)

Change, as John Dewey observed, is a basic fact of human experience.
We are temporal creatures, and the situations we find ourselves in,
the situations that make up the fabric of our lives, are always evolving
and developing. The omnipresence of change throughout all human
experience thus creates a fundamental problem for law, namely, how
can law preserve its integrity over time, while managing to address
the newly emerging circumstances that continually arise throughout
our history? If, following one extreme, we think of law as fixed, static,
and univocal in its content, then law runs the risk of losing its relevance to the new conditions and problems that face us each day.
However, the opposite extreme—that law is completely malleable—is
equally untenable, for that would make law nothing more than a tool
of those in power. Our problem, therefore, is how law can be both
stable and capable of growth.

[P]art of the answer to this foundational question is beginning to
emerge from recent research in the cognitive sciences. Human law
is a many-splendored creation of the human mind, that is, of human
understanding and reasoning. The primary business of the cognitive
sciences is to study empirically how the mind works. Therefore, cognitive science ought to give us insight into the nature of legal concepts and legal reasoning.[4] ...

I. The Need for a Cognitive Science of Law

[T]hings have changed dramatically over the past two decades in
light of the emergence of a second generation of cognitive science,

which has called into question virtually all of the major assumptions of the first-generation paradigm. Instead of seeing the mind as a disembodied computer program, the newer research reveals that our conceptualization and reasoning are grounded in our bodily experience and shaped primarily by patterns of perception and action.[5] There is a logic of our bodily experience that is imaginatively appropriated in defining our abstract concepts and reasoning with them. Imaginative processes of this sort depend on the nature of our bodies, our brains, and the patterns of our interactions with our environment. Imagination—which is the soul of human thinking—is therefore constrained and orderly, even though it can be flexible and creative in response to novel situations.

This new cognitive science of the embodied mind is predicated on the assumption that there is no human conceptualization or reasoning without a functioning human brain, which operates a living human body that is continually engaging environments that are at once physical, social, cultural, economic, moral, legal, gendered, and racialized. Our embodiment shapes both what and how we experience, think, mean, imagine, reason, and communicate. This claim is a bold one, and it directly challenges our received folk wisdom that what we call "mind" and "body" are somehow two fundamentally different kinds of entities. From a philosophical point of view, one of the hardest tasks you'll ever face is coming to grips with the fact of your embodiment because this fact requires a serious rethinking of the nature of mind, thought, and language. What makes this task so very difficult is the omnipresent idea of disembodied mind and thought that leaves its traces everywhere we turn, from claims about pure logical form, to pure concepts, to ideas of non-corporeal thought, to spectator views of knowledge, to correspondence theories of truth.

What is at stake here? Why should any of this matter? My answer is this:

1. A disembodied view of mind is often used to support a literalist and objectivist view of thought, concepts, and reason.
2. On the objectivist view, concepts are believed to have strict, fixed boundaries defined by necessary and sufficient conditions. This is what George Lakoff calls the "classical theory" of categories, according to which any concept is allegedly demarcated by a particular unique set of features that jointly identify some entity as falling under a specific concept.[6]
3. An objectivist/literalist paradigm supports a view of moral and legal reasoning as the application of literally-defined objective categories to situations in an all-or-nothing fashion, based on fixed criteria.

4. This objectivist/literalist theory is based on an empirically false view of cognition, mind, and language. It presupposes a dangerously false view of what a person is and how the mind works.

5. As a result, empirical research on the nature of cognition should have important implications for our understanding of moral and legal concepts and reasoning.

II. Where Does Meaning Come From?

If you think, as I do, that there is no mind without a body—a body in continuous interaction with ever-changing environments—then you've got to explain how this bodily activity gives rise to all our glorious abstract thoughts and symbolic interactions. I want to give a sketch of my version of certain key parts of this massive story of embodied meaning and thought and then suggest how this new view bears on our understanding of legal reasoning.

Second generation cognitive science has been developing a bold new theory of the bodily basis of meaning, imagination, and reason. Here, I can focus only on three of the most important aspects of human cognition that have potentially profound implications for law:

- Radially structured categories that manifest prototypicality effects.
- Image schemas, as a basis for embodied meaning and logical inference.
- Conceptual metaphors, by which we extend embodied meaning into our abstract conceptualization and reasoning.

III. Radial Categories and Prototypicality Effects

The classical theory of categories, which is the default view held by nearly everyone in our culture, is that categories have a fixed, stable, and objective structure. In this view, a concept like "dog" is believed to be defined by a set of features an object must possess to be that particular type of thing we call a dog. If some object has those features, then it is a dog, and not otherwise. Notice that assuming this view of concepts leads us to a very specific view of moral and legal reasoning. If a principle, rule, or law consists of a set of classically structured concepts, then that law would apply in a certain clear fashion solely to those situations where the defining conditions for the concepts were satisfied in our experience. . . . This classical objectivist view of categories, if it were true, would make law a neat little process of strict rule application. How a legal concept might grow without completely redefining the concept, and how legal judgment might change in a rational, stable manner, could never be explained using this view. . . .

Contrary to the classical objectivist view, there is now a massive and steadily growing body of empirical evidence supporting the proposition that large parts of human conceptualization and reasoning do not work in the way the classical theory requires. What the evidence shows is that many of our most basic concepts, from those for simple objects like cups and beds, all the way to abstract concepts in morality, politics, science, religion, and law, have complicated internal radial structures and exhibit what are known as "prototypicality effects."[7]

To illustrate my point about this complex structure of concepts, I want to tell an extremely sad story. Something awful happened this past summer. You know what I'm referring to, right? I'm talking about the planet Pluto, which—I can hardly utter the words—is now *not* a planet. . . . [T]hose planetary activists decided to ignore the obvious essence of planethood and brazenly declared Pluto kicked out of the planetary family . . . .

You thought Pluto was quite obviously a planet, right? Your whole astronomical education was based on this. And now what are we supposed to do with all those little solar system models we made with Styrofoam balls?

What happened to Pluto? The answer goes something like this. The concept of a planet has turned out to be just like nearly all of our other concepts. That is, it is defined relative to our history, values, interests, purposes, institutions, and philosophical views. The *fact* of what constitutes a planet turns out to depend quite substantially on the *values* certain people called astronomers hold dear. And smart people differ greatly about what those foundational values are. Let me explain. There are scads of small bodies circling the sun. Why do we call some of them planets and others not? One reason is that they have a certain size. Marble-sized bits of astrodust do not count. We could decide that astrodust should count, but we appear to have good reasons (and good values) for excluding it. In other words, astronomers have to decide just what importance size should play in defining the notion of a planet. For example, Pluto is apparently smaller than our moon. When Mike Brown of California Institute of Technology discovered 2003 UB313 (dubbed "Xena"), it looked like there was at least a 10th planet. Now, Xena is bigger than Pluto. Oh, no! What are we to do? Should we keep adding planets of a certain size, as we find them?

The next criterion that came into play for some, but not all, astronomers was whether the planet lies within the orbital plane of the other planets. It turns out, however, that Pluto's plane is slightly different than the plane shared by the other planets. Is that enough reason to boot it? Other astronomers propose other criteria, such as appropriate shape. This is actually a question about the formation of the planet—it has to be roughly spherical, which gives evidence that it was formed by a certain sequence of geological processes. So, two-hundred-mile-long slivers of rock do

Adam Foster, Nov. 8, 2009

Cute penguin couple

not count as planets. Some people even attribute metaphysical import to the spherical shape of planets, claiming that the sphere is the perfect shape in the great ontological scheme.

Okay, so maybe we can just say that planets are spheres that orbit the sun and not another body. However, it appears that this does not quite work for Pluto because it has a moon that is almost half its size, and it is not really clear whether the moon circles Pluto or whether, like two squirrels running around a tree trunk, they circle each other. It gets worse. Some astronomers then decided that it would be useful to stipulate that a true planet had to dominate its own orbit in a way that it would clear out other objects in its orbit.

I trust that the point I am trying to make is clear enough by now. It is starting to look as though our old, faithful idea of planets as balls of rock orbiting the sun is not arbitrary but defined relative to the history of our astronomy, our metaphysical systems, our observational technology, and a host of other facts and values. Those values and theoretical commitments show themselves, I am suggesting, in the fact that to answer the question—"Is Pluto a planet?"—depends, at the very least, on which of two competing orientations you choose: (1) the planetary scientists who are interested mostly in

> There is no absolute fact about what constitutes a planet. Any facts about planets are likely to be dependent on various values and theoretical commitments held by the people who get to decide the issue.

blmiers2's flickr photostream, March 4, 2012

Sure sign of spring

the composition and geologic processes of the celestial bodies or (2) the so-called "dynamicists" who are more interested in their mass, orbit, and their clearing out of their orbital plane. There is no absolute fact about what constitutes a planet. Any facts about planets are likely to be dependent on various values and theoretical commitments held by the people who get to decide the issue.

My point is that what we have just seen about the nature of planets reveals some very important insights about the nature of human conceptualization in general. Concepts can grow and change, but there are, nonetheless, various kinds of constraints on that growth. Accordingly, this is clearly not an arbitrary process. This is why I get upset when people complain that . . . the law means whatever judges say it means. And with what is [that idea] contrasted? [It is] contrasted with what the laws [supposedly] really mean when we understand the literal legal concepts correctly.

I cannot understand . . . this . . . notion of literal and objectively defined legal concepts as squaring with virtually any of the evidence I know of concerning how human conceptualization and reasoning work. It looks to me, instead, that most of our moral and legal concepts are more like the concept of a planet than they are anything like [our] classical [ideas about] categories. Concepts are ways we make distinctions and mark patterns. We do this for various purposes and relative to the developing situations in which we find ourselves. The proper application of concepts is an imaginative activity through and through.

But concepts are even more complexly structured than this. Consider the phenomenon known as "prototype effects" that was made famous by the work of Eleanor Rosch and her colleagues.[8] Rosch demonstrated that, from a cognitive perspective, people often build their categories around prototypical members, and they understand less-prototypical members by virtue of their relations

to the prototypes.[9] Rosch found, for example, that in America prototypical birds include robins and sparrows. Robins and sparrows
establish cognitive reference points for people's reasoning about
birds. Less-prototypical birds, such as chickens, emus, ostriches,
roadrunners, and penguins are cognized as lying at varying distances from the center of the category according to various principles of extension.[10] In some cases, there may even turn out to be no
univocal set of classical defining features shared by all members of
the category. Yet, we do manage to reason quite effectively by virtue
of our complex understanding of our radial categories and how they
apply to different situations.

This prototype characterization applies also to our most important abstract concepts, and not just to those for concrete physical
objects. Take, for example, the category "harm." At its conceptual
center are cases of direct physical injury to an organism, such that
the organism suffers some dysfunction, often accompanied by
bodily pain. But via principles of metaphorical extension, there
are also cases of nonprototypical harm, such as emotional harm,
psychological harm, social harm, economic harm, ethical harm,
legal harm, and so on. None of these is necessarily more experientially basic than any other, but from the viewpoint of how we cog-
nize things, some are more central and prototypical than others.

[W]e should think of our ethical and legal concepts as, for the
most part, having complex radial structures, manifesting prototype
effects. Such concepts are motivated by and grounded in our shared
bodily, social, cultural, moral, economic, and legal experience. But
there are body-based principles of extension that allow us to apply
our concepts to novel cases and sometimes also to expand our concepts. These principles of extension include image schema structure
and conceptual metaphor, which allow for cognitive flexibility in the
face of changing situations, even as they provide cognitive motivation and constraint for how we think creatively. This is how embodied imaginative meaning and understanding can grow. This is how
innovation is possible and how it is constrained. So, we need to look
at the role of image schemas and metaphor.

IV. Image Schemas[11]

Let us start with the fact that our experience is permeated with
hundreds of recurring sensory-motor patterns, known as "image
schemas," which give shape, connection, and significance to what
we experience. To illustrate this kind of meaningful structure, consider the "container" schema.[12]

Thousands of times each day we perceive, manipulate, and interact with containers, such as cups, boxes, briefcases, rooms, vehicles,
and even our own bodies. Via these recurrent vital interactions, we

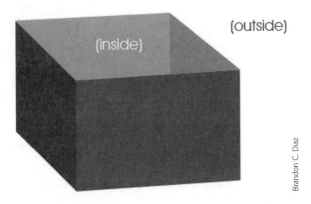

come to learn the meaning and logic of containment. The container schema consists of the following minimal structure:

1. A Boundary
2. An Interior
3. An Exterior[13]

To get schemas for concepts like "in" and "out," one must add structure that profiles various parts of the container schema.[14] The concept "in" profiles (highlights or activates) the interior of the container schema, whereas the concept "out" profiles the exterior that surrounds the boundary. "In" and "out" also require identification of a figure/ ground (or trajector/landmark) structure relative to the container schema. When we say, "The horse left the barn," the horse is the figure (trajector) relative to the barn, which is the ground (or landmark)."[15]

One crucial thing to notice is that, even for image schemas as elementary and simple as the container schema, there is already a definite spatial or bodily logic that is learned from our sensory-motor experience and that constrains our inferences about containers:

1. If an object, X, is in container A, then that object is not outside that container.
2. If an object, X, is within container A, and container A is within container B, then object X is within container B.
3. If an object, X, is outside of container B, and container A is inside container B, then object X is outside of container A.[16]

To emphasize just how much internal structure and thereby how much constraint on spatial logics there can be for even our most elementary image schemas, consider the "source-path-goal schema."[17] One could specify the minimal structure of the source-path-goal schema as follows:

1. A source point from which the path begins.
2. A path leading in some direction.
3. A goal, that is, an endpoint for the path.[18]

Described in this minimal way, you might think that the image schema does not have enough internal structure to support extensive inferences. However, actual source-path-goal schemas typically have considerable additional structure that can serve as the basis for a wide range of inferences, for example:

- A trajector that moves
- A source location (the starting point)
- A goal (the intended destination for the trajector)
- A route from the source to the goal
- The actual trajectory of motion
- The position of the trajector at a given time
- The direction of the trajector at that time
- The actual final location of the trajector when the motion is terminated, which may be different from the intended destination.[19]

This list leaves out other possible parameters that might play a role in various events, including speed of motion of the trajector, the trail left by the moving object, obstacles to motion, aids to motion, forces that move the trajector, multiple trajectors, and so on.[20]

An extremely important feature of image schemas is that they are topological in the sense that they can undergo a wide range of distortions or transformations while still retaining their image-schematic structure and logic.[21] For example, a path can be straight, or it can twist and turn back upon itself, or it can involve stop-and-go motion without losing its characteristic source-path-goal structure and without violating its characteristic spatial logic.[22]

Another crucial property of image schemas is their compositionality, that is, their ability to combine to produce other image schemas.[23] Via such composition, vast expanses of our experience and understanding of our mundane bodily experience are structured image-schematically. For example, as Lakoff and Nunez have shown, the concepts "into" and "out of" are blendings of the container schema with the source-path-goal schema.[24] The "into" schema is a composition of the "in" schema and the "to" schema, whereas the "out of" schema combines the "out" schema and the "from" schema:[25]

Into Schema

- The "in" schema: consisting of a container schema, with the interior profiled and taken as landmark.
- The "to" schema: consisting of a source-path-goal schema, with the goal profiled and taken as landmark.
- Correspondences: (Interior; Goal) and (Exterior; Source).

Out of Schema

- The "out" schema: consisting of a container schema, with the exterior profiled and taken as landmark.
- The "from" schema: consisting of a source-path-goal schema, with the source profiled and taken as landmark.
- Correspondences: (Interior; Source) and (Exterior; Goal).[26]

A full accounting of the image-schematic structure of our experience and understanding might extend to hundreds of structures. However, most of these would be complex combinations of a smaller number of more basic image schemas. In summary, there are four major points to keep in mind concerning the nature and activation of image schemas:

1. Image schemas characterize the recurring structure of much of our sensory-motor experience.

2. They are learned automatically through our bodily interactions with aspects of our environment, given the nature of our brains and bodies in relation to the possibilities for experience that are afforded us within different environments. Image schemas are meaningful to us even when, as is typical, they operate beneath the level of conscious awareness. (They are a basic part of embodied meaning.)

3. They have highly determinate "spatial" or "bodily" logics that support and constrain inferences.

4. They are compositional in that they combine and blend, yielding even more complex embodied meaning and inference patterns.

When I say that meaning is grounded in the body, I mean that the meaning of our experience emerges pre-reflectively from sensory experience and patterns of our bodily orientation, perceptual interaction, and movement. Image schemas constitute much of the inferential structure of this embodied understanding. All of this is tied intimately to the nature of our bodies and to the nature of the environments we inhabit. The range of image schemas is thus wide, but it is highly constrained and motivated by how our bodies are shaped. A full account of image schematic structures would include not just containment and source-path-goal, but a large array of schemas: attraction, repulsion, compulsion, blockage, verticality, right-left symmetry, balance, scalar intensity, straight versus curved, and so on.

V. Embodiment of Abstract Thought

Anyone who is convinced by the evidence for the embodiment of mind must then face the vexing problem of how abstract thought is tied to the body. How do we get from our perceptual and motor understanding to our most wonderful achievements of abstract conceptualization, reasoning, and creativity? . . . What we have found so far is that one of the central devices for human abstraction is what we call "conceptual metaphor," which involves a conceptual mapping from a highly structured source domain, typically some sensory-motor domain, to a less highly structured target domain, typically some abstract notion, such as justice, freedom, or mind.[27] Let me illustrate this with some basic examples.

VI. Conceptual Metaphors

It is not surprising that all our perceptual, spatial relations, and bodily movement concepts are intimately tied to our embodiment. Still, . . . [h]ow can we move from embodied meanings tied to our sensory-motor experience all the way to abstract concepts like love, justice, mind, knowledge, and freedom? How can we move from embodied spatial logic and inferences all the way to abstract logical relations and inferences?

[T]he general answer is that various imaginative structures and processes allow us to extend embodied meaning and thought to the highest level of abstraction possible for us, all the way up to science, philosophy, mathematics, logic, and law. Let us begin with a simple but suggestive example of how this works. Recall my earlier description of the structure and logic of the container schema. There is a commonplace metaphor—"categories are containers"—that is pervasive in our conceptual system and has its grounding in embodied container logic.[28] The conceptual metaphor "categories are containers" consists of a systematic mapping of entities and relations from the domain of spatial containment onto our understanding of conceptual categorization, as follows:

The Categories-Are-Containers Metaphor

Source Domain		Target Domain
Containers	>>>	Categories
Bounded regions in space	>>>	Categories
Objects inside bounded regions	>>>	Category members
One bounded region inside another	>>>	Subcategory[29]

Via this conceptual mapping, we can understand categorization as metaphorical placement within a container. For example, a certain animal can fall *within* one species but *outside of* another. We can identify an object as being *in* the category of living things. A subcategory is *part of* or is *contained in* a larger category There can be several subcategories *within* one more general category. Developing scientific research can move one organism *from* the plant category *into* the animal category.

Based on the source-to-target mapping, the spatial logic of containment that we mentioned above can carry directly over into the logic of abstract categories.[30] This gives rise to a series of correspondences of the following sort:

- "Every object is either within a container or outside of it" . . .
- "Given two containers A and B and an object X, if container A is in B and X is in A, then X is in B" . . .
- "Given three containers (A, B, C), if A is in B and B is in C, then A is in C" . . .
- "Given two containers A and B and an object Y, if A is in B and Y is outside B, then Y is outside A." . . .[31]

Notice that it is precisely this metaphorical container logic that is appropriated by the objectivist [formalist] view of legal reasoning that I mentioned earlier.

What this metaphorical logic of containment illustrates is the general principle that there are metaphorical and other imaginative structures that make it possible for us to understand abstract concepts and to reason about them using the spatial logics of various body-based source domains. For example, when we hear someone say, "Penguins fall outside the category of birds," in the context of talking about birds, "outside" activates the source-to-target mapping of the conceptual metaphor "categories are containers," and we thereby enlist the logic of containers as we process the next utterances of the speaker. . . .

VII. Metaphors Structuring Abstract Conceptual Systems

. . . The implications of the constitutive nature of conceptual metaphors are quite far-reaching. We come to see that even our most abstract theories are webs of body-based metaphors. . . . I want to offer an example of the type of category structure I am talking about here—one drawn from property law. . . . I had the good fortune to work with my colleague in the Law School, Carl Bjerre, as he was preparing a law review article on intellectual property law.[32] Here is a very small part of what we found in our analysis of the radial category of property.

At the center of the category are prototypical instances of property, such as a house, hand-tool, or land.[33] These cognitive prototypes are what are activated first for us when we read, hear, or think about the term "property." These prototypical instances satisfy a common idealized cognitive model in which property is:

- a discrete physical object or spatial expanse;
- that persists through time;
- is subject to exclusion from use by others;
- is alienable;
- and is useful.[34]

Extending out from the central prototypes are many noncentral members that do not possess all of the features specified by the central idealized cognitive model. Thus water is, in American culture, though not in certain Native American cultures, conceived of as potential property even though it is not a discrete object. The human body is often regarded as property, but we typically do not think of it as alienable or transferable. Garbage is apparently regarded by the law as property, although it seems somewhat at odds with our notion of prototypical property because it is not typically a discrete physical object and the notion of usefulness is suspect.[35] Extending even further out from the center are other types of property that are not physical entities. The primary principle of extension for most of these cases is conceptual metaphor. For example, we speak of intellectual property, such as ideas we have that can be copyrighted, patented, and excluded from use by others. Intellectual property is only metaphorically an entity, and it is only metaphorically transferable to another for their use. Pensions, stocks, and bonds are metaphorical property. We have an alleged right to utilize such abstract, metaphorically-defined entities for our own purposes under certain specifiable conditions. One's privacy is metaphorical property just like one's own name, and they both can become the subject of litigation.[36]

In addition to metaphorical principles of extension within the category, there are often metonymic principles coupled with the metaphors. For example, a share of stock stands metonymically for a share of the company, which is itself a metaphorical entity, and the company in turn stands metonymically for the company's assets. One's name is metaphorical property, but it is also metonymic for the person named.

One could go on an[d] on with such an analysis, but I hope that the key points are obvious. The concept "property" is not a classical category defined by a set of necessary and sufficient conditions. Instead, the concept is a vast, radially-structured category with a small number of central members or prototypical cases surrounded at various distances by noncentral members, according to principles of extension such as conceptual metaphor and metonymy.[37] Legal judgments in property law operate relative to this complex and potentially growing conceptual structure. Property is at least partially a metaphorically-defined concept.[38] You cannot practice property law without metaphor! . . .

Key Concepts

Radial structures
Prototypicality effects
Image schemas
The container schema
The source-path-goal schema
Conceptual metaphors

Discussion Questions

The material in this chapter and in the next one (on metaphor) is difficult, but "play" with it (remember the Falk excerpt from Chapter 1?) and see what you can do with it. Don't become anxious or frustrated just because it isn't immediately clear. "Play" with the ideas. Legal categories are the stuff of which briefs are made. The better you understand them, the better your briefs will be.

1. What does Llewellyn mean when he says that "to classify is to disturb"? To emphasize some things and de-emphasize others? To obscure some data and give fictitious value to others? How does that work? The excerpt from Johnson may help with the answer.

2. Here is a summary of some of the key points from the Johnson excerpt: (1) We often think about law as if it were a set of categories (harm, privacy). (2) We think of categories as if they were physical containers. (3) Physically, we experience containers (cups, briefcases) as having defined boundaries. (4) We think of things (our coffee, our work documents) as being either inside or outside those boundaries. (5) If legal categories are "containers," then they have clear boundaries. Circumstances are either "inside" or "outside" those clear boundaries. (6) But actually, many categories (legal or astronomical) do not have clear boundaries. It is only the confusion caused by the metaphor ("categories = containers") that causes us to think they do. This is the Pluto problem. (7) Therefore, the question of whether a certain event falls "inside" or "outside" the "category" of the Constitutional right to privacy is not so easy to know as we may have thought. We are working here on trying to understand our own process of thinking about law.

   Does this make sense to you? If so, what are the implications for the way we think about law?

3. Karl Llewellyn was one of the fathers of realism. In Chapter 13, we saw that one of the weaknesses of realism was its vulnerability to the idea that the law "depends on what the judge ate for breakfast." But if that describes our legal system, we cannot have confidence in its results or plan our lives. We need at least some consistency and predictability. This is the weakness of realism that prompted Professor Berger to say (in Chapter 3) that viewing law as rhetoric can give us a "place to stand" between formalism (the idea that the law is all rules) and realism (the idea that the law is nothing more than what a judge, who has the power to decide, will do). (Look back at the first paragraph of the Johnson reading in this chapter.)

   But notice here that Llewellyn, a founder of realism, has a very sophisticated view of the effect of categories. As you can see from this chapter, the study of categories is a key part of modern rhetoric. So if Llewellyn had such a sophisticated view of categories and if categories are such an important part of rhetoric, what is the difference between rhetoric and realism? In other words, why does the study of rhetoric (including categories) give us a "place to stand" that is different from legal realism?

   [A hint: Llewellyn says here that categories can be manipulated, but he does not mention whether there are any limits to that manipulation. Without limits, the judge seemingly can still do whatever she wants to do. But the study of modern rhetoric addresses the question omitted by Llewellyn: whether there are limits to the manipulation of categories. If there are, then the law is no longer simply what a judge will do. What might those limits be? Look again at the Berger excerpt in Chapter 3 and also at the Johnson excerpt from this chapter.]

Additional Suggested Reading

Ronald Chen & Jon Hanson, *Categorically Biased: The Influence of Knowledge Structures on Law and Legal Theory*, 77 S. Cal. L. Rev. 1103 (2004).

Laura E. Little, *Characterization and Legal Discourse*, 46 J. Legal Educ. 372 (1996).

Endnotes

1. *Popov v. Hayashi*, Ca. Sup. Ct., Dec. 18, 2002; *See generally* Paul Finkelman, *Fugitive Baseballs and Abandoned Property: Who Owns the Home Run Ball?* 23 Cardozo L. Rev. 1609 (2002).

2. 3 Cai. R. 175, 2 Am. Dec. 264 (N.Y. 1805).

3. *Citizens United v. Federal Election Commission*, 558 U.S. 08-205 (2010), 558 U.S. ——, 130 S. Ct. 876 (January 21, 2010).

4. For the most thorough treatment to date of the implications of cognitive science for law, see Steven L. Winter, *A Clearing in the Forest: Law, Life, and Mind* (U. of Chicago Press 2001).

5. George Lakoff & Mark Johnson, *Philosophy in the Flesh: The Embodied Mind and Its Challenge to Western Thought* 78 (Basic Books 1999).

6. George Lakoff, *Women, Fire, and Dangerous Things: What Categories Reveal About the Mind* 6 (U. of Chicago Press 1987).

7. *Id.* at 40-41.

8. Eleanor Rosch, *Cognitive Reference Points*, 7 Cognitive Psychology 532-547 (1975); *see* Lakoff, *supra* note 6, at 39-40.

9. Rosch, *supra* note 8, at 544.

10. Lakoff, *supra* note 6, at 44-45.

11. Selected parts of the following sections on image schemas are taken from chapter seven of . . . Mark Johnson, *The Meaning of the Body: Aesthetics of Human Understanding* (U. of Chicago Press 2007).

12. Lakoff & Johnson, *supra* note 5, at 31-32.

13. *Id.* at 32.

14. George Lakoff & Rafael E. Nunez, *Where Mathematics Comes From: How the Embodied Mind Brings Mathematics into Being* 31 (Basic Books 2000).

15. *Id.*

16. *Id.*

17. Lakoff & Johnson, *supra* note 5, at 32-33.

18. *Id.* at 33.

19. *Id.*

20. *Id.*

21. *Id.*

22. *Id.*

23. *See* Lakoff & Nunez, *supra* note 14, at 39.

24. *Id.*

25. *Id.*

26. *Id.*

27. Lakoff & Johnson, *supra* note 5, at 45.

28. Lakoff & Nunez, *supra* note 14, at 43.

29. *Id.*

30. *Id.* at 44.

31. *Id.*

32. Carl S. Bjerre, *Secured Transactions Inside Out: Negative Pledge Covenants, Property and Perfection*, 84 Cornell L. Rev. 305 (1999).

33. *Id.* at 357.

34. *Id.* at 358.

35. *See id.*

36. *See id.* at 359.

37. *See id.* at 357-360.

38. *Id.*

16. *Metaphor*

"What I am pointing out is that unless you are at home in the metaphor, unless you have had your proper poetical education in the metaphor, you are not safe anywhere. Because you are not at ease with figurative values: you don't know the metaphor in its strength and its weakness. You don't know how far you may expect to ride it and when it may break down with you."

—Robert Frost

"Metaphors in law are to be narrowly watched, for starting as devices to liberate thought, they end often by enslaving it."

—Judge Benjamin Cardozo[1]

Our work ("play") in Chapter 15 introduced categories, but it served as an introduction to the larger concept of metaphor as well. In this chapter, we'll look at metaphor more directly. Our first reading is from Professor Steven Winter, one of today's leading scholars working on law and metaphor. The themes in these two short paragraphs should be familiar by now, even if you are still working to grasp them completely.

Excerpt from

Steven L. Winter, *Preface, A Clearing in the Forest: Law, Life, and Mind*
xi-xvii (U. of Chicago Press 2001)

There is a virtual revolution going on within the cognitive sciences. Basic-level categorization, radial categories, image-schemas, conceptual metaphor—these and other findings are transforming our fundamental understanding of the mind. . . .

By far the most important conclusions to emerge from this recent work on cognition are two: first, that imagination is central to the cognitive process; and, second, that imagination is embodied. . . . On the one hand, we are discovering that human thought is irreducibly imaginative. On the other, we are learning that—contrary to the conventional wisdom—human imagination operates in an orderly and systematic fashion. This insight alters the contours of entire debates in disciplines such as law. . . .

The project rests on the straightforward premise that a better theory of the mind should facilitate a better understanding of the products of the mind. Law is one of those products. . . .

The promise of cognitive theory lies precisely in its ability to make explicit the unconscious criteria and cognitive operations that structure and constitute our judgment. It is by laying bare these cognitive structures and their impact on our reasoning that we can best aid legal actors—whether advocates or decision-makers—who wish to understand the law better so that they can act more effectively.

. . . The central question . . . is not *whether* we are rational but *how* we are rational. . . .

This understanding will yield a view of reason as grounded, but not determinate; as imaginative, but not free; as regular, but not entirely predictable. In short, it will yield a view of reason and knowledge as the profoundly human phenomena we know them to be. . . .

Our second reading is excerpted from a *N.Y. Times* article by Stanford's world-famous neurobiologist Robert Sapolsky. Dr. Sapolsky gives us a funny, accessible, and effective introduction to the cognitive science of metaphor.

Excerpt from

Robert Sapolsky, *This Is Your Brain on Metaphors*
N.Y. Times (Nov. 15, 2010)[2]

. . . There's another domain of unique human skills, and neuro-scientists are learning a bit about how the brain pulls it off. Consider the following from J. Ruth Gendler's wonderful "The Book of Qualities," a collection of "character sketches" of different qualities, emotions and attributes:

> Anxiety is secretive. He does not trust anyone, not even his friends, Worry, Terror, Doubt and Panic. . . . He likes to visit me late at night when I am alone and exhausted. I have never slept with him, but he kissed me on the forehead once, and I had a headache for two years. . . .

Or:

> Compassion speaks with a slight accent. She was a vulnerable child, miserable in school, cold, shy. . . . In ninth grade she was befriended by Courage. Courage lent Compassion bright sweaters, explained the slang, showed her how to play volleyball.

What is Gendler going on about? We know, and feel pleasure triggered by her unlikely juxtapositions. *Despair* has stopped listening to music. *Anger* sharpens kitchen knives at the local supermarket. *Beauty* wears a gold shawl and sells seven kinds of honey at the flea market. *Longing* studies archeology.

Symbols, metaphors, analogies, parables, synecdoche, figures of speech: we understand them. We understand that a captain wants more than just hands when he orders all of them on deck. We understand that Kafka's "Metamorphosis" isn't really about a cockroach. If we are of a certain theological ilk, we see bread and wine intertwined with body and blood. We grasp that the right piece of cloth can represent a nation and its values, and that setting fire to such a flag is a highly charged act. We can learn that a certain combination of sounds put together by Tchaikovsky represents Napoleon getting his butt kicked just outside Moscow. And that the name "Napoleon," in this case, represents thousands and thousands of soldiers dying cold and hungry, far from home.

And we even understand that June isn't literally busting out all over. It would seem that doing this would be hard enough to cause a brainstorm. So where did this facility with symbolism come from? It strikes me that the human brain has evolved a necessary shortcut for doing so, and with some major implications.

A single part of the brain processes both physical and psychic pain.

Consider an animal (including human) that has started eating some rotten, fetid, disgusting food. As a result, neurons in an area of the brain called the insula will activate. Gustatory disgust. Smell the same awful food, and the insula activates as well. Think about what might count as a disgusting food (say, taking a bite out of a struggling cockroach). Same thing.

Now read in the newspaper about a saintly old widow who had her home foreclosed by a sleazy mortgage company, her medical insurance canceled on flimsy grounds, and got a lousy, exploitative offer at the pawn shop where she tried to hock her kidney dialysis machine. You sit there thinking, those bastards, those people are scum, they're worse than maggots, they make me want to puke ... and your insula activates. Think about something shameful and rotten that you once did ... same thing. Not only does the insula "do" sensory disgust; it does moral disgust as well. Because the two are so viscerally similar. When we evolved the capacity to be disgusted by moral failures, we didn't evolve a new brain region to handle it. Instead, the insula expanded its portfolio.

Or consider pain. Somebody pokes your big left toe with a pin. Spinal reflexes cause you to instantly jerk your foot back just as they would in, say, a frog. Evolutionarily ancient regions activate in the brain as well, telling you about things like the intensity of the pain, or whether it's a sharp localized pain or a diffuse burning one.... Now instead, watch your beloved being poked with the pin. And your anterior cingulate will activate, as if it were you in pain.... When humans evolved the ability to be wrenched with feeling the pain of others, where was it going to process it? It got

Nalini Prasanna, May 4, 2007

Pencil art

crammed into the anterior cingulate. And thus it "does" both physical and psychic pain.

Another truly interesting domain in which the brain confuses the literal and metaphorical is cleanliness. In a remarkable study,[3] Chen-Bo Zhong of the University of Toronto and Katie Liljenquist of Northwestern University demonstrated how the brain has trouble distinguishing between being a dirty scoundrel and being in need of a bath. Volunteers were asked to recall either a moral or immoral act in their past. Afterward, as a token of appreciation, Zhong and Liljenquist offered the volunteers a choice between the gift of a pencil or of a package of antiseptic wipes. And the folks who had just wallowed in their ethical failures were more likely to go for the wipes. In the next study, volunteers were told to recall an immoral act of theirs. Afterward, subjects either did or did not have the opportunity to clean their hands. Those who were able to wash were less likely to respond to a request for help (that the experimenters had set up) that came shortly afterward. Apparently, Lady Macbeth and Pontius Pilate weren't the only ones to metaphorically absolve their sins by washing their hands.

Anna Sattler (G & A Sattler's flickr photostream, Aug. 17, 2007)

Homemade cleaning wipe supplies

This potential to manipulate behavior by exploiting the brain's literal-metaphorical confusions about hygiene and health is also shown in a study by Mark Landau and Daniel Sullivan of the University of Kansas and Jeff Greenberg of the University of Arizona. Subjects either did or didn't read an article about the health risks of airborne bacteria. All then read a history article that used imagery of a nation as a living organism with statements like, "following the Civil War, the United States underwent a growth spurt." Those who read about the scary bacteria before thinking about the U.S. as an organism were then more likely to express negative views about immigration.

Another example of how the brain links the literal and the metaphorical comes from a study[4] by Lawrence Williams of the University of Colorado and John Bargh of Yale. Volunteers would meet one of the experimenters, believing that they would be starting the experiment shortly. In reality, the experiment began when the experimenter, seemingly struggling with an armful of folders, asks the volunteer to briefly hold their coffee. As the key experimental manipulation, the coffee was either hot or iced. Subjects then read a description of some individual, and those who had held the warmer cup tended to rate the individual as having a warmer personality, with no change in ratings of other attributes.

Another brilliant study by Bargh and colleagues concerned [sensations related to the sense of touch]. Volunteers were asked to evaluate the resumes of supposed job applicants where, as the critical variable, the resume was attached to a clipboard of one of two different weights. Subjects who evaluated the candidate while holding the heavier clipboard tended to judge candidates to be more serious, with the weight of the clipboard having no effect

dyobmit's flickr photostream, June 10, 2005

Coffee

on how congenial the applicant was judged. After all, we say things like "weighty matter" or "gravity of a situation."

What are we to make of the brain processing literal and metaphorical versions of a concept in the same brain region? Or that our neural circuitry doesn't cleanly differentiate between the real and the symbolic? What are the consequences of the fact that evolution is a tinkerer and not an inventor, and has duct-taped metaphors and symbols to whichever pre-existing brain areas provided the closest fit?

Markusram's flickr photostream, July 19, 2010

Ice-cold gin and tonic

xcode's flickr photostream, Oct. 14, 2009

Cockroach

Jonathan Haidt, of the University of Virginia, has shown how viscera and emotion often drive our decision-making, with conscious cognition mopping up afterward, trying to come up with rationalizations for that gut decision. The viscera that can influence moral decision-making and the brain's confusion about the literalness of symbols can have enormous consequences. Part of the emotional contagion of the genocide of Tutsis in Rwanda arose from the fact that when militant Hutu propagandists called for the eradication of the Tutsi, they iconically referred to them as "cockroaches." Get someone to the point where his insula activates at the mention of an entire people, and he's primed to join the bloodletting. . . .

This neural confusion about the literal versus the metaphorical gives symbols enormous power, including the power to make peace. . . . Hope for true peace in the Middle East didn't come with the news of a trade agreement being signed. It was when President Hosni Mubarak of Egypt and King Hussein of Jordan attended the funeral of the murdered Israeli prime minister Yitzhak Rabin. That same hope came to the Northern Irish, not when ex-Unionist demagogues and ex-I.R.A. gunmen served in a government together, but when those officials publicly commiserated about each other's family misfortunes, or exchanged anniversary gifts. And famously, for South Africans, it came not with successful negotiations about land reapportionment, but when black South Africa embraced rugby and Afrikaans rugby jocks sang the A.N.C. national anthem.

Nelson Mandela was wrong when he advised, "Don't talk to their minds; talk to their hearts." He meant talk to their insulas and cingulated cortices and all those other confused brain regions, because that confusion could help make for a better world.

Our last three excerpts bring us back to specific areas of the law. First, we hear again from Professor Linda Berger on the topic of how corporations came to be people; how speech came to be a product in a marketplace; and what implications these metaphors may have for law.

Excerpt from

Linda Berger, *What Is the Sound of a Corporation Speaking? How the Cognitive Theory of Metaphor Can Help Lawyers Shape the Law*
2 J. ALWD 169 (Fall 2004)

Evolution of a Metaphor: An Artificial Entity Becomes a Person Protected by the First Amendment

The marketplace of ideas in which corporations speak is so central to First Amendment doctrine that it is necessary to remind ourselves that these concepts derive from metaphor. . . . So conventionalized is the market metaphor that it is difficult to discuss free speech values in the United States without referring to competition among speakers, free trade in ideas, and the power of thought to be accepted in the market. This section examines the contribution of these metaphors to the development of First Amendment protection for corporate speech.

Given a metaphorical target on which the economic market's structure and assumptions have been mapped, it seems only natural to treat a corporation as an equal competitor. . . .

The metaphorical grant of personhood to corporations has some backing. Treating an object or an abstraction as a person is a basic conceptual metaphor; it allows us to comprehend unfamiliar experiences in terms of familiar "human motivations, characteristics, and activities." . . . Moreover, personification "works" to some extent; it may seem fair, for example, to make a corporation that does business in a state subject to jurisdiction in that state. But as the metaphor becomes entrenched, it entails many assumptions: a corporation can be somewhere; it can act and move, sue and be sued; it can see, hear, speak; it can perceive and understand; it can formulate ideas and adopt views; it can express those ideas and views. And because it can do all these human things, the corporation must be treated as an equal participant in the free market of ideas.

Theories of Corporate Being

Because an abstraction cannot sue or be sued, the corporation had to become some "thing." For legal purposes, as John Dewey wrote, using the word "person" to stand for a corporation could have meant nothing more than designating it as a unit with rights and obligations, with the extent of each right and obligation to be determined by its fit with the nature and characteristics of the unit.[5]

Instead of such an approach, three inherently consequential theories of corporate being have been followed: [1.] treating the corporation as an artificial entity that is a creature of the state; [2.] treating the corporation as a group aggregating a number of individuals; and [3.] treating the corporation as a real and discrete entity similar to a person.

Viewed as an artificial entity that is purely a creation of state statute, the corporation receives little First Amendment protection; free speech values in corporate expression are limited to the public interest in the free exchange of ideas, and limits on corporate speech might well be acceptable. Under the artificial entity theory, judicial decisions were based primarily on the corporation's relationship with the state. In *Trustees of Dartmouth College v. Woodward*, for example, the Supreme Court limited the corporation's power to the original charter granted by the state: "A Corporation is an artificial being, invisible, intangible, and existing only in contemplation of law. Being the mere creature of law, it possesses only those properties which the charter of its creation confers upon it, either expressly or as incidental to its very existence."[6]

Viewed as a group of individuals or as a real and discrete entity with attributes similar to those of a person, a corporation gains First Amendment rights that are indistinguishable from those of individuals.[7] Under the group theory, courts emphasize that human individuals constitute the corporation, with the corporation protecting those individuals' rights.[8]

The third approach treats the corporation as an autonomous and real entity, separate from its creation by the state and from the individuals who work for it. Without examination, the Supreme Court has consistently followed this approach to corporate property rights.[9] In the case cited for establishing the principle that a corporation is a person, Santa Clara County sued a railroad company for failure to pay taxes. The railroad argued six defenses, including that corporations were persons.[10] One of the other five defenses was found successful. Although not included in the reported opinion, Chief Justice Waite apparently told the attorneys waiting to hear the opinion that the court "does not wish to hear argument on the question whether the provision in the Fourteenth Amendment to the Constitution . . . applies to these corporations. We are of [the] opinion that it does."[11] Because the court reporter included a commentary note stating that the defendant corporations were persons within the intent of . . . the Fourteenth Amendment to the Constitution, the case now stands for a long-established proposition: that corporations are persons.[12]

More debate accompanied the extension of individual liberty rights to corporate persons.[13] In the 19th century, courts usually rejected attempts to grant corporations rights that seemed to derive from exclusively human interests. In the 20th century, though some justices pointed out the irony of extending to corporations the protections that were intended to eliminate racial discrimination,[14] the Supreme Court incrementally did so. Corporations count as persons for the Fourth Amendment's protection against unreasonable searches, the Fifth Amendment's protection against double jeopardy, and the Seventh Amendment's right to trial by jury in civil cases.[15] Whether viewed as metaphor or as a convenient legal fiction, this concept has grown "to influence or even control how we think or refuse to think about basic matters."[16]

Theories of Corporate Speaking

In its early applications, the First Amendment protected individuals with unpopular or dissenting views. Under current commercial speech doctrine, the First Amendment protects the speech rather than the speaker.

The article here explains the three steps taking the First Amendment from the protection of individuals to the protection of the message: (1) The assumption that there were only two categories of speakers, private and public, and that the Amendment's purpose was to protect private speakers from governmental regulation; since a corporation is not the government, it must be in the category of private speakers, protected against the government. (2) The assumption that spending money is protected speech because it is a method of speech. (3) The assumption that the rights of listeners were as important as the rights of speakers.

By taking these three steps, the Supreme Court moved from protecting the rights of individuals to speak freely to protecting speech itself, thus supporting the free market of information by prohibiting the government from limiting the stock of information available to consumers and voters.[17]

As a result, although in 1942 the Court had ruled that "the Constitution imposes no . . . restraint on government as respects purely commercial advertising,"[18] by 1976 the Court was extending First Amendment protection to the communication, its source, and its recipients because "the free flow of commercial information is indispensable to the functioning of a free market economy."[19] The flow of information to consumers remains the primary rationale for protecting corporate speech. . . .

In *First National Bank v. Bellotti*,[20] the Court explicitly held that the First Amendment protects corporate speech by relying on the rights of listeners in the market. In *Bellotti*, a state criminal statute prohibited corporate contributions or expenditures to influence referenda not affecting the corporation's business or assets. Writing for the majority, Justice Powell rephrased the question; it was not whether corporations have First Amendment rights. Instead, because the First Amendment "serves significant societal interests," the question was whether the Massachusetts statute "abridges expression that the First Amendment was meant to protect" or "whether the corporate identity of the speaker deprives this proposed speech of what otherwise would be its clear entitlement to protection."[21] Because speech about the referendum issue was core First Amendment Speech, "[t]he inherent worth of speech in terms of its capacity for informing the public does not depend upon the identity of its source, whether corporation, association, union, or individual."[22] Justice Powell acknowledged that some "purely personal guarantees" of the constitution were limited to individuals[23] but was unswayed by Justice White's argument that "what some have considered to be the principal function of the First Amendment, the use of communication as a means of self-expression, self-realization, and self-fulfillment, is not at all furthered by corporate speech."[24]

After *Belloti*, protected speech included a corporation's spending of money for lobbying, political advertisements, and other attempts to influence the political process.[25] . . .

Metaphors for Free Expression

Just as corporations were not always persons protected by the First Amendment, First Amendment values were not always viewed through the prism of the free market.

The article here summarizes the work of John Milton and John Stuart Mill, who helped lay the foundation for thinking of truth and falsehood as a battle between foes and truth as a stream flowing freely, leading to Justice Holmes's introduction of the free trade metaphor:

Dissenting from the affirmance of a conviction under the espionage act, Justice Holmes wrote that "the ultimate good desired is better reached by free trade in ideas—that the best test of truth is the power of the thought to get itself accepted in the competition of the market."[26] Although Justice Holmes wrote about the "free trade in ideas" and "the competition of the market" in 1919, it was Justice Brennan who first wrote about the "marketplace of ideas" in 1965.[27] . . .

Although the metaphor was new, it contained basic conceptual metaphors, the **Mind is a Container** and **Ideas are Objects.** These basic metaphors in turn help generate new and different metaphors. . . . They combine with the economic experience of the market to "entail" a whole set of associations and inferences: "ideas are commodities; persuasion is selling; speakers are vendors; members of the audience are potential purchasers; acceptance is buying; intellectual value is monetary value; and the struggle for recognition in the domain of public opinion is like competition in the market."[28] . . .

Why the Metaphors Matter

. . . Referring metaphorically to the corporation as a person allows the decision-maker to treat the corporation as if it were identical for all purposes to individual human beings. Referring metaphorically to the marketplace of ideas suggests that the corporation needs protection from government regulation because its voice is necessary to the debate from which truth will emerge.

Because personhood provides a simple answer to the question of how to regard a corporation, it diverts attention away from the differences among forms of organization and from the different treatments that should result.[29] Instead of considering complex questions and making relevant distinctions, decision-makers simply apply to institutions the ideas and rules that grew out of an individualistic context.[30] Moreover, the declaration of personhood not only carries rights and obligations but also shapes social values and can diminish the rights of others.[31] Conferring Bill of Rights protections on corporations legitimizes various acts and functions of corporations. This message reflects existing values, influences future behaviors, and generates new values. Finally, granting corporations such protection poses a greater danger if "the extension of corporate constitutional rights [becomes] a zero-sum game that diminishes the rights and power of real individuals." If that is the case, "[t]he corporate exercise of first amendment rights frustrates the individual's right to participate equally in democratic elections. . . ."[32]

> *Because personhood provides a simple answer to the question of how to regard a corporation, it diverts attention away from the differences among forms of organization and from the different treatments that should result.*

Among other points, the article then summarizes some of the reasons that complete acceptance of corporate personhood might be inappropriate: (1) sacrificing some of the purposes of freedom of expression, such as self-fulfillment and broad civic participation; (2) inappropriately viewing corporations as subjects rather than objects of political actions; (3) assuming without analysis the idea that corporations need the same kind of protection from the state that individuals need; (4) assuming incorrectly that large corporations are groups of individuals joined together for a common commercial purpose, not as instruments of expression. The point here, however, is not whether the legal results of corporate personhood are appropriate but, instead, the way that the metaphor hides key differences between a corporation and a human being and therefore can prevent discussion of key questions about how far the metaphor can or should take us. The metaphor obscures those questions and is, therefore, a powerful tool of persuasion, both helpful and dangerous. Understanding its largely unconscious work is critically important for advocates, judges, and citizens alike.

Professor Berger's article has invited us to look back in time and notice the significant implications a set of metaphors has had on the First Amendment. Next, Professor Carol Parker invites us to look forward at possible future legal implications of the newly popular cultural metaphor, the "perfect storm."

Excerpt from

Carol Parker, *The Perfect Storm, the Perfect Culprit: How a Metaphor of Fate Figures in Judicial Opinions*
43 McGeorge L. Rev. _____ (2011)

In 1991, the *Andrea Gail*, a sword-fishing boat, was lost in a storm at sea. No one knows what happened or why. The cause could have been (1) reckless decisions made by the captain, who was obsessed with getting a catch; (2) reckless modifications the owner made to the ship several years earlier, making her less seaworthy; or (3) forces of nature beyond human agency, making the loss inevitable and therefore relieving all potential defendants of any responsibility.

A meteorologist reporting on the storm referred to it as a "perfect storm," implying a convergence of unusual and intense natural forces that are impossible to resist. The phrase promptly became a part of the popular culture and at the time of Professor Parker's writing had appeared in more than 130 judicial opinions. Interestingly, however, in those opinions, the phrase often describes circumstances of entirely human origin, circumstances in which we would normally attribute causation and assign liability. Is the phrase (and the event to which it originally referred) changing the way we think about legal causation?

The following section of Professor Parker's article is taken from a pre-publication draft:

The Perfect Storm as Explanatory Metaphor

[After the release of the book and the movie, there was a marked increase in the use of the phrase in judicial opinions.] Not only the frequency, but also the character of these references is different from the earlier references. While an occasional opinion written after 2000 uses "perfect storm" as a bit of dramatic imagery to describe the intensity of an event, in the great majority of cases, the term alludes to additional elements of the story of the Halloween Gale of 1991, as told in Junger's book, published in 2000, and later in the movie based on that book, released in 2002. Understood within the context of those narratives, "perfect storm" is more than a vivid descriptor, it is a story complete in itself.

The "perfect storm" has come into popular discourse as what researchers George Lakoff and Mark Johnson have termed a "new metaphor."[33] Lakoff and Johnson state, "New metaphors have the power to create a new reality. This can begin to happen when we start to comprehend our experience in terms of a metaphor, and it becomes a deeper reality when we begin to act in terms of it."[34] Like any metaphor, it is employed to represent one concept in terms of another, more concrete, image that is closer to our visceral experience, providing a structure that emphasizes certain aspects of experience over others. Unlike conventional metaphors, however, a new metaphor is not—or not yet—systematically embedded in our conceptual system. . . .

Rather, a new metaphor is one that offers a new imaginative understanding of experience.[35] The "facts" embodied in the metaphor correspond to aspects of the experience in the form of metaphoric entailments. "[T]hese 'new metaphors' are outside our conventional conceptual system and are capable of giving us a mew understanding of our experience."[36]

Aspects of the metaphoric concepts provide a structure for making sense of the actual experience. For example, Lakoff and Johnson explain how we intuitively understand statements such as "We have covered a lot of ground in our argument" in terms of the metaphor, "An-Argument-is-a-Journey," based on experiential rather than objective similarities:[37]

The Facts About Journeys	*The Metaphoric Entailments*
A journey defines a path	An argument defines a path.
The path of a journey is a surface.	An argument's path is a surface.[38]

Framing the facts of a case in terms of a perfect storm requires coherence between a perfect storm and the situation giving rise to the dispute. Based on Junger's narratives of the loss of the *Andrea Gail* in the Halloween Gale of 1991, the attributes of the perfect storm may be set out as follows:

- A singular or highly unusual event
- Involving the convergence of multiple forces
- Which could not have been foreseen

- Having devastating consequences
- Which could not have been prevented

Analyzing the effect of the perfect storm metaphor in judicial opinions raises questions, including these: (1) How do the facts of cases line up with those attributes? (2) Which aspects of the narrative are emphasized? and (3) Of what significance is the metaphor to the court's reasoning?

A corollary and equally important question asks which facts of the case are de-emphasized by the metaphor. As Lakoff and Johnson have written, "The very systematicity that allows us to comprehend one aspect of a concept in terms of another . . . will necessarily hide other aspects of the concept."[39] Accordingly, a "carelessly invoked metaphor" may be a means to obscure analysis or "avoid explicit consideration of a decision's consequence."[40] As Steven Winter cautioned, "Metaphor can . . . have as great a potential to mislead as to enlighten."[41]

The article then explores examples of the post-2002 use of the "Perfect Storm" metaphor in judicial opinions, particularly with regard to the metaphor's attributes (stated above) and how they have tended to affect decisions about causality and liability. Here is the article's conclusion:

Following publication of the book and release of the movie entitled *The Perfect Storm* the phrase, "it was a perfect storm," entered the popular culture in apparently limitless contexts, including more than 139 judicial opinions. Although no one knows what happened to the *Andrea Gail* and its crew, the narrative set out in Sebastian Junger's non-fiction novel *The Perfect Storm* suggests what may have happened and provides a conceptual structure for the metaphor.

Apparently even by those who have never read the book, a reference to "the perfect storm" is understood to embody that story, in which multiple forces converged in a singular event to produce devastating consequences which could not have been foreseen or prevented. The metaphor embodies the visceral experience of a violent storm and imports that physical response to the new set of circumstances, highlighting those aspects of a current situation that [may be interpreted to] line up with the attributes of the storm story: a singular event involving a convergence of forces which could not have been predicted or prevented, resulting in devastating harm.

In highlighting those aspects of experience, though, the metaphor may obscure others. By emphasizing the convergence of forces, the metaphor promotes a view of multiple causation as "perfect"—and separate from human agency. By emphasizing the singular quality of the storm, the metaphor invites a highly contextualized reading

> "The perfect storm" is understood to embody that story, in which multiple forces converged in a singular event to produce devastating consequences which could not have been foreseen or prevented.

and suggests that a perfect storm is unlikely to recur, and therefore that any precedential effect of the case so described will be minimal. By conjuring up the awesome and mysterious forces of nature, the metaphor may work to absolve individuals of responsibility for their own actions. This view rejects the stories of the reckless sea captain and the negligent employer's unseaworthy vessel, which assert that events are attributable to human causation, danger is predictable, and harm can be prevented.

Still, a question posed earlier in this essay lingers: of the narratives available to explain the loss of the *Andrea Gail*, why would litigants choose this narrative of fateful coincidence? Why not prefer a story of a reckless sea captain or a negligent employer's unseaworthy vessel? . . .

Perhaps those alternative accounts are less satisfying because they fail to fully explain the loss in the way that Neal Feigenson has described as a "simple, indeed monocausal, account[] of events [that] point[] toward a melodramatic conception of accidents, in which one and only one party is to blame."[42] Where multiple forces converge with unexpected consequences, the process of assigning blame is difficult and uncertain. Perhaps the answer to my question is that we prefer the complete solution offered by a version of the story in which "the Perfect Storm" is the culprit.

Indeed, the perfect storm is the perfect culprit because it absolves human actors of responsibility to compensate victims for their loss. If the result is inevitable, there is no point to a post-mortem dissection of contributing factors. The appeal of this line of argument is reflected in other popular figures of speech that minimize the value of allocating responsibility to human agency. For example, a fault-based analysis may be dismissed as an exercise in "the blame game." Instead we may say "it is what it is." The past is beyond our reach, and to attempt to sort out responsibility for past actions is to look backward, perhaps missing the opportunity to act effectively in the present. It is preferable to "move on."

On one hand, the popularity of these figures of speech may suggest a trend toward the erosion of personal responsibility or simply laziness in our habits of mind. On the other hand, though, it may seem to us as increasingly possible that events really *are* too complicated, their causes too intertwined, to be sorted out. To say that a result might have been different had one actor behaved differently assumes that the actor *could* have changed the outcome. But maybe that isn't so; maybe no one had that power. In his recent book, *The Age of the Unthinkable*, Joshua Cooper Ramo writes,

> Part of the reason a direct, head-to-head approach fails is that today we often can't find or name the threats we face. . . . The new-spun mashup risks of modernity, everything from greedy hedge funds to

accidental bioreleases, can barely be understood, let alone confronted, in one place at one time. And often, the threats morph
into something unrecognizable and even harder to name or
confront.[43]

The alternative to a direct approach, Ramo argues, is "to look holis-
tically instead of narrowly and then . . . to focus on our own resilience instead of trying to attack everything that looks scary."[44]
Ramo's view is reflected in both the resilience and the fatalism of
the fisherman described in Junger's book and may explain the res-
onance of his narrative of fateful coincidence and tragic heroes.
Perhaps the idea that a devastating loss could have been
prevented—was not inevitable—is too much to bear.

    The implicit message of the perfect storm metaphor is troubling
within a legal context. The perfect storm metaphor offers not only a
way to avoid assigning blame but also a rationale for inaction and
rough justice: a perfect storm cannot be undone, and its victims
cannot be compensated, however deserving of compassion they
may be. Conceptualizing a legal question in terms of a perfect
storm suggests that the normal rules cannot apply—and perhaps
that the legal system is incapable of reaching a just result.

    In judicial opinions, the perfect storm image has been con-
sciously invoked as a new metaphor; the audience is aware that it
is offered for purposes of persuasion, and if the popularity of the
phrase wanes, it may well cease to appear in judicial opinions.
However, if the new metaphor becomes embedded in legal discourse so as to serve as a stand-in for some aspect of legal analysis,
the audience will be less conscious of its effect, and the impact of
the metaphor will be more powerful.

Finally, we'll finish this chapter by adding a visual component with a
short excerpt from Professor Lucy Jewel and with the iconic "perfect
storm" image.

Excerpt from

Lucille A. Jewel, *Through a Glass Darkly: Using Brain Science and Visual Rhetoric to Gain a Professional Perspective on Visual Advocacy*

19 So. Cal. Interdisc. L.J. 237, 263 (2010)

This fascinating article explains a great deal of the cognitive science on the
subject of how visual persuasion affects our decision-making processes,
especially how it works unconsciously and outside the normal processes
of rational thought. Here is the article's summary of part of the research:

"Seeing is
believing."

To briefly summarize the foregoing, our perceptions are fallible for three broad reasons. First, the rules we unconsciously use to make sense of . . . visual information . . . sometime lead to mistakes.[45] Second, we process sensory information rapidly and unconsciously, in a way that we cannot cognitively comprehend or analyze with logic. Sometimes, we are unable to rationally consider how images affect our emotions or our decision-making process. As we are processing an image in our pre-conscious sensory system, that image can activate an emotional reaction in our mind without [our] even knowing about it.[46] Or, as we view sensory information, we might reach a decision on its substantive meaning in a mere split second and that decision might be the product of unconscious bias.[47] Third, . . . what we perceive is highly influenced . . . by [unconscious] pre-existing biases and expectations[48] that we are often unaware of.[49] Thus, whether our perception is created due

The Perfect Storm © Warner Bros., a division of TimeWarner Entertainment Company, L.P. All rights reserved. Used by permission.

to unconscious visual processing or visual processing that is unconsciously influenced by our expectations and beliefs. The bottom line is that we may not have much conscious control over what we see.

Despite the fallibility of human perceptions, we nonetheless give great weight to what we see and do not tend to critically evaluate it unless highly motivated to do so.[50] Even though our vision is not perfect, our minds tell us that it is seamless.[51] This idea of "seeing is believing" has been referred to as the phenomenological fallacy of perception.[52] ... When faced with a visual argument or visual evidence that needs to be countered, lawyers need to challenge the "seeing is believing" mentality and urge the audience to confront the imagistic material and rationally consider its logic. Lawyers must also understand the instances where unconscious biases and processes might affect a person's understanding of an image.

Now that you have read this summary of part of Professor Jewel's article (or the whole article, if you have time), remember the poster for the movie *The Perfect Storm*.

You may recall that it entered popular culture as the most common advertisement for the movie. Is it likely that this or other images from the film might be activated in our brains when we hear the phrase "the perfect storm"? Will the unconscious cognitive processes of visual persuasion add force to the already powerful semantic metaphor described in Professor Parker's article? If so, the "perfect storm" metaphor may be even more potentially powerful than we had first imagined.

Key Concepts

Mind = container
Ideas = objects

Discussion Questions

1. In the Winter excerpt, we read about a view "of reason as grounded, but not determinate; as imaginative, but not free; as regular, but not entirely predictable." What does that mean? Is it related to the discussion questions at the end of Chapter 15? And Professor Berger's "place to stand" from Chapter 3? How would you describe the "ground" of reason and its "regularity"?

2. What does Winter mean when he says that imagination is "embodied"?

3. What is your reaction to the *N.Y. Times* excerpt from Robert Sapolsky? What surprised you most? What implications for lawyering (and life) occur to you?

4. Read the majority and dissenting opinions in *Citizens United v. Federal Election Comm.*, 558 U.S. 08-205 (2010), 558 U.S. ___, 130 S. Ct. 876

(January 21, 2010). Look for and critique the metaphors you find there. The point isn't to decide which opinion is "correct" but rather to examine how the metaphors constrain the reasoning in both opinions.

5. Turn back to the list of characteristics originally associated with the "perfect storm" metaphor. It looks like a list of legal elements for avoiding causation, doesn't it? Do you remember seeing anything like that in your torts class, in the part of the semester when you studied causation by multiple parties?

6. Have you experienced the popular usage of the term "the perfect storm" to refer only to the convergence of three problems, without necessarily meaning that the causes were unforeseeable, unpreventable, or unrelated to human agency? If the popular usage of the metaphor shifts, so as to drop or deemphasize the effects of human agency, what changes in the law of causation might occur? Might some parties avoid liability who might have been held liable otherwise? And perhaps with less analysis undergirding the shift?

Additional Suggested Reading

Linda Berger, *How Embedded Knowledge Structures Affect Judicial Decision Making: An Analysis of Metaphor, Narrative, and Imagination in Child Custody Disputes*, 18 S. Cal. Interdisc. L.J. 259 (2009).

Linda Berger, *Of Metaphor, Metonymy, and Corporate Money: Rhetorical Choices in Supreme Court Decisions on Campaign Finance Regulation*, 58 Mercer L. Rev. 949 (2007).

Haig Bosmajian, *Metaphor and Reason in Judicial Opinions* (So. Ill. U. Press 1992).

Lisa Eichhorn, *A Sense of Disentitlement: Frame-Shifting and Metaphor in* Ashcroft v. Iqbal, 62 Fla. L. Rev. (2010).

Michael Frost, *Greco-Roman Analysis of Metaphoric Reasoning*, 2 Legal Writing 113 (1996).

Julie A. Oseid, *The Power of Metaphor: Thomas Jefferson's "Wall of Separation Between Church & State,"* 7 J. ALWD 123 (2010).

J. Christopher Rideout, *Penumbral Thinking Revisited: Metaphor in Legal Argumentation*, 7 J. ALWD 155 (2010).

Louis J. Sirico, Jr., *Failed Constitutional Metaphors: The Wall of Separation and the Penumbra*, 45 U. Rich. L. Rev. 459 (2011).

Michael R. Smith, *Levels of Metaphor in Persuasive Legal Writing*, 58 Mercer L. Rev. 919 (2007).

Endnotes

1. Judge Benjamin Cardozo in *Berkey v. Third Avenue R. Co.*, 155 N.E. 58, 61 (N.Y. 1926).

2. http://opinionator.blogs.nytimes.com/2010/11/14/this-is-your-brain-on-metaphors/?emc=.

3. Chen-Bo Zhong & Katie Liljenquist, *Washing Away Your Sins: Threatened Morality and Physical Cleansing*, 313 Science no. 5792, pp. 1451-1452 (Sept. 2006), http://www.sciencemag.org/content/313/5792/1451.short.

4. http://www.yale.edu/acmelab/news.html (Automaticity in Cognition, Motivation, and Evaluation).

5. John Dewey, *The Historic Background of Corporate Legal Personality*, 35 Yale L.J. 655, 656 (1926).

6. 17 U.S. 518, 636-637 (1819).

7. Charles D. Watts, *Corporate Legal Theory Under the First Amendment:* Bellotti *and* Austin, 46 U. Miami L. Rev. 317 362-363 (1991).

8. *See e.g., Bank of the U.S. v. Deveaux*, 9 U.S. 61, 86 (1809) (rejecting the argument that corporations were citizens within the meaning of the Constitution but allowing corporate litigants to plead as parties for diversity purposes).

9. Watts, *supra* note 7, at 336-340.

10. *Santa Clara Co. v. Southern Pacific Railroad Co.*, 118 U.S. 394 (1886).

11. *See* Thom Hartmann, *Unequal Protection: The Rise of Corporate Dominance and the Theft of Human Rights* 104 (Rodale 2002).

12. *Id.* at 107-109.

13. Student Author, *What We Talk About When We Talk About Persons: The Language of a Legal Fiction*, 114 Harv. L. Rev. 1745, 1751-1752 (2001).

14. *See e.g., Wheeling Steel Corp. v. Glander*, 337 U.S. 563, 578 (1949) (Douglas, J., dissenting); *Conn. Gen. Life Ins. Co. v. Johnson*, 303 U.S. 77, 85-90 (1938) (Black, J., dissenting). . . .

15. See the cases listed in Student Author, *supra* note 13, at 1752 n.49, and Carl J. Mayer, *Personalizing the Impersonal: Corporations and the Bill of Rights*, 41 Hastings L.J. 577, 664-665 (1990).

16. Aviam Soifer, *Reviewing Legal Fictions*, 20 Ga. L. Rev. 871, 877 (1986).

17. *Virginia State Bd. of Pharmacy v. Virginia Citizen's Consumer Council*, 425 U.S. 748, 783 (1976).

18. *Valentine v. Chrestensen*, 316 U.S. 52, 54 (1942).

19. *Virginia State Bd. of Pharmacy*, 425 U.S. at 765.

20. *First National Bank v. Bellotti,* 435 U.S. 765 (1978).

21. *Id.* at 775.

22. *Id.* at 777.

23. *Id.* at 778 n.4.

24. *Id.* at 804-805 (White, J., dissenting).

25. *See* Martin H. Redish & Howard W. Wasserman, *What's Good for General Motors: Corporate Speech and the Theory of Free Expression*, 66 Geo. Wash. L. Rev. 235, 243 (1998). . . .

26. *Abrams v. U.S.*, 250 U.S. 616, 630 (1919).

27. *Lamont v. Postmaster General*, 381 U.S. 301, 308 (1965). . . .

28. Steven L. Winter, *A Clearing in the Forest: Law, Life, and Mind* 272 (U. of Chicago Press 2001).

29. Meir Dan-Cohen, *Rights, Persons, and Organizations: A Legal Theory for Bureaucratic Society* 44 (U. of Cal. Press 1986).

30. *Id.* at 5.

31. Student Author, *supra* note 13, at 176.

32. Mayer, *supra* note 15, at 658.

33. George Lakoff & Mark Johnson, *Metaphors We Live By* 139-146 (1980).

34. *Id.* at 145.

35. *Id.* at 139.

36. Chad M. Oldfather, *The Hidden Ball: A Substantive Critique of Baseball Metaphors in Judicial Opinions*, 27 Conn. L. Rev. 17, 20 n.8 (1994).

37. Lakoff & Johnson, *supra* note 33, at 153-154.

38. *Id.* at 91.

39. *Id.* at 10.

40. Oldfather, *supra* note 36, at 30.

41. Steven L. Winter, *The Metaphor of Standing and Problem of Self-Governance*, 40 Stan. L. Rev. 1384, 1387 (1988).

42. Neal Feigenson, *Legal Blame* 92 (American Psychological Association 2000).

43. Joshua Cooper Ramo, *The Age of the Unthinkable* 204 (Little, Brown and Company 2009).

44. *Id.* at 205.

45. Zenon W. Pylyshyn, *Seeing and Visualizing: It's Not What You Think* 3 (Bradford Books 2003).

46. Ann Marie Seward Barry, *Visual Intelligence, Perception, Image, and Manipulation in Visual Communication* 18 (State Univ of New York Press 1997); Joseph LeDoux, *The Emotional Brain* 61-62 (Simon & Schuster 1998).

47. Malcolm Gladwell, *Blink* 11-12 (Little, Brown and Company 2005).

48. Pylyshyn, *supra* note 45, at 40, 49-50.

49. Anthony G. Greenwald & Linda Hamilton Krieger, *Implicit Bias: Scientific Foundations*, 94 Cal. L. Rev. 945, 948 (2006).

50. Barry, *supra* note 46, at 18; Jerome S. Bruner, *On Perceptual Readiness*, in *Beyond the Information Given: Studies in the Psychology of Knowing* 7, 10 (Jeremy M. Anglin ed., W.W. Norton Co. 1973); Pylyshyn, *supra* note 45, at 41; Tom Stafford & Matt Webb, *Mind Hacks* 134 (O'Reilly Media 2004).

51. Stafford & Webb, *supra* note 50, at 134.

52. Barry, *supra* note 46, at 19.

17. *Storytelling*

Beginning with this chapter, we're back in more familiar terrain. We've been storytellers and story-listeners all our lives, so we don't have to learn a complicated new set of terms. That doesn't mean, though, that the ideas and implications won't be big.

We begin with a short excerpt from Professor Philip Meyer on the idea that our sense of justice (both generally and in a particular case) comes from and is maintained by story. If so, says Professor Meyer, brief-writers should take some time to learn how stories work.

Excerpt from

Philip N. Meyer, *Vignettes from a Narrative Primer*
12 Legal Writing 229, 229-230 (2006)

Let me begin by positing a broad initial claim: Attorneys, especially litigation attorneys, work in what is largely a storytelling or narrative culture. Legal arguments are, perhaps, best understood as disguised and translated stories. Even arguments whose structure is seemingly more formal and legalistic (as in appellate briefs or the judicial rhetoric of a United States Supreme Court opinion) may be best understood as narrative. It may appear initially that paradigmatic forms of legal reasoning "tame" narrative[1] and bring narrative impulses under control, translating and reshaping the story for purposes of argumentation. But let us assume, momentarily, that our notions of justice and right outcome are fundamentally grounded in and governed by narratives. Let us assume that we are truly narrative creatures and that we construct our sense of how the world works, of who we are, and of how events transpire, with the stories that are told to us, that we tell to others, and that we tell to ourselves. We use stories to order and mediate overwhelming environments of perceptions, informational data, and factual noises that might otherwise be incomprehensible. Stories are enabling and empowering and, indeed, fundamental to how we fashion our beliefs and how we act upon them.

Further, assume that our determination of the appropriate law governing a particular case, what is "right" in a particular case, what the outcome "should be," is likewise shaped by stories. Thus, perhaps more often than we care to admit, it is narrative that truly does the persuasive work in legal advocacy. If this is so, then it behooves [us] to better understand how stories work, and to develop a narrative tool kit supplementing the analytical skills traditionally taught in law school. . . .

So is that claim true? More specifically, are appellate judges actually persuaded by narrative? In our second excerpt, Professor Kenneth Chestek reports on his 2008 study to gauge the persuasive nature of narrative in appellate briefs.

The test instruments were four appellate briefs written for the same hypothetical case raising a pure question of law. Two briefs were written on behalf of the petitioner and two on behalf of the respondent. Of the two briefs written for each party, one contained only the legally relevant facts, those facts which set up the pure question of law. The other brief included expanded facts that told a story about that party and included a narrative theme. Study participants (appellate judges, appellate law clerks, appellate court staff attorneys, appellate practitioners, and law professors) were asked to compare the two briefs written on behalf of the same party.

What do you think Professor Chestek found? While the sample size was small, the study yielded some interesting results:

Excerpt from

Kenneth D. Chestek, *Judging by the Numbers: An Empirical Study of the Power of Story*
7 J. ALWD 1, 10-22 (2010)

. . . For my study, I attempted to write two "information-based narratives" (which I will refer to below as the "logos briefs") and two "story briefs." Each pair of briefs addressed opposite sides of a hypothetical case in a fictional jurisdiction. . . . A county in the fictional state of West Dakota had adopted (by voter referendum) an ordinance purporting to prohibit corporations from [exercising free speech rights to seek] to influence local government officials, on the theory that corporations are not "persons" protected by either the United States or West Dakota Bill of Rights. The corporate defendant, a retail hardware store, had the "easy case" to make (reliance on the doctrine of stare decisis and a 130-year-old Supreme Court precedent), while the county had a much harder case to make (seeking to overturn that long-settled principle of law).

The logos briefs were intentionally spare; they provided just the legally relevant facts . . . and focused tightly on the legal precedents and logical reasoning. . . . For example, the statement of the case in the logos briefs for both the hardware store and the county recited these bare but legally relevant facts: that the county voters had adopted Proposition 3 [purporting to deprive corporations of the right to speech designed to influence local government decisions]; that the hardware store had sought a rezoning for a parcel of land; that it had purchased a full-page advertisement in the local newspaper seeking to gain popular support among the local citizens for the rezoning request; that the rezoning request had been denied; and that because the advertisement violated the ordinance, the county had levied a fine against the hardware store. . . . While the store's and the county's briefs varied some of the word choices, sentence structures and selection of the facts in order to put more emphasis on the facts each side felt were more helpful to their sides, the end result was that the statements of facts in the two logos briefs were pretty similar.

The fact sections of the story briefs, however, were very different [from each other. Both briefs set out] a satisfying pre-existing condition that was lost when the controversy arose. [In both briefs, the fact statement subtly implied that the opposing party was responsible for the disruption. The narrative appeals to the court to restore the original narratively satisfying situation. Each story brief relies on the appealing theme of freedom. The brief for the county relies on a theme of freedom to make local decisions, and the brief for the corporation relies on the free market ideal.] . . .

A. Overall Results

My first hypothesis was that the story brief would prove to be more persuasive than the pure logos brief. The overall data suggest that hypothesis is correct:

Table 2: All Participants

Brief	More persuasive (n)	%
Logos brief	29	30.5%
Story brief	61	64.2%
Neither	5	5.3%
TOTAL	95	100%

My second hypothesis was that the story brief would have a greater impact on the Respondent side of the case, since the law favored Petitioner. Table 3 breaks down the results between Petitioner and Respondent briefs.

Given the sample size, these results likely fall within the margin of error for this study. In short, my second test hypothesis appears to have been disproven; there was no significant difference between the Respondent briefs and the Petitioner briefs. Storytelling seems to work in all cases, not just hard ones.

Table 3: Petitioner vs. Respondent

Brief	More persuasive (n)	%
Respondent briefs		
Logos brief	16	33.3%
Story brief	30	62.5%
Neither	2	4.2%
TOTAL	48	100%
Petitioner briefs		
Logos brief	13	27.7%
Story brief	31	66.0%
Neither	3	6.4%
TOTAL	47	100%

B. Differences by Job Function

One of the main purposes of this study was to determine, if possible, whether stories persuaded the primary audience for briefs: appellate judges.

Unfortunately, while 23 appellate judges initially registered for the study, only 13 ultimately read the briefs and completed the study. Thus, in an effort to get a larger sample, I initially combined the categories of appellate judges, appellate court staff attorneys, and appellate law clerks into a category of "readers of briefs." I then compared those results with "writers of briefs" (the appellate practitioners), and the law professor category. These results are displayed in Table 4.

Table 4: Responses by Participant Group

Brief	"Readers"		"Writers"		Law Profs	
Logos	12	36.4%	8	21.6%	9	36.0%
Story	19	57.6%	27	73.0%	15	60.0%
Neither	2	6.1%	2	5.4%	1	4.0%
TOTAL	33		37		25	

In this grouping, it appeared that the law professors reacted to story in almost exactly the same way that the readers group did. Upon reflection, however, I wondered if the readers group was as homogeneous as I thought. I therefore did another chart, breaking the readers group down into its constituent parts. The results of that analysis are shown in Table 5.

The most interesting difference revealed in Table 5 is the wide discrepancy between law clerks and other "readers" as to how persuasive the logos brief was to them. . . .

Table 5: Responses by Participant Type

Brief	Appellate Judges		Law Clerks		Staff Attorneys		Practitioners		Law Profs.	
Logos	4	30.8%	6	50.0%	2	25.0%	8	21.6%	9	36.0%
Story	7	53.8%	6	50.0%	6	75.0%	27	73.0%	15	60.0%
Neither	2	15.4%	0	0.0%	0	0.0%	2	5.4%	1	4.0%
TOTAL	13		12		8		37		25	

C. Gender Differences

I was also curious to see if there was any gender-based difference in the responses. Stereotypically, women are perceived to be more emotional; would they respond to the story brief in greater numbers than the male participants? It appears that gender made absolutely no difference; men and women reacted to the briefs in virtually identical ways. Table 6 analyzes all participants by gender.

Table 6: Gender Differences

Brief	More persuasive (n)	%
Male participants (n = 56)		
Logos brief	17	30.4%
Story brief	36	64.3%
Neither	3	5.4%
Female participants (n = 39)		
Logos brief	12	30.8%
Story brief	25	64.1%
Neither	2	5.2%

D. Job Longevity

One of the demographic questions asked participants how long they had held their current job. I was curious to see if participants got more jaded over time, favoring pure logic over the "softer" story briefs. Surprisingly, I found the opposite to be true. It appears that the longer one works in a particular job, the more the story of the case is persuasive. Table 7 breaks down the responses by the number of years each participant had held his or her current job.

Table 7: Responses by Experience in Job

Brief	0-4 yrs.		5-9 yrs.		10-14 yrs		15-19 yrs.		20-24 yrs.		25+ yrs.	
Logos	11	30.8%	5	33.3%	4	26.7%	1	10.0%	6	35.3%	2	14.3%
Story	13	53.8%	9	60.0%	9	60.0%	9	90.0%	10	58.8%	11	78.6%
Neither	0	15.4%	1	6.7%	2	13.3%	0	0.0%	1	5.9%	1	7.1%
TOTAL	24		15		8		10		17		14	

Grouping the two ends of the spectrum together reveals an interesting pattern:

Table 8: Responses by Experience Groups

Brief	More persuasive (n)	%
0-9 years' experience (n = 39)		
Logos brief	16	41.0%
Story brief	22	56.4%
Neither	1	2.6%
15+ years' experience (n = 41)		
Logos brief	9	22.0%
Story brief	30	73.2%
Neither	2	4.9%

The article then summarizes the study's main findings:

1. The story briefs were more persuasive than the logos briefs.
2. There were no gender differences.
3. The more experience the reader had, the more likely the reader would find the story brief more persuasive than the logos brief.

So it looks as if perhaps stories are persuasive to appellate judges, and if so, Professor Meyer is right that we should learn something about the way our brains process stories. This excerpt from Professor Jennifer Sheppard gives us a good summary of some of these cognitive concepts. The article begins with a principle that should sound familiar by now: that in order to construct meaning, the human mind requires an interpretive framework:

Excerpt from

Jennifer Sheppard, *Once Upon a Time, Happily Ever After, and in a Galaxy Far, Far Away: Using Narrative to Fill the Cognitive Gap Left by Overreliance on Pure Logic in Appellate Briefs and Motion Memoranda*
46 Willamette L. Rev. 255, 259-263 (2009-2010)

According to cognitive researchers, human perception and cognition require some interpretive framework with which to construct meaning and reality.[2] Consequently, humans make sense of new experiences by fitting them into "cognitive structures," or "categories in the mind," called schemas.[3] Schemas are "mental structure[s] which contain[] general expectations and knowledge of the world"[4] and are based on "simplified models of experiences [an individual has] had before."[5] Thus, schemas serve as "mental blueprints" that organize an individual's experiences and knowledge of the world into an existing framework that allows him or her to assess new situations and ideas without having to "interpret things afresh."[6] Thus, schemas allow an individual to conserve mental energy by functioning as a form of "shorthand that transcribes [an individual's] stored knowledge of the world. . . ."[7] Schemas also help the individual understand people, events, objects, and their relationships to each other in a way that is meaningful "based on what [that individual has] come to believe is natural through experience within a particular culture."[8] Schemas, therefore, function as cognitive "shortcuts" that transform unfamiliar situations into events that are within an individual's range of experience.[9]

In order to construct meaning in a new situation, an individual must go beyond the information that the new situation supplies.[10] That is where schemas come into play; schemas allow an individual to fill in the gaps and to "draw inferences about what has happened in the past and about what is likely to happen in the future."[11] For example, consider the following situation: "John went to a party. The next morning he woke up with a headache."[12] While no explanation is offered regarding why John had a headache the morning after the party, an individual will have no trouble supplying one.[13] A schema quickly provides the explanation. . . . The schema fills in the gap by tapping into [preexisting] knowledge and providing an explanation that goes beyond the information given.[14]

These schemas, or interpretative frameworks, are always at work helping individuals to quickly assess what they "should be seeing and feeling in a given situation."[15] Consequently, schemas constantly filter and affect what [an individual] see[s] and think[s]."[16] They function on an unconscious level, shaping an individual's perceptions and reasoning processes[17] "like a 'hidden hand' that shapes how [the individual] conceptualize[s] all aspects of [his or her] experience."[18]

Narratives, or stories, serve as an interpretative framework in which multiple schemas are operating at once. Humans have a "predisposition to organize experience into narrative form";[19] in fact, "this predisposition toward narrative is . . . as natural to human comprehension of the world as [an individual's] visual rendering of what the eye sees."[20] Consequently, narrative form is "an innate schema" for the organization and understanding of human experience.[21] Because humans learn by interacting with their environment,[22] they understand concepts expressed in the form of stories better than they understand abstract principles.[23] Thus, narratives are "central to [an individual's] ability to make sense out of a series of chronological events."[24]

Stock stories, also referred to as master stories or myths,[25] provide ways for an entire culture to interpret certain experiences[26] and are "infused with social meaning."[27] Stock stories serve as "an idealized cognitive model" of a story that provides a template, or path, for a wide variety of other similar stories to follow.[28] They supply a way of viewing events that allows individuals to understand their experiences and to predict the outcome,[29] offering "mental models" of the ordinary course events should take[30] based on individuals' preconceived "understandings of common events and concepts, configured into a particular pattern of story-meaning."[31] These narratives serve as "recipes for structuring experience itself, . . . for . . . guiding the life narrative up to the present [and] directing it into the future."[32] Thus, narratives not only allow individuals to predict what will happen in a particular situation, but what they will need to do in response to the circumstances.[33] Moreover, "[s]tock stories not only contain standard models for human action but also allow generalizations about the meaning of those actions."[34] . . .

Narratives, like other schemas, generally operate on a subconscious level. They affect how an individual thinks in any given situation without the individual being aware of their impact.[35] The subconscious effect of narrative allows an individual to make sense of new situations. . . . Thus, stock stories not only function as cognitive shortcuts that provide meaning to a set of events that would otherwise seem random, but they also reinforce traditional cultural and societal values. . . . Once the individual's cognitive mind has selected a stock story within which to interpret the situation, that individual's judgments will be based on the assumptions derived from the social knowledge embedded in the story rather than on the unique characteristics of the current situation.[36] Furthermore, the outcome suggested by the stock story will seem inevitable, as though it is the natural result of the events that preceded it.[37] . . .

Is There Such a Thing as an "Objective" Recitation of Facts?

So far, it might seem that a judge starts with an "unbiased" view of the facts and that a lawyer's job is to trigger a stock story that will "bias" the judge's view of the facts. But actually, as much she might like to, the judge does not start with an unbiased view. There is no such thing as an unbiased view. We cannot become aware of a set of facts without selecting language for those facts, focusing on particular events and details, and organizing them into something that resembles a plot. The moment the judge becomes aware of the facts, these pivotal story-creating actions automatically happen. When does that happen? Kendall Haven describes research by University of Texas neurobiologist Dr. David Engleman:

> . . . Engleman's research has shown that the brain lives just a little bit in the past. A human brain collects a lot of information and then pauses for a moment to organize it before releasing the processed information to the

conscious mind. "Now" actually happened a little while (several milli-seconds) ago.

To demonstrate this to yourself, tap your finger on a tabletop at arm's length. Light travels faster than sound. So the sight actually reached you a few milliseconds before the sounds. However, your brain synchronized the two to make them *seem* simultaneous. The same thing happens when you watch someone's lips move as they speak. During these microsecond pauses the brain/mind constructs a plausible story to make the incoming information make sense. Sensory impressions enter the brain; stories exit to the conscious mind for interpretation and action. A significant part of what the brain does for the conscious mind is structure experience into story.[38]

So is writing a fact statement that tells a story an attempt to bias the judge? To take the judge from an "unbiased" position to a "biased" position? No. Here is how Kendall Haven puts it:

> There is no such thing as "the truth, the whole truth, and nothing but the truth."[39] Bruner agreed when he stated, ". . . language . . . can never be neutral. It imposes a point of view not only about the world to which it refers but also toward the use of mind in respect to that world."[40] The act of selecting certain words and images to include and/or to exclude from a story automatically places both a personal bias and set of values into the writing that will color the reader's images and thus, technically, fictionalize the writing. The myth of the dispassionate, neutral observer is just that, a myth, a fiction that never actually existed.[41]

In other words, from the first moment of becoming aware of an event, we start with an assumed perspective and, most likely, a stock story or schema. The question is not *whether* to persuade a judge to see the events through a schema but *which schema* the judge will use. If a judge does not realize that there is more than one way to see the facts, the judge will remain unconsciously captive to a set of unexamined narrative assumptions. The lawyer's job is to give the judge the chance to examine those assumptions. Harvard Law School's Dean, Martha Minow, writes:

Language can never be neutral.

> The Rabbi hears in his study a dispute between two congregants. He listens to the first person carefully and comments, "You're right." Then he listens to the second person and concludes, "You're right." The Rabbi's wife, over-hearing it all from the kitchen, calls out, "They can't both be right." "You're right also," says the Rabbi.
>
> Offered as an illustration of the limitation of stories themselves to guide the evaluation of stories, this story also suggests a guide to the entire set of dilemmas that I have described. The guide is a posture of humility and acknowledgment of the partiality of truths. To generalize far beyond the context of that story, let me suggest the following: Modes of analysis and argument that maintain their exclusive hold on the truth are suspect. By casting doubt on alternative modes, they shield themselves from challenge and suppress alternative ways of understanding. They also render ordinary and explicable all they encounter: "To a hammer, everything looks like a nail." But some things are extraordinary and call for extraordinary responses.

Methods of analysis that smooth out the bumps and subsume all under generalizations risk not only making this mistake but hiding it from view.[42]

The Role of Narrative in Other Forms of Legal Reasoning

It might be tempting to think that narrative is inconsistent with rule-based and other forms of legal reasoning, but as Professor Nancy Levit says, it's stories all the way down:

> Philosopher William James once explained what an "absolute moralist" believed by describing a series of rocks, one rock resting atop another one: "it was rocks all the way down."[43] A perhaps apocryphal story growing out of this, maybe influenced by Hindu cosmology which posits that the Earth rests on the back of a giant turtle . . . is that "It's turtles all the way down."[44] This metaphor became important in jurisprudence circles when critical legal studies scholars began to explain how power worked.[45] It is an explanation that applies to narrative as well. Everyone tells stories: People in power tell stories too. It's stories all the way down.[46]

How can that be? How can we say that rules and analogies and policies are made up of narrative? That's a huge question. Here are just a few thoughts:

Excerpt from

Linda H. Edwards, *The Convergence of Analogical and Dialectic Imaginations in Legal Discourse*
20 Legal Stud. F. 7, 20-27 (1996)

This second use of narrative reasoning—using the reasoning to create and announce a rule of law—is more common. In this situation, the judge uses parts of the narratives presented by the facts to create or modify a legal rule. Then the judge applies that rule to reach a result in the pending case. Often the rule provides evidence of its narrative origin by its presentation in a casuistic, "if/then" structure, a blatantly narratival form. A rule in a casuistic structure describes a set of circumstances and then pronounces a result: If A, B, and C occur, then Y is the legal conclusion. . . . Consider, for instance, the rule defining the elements for a cause of action based on fraud. A common articulation of the rule provides that a defendant has perpetrated a fraud if:

1. the defendant made a representation;
2. the representation was false;
3. the defendant knew the representation was false when making it;
4. the defendant intended that the hearer rely on the representation;
5. the hearer did rely;
6. the reliance was justified;
7. damage resulted.

These elements tell the story of a plaintiff entitled to relief in a cause of action for fraud. If one could locate the first successful fraud case articulating these elements, one would probably find that these elements tell the story of that individual plaintiff.

Rules born of narrative seldom arrive fully formed. After a judge has created a legal rule from a narrative, the rule is often modified by future narratives. In subsequent cases, the narratives of future litigants bump up against the rule created from the narratives of the first set of litigants, with the result that the rule becomes more and more refined. In resolving the tensions between present narratives and the original narrative (now in the form of the rule), judges define terms, add criteria, and develop exceptions.

Rules are mini-stories.

For instance, the articulation of the elements for a fraud claim might not have originally included all of the seven listed elements. That first court might have stated the elements more simply, perhaps articulating only that the defendant must have made a false representation and the hearer must have relied upon it to her damage. The elements requiring that the defendant knew of the falsity, that the defendant intended that the hearer rely, and that reliance was justified may have been added to the rule when the stories of subsequent litigants raised those issues for the first time.

Thus, subsequent stories call into question the adequacy of the rule crafted from the first story. Each succeeding story refines the rule further, as new plot twists test or define the existing rule. Must the defendant have actual knowledge of the falsity or will reckless disregard be enough? Must the representation be express or can failure to speak be sufficient? Is "reasonableness" judged by an objective or a subjective standard? Must the defendant be of the age of majority or can a minor who has reached a lesser age, an age of discretion, be held responsible for a false representation? At each stage, the newly-created or newly-modified rule becomes the standard for evaluating future litigation stories. In this sense, the rule comes to constitute a form of literary criticism. . . .

[Forms of reasoning other than rule-based reasoning] have narrative roots as well, though in each case the reasoning is several steps removed from the narrative.

Analogical reasoning is explicitly narratival, for it compares the present story to the stories of other litigants in other cases. . . .

Consensual normative reasoning [supporting a result by appealing to culturally recognized attitudes and practices] also grows from narrative roots because it compares the litigant's story with the stories that are customary in similar situations. . . .

Next, consider policy-based reasoning, perhaps the most complex of the forms of reasoning. Policy-based reasoning relies on many components that are not directly narratival: aesthetic

Library of Congress (circa 1900-1930)

Wild fox

principles, scientific models, social organization, economic analysis, efficiency concerns, political realities, and predictable psychological reactions. However, even policy-based reasoning has narratival roots. First, much of policy-based reasoning is a way of articulating and valuing the stories of non-parties. These non-parties may be real characters or hypothetical characters designed to represent the interest of other real groups. But much of policy-based reasoning is directly drawn from the stories of these real or fictional characters. For instance, in *Pierson v. Post* [the famous fox hunting case from the first-year Property course], the majority based its rejection of the claim of Post's individual story on the imagined stories of future fox hunters who would be arguing with each other, perhaps coming to blows, and prolonging their disputes with litigation over whether hunter A or hunter B had been first in pursuit of the fox. The majority decided that it was more important to prevent these future stories than to redress the inequities of the present individual stories.[47]

The policy-based reasoning that forms almost the entire basis of the dissent in *Pierson v. Post* is even more directly narratival. Judge Livingston spent more time describing the [imagined] stories of three non-parties or groups of non-parties [farmers, foxes, and future hunters] than he spent in describing the stories of Pierson and Post. . . .

Second, the cognitive process of realizing the existence of these other stories is a narratival activity. Gary Saul Morson, a leading scholar of Russian and comparative literature, has dubbed this activity "sideshadowing."[48] Sideshadowing defines a field of possible stories, not what *did* happen but what *might* have happened.

These other possible stories shadow the actual stories, and demand adjudicative attention. Realizing what did not, but might have happened in the pending case, is part of the process of realizing and evaluating these other possible stories. And considering these other possible stories frees the law from a result that might have seemed preordained by the stories of the present litigants. Thus, part of the value of policy-based reasoning is to loosen the grip of the individual narratives and enlarge the narrative options to include other possible stories.

side shadowing

Third, policy-based reasoning includes consideration of moral principles, and as Robert Cover has explained, moral value originates in myth and cultural narrative.[49] Like Cover, moral theologian Stanley Hauerwas argues that our convictions about how we ought to behave socially and politically are rooted in values encoded in cultural narratives which define and form our character.[50] . . .

The "Voices" Brief

We saw in the Bartrum excerpt in Chapter 14 that one of the pivotal moments in the history of brief-writing came in the case of *Muller v. Oregon*,[51] when Louis Brandeis filed the brief for the Defendant in Error, the brief which almost immediately became known as "the Brandeis Brief." That brief is credited with creating a new form of express argument based on policy and social science evidence. Just as the Brandeis Brief taught us how to use policy to argue a question of law, we might think of the amicus brief filed by the National Abortion Rights Action League (the "Voices" brief)[52] as showing us a new way to use stories to support an argument on a pure question of law. In "Theorizing and Litigating the Rights of Sexual Minorities,"[53] Professor Nancy Levit describes the brief this way:

> . . . This brief was primarily a collection of stories of women from all walks of life who had abortions both legally and illegally. These were teenagers, women who were raped when they sought abortion services, women who were prosecuted when they had illegal abortions, those who had abortions

in unsafe conditions when abortions were illegal, those who had abortions after Roe v. Wade in safe, clean, and supportive environments, women who had health problems that made childbirth dangerous, those who did not have financial resources to raise children, some who had cancer while pregnant, divorced professional women, married women with physically abusive spouses, some who suffered failed birth control methods, women who were pregnant as a result of rape (including a former nun raped by a priest), those afflicted with severe illnesses that necessitated abortion to save their lives, some who were addicted to drugs or alcohol, and some who carried fetuses with genetic diseases such as Tay-Sachs. These were not paradigm plaintiffs; they were Everywoman. The brief, directed at a Court composed at the time of seven older men and two older women (none of whom, presumably, had ever had an abortion), was intended to show that abortion decisions are not made frivolously or easily and to illuminate the many circumstances in which abortion is a justifiable choice.

The storytelling technique in the Voices Brief was based on the idea that "moral convictions are changed experientially and empathically, not through argument."[54] Although no member of the Court has ever cited the Voices Brief, it may have encouraged some empathetic understanding. For instance, when the Court struck the spousal notification law in *Planned Parenthood of Southeastern Pennsylvania v. Casey*, the plurality recognized some married women who were the victims of domestic violence might have good reason not to tell their spouses about their pregnancies.[55]

Professor Robin West, who teaches the brief every year, wrote:

Every year, at least one student . . . tells me that the brief changed his mind on abortion. . . . [The Voices brief] does something that Sunstein's book[56] simply does not even attempt: it *shows*—illustrates—the terrible consequences of rolling back *Roe v. Wade*. Obviously, one does not have to have *been there* to understand what those consequences might be. However, one must indeed somehow be shown those consequences. The consequence that matters is that, in a world of illegal abortion, some of us, but only some of us, live out a regime of terror, torture, and unnecessary death. This is not a hard point to grasp. But, to be grasped, it must be shown. Principles and reason do not make the case.[57]

Discussion Questions

1. Look back at the results of Professor Chestek's study. Which results would you have predicted? Which results surprised you? Why?
2. What commonalities do you see between the material in this chapter and the material in our prior chapters on categories and metaphor (Chapters 15 and 16)? Given what we've read, how much can we trust our own perceptions and opinions? Should we try to hold our own perceptions and opinions lightly, perhaps even with some degree of skepticism?
3. What does the material in this chapter teach us about persuasion in general and persuasion of judges in particular?

Additional Suggested Reading

Jerome Bruner & Anthony Amsterdam, *Minding the Law* (Harv. U. Press 2002).

Robert Cover, *Nomos & Narrative*, 97 Harv. L. Rev. 4 (1983).

Linda H. Edwards, *The Convergence of Analogical and Dialectic Imaginations in Legal Discourse*, 20 Leg. Stud. F. 7 (1996).

Jeanne M. Kaiser, *When the Truth and the Story Collide: What Legal Writers Can Learn from the Experience of Non-Fiction Writers About the Limits of Legal Storytelling*, 16 Legal Writing 163 (2010).

Krieger & Neumann, *Essential Lawyering Skills* (Wolters Kluwer 2007).

Michigan Storytelling Symposium, 87 Mich. L. Rev. 2073 (1988-1989).

J. Christopher Rideout, *Storytelling, Narrative Rationality, and Legal Persuasion*, 14 Legal Writing 53 (2008).

Endnotes

1. Jerome Bruner, *Actual Minds, Possible Worlds* 11-43 (Harvard U. Press 1986); Jerome Bruner, *On Knowing: Essays for the Left Hand* (Belknap Press of Harvard U. Press 1964).

2. Richard K. Sherwin, *The Narrative Construction of Legal Reality*, 18 Vt. L. Rev. 681, 717 (1994).

3. Clive Baldwin, *Who Needs Facts When You've Got Narrative? The Case of* P, C & S v. United Kingdom, 18 Int'l J. Semiotics L. 217, 236 (2005); Linda L. Berger, *How Embedded Knowledge Structures Affect Judicial Decision Making: A Rhetorical Analysis of Metaphor, Narrative, and Imagination in Child Custody Disputes*, 18 S. Cal. Interdisc. L.J. 259, 264 (2009).

4. Ronald Chen & Jon Hanson, *Categorically Biased: The Influence of Knowledge Structures on Law and Legal Theory*, 77 S. Cal. L. Rev. 1103, 1133 (2004) (quoting Martha Augoustinos & Iain Walker, *Social Cognition: An Integrated Introduction* 34 (Sage Publications 1995)).

5. Sherwin, *supra* note 2, at 700.

6. *Id.*; Berger, *supra* note 3, at 265.

7. Sherwin, *supra* note 2, at 700.

8. Berger, *supra* note 3, at 265.

9. *Id.*

10. Sherwin, *supra* note 2, at 700-701.

11. Baldwin, *supra* note 3, at 236; Chen & Hanson, *supra* note 4, at 1133. . . .

12. Sherwin, *supra* note 2, at 700.

13. *Id.*

14. *Id.* at 701.

15. *Id.* at 700.

16. Berger, *supra* note 3, at 266; Sherwin, *supra* note 2, at 717.

17. Berger, *supra* note 3, at 262.

18. George Lakoff & Mark Johnson, *Philosophy in the Flesh: The Embodied Mind and Its Challenge to Western Thought* 13 (Basic Books 1999).

19. Jerome Bruner, *Acts of Meaning* 45 (Harvard U. Press 1990); Robert P. Burns, *A Theory of the Trial* 159 (Princeton U. Press 1999); J. Christopher Rideout, *Storytelling, Narrative Rationality, and Legal Persuasion*, 14 Legal Writing 54, 57 (2008).

20. Rideout, *supra* note 19, at 58.

21. Burns, *supra* note 19, at 159; Rideout, *supra* note 19, at 55, 58.

22. Michael R. Smith, *Advanced Legal Writing: Theories and Strategies in Persuasive Writing* 260 (Wolters Kluwer 2002).

23. *Id.* at 259.

24. Berger, *supra* note 3, at 266; Anthony Amsterdam & Jerome Bruner, *Minding the Law* 30-31 (Harvard U. Press 2000).

25. Linda H. Edwards, *Once Upon a Time in Law: Myth, Metaphor and Authority*, (77 Tenn. L. Rev. 885 (2010)).

26. Berger, *supra* note 3, at 268; Judith Olans Brown et al., *The Mythogenesis of Gender: Judicial Images of Women in Paid and Unpaid Labor*, 6 UCLA Women's L.J. 457, 457-458 (1996). . . .

27. Rideout, *supra* note 19, at 59.

28. Steven L. Winter, *A Clearing in the Forest* 106-113; Steven L. Winter, *Making the Familiar Conventional Again*, 99 Mich. L. Rev. 1607, 1629 (2001); Berger, *supra* note 3, at 268.

29. Anthony Amsterdam & Jerome Bruner, *Minding the Law* 17 (Harvard U. Press 2000); Berger, *supra* note 3, at 268.

30. Berger, *supra* note 3, at 268.

31. Rideout, *supra* note 19, at 59; Winter, *Making the Familiar Conventional Again*, *supra* note 28, at 1628-1629.

32. Berger, *supra* note 3, at 266; Jerome Bruner, *Life as Narrative*, 71 Soc. Res. 691, 708 (2004).

33. Berger, *supra* note 3, at 266.

34. Rideout, *supra* note 19, at 68. . . .

35. Berger, *supra* note 3, at 268; Brown, *supra* note 26, at 458.

36. Berger, *supra* note 3, at 299; Chen & Hanson, *supra* note 4, at 1231.

37. Berger, *supra* note 3, at 265; *see, e.g.*, David F. Chavkin, *Fuzzy Thinking: A Borrowed Paradigm for Crisper Lawyering*, 4 Clinical L. Rev. 163 (1997).

38. Kendall Haven, *Story Proof: The Science Behind the Startling Power of Story* 22 (Libraries Unlimited, Greenwood Publ. Group 2007).

39. M. Freeman, *Rethinking the Fictive, Reclaiming the Real: Autobiography, Narrative Time, and the Burden of Truth*, in *Narrative and Consciousness: Literature, Psychology and the Brain* 37-52 (G. Fireman et al. eds., Oxford U. Press 2003).

40. Jerome Bruner, *Actual Minds, Possible Worlds* (Harvard U. Press 1986).

41. Haven, *supra* note 38, at 128.

42. Martha Minow, *Stories in Law* 35, in *Law's Stories* (Peter Brooks & Paul Gewirtz eds., Yale U. Press 1996).

43. Roger C. Cramton, *Demystifying Legal Scholarship*, 75 Geo. L.J. 1, 1-2 (1986) (quoting William James, *The Will to Believe* 85 (Dover Publications 1979)).

44. Clifford Geertz, *The Interpretation of Cultures* 28-29 (Basic Books 2000); Stephen W. Hawking, *A Brief History of Time* 1 (Bantam 1988).

45. *See, e.g.*, Joseph William Singer, *Radical Moderation*, 1985 Am. B. Found. Res. J. 329, 329-330.

46. Nancy Levit, *Reshaping the Narrative Debate*, 34 Seattle U. L. Rev. 751, 755 (2011).

47. 3 Cai. R. 175, 2 Am. Dec. 264, 267 (Sup. Ct. N.Y. 1805).

48. Gary S. Morson, *Narrative and Freedom: The Shadows of Time* 6-9 (Yale U. Press 1994).

49. Robert M. Cover, *Nomos and Narrative*, 97 Harv. L. Rev. 4, 4-5 (1983).

50. Stanley Hauerwas, *A Community of Character* (U. of Notre Dame Press 1981).

51. 208 U.S. 412 (1908).

52. Brief of Amici Curiae National Abortion Rights Action League et al., *Thornburgh v. American College of Obstetricians & Gynecologists*, 476 U.S. 747 (1986) (Nos. 84-495 & 84-1379), *reprinted in* 9 Women's Rts. L. Rep. 3 (1986).

53. Nancy Levit, *Theorizing and Litigating the Rights of Sexual Minorities*, 19 Colum. J. Gender & L. 21, 40 (2010).

54. Robin L. West, *The Constitution of Reasons*, 92 Mich. L. Rev. 1409, 1436 (1994).

55. 505 U.S. 833, 888-893 (1992).

56. This article is a review of Cass R. Sunstein, *The Partial Constitution* (Harvard U. Press 1993).

57. Robin L. West, *The Constitution of Reasons*, 92 Mich. L. Rev. 1409, 1436 (1994).

18. *Clients' Stories*

"To understand all is to forgive all."

—French proverb

Story: n.: A detailed, character-based narration of a character's struggles to overcome obstacles and reach an important goal.

—Kendall Haven[1]

In Chapter 17 we saw that narrative is foundational to the way we see the world. The most obvious places for legal storytelling are in issue statements, fact statements, and procedural statements. In order to tell good stories there, we should be aware of the key elements of a story:

Key Elements of a Story

In his excellent and accessible book, "Story Proof," Kendall Haven identifies five core elements of a story:[2]

1. Characters, with enough detail to establish emotional states, beliefs, and attitudes and including a character from whose viewpoint (i.e., perspective) you will tell the story;
2. Intent (i.e., motives—what the characters seek and why);
3. Actions (what the characters do);
4. Struggle, which means there must be something to struggle against;
5. Details to create the mental imagery for envisioning and evaluating the story.

Haven uses a simple but powerful example of these elements:[3] We start with an action: Mother pours milk into a glass. This simple action does not constitute a story. But what if we add the five core elements? What if Mother has had a stroke which left her partially paralyzed? After months of in-patient physical therapy, she comes home with her young son. It is a school day, and her son comes into the kitchen for breakfast. Mother's arm is weak, and her grip is uncertain. Here is the scene:

> The milk carton . . . is heavy and slippery. It slips and falls; she spills; she misses the glass; she overfills it, sending a white flood across the counter and dribbling onto the floor. Through tears of embarrassment and frustration, she is determined to pour a simple glass of milk for her son. She *has* to. She struggles to will her arm to make one more try.[4]

As Haven says, now this simple action is becoming a story. We want to know what happens. Mother has become a character, through whose perspective we experience the scene. She has a goal. She acts. She struggles. And we have powerful details to carry home the other core elements. In order to complete the story, we'll need a resolution, of course, but notice how the addition of the core elements of story have created an urgency to know what happens—a strong desire to see Mother succeed. This kind of desire is part of the reason that narratives are so persuasive. So what makes a story good? We'll get some help from our next readings:

Plot

Excerpt from
Anthony G. Amsterdam & Jerome Bruner, *Minding the Law*
113-114 (2000)

[A narrative] needs a *plot* with a beginning, a middle, and an end, in which particular characters are involved in particular events. The unfolding of the plot requires (implicitly or explicitly):

1. an initial *steady state* grounded in the legitimate ordinariness of things
2. that gets disrupted by a *Trouble* consisting of circumstances attributable to human agency or susceptible to change by human intervention,
3. in turn evoking *efforts* at redress or transformation, which succeed or fail,
4. so that the old steady state is *restored* or a new (*transformed*) steady state is created,
5. and the story concludes by drawing the then-and-there of the tale that has been told into the here-and-now of the telling through some *coda*—say, for example, Aesop's characteristic *moral of the story*.

That is the bare bones of it. One could add more, though not without getting into quarrels with some narratologist or other. For example, does a narrative imply a narrator with a *point of view*? Well, perhaps, though novelists until recently tried to create the illusion that their

Library of Congress (Harris & Ewing, circa 1913-1917)

Tornado

narrator was omniscient and therefore needed no point of view. Or, does narrative imply "commitment" or caring in its characters (*Sorge*, as Ricoeur calls it)?[5] To those who say yes, postmodernists say no.[6] We think our present list of features is long enough to provide ample room for thought about such matters later.

_____

Themes and Characters

The idea that a brief should have a theme is surely familiar advice. Nor need we spend much time explaining what we mean by a theme in the context of a brief. The theme is drawn from the perspective and the plot. It is a tightly compressed expression of why the story should end in a particular way. It is often the answer to this question: What is this case about? If you can answer that question in a way that convinces your reader of your desired outcome, you have found a theme.

Characters may be the most important elements of a story[7] because they are the actors who make the theme "work." As we shall see in the later excerpt on "showing and telling," the best way to establish character is not to assert particular character traits, but rather to use events and details to paint a picture for the reader, allowing the reader to create an image that is seemingly her own. Identify the main characters of your story, and ask yourself what kind of people you want your reader to think they are. Then find and use the pieces of the story that can help you help the reader come to that same conclusion. Finally, remember that at least some of your characters can and perhaps should change during the course of the story. Change in a key character can drive the plot, add narrative energy, and help you build a theme.

Other Story Elements

Excerpt from
Philip N. Meyer, *Vignettes from a Narrative Primer*
12 Legal Writing 229, 241, 250-251 (2006)

We often hear that the best and most appropriate perspective for telling a legal story is that of the client. Generally, this advice is meant to say that we want the reader to understand the story as our client likely experienced it. That advice is nearly always true. But we can learn more about perspective, especially if we think of it as related to who is doing the reporting. Great brief-writers often adopt the perspective of others, including potentially "neutral" observers like governmental agents, social workers, doctors, or police officers. This reading helps us think more deeply about perspective, or point of view:

Perspective

David Lodge observes, "The choice of the points(s) of view from which the story is told is arguably the most important single decision that the [writer] has to make, for it fundamentally affects the way readers will respond, emotionally and morally."[8] . . . What, exactly, is point of view? . . . What are the advantages and disadvantages of differing perspectives, and their possible utility in the tool kit of the legal storyteller? Is it possible, or appropriate, to shift points of view within the text of an argument without "breaking the frame" of the narrative?

A starting point for answers to such questions appears in Gardner's identification of five common points of view or perspectives in narrative composition.[9] The "first person" is, perhaps, the most "natural" voice, because it allows the writer to write as he thinks and talks, and to write simply about how he perceives the world.[10] The second often-adopted narrative perspective, according to Gardner, is the "third person subjective, a point of view in which all the 'I's' are changed to 'he's or she's' and emphasis is placed on the character's thoughts."[11] The third "point of view" or perspective Gardner labels is the "third-person objective," which is "identical to the third-person subjective except that the narrator not only never comments himself but also refrains from entering any character's mind. The result is an ice-cold camera's-eye recording. We see events, hear dialogue, observe the setting, and make guesses about what the characters are thinking."[12] Fourth, there is the "authorial omniscient point of view."[13] In this fourth voice,

> [t]he writer . . . sees into all his characters' hearts and minds, presents all positions with . . . detachment, occasionally . . . gives the reader an immediate sense of why the character feels as he does, but reserves to himself the right to judge (a right he uses sparingly).[14]

Finally, Gardner identifies the "essayist omniscient" and differentiates this perspective from that of the authorial omniscient: "The language of the authorial-omniscient voice is traditional and neutral. . . . Every authorial-omniscient voice sounds much like every other."[15] In contrast, "[t]he essayist-omniscient voice, though it has nearly the same divine authority, is more personal."[16] The "essayist-omniscient" voice is more personal because the fact of a speaker, and the identity of the speaker, is intimated by "personal" qualities in the "voice" of the writer.

We have thought now about themes, characters, and perspectives, so it is time to think about how these story elements can be conveyed. Here are several important ways. The first, "showing and telling," may be the most important lesson beginning legal storytellers should learn. The idea is that the writer should decide, strategically, which points will be shown to the reader and which points will be stated by the writer. Generally, the more important the point is to the client's case, the more the brief should avoid stating the narrative's conclusion. Rather, the story itself should show the reader the conclusion, so that the reader comes to those conclusions herself. Conversely, the less the conclusion is favorable, the more likely that the brief should tell the conclusion rather than show it.

"Showing and Telling"

In [an] essay for writers entitled *Showing and Telling*, David Lodge identifies the virtues and vices of "showing" as compared to "telling."[17] Initially, he observes, the "purest form of showing" is "quoted speech of characters, in which language exactly mirrors the event," while the "purest form of telling is authorial summary, in which the conciseness and abstraction of the narrator's language effaces the particularity and individuality of the characters and their actions."[18] The sophisticated brief writer employs the "virtues" of each technique, often choosing to build briefs largely from verbatim excerpts of transcripts, direct quotations from opinions, and from external and purportedly objective sources.

Lodge admonishes the young writer that overuse of authorial summary is . . . deadening. . . .[19] Nevertheless, summary has its uses, [such as accelerating] the tempo . . . , "hurrying us through events which would be uninteresting, or *too* interesting—therefore distracting, if lingered over."[20]

Later in the article, we see an example of how to show rather than merely tell:

. . . For example, . . . raising powerful mitigating evidence that was not presented in the capital sentence in *Williams v. Taylor*,[21] defendant's counsel first speaks of omitted evidence abstractly, based upon a "traumatic childhood," and a mother who "drank herself into a stupor almost daily while pregnant with him."[22] By itself, these abstractions are merely cliché and without impact upon the reader. However it is the imagery and details from "uncontroverted juvenile records,"[23] presumably from the notes and direct observations of an "objective" social worker who had visited the family's home, and who was charged with protecting the children on behalf of the State, that visually capture the quality of Williams's childhood, and manage to bring "the sordid conditions of Williams's home" to life for the reader:[24]

> Lula and Noah [the parents] were sitting on the front porch and were in such a drunken state, it was almost impossible to get them up. They staggered into the house to where the children were asleep. Terry, age 1, and Noah Jr., age 3, were asleep on the sofa. There was an odor of alcohol on the breath of Noah Jr. . . . [Olivia] had just awakened and was very sick. She said she was hungry and had been drinking whiskey. Ohair was completely passed out and never could be awakened. He did not have on any clothes. . . .
>
> The home was a complete wreck. . . . There were several places on the floor where someone had had a bowel movement. Urine was standing in several places in the bedrooms. There were dirty dishes scattered over the kitchen, and it was impossible to step any place on the kitchen floor where there was no trash. . . . The children were all dirty and none of them had on under-pants. Noah and Lula were so intoxicated, they could not find any clothes for the children, nor were they able to put the clothes on them. There was stuffed pickle scattered on the floor in the front bedroom.
>
> Noah and Lula were put in jail, each having five charges of neglect placed against them. The children had to be put in Winslow Hospital, as four of them, by that time, were definitely under the influence of whisky. When Dr. Harvey examined them, he found that they had all been drinking bootleg whiskey. They were all hungry and very happy to be given milk, even the baby [Terry] drank a pint of milk before stopping. [Olivia] said they had not had any food all day. Ohair was still so drunk he could not talk.[25]

The writer . . . does not comment upon the meaning of this evidence. But he has the confidence to present the images, and simply conclude, "Williams'[s] parents were jailed for criminal neglect, and the children were placed in a foster home where they were badly treated before being returned to their parents three years later."[26] The understatement serves the vivid imagery well, as it is left to the reader to understand the defendant as a product of his bleak social history. The imagery, conveyed through hard visual detail *invites*—but the understated framing language does not *force*—the reader to enter momentarily into the horrific world of the defendant as a small boy.

A second method for creating theme, characters, and perspective is the conscious decision about what voice to use to convey different facts:

Telling in Different Voices

Often, the strongest narratives are not created through the voice of the author. Rather, they are provided by the voices of other speakers and writers. The brief writer must assemble and transform compelling collages of quotations into structured compositions of pieces, developed from previous tellings and retellings of the story. These pieces are often reconfigured in some new way that makes this retelling compel the responsiveness of the court. The voices that speak through the brief are often in the form of quotations from transcripts, testimony, and judicial opinions. The use of other voices, from purportedly objective or disinterested sources, like prior appellate opinions, is a powerful narrative tool. In an important sense, the brief writer is rendering the statement of the case through the use of quotation, another technique employed in non-fiction, in which the art is often in the quality of the investigation, and in the meticulous exploration and reassembly of what the pieces of testimonial evidence reveal. . . .

Sometimes—perhaps, for example, when a domestic violence client seeks a protective order—the most effective theme may be the story of the client's heroic struggle toward transformation and a better life. In such cases, consider using Professor Ruth Anne Robbins' suggestions in this next reading:

Excerpt from

Ruth Anne Robbins, *Harry Potter, Ruby Slippers, and Merlin: Telling the Client's Story Using the Characters and Paradigm of the Archetypal Hero's Journey*
29 Seattle L. Rev. 767 (Summer 2006)

What can Harry Potter[27] teach us about how to represent our clients? Potentially, quite a lot. . . . There is a reason why *Harry Potter* novels topped the fiction bestseller lists for so many months just as there is a reason why so many high-earning movies share a common

plot development.[28] Memorable pop-culture protagonists such as
Harry Potter, Dorothy Gale, Luke Skywalker and Frodo Baggins all
share commonalities in their personalities and quests. And, as storytellers in the law, lawyers should understand and appropriately utilize that phenomenon. . . .

This article focuses on the relationship of mythology and folklore
heroes to everyday lawyering decisions regarding case theory when
the audience is a judge or panel of judges rather than a jury. [Using
myth and archetype] provides a scaffold to influence the judge at
the unconscious level by providing a metaphor for universal themes
of struggle and growth. . . .

Franck Chicot, June 14, 2008

Once upon a time

According to linguistics experts, summoning the imagery of a
hero employs metaphoric reasoning.[29] . . . As Professor Steven Winter wrote, "The attraction of narrative is that it corresponds more
closely to the manner in which the human mind makes sense of
experience than does the conventional, abstracted rhetoric of
law."[30] The story is not a parlor trick used to draw attention away
from the logic of law. It is part of the logic itself. . . .

A Primer on the Development of Heroic Archetypes as a Discourse

Heroic archetype, the myth of the hero, has been introduced to everyday culture through the interdisciplinary studies of many individuals but most famously by mythologist Joseph Campbell. Campbell made his hypotheses and reached many of his conclusions by combining the psychological work of Carl Jung with earlier publications of nineteenth century anthropologists such as Adolph Bastian.[31]

Jung believed that individual and social behavior and thought have their roots in a common pattern of characters.[32] He emphasized the universal psychological forces working within the individual to shape his or her personality.[33] These archetypal patterns were present in every culture he studied and in each time period in recorded history. Jung saw these common recurring patterns as manifestations of what he called "the collective unconscious."[34] Anthropologist Adolph Bastian first proposed the idea that myths from all over the world seem to be built from the same "elementary ideas." Subsequently, Sir James Frazer similarly observed that there was an unexplainable similarity that existed in certain tribal rituals in tribes so separate that no contact had ever taken place. He concluded that the rituals encapsulated the imaginative story of human connection to the universe.[35] More recently, the prolific psychologist and writer, James Hillman, opined that the study of basic human nature necessarily includes learning about a society's mythology.[36]

Joseph Campbell coalesced these related psychological and anthropological theories into an analysis of human religion and spirituality. His tome, *The Hero with a Thousand Faces*, is considered a seminal publication in the field.[37] Campbell believed that within all of the world's mythologies there are heroes whose journeys follow a predictable pattern. He opined that the storytellers of the different eras and cultures were trying to tell us, through symbolism and metaphor, of our own journeys toward individuation.[38]

According to Campbell, myths can serve a pedagogical function, informing us of how to live in our society under any circumstances.[39] ... In terms of persuasion, we walk in the shoes of the protagonist. If we can marry the concepts of storytelling to the "collective unconscious" in our statements of the case, we will potentially create powerfully persuasive undercurrents [and] persuade in a more subtle way.

The Lawsuit Casting Call: One Story, One Hero

... The lawsuit, like the hero's journey, necessarily includes a predictable cast of characters. ...

A Hero: The Client's Role

Heroes are those who transform themselves or their societies through a search for identity and wholeness.[40] They can do this through internal reflection or through outward action. Heroes are termed as such because they all similarly embark on some sort of transformative journey. That journey can take place externally or internally. . . .

Because the hero is the person in the story with whom the reader most closely identifies, the writer must grant the hero universal qualities and emotions that most readers have either experienced or understand. . . . Heroes start out as somehow flawed at a fundamental level that affects their daily life and/or prevents them from living up to their potential.[41] The hero, then, represents a search for identity and wholeness.[42] Emotions and motivators at both ends of the spectrum are available to the hero; everything from love and joy to anger and a thirst for revenge to the middle emotions of loneliness, despair and the feelings of oppression.[43] A hero is imperfect by definition, and audiences admire the hero all the more for striving to overcome these flaws.

The hero represents a search for identity and wholeness.

Casting the client as the main character and hero of the lawsuit story gives the client permission to be imperfect. . . . The character flaw does not ultimately define a hero, assuming the hero can overcome it, but the hero is allowed to have that flaw at least at the outset. . . .

Types of Heroes

. . . In modern application there are several authors who have proffered a variety of heroic archetypes. Each of these archetypes,

epSos.de's flickr photostream, Dec. 2, 2009

Life-size religious king statue with spear

though pursuing different goals and possessing different character traits and flaws, nevertheless shares some significant commonalities with other archetypes. Each different type of hero character has its own quest and fear and each has its own proverbial dragon that the hero must, metaphorically or literally, slay. This article relies on Dr. Carol Pearson's work, which suggests twelve different hero types.[44] . . .

The article then lists the following types:

1. *Warrior (Luke Skywalker from* Star Wars*)*
2. *Creator (writer or artist struggling to succeed)*
3. *Caregiver/Martyr (mother taking care of her family against odds; religious figures)*
4. *Every person/Orphan (orphan looking for his birthright and a sense of family and identity; Harry Potter)*
5. *Outlaw/Destroyer (Robin Hood)*
6. *Sage/Scholar (student trying to do well in school or professor trying to get tenure)*
7. *Explorer/Wanderer/Seeker (early colonists and pioneers; astronauts; Daniel Boone)*
8. *Magician (Merlin)*
9. *Ruler (King Arthur)*
10. *Lover (Cinderella variations; Princess Diana)*
11. *Jester/Fool (leads in comic movies)*
12. *Innocent (young, happy, well-cared-for child; Dorothy from* The Wizard of Oz*)*

Just as there is more than one story module, there are multiple hero types. According to archetypal psychologists, we are each on different heroic quests throughout our lives as we mature and transform ourselves. The process is not linear or absolute. Instead, we may ourselves be more than one type of hero at any given point in time. This is good news for lawyers working with their clients, because the lawyer is not limited to casting the client in the role of Luke Skywalker. . . .

Example of Heroic Archetype Selection: Clients Seeking Domestic Violence Protective Orders

This particular area of law provides a conundrum to the storyteller. How do we make the domestic violence plaintiff look like a hero, especially if she acted imperfectly herself . . . ? Since a hero cannot be passive, how do we make that client look active? . . . [P]lacing the plaintiff in a "victim" role . . . cast[s] the client as the damsel-in-distress rather than as the hero of her own story. [That casting decision] awards the role of hero to the judge, whose job it becomes to save the damsel from her distress. However, a hero will save only a true and pure damsel and not one who shows herself to have impurities.[45] Consequently, when the client acted imperfectly, a judge cast in the role of hero may conclude that the client is no true damsel who deserves saving. . . .

Casting the client as the hero is the option, then, that allows the client to have flaws. . . .

The article then explores the selection of which type of hero might work best for a domestic violence client.

Mentor: The Judge

If the judge cannot be the hero of the client's story, the next best role . . . is as the hero's mentor. The mentor is a former hero who now serves as the sage advice-giver to the next hero. . . . [T]he mentor teaches and tests the hero and offers the gift of an amulet or talisman needed to help conquer the so-called villain or dragon. . . . Casting the judge as mentor allows the judge to symbolically and literally deliver a talisman to the client in the form of a judgment and opinion. In myth and story, the symbolic gifts must be earned by the hero by demonstrating the learned lesson of commitment. In the lawsuit scenario, so too the hero client earns the judge's favorable opinion only after going through the tests of the legal process. . . .

Finally, by casting the judge in the role of mentor, we are also acknowledging the judge's own heroism. Mentors in myth may be heroes themselves from a different quest who now impart the knowledge they have gained to the next generation of hero. . . . In a sense, all judges are scholar heroes. . . .

Villain or Dragon: Not Necessarily the Opposing Party's Role

Villains or dragons, also called shadows, represent darkness and suppression.[46] The hero must confront the villain in order to complete the transformation. Depending on the type of journey, the villain may be an internal dragon.[47] Internal struggles include an addiction or perhaps a character trait that the hero needs to overcome. . . .

Pigeonholing the opposing party as villain may also risk the lawyer entering the world of damaging hyperbole.

Library of Congress (Woodcut, circa 1405-1475)

The article goes on to suggest other possible casting decisions for the opposing party, such as threshold guardian (gate-keeper) or shape-shifter (trickster), and to identify helpful friends as archetypal companions.

A Hero's Transformative Journey

Part of the lawyer's lesson in preparing to tell the client's story lies in . . . understanding the lawsuit's place in the client's journey. Any hero, no matter the specific type, follows a similar path. . . . The journey, then, changes the hero, and potentially also the hero's society.[48] . . .

The three main stages of the journey include the departure, the initiation, and the return.[49] The departure stage involved the hero leaving the ordinary and journeying to the new world, whether voluntarily or involuntarily. During the initiation stage, the hero faces tests designed to teach the hero how to face and overcome the dragon; at the end of that stage, the hero does exactly that. Finally, during the return stage the hero either goes back to the ordinary world to transform it with the knowledge and gifts that the hero has learned along the journey, or the hero remains in the new world and helps that society heal or change.[50] . . . Part of deciding how to cast the client necessarily involves the lawyer understanding what role the lawsuit itself plays in the client's overall hero journey. Is winning the lawsuit the same as obtaining the ultimate boon? In reality, this is probably only the case on rare occasions. It is more likely that the lawsuit represents one test the client must face along the road of trials. . . .

The article then discusses the three stages of the journey—departure, initiation, and return, providing examples of each.

Conclusion

These concepts of hero and journey provide lawyers with a framework to do factual investigation. . . . [L]awyers can use the journey premise as a foundation or scaffold for starting to strategize a theory of the case. . . . I do not intend for this Article to stand for the sum total of the discussion about heroic archetypes . . . it is intended to start the conversation. . . . Heroic journeys provide one possibility for conceptualizing the client's story and the theory of the case. . . . The true point is that lawyers should have a methodology for story building. . . . The possibilities truly are infinite.

Key Concepts

Kendall Haven's five core elements of a story: characters, intent, actions struggle, details
Amsterdam and Bruner's plot structure: steady state, trouble, efforts, restoration or transformation, coda
Showing vs. telling
Perspective/point of view
Hero archetype
Departure, initiation, and return

Discussion Questions

1. Will knowing some terms for the core elements of a story and a particular kind of plot structure help you think more clearly and strategically about the fact statements you write? If so, how?
2. Were you surprised by the advice in the section on showing and telling? How? What do you think of it?
3. Might it be effective sometimes to tell the story from the perspective of someone other than the client? The answer to that question probably depends entirely on the kind of case you are handling and the facts you have to work with. What kinds of cases might be best told from the client's perspective? What kinds of cases might be exceptions to that approach?
4. What do you think of the idea of conceptualizing the fact statement in archetypal terms?

Exercises

1. Read the fact statement in the Petitioner's brief in *Atkins v. Virginia*,[51] and be prepared to comment on how the author used what we have learned about plot, theme, character, perspective, showing vs. telling, and the use of different voices.
2. Compare the fact statements in the Petitioner's and Respondent's briefs in *Wards Cove Packing Co. v. Atonio*.[52] What differences do you notice? What worked well and what did not? Read the description of the facts in the Court's majority opinion. Does it resemble one of the briefs? Read Justice Blackmun's dissent. If you were going to rewrite Atonio's brief, what approach would you take?

Additional Suggested Reading

Stacy Caplow, *Putting the "I" in Wr*t*ng: Drafting an A/Effective Personal Statement to Tell a Winning Refugee Story*, 14 Legal Writing 249 (2008).

Kenneth D. Chestek, *The Plot Thickens: Appellate Brief as Story*, 14 Legal Writing 127 (2008).

James Parry Eyster, *Using Significant Moments and Obtuse Objects to Enhance Advocacy*, 14 Legal Writing 87 (2008).

Brian Foley & Ruth Anne Robbins, *Fiction 101: A Primer for Lawyers on How to Use Fiction Writing Techniques to Write Persuasive Facts Sections*, 2 Rutgers L.J. 459 (Winter 2001).

Michael J. Higdon, *Something Judicious This Way Comes: The Use of Foreshadowing as a Persuasive Device in Judicial Narrative*, 44 U. Rich. L. Rev. 1213 (2010).

Elyse Pepper, *The Case for "Thinking Like a Filmmaker": Using Lars von Trier's* Dogville *as a Model for Writing a Statement of Facts*, 14 Legal Writing 171 (2008).

Michael R. Smith, *Advanced Legal Writing: Theories and Strategies in Persuasive Writing* ch. 3 (2d ed., Aspen 2008).

Shaun B. Spencer, *Dr. King, Bull Connor, and Persuasive Narratives*, 2 J. ALWD 209 (2004).

Endnotes

1. Kendall Haven, *Story Proof: The Science Behind the Startling Power of Story* 79 (Libraries Unlimited, Greenwood Publ. Group 2007).
2. *Id.* at 75-77.
3. *Id.* at 77 (citing to M. Turner, *The Literary Mind: The Origins of Thought and Language* (Oxford U. Press 1996)).
4. *Id.* at 77.
5. Paul Ricoeur, *Time and Narrative*, vol. 1 (Kathleen McLaughlin & David Pellauer trans., U. of Chicago Press 1984); Paul Ricoeur, *Oneself as Another* (Kathleen Blamey trans., U. of Chicago Press, 1992).
6. Vincent Crapanzano, *Hermes' Dilemma and Hamlet's Desire* (Harvard U. Press 1992). See also Kenneth Gergen, *The Saturated Self* (Basic Books 1992).
7. David Lodge, *The Art of Fiction* 67 (Penguin Books 1992).
8. *Id.* at 26.
9. John Gardner, *The Art of Fiction* 155-159 (1st Vintage Bks. Ed. 1985).
10. *Id.* at 155.
11. *Id.*
12. *Id.* at 157.
13. *Id.* at 157-158.
14. *Id.* at 157.
15. *Id.* at 158-159.
16. *Id.* at 159.
17. Lodge, *supra* note 7, at 122.
18. *Id.*
19. *Id.*
20. *Id.* (emphasis added).
21. 529 U.S. 362 (2000).
22. Br. For Petr. At 3, *Williams v. Taylor*, 529 U.S. 362 (2000).
23. *Id.*
24. *Id.*
25. *Id.* at 4.
26. *Id.* at 4-5.
27. [Harry Potter was introduced to the world in J.K. Rowling's first novel, *Harry Potter and the Sorcerer's Stone* (Scholastic 1997)].
28. *See* Stuart Voytilla, *Myth and the Movies: Discovering the Mythic Structure of 50 Unforgettable Films* (Michael Wiese Prod. 1999). . . .
29. George Lakoff & Mark Johnson, *Metaphors We Live By* 115-119 (U. of Chicago Press 2003).
30. Steven L. Winter, *The Cognitive Dimension of the* Agon *Between Legal Power and Narrative Meaning*, 87 Mich. L. Rev. 2225, 2228 (1989).
31. Joseph Campbell, *The Hero with a Thousand Faces* (Princeton U. Press 1990).
32. According to a traditional definition, archetypes are the "primary form that governs the psyche." James Hillman, *Archetypal Psychology: A Brief Account* 1 (Spring Pub. 1985).
33. *Id.* at 11.
34. Carl G. Jung, *The Portable Jung* 59-60 (Joseph Campbell ed., Penguin Books 1976). . . .
35. Campbell, *supra* note 31, at 18-19. . . .
36. Hillman, *supra* note 32, at 3.
37. Campbell, *supra* note 31.
38. *Id.*
39. Richard L. Sartore, *Joseph Campbell on Myth & Mythology* 5 (U. Press of Am. 1994).
40. Christopher Vogler, *The Writer's Journey* 35 (2d ed., Michael Wiese Prod. 1998).

41. *Id.* 90-94.

42. *Id.* at 35.

43. *Id.* at 36-38.

44. Carol S. Pearson, *Awakening the Hero Within: Twelve Archetypes to Help Us Find Ourselves and Transform Our World* 4 (HarperCollins 1991).

45. Carol Pearson & Katherine Pope, *The Female Hero in American and British Literature* 25-32 (R.R. Bowker Co. 1981).

46. *Id.* at 15; Vogler, *supra* note 40, at 71.

47. Joseph Campbell with Bill Moyers, *The Power of Myth* 183-184 (First Anchor Books ed., Random House 1999). . . .

48. *Id.*

49. Campbell, *supra* note 31, at 245.

50. *Id.*

51. *Atkins v. Virginia*, 536 U.S. 304 (2002). The defense brief is found on the website associated with this book.

52. *Wards Cove Packing Co. v. Atonio*, 490 U.S. 642 (1989). The briefs are found on the website associated with this book.

19. Law's Stories

If we see the world though stories, do we tell stories about the law as well? Remember from Chapters 15 and 16 that we think about abstract ideas (like legal theories, for example) metaphorically. Does that mean we can think about law narratively?

Excerpt from

Linda H. Edwards, *Once Upon a Time in Law: Myth, Metaphor, and Authority*
77 Tenn. L. Rev. 885 (2010)

. . . [T]he law has stories. . . . We have long known that *client* stories are crucial in litigation. Lawyers and judges hear, transform, and represent those stories in fact statements of briefs and judicial opinions. But later in those same documents, lawyers and judges also tell stories about the law itself. In discussions of cases, statutes, and constitutional provisions, there are stories of birth, death, battle, betrayal, tricksters and champions. In fact, we may not be able to talk about these sources of law without telling stories about them. These [legal] stories do their narrative work beneath the surface of routine law talk and lead straight to the conclusions that become the law.

Discussions of law do not *sound* like stories, of course. They state an issue, cite authority, and purport to rely on a legal rule. But when we talk about legal authority, using the logical forms of rules and their bedfellows of analogy, policy, and principle, we are actually swimming in a sea of narrative, oblivious to the water around us. [This is not surprising.] As the old Buddhist saying goes, we don't know who discovered the ocean, but it probably wasn't a fish.

This article teases out several familiar myths often hidden in discussions of legal authority. These myths are simultaneously true and false, world-shaping yet always incomplete. The choice of which stories we tell about the law matters greatly. Why? Because we so seldom question familiar narratives, and these myths practically run in our veins. We would be wise to learn to recognize and interrogate these stories, attuned to their truths, alert to their limitations, and ready, when necessary, to seek other more accurate and complete stories for the law. . . .

[This article] will explore the birth story from the Petitioner's Brief in *Miranda v. Arizona*[1] and then the rescue story from the Respondent's Brief in *Bowers v. Hardwick*.[2] The final section of the article will compare the ... ways these two stories function and identify some of fundamental questions raised by the idea that narrative plays an important, but hidden, role in shaping our view of legal authority. First, though, it will be helpful to review some basic concepts about story structures, cultural myths, and how metaphor works when we think about law.

We don't know who discovered the ocean, but it probably wasn't a fish.

Stories, Myths, and Metaphors

... [S]tories are among the primary ways of making sense of the world, including the world of law. A story's two most important components for doing this formative work are character and plot. At the very least, a story needs a protagonist ... and a difficult challenge to overcome. Something important must be happening, some narrative movement from an inadequate state of affairs to a resolution of that inadequacy, taking place over a period of time.[3]

Library of Congress (Daniel Carter Beard, circa 1889)

Knight in armor tilting at modern man in tree for refuge

One classic plot structure begins with a struggle toward a specific goal. Right from the opening scene, the world (or at least the protagonist's world) needs fixing or lacks something important.[4] Journey stories, for example, often use this structure. The opening scene may find the protagonist far from home, facing a long journey. Homer's epic poem, the *Odyssey*, is a prototypical example.[5] As the story begins, Troy has just fallen, and the warrior Odysseus is standing on the distant shore, ready to return home. The story describes his struggles as he undertakes the ten-year journey back to Ithaca and to his family there. . . .

Late September road, Maryland

In another common plot structure, the key characteristic of the story's opening scene is its normality and stability. The world is not incomplete; rather life is more or less as it should be. This initial stable world enters a stage of disequilibrium, however. Amsterdam and Bruner speak, for instance, of a "steady state" followed by "trouble."[6] The steady state is, by definition, legitimate. . . . In narrative terms, whatever disrupts a steady state is bad. The story describes the struggle to resolve the disequilibrium and return to some version of legitimate stability—either to the original steady state (restoration) or to some other good and stable place (transformation).[7] [For example, in] *Murder on the Orient Express*, Hercule Poirot boards the train in Istanbul. The train proceeds normally along the scheduled journey until the second night, when a murder occurs. Poirot undertakes to solve the murder. In the end, rough justice is done, and the lives of Poirot and the passengers proceed as we are meant to think they should.[8]

Client stories easily lend themselves to such plot structures. For instance, in *Bowers v. Hardwick*,[9] Michael Hardwick was safely at home (the steady state). The police entered his home, and he was arrested under Georgia's sodomy law (the trouble). By enforcing a right to privacy, the Court can return Hardwick to the safety and sanctity of his home (the restoration).

But the law has such stories too. Just like any other story, the law's story will need characters and a plot and perhaps a prop here and there. Metaphor can help provide all of these elements of the story. . . . [W]e think about abstract ideas in metaphors.[10] So when we think about a legal theory or a statute or the holding of a case, we think about it metaphorically, as if it were a sentient being or a concrete thing. . . . Ideas are grounded in concrete physical experience and cannot otherwise exist.[11] This understanding of metaphor reveals something important about the law's stories: Characters can be entities, like courts or legislatures or prosecutors' offices or even abstract concepts, like a principle or a policy, a statute or a case holding. So there might be characters in a legal discussion after all, and those characters might be doing something—something that might amount to a plot.

One other concept—myth—will help with both characters and plot. The term "myth" has been used in a variety of ways with a variety of definitions. Here I use it to mean particularly an archetype or other master story. Myths or archetypes may be simply cultural, soaked up by living in a particular place and time, or they may be encoded at birth. For this article's purposes, their origin and possible universality matter little. Either way, by the time we are old enough to think about law, myths have become part of us, and they are ready to orchestrate our understanding of the world, including the world of law.[12]

. . . Myths and narrative archetypes such as birth, death, re-birth, journey or sacrifice provide templates for plots. They establish a particular view, a narrative perspective on the events of a story, creating the context in which ideas or events will be interpreted.[13] We carry the blueprints of these archetypal situations, and when events trigger those archetypes, we create at least the rough outlines of a particular mythological story through which we view those events.[14] In other words, we mentally create an archetypal plot line. Myth, too, provides a ready stock of characters to "people" those plots with champions, children, tricksters, mentors, kings, mothers, demons, and sages. These character templates also stand ready, inviting us to cast both people and things in particular archetypal roles.

To summarize: If the law is to have a story, it needs at least characters and a plot. But because we think metaphorically, the story's characters can include institutions or reified ideas, and these institutions or ideas may be doing things that constitute a plot. Nor are we left adrift to create a plot or cast the characters. Instead, we are programmed with mythological plots and characters, and we are inclined to see both events and ideas as fitting into those archetypal stories. Finally, and perhaps most importantly, this process of story creation is usually unconscious, which makes its operations all the more significant.[15] If we are not aware that we are inside a story, we cannot decide to step out of it long enough to ask whether there might be other possible stories and whether those other stories might make better sense of the situation.

Miranda v. Arizona as a Creation or Birth Story

With these basic concepts of myth and metaphor in mind, it is time to ask what kind of characters and plots the law can have. There are a number of common myths about the law, and this article will consider two of them: birth and rescue. First, the birth story told in the Petitioner's Brief in *Miranda v. Arizona*.[16]

Ernesto Miranda was brought to police headquarters and taken into Interrogation Room 2. The door was closed, and he was alone with two officers. Two hours later he came out, having signed a confession. At that point, a lawyer was appointed,[17] but Miranda's fate was already sealed. The author of the Petitioner's Brief, John Paul Frank, tells Miranda's story . . . in compelling terms. But Frank tells another story too—a story about the governing law. It is the story of the growth and development of the right to counsel.

Appreciating Frank's story calls for a comparison of its structure with an alternate structure of legal analysis. In that alternate structure, a writer would begin with the current governing law supported by a discussion of the most recent authorities. If the current law is favorable, the writer would add a policy discussion to support it. If not, the writer would argue for change using other authorities and policy discussions. It would seem that there is no plot, no action, nothing happening there. The discussion forgoes most of the influence of narrative to affect perception. The problem is particularly troubling if the writer wants to change current law because in narrative terms, the argument may have presented the current law as the steady state. . . . Having done so, the writer now must unseat her own implicit narrative admission that the current law is legitimate.

Frank's story, though, begins not by explaining the current status of the right to counsel, but with this sentence: "We deal here with growing law, and look to where we are going by considering where we have been."[18] Notice the narrative move in that first sentence. It takes us from the distant past straight to an imagined future. What is missing is the troublesome state of the current law, which did not preclude admission of Miranda's confession. Rather than setting up current law as the legitimate steady state, the story treats current law, by omission and therefore by implication, as merely one of many interim stages in the ongoing growth of constitutional doctrine and thus not worthy of any particular importance. From the argument's first sentence, we are in narrative motion.

After this panoramic introductory view, the brief begins the story of creating constitutional protections against pressured confessions.

Starting with the 15th Century, we watch the doctrine grow, case by case by case.[19] The narrative pace is steady. One after another come [seven] cases the Court has decided. . . . Metaphorically, we can almost see the Court fashioning each new facet of the doctrine. The story brings us then to *Haley v. Ohio*,[20] and here the pace slows. The discussion spends some time with the *Haley* opinion, naming the four subscribing justices, and then pauses so the narrator can underline the dramatic significance of the case:

> We assume that the opinion in *Haley*, had it been of five Justices, would totally control in the instant situation. . . . But there were not five. Justice Frankfurter concurred specially. . . . He concluded that the confession should be barred because of specialized circumstances in the particular case, without reaching the broader question.[21]

Perhaps we feel a little disappointment. The birth labor has slowed. The Court was on the verge of completing a long, hard process, but at the last moment, one of the justices hesitated. Notice the first appearance here of another narrative principle—the principle of the gap. As Peter Brooks put it, a gap "demands to be filled; it activates the interpreter's ingenuity."[22] When a reader sees a gap in a story, the reader wants to fill in that gap, and that, of course, is exactly what John Frank wants the present Court to do.

After identifying the gap, the story resumes:

> In 1957, two new voices were added in this Court on the right to counsel at the interrogation [stage]. The case was *In re Groban's Petition*. . . . The majority opinion, by Justice Reed on his last day on the Court, found distinctions because this was an administrative hearing and therefore did not reach the principal question. [Justices Black, Warren], Douglas and Brennan did.[23]

Disappointment again; another opportunity to fill the gap, missed once again by so close a margin. The pace now quickens:

> These same dissenting Justices expressed their views again in *Crooker* . . . and [then again in] *Cicenia*. . . . [Justices Douglas, Warren, Black, and Brennan] gave an emphatic and detailed analysis of the absolute need for counsel at the pretrial stage. . . .[24]

Notice that since the discussion of *Haley v. Ohio*, the argument has begun to name the justices who are working to complete the doctrine. Naming the justices helps us identify the characters, understand their goals, and share some of their frustration. This naming continues as the pace picks up speed again, now with added strength and urgency:

> Soon after *Crooker* and *Cicenia*, the tide which was to overrule *Betts*[25] began to flow with new vigor. . . . Justices Douglas and

Brennan called outright for the overruling of *Betts*. . . . Justices Frankfurter and Stewart . . . held that a confession should not be admitted. . . . Justices Douglas and Black wished to rest frankly on the principle [of the right to consult a lawyer before interrogation]. . . . [T]hese Justices felt that all defendants are entitled to know their constitutional rights.[26]

In this description, we hear the voices of these four justices urging their positions, each speaker breaking in when the prior speaker stops to take a breath. There is narrative energy here. It is a noisy scene with animated voices making their points. . . .

[T]he story continues, as *Gideon* takes the crucial developmental step of overruling *Betts*:

In overruling *Betts*, Justice Black . . . closed the [procedural] circle by applying the principle of his own 1938 opinion of *Johnson v. Zerbst* to state proceedings. . . . It follows that, so far as the Sixth Amendment is concerned, after March 18, 1963, there is no difference between the right to counsel . . . in the two court systems.[27]

Then and only then, after the story of this long process, do we learn the current state of the law. Our narrator tells us, in tabulated form, that as of the spring of 1963:

1. Defendants were entitled to counsel at all trials in the federal courts. *Johnson v. Zerbst*.
2. Defendants in state courts were entitled to counsel in all trials. *Gideon v. Wainwright*.
3. Persons were entitled to counsel in all federal arraignments . . . and in all arraignments or analogous proceedings under state law at which anything of consequence can happen. *Hamilton v. Alabama*; *White v. Maryland*.
4. Several Justices believed that in all cases, a person who requested counsel at pre-arraignment investigation was entitled to it. . . . *Crooker v. California*; *Cicenia v. La Gay*.
5. Several Justices believed that, requested or not, a person has a right to counsel upon interrogation unless he intelligently waived that right. *In re Groban's Petition*; *Crooker v. California*; *Cicenia v. La Gay*.

Situation 5 is that presented in the instant case.[28]

Here is the drum-roll. The legal discussion goes on to offer policy reasons for why the Court should resolve "Situation 5," but the story of the slow, careful development of the law has prepared us to hear those policy arguments. The story began five hundred years ago. We heard how, bit by bit, the right to counsel grew. The story has brought us now to the *pleroma*—the fullness—of time, when the crucial decision will be made. The long story of the law has met Ernesto Miranda's case.

In this story, every part of the doctrine has been added except one. But that last part—Miranda's part—need not be created from whole cloth, because to listen to a creation story is to have already imagined the fully developed doctrine the characters are creating.[29] The doctrine actually exists. It remains only to bring it out of our minds and onto the pages of an opinion. Here is how the brief states it several pages later:

> The right does exist. It is the same. This is not the result of a single case, *Escobedo* or any other. Rather there is a tide in the affairs of men, and it is this engulfing tide which is washing away the secret interrogation of the unprotected accused.[30]

The bold assertion that began the Summary of the Argument pages earlier makes sense:

> There is a right to counsel for arrested persons when interrogated by the police. The law has been growing in this direction for more than thirty years.[31]

At first those two sentences seemed inconsistent; surely to say that the law has been growing in this direction is to implicitly admit that no authority has yet declared the principle. Yet it is exactly that growth that has created the right, positioning it as the *telos*, the consummation, the destiny to which the "affairs of men" inevitably lead. All that remains is to recognize it formally.

Compare the movement of that plot to a more formalistic structure of legal analysis. Without the story, the writer likely would begin by baldly articulating the current law with no action happening anywhere in the discussion. The argument would set out the troublesome current law as the implicitly legitimate "steady state" and move us nowhere from there. We would have to seek a legal change with only abstract policy arguments instead of with a story that encodes the argument's message: that the process must be completed—as any birth process must be completed—with the right to counsel fully and finally recognized.

Frank's argument is a creation or birth story, a primary archetype. In fact, at the end of the argument section, the brief becomes explicit. It quotes Justice Douglas when he referred to the right to counsel as "yet unborn"[32] and later refers to the "birth"[33] of the right to counsel at the interrogation stage. A birth narrative like this one is inherently powerful. It rings true to us on a deep and unconscious level because it is a primary archetype.

Who are the characters of this story? The protagonists include the many nameless lawyers and judges involved in all those cases throughout the years, and perhaps especially the Justices who sat in the minority for so long, coming so close to a majority time and again. In fact, in an important sense, this is a story about the

The long story of the law has met Ernesto Miranda's case.

Court itself. The brief is telling the Court a story about who it is and about the important work it has been doing. In fact, it may be that almost all stories written to the Court are, ultimately, stories about the Court itself.

Will the work be completed? As we hear the story of the struggle, we find ourselves rooting for the protagonists, in part because of the struggle itself, for when we watch someone trying to do something difficult, we almost automatically want them to succeed. The climax is not resolved in the brief, of course. If it were, the tension the brief worked so hard to build would be dissipated, leaving little narrative impetus for the Court to act. Instead, the brief brings the tension of the story to its climactic height, and presents that tension to the Court. It is that height of tension that urges the Court to complete the story, to bring about the destiny toward which the story has been moving. And of course, that is just what the Court in *Miranda* did.[34]

Bowers v. Hardwick as a Rescue Story

Unlike the birth story in Miranda, a rescue story is often less obviously narratival. In a birth story, the facts usually are presented as a chronology. Key events are set out as challenges that are faced and overcome. First this, then that, then something else, moving us on to an anticipated culmination. If we simply stop to notice, we can tell that we are reading a story. A rescue story, however, may be harder to recognize because it may not be signaled by a chronology. To create a narrative situation, a rescue story may depend not so much on reciting a series of historical events as on presenting particular kinds of characters set in particular kinds of narrative situations. The plotline does not appear on the page, but the reader will supply it, unconsciously choosing from the ready supply of master stories in the shared culture.

Rescue stories can be told overtly or by implication. Either way, the story happens in the midst of danger from evil forces bent on domination or destruction. A band of the faithful—usually outnumbered and outgunned—resists. The object of rescue might be a person; someone we care about is in danger, vulnerable to harm or already captured. The protagonists' task is to save the vulnerable character. A classic example from world literature is the ancient Sanskrit epic story of Ram's rescue of his wife, Sita, who had been captured by the evil Ravana, the King of the Demons.[35] . . .

The object of rescue might also be an item of great value, such as a talisman or an amulet worn for protection or to enable its possessor to exercise great power. The antagonist is trying to take or destroy the talisman, and the protagonists must retrieve or safeguard it, either for its protective power or to keep its power from hands that would misuse it. Examples of talisman stories abound in literature and film. Most obvious are fantasies such as *The Lord of the Rings*, Tolkien's trilogy in which Frodo Baggins and his faithful friends must keep the One Ring from the hands of the Dark Lord Sauron, who intends to use it as the ultimate weapon to rule and brutally oppress Middle-Earth.[36] Battles over the possession of a talisman or some other all-important item exist outside of fantasy as well, for instance, in stories about the possession of a nuclear warhead[37] or an important scientific formula.[38]

Whether the goal is to safeguard a talisman or to save a character in danger, the [narrative task] is the same: rescuing someone or something important. That is the [task presented] by Laurence Tribe, Kathleen Sullivan, and Brian Koukoutchos, the authors of Michael Hardwick's brief in *Bowers v. Hardwick*.[39] In *Hardwick*, the issue was the right to privacy in intimate relationships.[40] Surprisingly, the brief portrays the right as already established. The Eleventh Circuit had recognized the right in the *Hardwick* opinion below,[41] so Tribe, Sullivan, and Koukoutchos could position the right as the narrative's "steady state." Immediately, though, we learn that the right is in danger:

> The State of Georgia urges this Court to overturn that ruling and declare that a law reaching into the bedroom to regulate intimate sexual conduct is to be tested by no stricter a standard than a law that regulates the community environment outside the home: namely, a standard of minimal scrutiny. In the State's view, the most private intimacies may thus be treated as public displays,

and the sanctum of home and bedroom merged into the stream of commerce—all subject to regulation whenever there is any conceivable "rational relationship" to the promotion of "traditional" or "prevailing" notions of "morality and decency."[42]

And again, in the first line of the Argument section:

[T]he State of Georgia has criminalized certain sexual activities defined solely by the parts of the body they involve, no matter who engages in them, with whom, or where. Georgia threatens to punish these activities with imprisonment even if engaged in by two willing adults—whether married or unmarried, heterosexual or homosexual—who have secluded themselves behind closed bedroom doors in their own home, as Michael Hardwick did. All that is at issue in this case is whether a state must have a substantial justification when it reaches that far into so private a realm.[43]

First, notice the powerful metaphor of the State "reaching . . . into a private realm." In one sentence, the metaphor takes the visceral reaction some readers in 1986 likely would have to the act of sodomy and turns that reaction back on the challenged statute. It casts the State of Georgia as the sodomizer of its own citizens. The act is more than metaphorical sodomy, in fact, because unlike the lovers in the case, the State's act is violent and nonconsensual. The image recurs throughout the entire legal discussion with phrases like "a law that so thoroughly invades individuals' most intimate affairs";[44] or a law that "intrudes the grasp of the criminal law deep into" such an area;[45] . . . or the "State of Georgia contends that it may extend its criminal authority deep inside the private home."[46]

In the midst of the violent world these images create, characters are playing out a story. The battle scene is set by the procedural statement, in which we learn that the Eleventh Circuit opinion had established a right to privacy but the State of Georgia has appealed, arguing that no such right should exist here. Hardwick and his lawyers are the protagonists, struggling to protect the right to privacy. The antagonist is "the State of Georgia," a character with a flawed reputation before the Court.[47] The brief personalizes Georgia and capitalizes on its flawed reputation. Repeatedly we hear that the "State of Georgia" has done or is doing something. In fact, the other characters hardly act at all; Georgia is the primary actor in the drama: "The State of Georgia [sent] its police into a private bedroom."[48] "Georgia threatens to punish . . ."[49] "Georgia [reads] *Griswold*."[50] "Georgia argues . . ."[51] "Georgia alludes . . ."[52] "Georgia has never explained . . ."[53] Instead of referring to what "the statute" does or says, the brief seldom misses a chance to personalize, casting "Georgia" as the bad actor in this drama.

The story has protagonists and an antagonist, but the story needs someone or something to rescue or protect. One analysis would cast the right to privacy as the talisman still precariously held by the protagonists but in great danger of destruction by the State of Georgia. This talisman alone provides protection against Georgia's violation of its citizens, who will otherwise be defenseless against the power of the State. Georgia has mounted a forceful campaign to destroy the right or neutralize its protective power. The battle's purpose is to keep the talisman and its protection in the hands of those who need it.

The concept of the talisman is an easy fit here and works more than adequately to explicate the narrative in the legal argument, but another possible analysis adds interesting narrative dimensions. The Right to Privacy might be seen as a character rather than as a tangible thing; it may, in fact, function as the archetypal Divine or Magic Child.[54] The Magic Child is young, small, and vulnerable, even powerless. She often comes from an unlikely source, such as low social status or some kind of scandal. In the archetypal story, evil forces are out to kill the Divine Child, but if the Child can be saved, she proves to have the power to save or transform us all. There is often an element of surprise in the Child's power to save. The protagonists may initially be acting for important but less grand reasons, such as the "mere" protection of a child. Only as the story progresses do we learn that what is at stake here is much bigger than the safety of one small character.

If the Child can be saved, she proves to have the power to save or transform us all.

Library of Congress (Engraving, John C. McRae, circa 1855)

"My Child! My Child!"

Culturally, we see the Divine Child in [stories] such as those surrounding the births of Jesus[55] and Moses.[56] Both Jesus and Moses were powerless infants, completely vulnerable. Both came from unlikely origins, including low social status and even scandal. Strong forces are out to hurt both, but both are saved and protected by a small, brave group. Then each proves to have the power to save or transform the larger group.[57] . . .

Modern versions of archetypal stories often include a Magic Child component as well. For instance, at the cost of her own life, Harry Potter's mother saves the infant Harry from Voldemort. Then other brave caretakers protect him during his childhood. As he grows, Harry develops unusual powers, which he ultimately uses to save the wizard world from Voldemort's brutal domination.[58] Another modern example is the story of the American cultural icon "Superman," . . . . "Superman" was born on Krypton. As an infant named Kal-El, he was saved from his planet's destruction when his father put him in a rocket and sent him to Earth. There he was found and adopted by a simple farming couple, who raised him with a new name, Clark Kent. It soon became apparent that he possessed superhuman powers, which he subsequently used to protect others in danger.[59]

So is there a Divine Child in Michael Hardwick's brief? If [we] are right that people reify ideas, then a constitutional principle, or a line of cases, or even one important case holding might be cast as the character of the Divine Child. Like the archetypal Divine Child, a constitutional doctrine is not able to protect itself. It is constantly vulnerable to erosion or even destruction. But if citizens and the Court protect the doctrine, it will ultimately protect and save us all. The Hardwick brief casts the right to privacy as the Divine Child. The argument quotes Justice Harlan's reference to liberty under the Due Process Clause as "a living thing."[60] It establishes the right's supreme importance by quoting Justice Brandeis:

> This case is thus about the very core of that "most comprehensive of rights and the right most valued by civilized man," namely, "as against the Government, the right to be let alone."[61]

Like the archetypal Child, the right is very young, having been born only a few months earlier in the decision below. It is especially vulnerable precisely because of its recent birth. It is not a doctrine of long standing, which would be harder to overturn. Rather, the Court could simply reverse the holding below. It would not need even to overturn a holding from an earlier case.

Also like the archetypal Child, the right was associated in the 1980's with a situation of low social status tainted with scandal. It was invoked to protect the world of alternative sexualities, a world driven underground by the law and therefore relegated to metaphorically dark places and peopled by the scorned and the outcast.[62] But again like the myth of the Magic Child, the right to privacy has the power to transcend particular situations and to extend its protection to all who need it. Throughout the argument are nearly constant implied images that any of us could be next, that Georgia's police could soon be invading our own bedrooms. The argument describes the issue as what Georgia can do to its citizens rather than what it has done to Michael Hardwick. The brief speaks of bedrooms (plural). It reminds us that the statute applies to any "two willing adults—whether married or unmarried, heterosexual or homosexual—who have secluded themselves behind closed bedroom doors in their own home."[63] It makes ample use of plural first-person pronouns: "such casual state control of our most private realm";[64] "our government cannot lightly trespass in the intimacies of our sexual lives—whether or not our conduct of those intimacies at any given moment involves a choice about conceiving a child."[65] "When we retreat inside that line [the door of our homes]. . . ."[66] "The home not only protects us from government surveillance, but also 'provide[s] the setting for [our] . . . intimate activities . . . ."[67] "The home surely protects more than our fantasies alone."[68] Thus, protecting the right to privacy here will protect each reader from violation by the State.

Whether this rescue story is a struggle over protection of a talisman or a Divine Child, the battle is intense. The right to privacy is under attack by the Evil Antagonist (the State of Georgia). The doctrine is utterly unable to protect itself. A small band is working to protect it. Ultimately, the only savior is the story's Champion, the Supreme Court, who is asked to come to the rescue. The archetype promises that if this Champion will here protect the right to privacy, the right will survive to later protect us all.

This masterful brief very nearly won this difficult case. The decision was five-to-four, and Justice Powell had vacillated throughout the deliberations.[69] When asked about the decision four years later, Powell said, "I think I probably made a mistake on that one."[70] Asked for clarification, he said, "When I had the opportunity to reread the opinions a few months later, I thought the dissent had the better of the arguments."[71] Had Justice Powell gone the other way, the right to privacy in intimate relationships would have been established in 1986, long before *Lawrence v. Texas.*[72]

Telling Stories About Law

Unearthing the stories beneath the legal arguments in *Miranda* and *Hardwick* expands our academic understanding of how law develops. But our interest in legal narratives is greater than mere academic curiosity if these alternative stories operate differently in legally significant ways. As it turns out, that is in fact the case.

Birth stories and rescue stories each have particular limitations and each bring particular advantages to the task of persuasion and thus to the development of law. At the very least, these stories differ in how they treat current law; in the outcomes they desire; in the degree of their implied legitimacy; in the degree to which they require the court to identify with a party; and in the degree to which they can create dramatic tension.

A foundational difference is that a rescue story calls for reaffirming existing law or at least existing policy. In a rescue story, the antagonist is the character seeking change, while the protagonists seek protection for something that already exists, albeit in a vulnerable situation. The story uses a steady state/trouble plot structure, so it can position itself as conservative, a particularly helpful rhetorical posture. Such a story asks only for a return to normal, legitimate, ordinary life, a request that seems little enough to ask.

A birth story, on the other hand, calls for a change in the law, but the change is presented as the natural culmination of a normal process. A birth story, then, offers a way to make a call for change seem more conservative. This is no revolution, says the analysis. This is merely the culmination of a natural and inevitable process in which the law has been engaged for a long time. This normal, natural process is moving the law in a trajectory toward a future that has been preordained from the start. In a birth story, there is nothing unusual or alarming about that forward movement. In fact, the end result is nothing more than our path toward establishing an anticipated steady state, the preordained legitimate ordinary. In a narrative sense, a birth story allows the narrator to use the idea of a steady state even when it does not yet exist.

A related point of comparison, then, is how the two stories are able to treat current law. As Miranda's brief demonstrates, a birth story deemphasizes inconvenient current law. In fact, the story can make current law almost disappear in the course of the narrative sweep from the distant past to a preordained future. A typical rescue story, on the other hand, bolsters current law, arguing that it is vital to society's shared enterprise and to the welfare of many. Those attacking current law are seeking to eviscerate its protection, perhaps by disregarding the careful developmental work that created normative legal standards.

The stories differ also in the source of the desired outcome and the degree of implied legitimacy that outcome can claim. For a rescue story, the litigants are in a battle, which places them initially in a rhetorically equal setting. The simple fact that a battle is occurring gives no narrative hint of how the battle should end. A leaning in favor of protection arises once a reader begins to relate to the battle as a rescue story, but because that leaning may not seem preordained, it needs an affirmative case showing the worthiness of the person or doctrine to be protected. A birth story, too, must be accompanied by an affirmative case, but in a birth story, the legitimacy of the desired outcome (the culmination of an ongoing birth process) is embedded in the narrative itself. And since this narrative assumption happens outside the reader's notice, it is less subject to the reader's resistance.

The stories also differ in the degree to which they must remain mired in combat. A birth story need not rely primarily on casting opposing armies, with one army intent on doing harm. It can rise above the fray of the litigation, leaving behind much of the ugliness of conflict, and therefore reducing the focus on the opposing arguments. It can work instead in the much more abstract, rarified setting of law creation, transcending the current case and inviting the reader to join in a larger, purer effort. A rescue story, however, nearly always takes place in the context of a heated battle, and taking a side means participating on a battlefield.

On a closely related point, the reader of a birth story may not have to choose sides quite so blatantly since the story does not rely primarily on casting opposing forces. A reader has already participated implicitly in the creative effort by imagining the end result of the birth process. Therefore, on some level, the reader has already been cast as a part of the protagonists' creative effort. Rather than listening to a dispute from the narrative perspective of a removed arbiter, the story casts the reader as having joined the creative team long ago. This assumption, too, happens outside the reader's notice and therefore is less susceptible to resistance.

The stories differ in the degree to which they can distance themselves from litigants with whom a reader may have trouble identifying. A birth story is about the completion of an historic process. A reader can be invested in the process without identifying with a particular group of litigants, so there is less pressure on the narrator to successfully characterize a particular group as worthy of protection. Additionally, judges as characters draw attention away from the litigants themselves. For instance, in Miranda's brief, one almost feels that the State of Arizona is litigating against Justices Douglas, Brennan, Frankfurter, and Stewart rather than against Ernesto Miranda, a convicted felon with a long rap sheet. A rescue story, however, depends more on the reader's acceptance of the need to protect someone. Characters must be cast as good guys and bad guys, which may not always be easy and may be less persuasive when the court has a natural tendency to identify more with one side than the other. It may be more important, then, for a rescue story to broaden the group in need of protection by the talisman or Magic Child, as the brief in Hardwick tried to do.

Finally, the two kinds of stories differ in their relative ease of creating the necessary dramatic tension. A creation story may need to do extra work to convince the reader that the outcome of the process matters. A reader's investment in a creation story derives from watching a creative process unfold, and the story will have to work to keep that process from seeming bland. Ideally, a compelling birth or creation process would be long and difficult, and its direction should be consistent, with no backward steps. The relevant legal authorities may or may not make such a depiction realistically possible. In a battle or rescue story, by contrast, the reader's investment derives from watching a metaphorically violent struggle, where one side is vulnerable to great harm. Generally, the impulse to protect someone we already know from danger is stronger than an impulse to create something new. The danger in a rescue story makes it seem that there is more at stake. The difference between a weak birth story and a well-told rescue story is like the difference between watching an anonymous artist painting a picture and watching Bruce Willis sweating and bleeding in *Die Hard*. Many viewers would find the *Die Hard* story far more riveting as they wonder whether John McClane (Willis) and his wife Holly (Bonnie Bedelia) will live or die.

The choice of underlying myth, then, can play a significant role in persuasion and thus in the development of the law. The operative narrative and its accompanying metaphors create the lens through which we view a legal issue and the context within which we imagine it operating. Myth and metaphor provide characters, give those characters motives, and identify the "right ending" for the story of the law. . . . [The article here goes on to raise some of this idea's implications for legal theory.]

Conclusion

This article has unearthed two master narratives and some unexpected characters in the legal analyses from the landmark briefs in *Miranda v. Arizona* and *Bowers v. Hardwick*. These legal characters and plots are disguised in the routine language of law talk, but their impact is all the more important for that disguise. Because narrative's power in the sacred domain of legal authority is so effectively hidden, the law needs a well-honed narrative sensibility, including a sensibility to the role of myth and metaphor in law's stories.

We need this legal narratology for several reasons. Certainly, in law practice, an understanding of narrative's powerful role in the analysis of authority will produce more skilled advocates and more sophisticated opinion writers. In judicial decision-making, an understanding of how narrative creates and constrains legal argument will produce judges far more skilled in evaluating competing arguments and selecting wisely from among them.

A better understanding of narrative's constructive role, in both senses of that word, will help us understand the roles and limits of articulated rules and other forms of traditional legal analysis. We talk in the language of rules, analogies, and policies. That language gives us a sense of stability and some hope of applying the law consistently.[73] But myth and metaphor create the narrative world that gives the law its life, and they provide an ever-present measuring rod to be sure the law is still doing its job.

Finally, we need a narratology so we can recognize these constitutive stories and be prepared to interrogate them bravely and without blinking. If we do, we will see that, like the cowmen and the farmers of the Old West, narrative and formal legal reasoning can be friends, and our understanding and use of legal authority will be the better for it.

> We need a narratology so we can recognize these constitutive stories and be prepared to interrogate them bravely and without blinking.

Discussion Questions

1. Have you thought before about telling stories in the part of your brief where you are setting out the legal authorities? Birth and rescue do good work in the two briefs discussed here. Look at the legal discussions of some of the briefs covered by this book. Do you see hidden stories there?

2. The article identifies two kinds of plot structures, one beginning with things being more or less as they should be and the other beginning with a problem to be solved. Which kind of plot structure would tend to be more helpful for a party arguing for an expansion or limitation of existing authority? Why?

3. If even our understanding of legal authorities can be affected by stories, is there any kind of thinking that is unaffected by narrative?

Endnotes

1. *Miranda v. Arizona*, 384 U.S. 436 (1966).
2. *Bowers v. Hardwick*, 478 U.S. 186 (1986).
3. Steven L. Winter, *The Cognitive Dimension of the* Agon *Between Legal Power and Narrative Meaning*, 87 Mich. L. Rev. 2225, 2237 (1989).
4. *Id.*
5. Homer, *The Odyssey* 1 (Robert Fitzgerald trans., 1998).
6. Anthony G. Amsterdam & Jerome Bruner, *Minding the Law* 113 (Harvard U. Press 2000).
7. *Id.*
8. Agatha Christie, *Murder on the Orient Express* (Dodd, Mead & Company 1934).
9. *Bowers v. Hardwick*, 478 U.S. 186 (1986).
10. *See, e.g.*, George Lakoff & Mark Johnson, *Metaphors We Live By* 47 (U. of Chicago Press 1980).
11. *Id.*
12. *See generally* Chapters 16-18 of this book.
13. Steven L. Winter, *A Clearing in the Forest: Law, Life and Mind* 128 (U. of Chicago Press 2001).
14. *Id.*

15. Kathryn M. Stanchi, *The Science of Persuasion: An Initial Exploration*, 2006 Mich. St. L. Rev. 411, 422 (2006).

16. Brief For Petitioner, *Miranda v. Arizona*, 384 U.S. 436 (1966) (No. 65-759), 1966 WL 100543. Because few readers will have access to the pagination of the original brief filed with the Court, citations to the brief will be made to the Westlaw document. Further, for ease of reading and better focus on the narrative moves, quotations from the briefs here will sometimes omit internal citations.

17. *Id.* at 3-4.

18. *Id.* at 11.

19. *Id.* at 11-33.

20. *Haley v. Ohio*, 332 U.S. 596 (1948).

21. Brief for Petitioner, *supra* note 16, at 21.

22. Peter Brooks, *Storytelling Without Fear? Confession in Law and Literature*, in *Law's Stories: Narrative and Rhetoric in the Law* 117 (Peter Brooks & Paul Gewirtz eds., Yale U. Press 1996).

23. Brief for Petitioner, *supra* note 16, at 21-22.

24. *Id.* at 23.

25. *Betts v. Brady* had held, in part, that the Sixth Amendment did not apply to state criminal proceedings. 316 U.S. 455, 464 (1942).

26. Brief for Petitioner, *supra* note 16, at 25-26.

27. *Id.* at 27.

28. *Id.* at 27.

29. *See generally* Michael J. Higdon, *Something Judicious This Way Comes . . . The Use of Foreshadowing as a Persuasive Device in Judicial Narrative*, 44 U. Rich. L. Rev. 1213 (2010) (discussing the cognitive science behind this kind of foreshadowing).

30. Brief for Petitioner, *supra* note 16, at 34. The argument's first point heading baldly states, "There Is a Right to Counsel for Arrested Persons When Interrogated by the Police." *Id.* at 11.

31. *Id.* at 6.

32. *Id.* at 30.

33. *Id.* at 30.

34. *Miranda*, 384 U.S. at 499.

35. Valmiki, *The Ramayana* (Arshia Sattar trans., Penguin Books 1996).

36. J.R.R. Tolkien, *The Lord of the Rings* (Geo. Allen & Unwin 1954-1955).

37. *Thunderball* (United Artists 1965) (James Bond retrieves two thermonuclear weapons stolen from NATO and planned to be used to start World War III); *For Your Eyes Only* (1981) (James Bond retrieves a stolen British missile command system sought by the KGB).

38. *The Saint* (Paramount Pictures 1997) (the formula for cold fusion).

39. Brief for Respondent, *Bowers v. Hardwick*, 384 U.S. 436 (1966) (No. 85-140), 1986 WL 720442. Because few readers will have access to the pagination of the original brief filed with the Court, citations to the brief will be to the Westlaw document. Further, for ease of reading and better focus on the narrative moves, quotations from the briefs here will sometimes omit internal citations.

40. More precisely stated, the issue was whether the state must prove a compelling interest in order to restrict the right of privacy in intimate relationships within the home.

41. *Hardwick v. Bowers*, 760 F.2d 1202 (11th Cir. 1985).

42. Brief for Respondent, *supra* note 39, at 5-6.

43. *Id.* at 5.

44. *Id.* at 4.

45. *Id.* at 19.

46. *Id.* at 14.

47. The Court had already struck Georgia's attempt to criminalize the purely private possession of obscene materials within the home, *Stanley v. Georgia*, 394 U.S. 557, 559 (1969), and for years, the Court had been watching and participating in civil rights cases arising throughout the Deep South.

48. Brief for Respondent, *supra* note 39, at 1.

49. *Id.* at 5.

50. *Id.* at 10.

51. *Id.* at 7.

52. *Id.* at 27.

53. *Id.* at 13.

54. *See generally* C.G. Jung, *The Archetypes and the Collective Unconscious* (2d ed., R.F.C. Hull trans., Princeton U. Press 1980).

55. *See Matthew* 1:18-2:11.

56. *See Exodus* 2:1-10.

57. *Exodus* 1:1-40:38 and *Matthew* 1:1-2:18.

58. J.K. Rowling, *Harry Potter and the Sorcerer's Stone* (Scholastic 1998); J.K. Rowling, *Harry Potter and the Chamber of Secrets* (Scholastic 1999); J.K. Rowling, *Harry Potter and the Prisoner of Azkaban* (Scholastic 1999); J.K. Rowling, *Harry Potter and the Goblet of Fire* (Scholastic 2000); J.K. Rowling, *Harry Potter and the Order of the Phoenix* (Scholastic 2003); J.K. Rowling, *Harry Potter and the Half-Blood Prince* (Scholastic 2005); J.K. Rowling, *Harry Potter and the Deathly Hallows* (Scholastic 2007).

59. The modern film version is *Superman* (Warner Bros. 1978).

60. Brief for Respondent, supra note 39, at 8, citing *Poe v. Ullman*, 367 U.S. 497, 542 (1961) (Harlan, J., dissenting).

61. *Id.* at 7, quoting *Olmstead v. United States*, 277 U.S. 438, 478 (1928) (Brandeis, J., dissenting).

62. Early black-and-white scenes in the movie *Milk* paint a dismally instructive picture of the consequences of the law's treatment of LGBT communities during the time frame leading up to the Hardwick brief. *Milk* (Universal Pictures 2008).

63. Brief for Respondent, supra note 39, at 15-16 (quoting *Oliver v. United States*, 466 U.S. 170, 179 (1984)).

64. *Id.* at 6.

65. *Id.* at 12.

66. *Id.* at 15.

67. *Id.* at 15-16 (quoting *Oliver v. United States*, 466 U.S. 170, 179 (1984)).

68. *Id.* at 16.

69. John C. Jeffries, Jr., *Justice Lewis F. Powell, Jr.* 513-530 (Scribner's Sons 1994).

70. *Id.* at 530. Jeffries describes how Justice Powell had been unable to understand gay men on a human level. At least twice, he made the remarkable proclamation that he had never known a homosexual. He did not know that he had, in fact, had gay men as clerks in the past and had a gay man as a clerk at the time of the deliberations in *Bowers v. Hardwick.* Because Powell perceived that this clerk was more liberal than the others, Powell had initiated several conversations with him, trying to understand what it meant to be gay. Jeffries reports that Powell was never able to come to terms with homosexuality as "a logical expression of the desire and affection that gay men felt for other men." *Id.* at 521. In other words, in the case of Justice Powell, the necessary narrative component of identification had failed.

71. *Id.* at 530.

72. *Lawrence v. Texas*, 539 U.S. 558 (2003). Prior to *Lawrence v. Texas*, the Georgia Supreme Court struck the Georgia sodomy statute as unconstitutional under the Georgia Constitution. Ironically, that case was styled *Powell v. Georgia*, 510 S.E.2d 18 (1998).

73. I leave for another day the topic of how misleading this sense of stability and consistency may be.

Our Lives in the Law

Our last chapter is the culmination of all the work we've done. If our work is creative at its core, and if, through it, we actually "constitute" the law, then being a lawyer is both endlessly intellectually interesting and morally and emotionally rewarding. On its largest scale, this rhetorical work is the stuff that creates and maintains a society. And case by case, it serves our clients when they need our help the most. Definitely a life worth living.

20. *A Life in the Law*

"How we spend our days is, of course, how we spend our lives."

—Annie Dillard, *The Writing Life*

And now one last excerpt from Professor James Boyd White as he looks back on his life in the law.

Excerpt from
James Boyd White,[1] *An Old-Fashioned View of the Nature of Law*
12 Theoretical Inquiries L. 381 (2011)

The law is not an abstract system or scheme of rules, as we often speak of it, but an inherently unstable structure of thought and expression. It is built upon a distinct set of dynamic and dialogic tensions, which include: tensions between ordinary language and legal language; between legal language and the specialized discourses of other fields; between language itself and the mute world that lies beneath it; between opposing lawyers; between conflicting but justifiable ways of giving meaning to the rules and principles of law; between substantive and procedural lines of thought; between law and justice; between the past, the present, and the future. Each of these tensions is present whenever a lawyer or judge goes to work. None of them can be resolved by resort to a rule or other directive, but must be addressed anew by the lawyer and judge in each case as it arises by the exercise of an art of language and mind that is defined by these tensions themselves. . . .

. . . I have spent a lot of energy in the course of my career trying to connect the Western literary and humanistic tradition with the teaching and study of law. To some people this work has naturally seemed a bit puzzling, even idiosyncratic. "What can literature possibly have to do with law?" is a question I have been asked over and over. From my point of view, such a questioner often misunderstands what literature is, and can do—maybe seeing it only as a form of aesthetic consumption, not as *about* anything important except the pleasure it gives. . . .

But I think such a questioner also often misunderstands what law is, and can do, or at least understands these things differently from the way I do, and it is mainly law that I wish to talk about this evening. My idea is to render more explicit than I have done so far the vision of law itself out of which I have been functioning: what I call in my title an old-fashioned view of the nature of law.

What I shall say, in a phrase, is that law is not at heart an abstract system or scheme of rules, as we often think of it; nor is it a set of institutional arrangements that can be adequately described in a language of social science; rather, it is an inherently unstable structure of thought and expression, built upon a distinct set of dynamic and dialogic tensions. It is not a set of rules at all, but a form of life. It is a process by which the old is made new, over and over again.

I think I can best give content to this perhaps puzzling summary by explaining where the view I describe comes from. This will require me to be a bit autobiographical, but I hope you can see that here my real subject is not me, but the law.

I. Law as an Activity of Mind and Language

I came to law from the study of English literature and Classics, especially ancient Greek. In both of these fields my focus was on language, most obviously so with respect to Greek.

In working on Greek I naturally asked questions like the following: How was this language put together? What were its key terms of value, of social and natural description, of psychology, and what did they mean? What were its principles of grammar and syntax, governing the way in which sentences could be composed? What were the forms of thought and imagination that this language invited and made possible? What, in short, could be said and done in this language that could not be said and done in English? *(Do you see that the same questions could be asked of the law?)*

The activity of translation, in which I was constantly engaged, captures the essence of the problem I was facing: How much, or how little of what Homer does in the *Iliad*, say, can be brought into English? When we try to bring this poem into English, how do we distort or damage the original? How do we add to it?

I could see that I simply had to learn to read Homer in his language if I were to begin to understand what he said and did.

As I did that, what did I begin to see or experience? Certainly not what might be called an art-object, as some might think, offering itself to our aesthetic delectation, as a fine wine offers itself to our palate. The *Iliad* is beautiful, but it is also hideous, and it certainly is not about beauty as an aesthetic ideal. The same I think is true as a general matter of virtually any imaginative literature worth reading.

What the *Iliad* offered, as I saw it, was an engagement with what seemed like everything: the way a culture (in this case the heroic culture it describes and celebrates) is formed and works; the nature of cultural imperatives, and the way they can lead us into war and murder; the way an individual, necessarily formed in large part by his culture, can find himself almost by accident, as Achilles does, suddenly on the edge of that culture, in a position from which it can be seen and in some sense criticized and resisted; the character of human life itself, bounded as it is by death; and the achievement of art, by which this universal fact of human mortality can to some extent be defeated.

As the French philosopher Simone Weil says, the *Iliad* is a poem of force:[2] showing us the roots of war in the ideologies by which we dehumanize each other—a dehumanization the poem itself heroically reverses, in seeing, and bringing the audience to see, against the force of the military culture itself, the common humanity of Greek and Trojan.

So for me the *Iliad* was not literature as aesthetic consumption or display, but a powerful form of thought and education about the most important things in human life.

What I say of the *Iliad* was true in a general way of the best of the other books I read:[3] they offered engagement with human thought of the deepest and best kind about the most important matters in our individual and collective lives. In the work I admired—from Virgil to Shakespeare to Jane Austen to Robert Frost—I found people talking as well as they could about what was most important to them, constantly confronting their own limits of perspective, of knowledge, of mind—and the limits of their language too. Reading these texts in this way was for me a school for thinking well, reading well, writing well, and always about what mattered most in human life.[4] *(Can you imagine that I would come to say the same thing about law?)*

I went to graduate school in English literature, hoping to make a life out of this kind of engagement with the writing I loved, but I was disappointed, in part because to me this profession felt disconnected from what I thought of as the real world, and for that reason was, I thought, unable to respond deeply and well to the texts to which it was supposed to be devoted. I may have been wrong, but this is what I felt, and I left for law school.

In law school I felt that I came back to my own mind, and to a life I recognized. I was learning law, a new language, a language in which to think about and debate many of the most important questions of our shared existence. It was like learning Greek, except that I was learning it for use in the world, rather than as a way of engaging with literary and philosophic texts.

> It was like learning Greek.

This was not for me an academic or purely intellectual activity, but training in a profession that I intended to practice. I thought of this future most readily in rather small-town terms: I could imagine a client coming in off the street with a problem—a sense of threat or frustration or loss—that he or she could not handle without help. Law was the language into which this problem would have to be translated: it was the language I would use to define the problem and to make sense of it, and of its larger context too. It would ultimately be a language of power, producing a result authorized and enforced by the government.

The questions for me were these. What is this language of the law, and how does it work? What can be said and done in this language that cannot be done in ordinary English? How, in particular, does law work as a process of translation: with what losses, what gains, what distortions?[5] What will it mean to me to give myself the mind and character of a lawyer?

As I imagined it, in practice I would be talking about what really mattered, in competition (and cooperation) with others who were doing likewise, before judges who were also talking about what really mattered. For what we were talking about was important not only to our clients, which it surely was—would they be compensated for their injury, or hold on to their land, or lose their inheritance?—but to the world: and this not so much because the outcome of the particular case mattered, but because it always matters very much to the world how such cases are debated and resolved. Every case performs an answer to the question: What are our institutions of justice? How well—how justly—do they work? How should they work? And nothing is more important to a healthy community than justice.

I saw the law as a wonderful system in which power worked through conversation, through open argument and persuasion. In principle at least, everyone got his or her opportunity to present the case in the best way possible, and to answer what was said on the other side. In a legal hearing one could say whatever it was necessary or crucial to say about this injury, this divorce, this failed agreement, this event in the real world.[6]

To engage in this complex activity it was crucial that I should be able to learn and speak and use the language of the law well, and in two senses: that I should be an effective counselor and advocate; and that in doing so I should conceive of myself as doing something of value not only to my client but to the world: contributing to the maintenance of our institutions of justice, indeed contributing to the realization of justice itself.

Of course, as in all language use, all translations, I could see that the conversation of the law would always be imperfect: there would always be something left out, something out of tune, something stuck in, always a deep imperfection. Sometimes I thought that the legal language I was given to use was itself hopelessly dead and inadequate. Even where it did seem to have wonderful resources, these were not always taken advantage of by lawyers and judges—who sometimes spoke in the dead ways familiar to all of us, full of clichés and empty formulas.

But both things—the inherent failings of the language and our failings in our use of it—seemed to me to present challenges for a life of value, the aim of which was to define and express meaning: the meaning of the experience of our clients; the meaning of the collection of authoritative texts and traditions and understandings that are the embodiment of the law; the meaning of the institutions of thought and argument in which these questions were presented and addressed.[7]

When I went into law practice the view I describe was confirmed: the heart of my work was reading and writing, not in a trivial or mechanical sense, not as the exercise of skill alone, but as the fullest and most important expression of a mind engaged in the world. It was hard to do it well, impossible to do it perfectly.

My view of law was internal, from the inside, from the point of view of someone actually doing it. The law can of course be looked at from the outside too, by sociologists and political scientists and anthropologists and others, and they are entitled to look at it differently: as a social or political process, or as a structure of rules reflecting certain policies. But the way they look will define what they see, and it will not be the law as I know it. They will not be doing law, but something else entirely.

Law is an activity.

I saw law, as I continue to see it, as an activity of mind and language: a kind of translation, a way of claiming meaning for experience and making that meaning real. It is not a system of rules, as I said earlier, but a structure of thought and expression built upon a set of inherently unstable, dynamic, and dialogic tensions. In this it is like a poem.

MyTudut's flickr photostream, Aug. 22, 2006

Two men shaking hands

So for me law was a language that one could learn, well or badly, a structured activity of mind one could perform well or badly. One could use this language to carry on conversations in the world, conversations that produced results in the form of judicial decisions, settlement agreements, contracts, and the like; results that mattered, sometimes acutely to actual people, especially the clients; and results that mattered in another way to the whole polity, for one question always present in the conversation was what justice should require, what the law should be. The object of our work was to reconstitute the material of the past to claim new meaning in the present and future.

II. Tensions in Legal Thought and Expression

Exactly what are the tensions of which I speak, and how do they work? How are they to be addressed? What does it mean that the law is built upon them? These are my next questions.

I should tell you at the outset that much of what I am going to say about them may seem very basic. Indeed it *is* basic. At one time perhaps we could even have taken much of what I am going to say for granted. This set of perceptions might not have been wholly conscious, but I think it was there in the legal culture, and did not need stating. This is why I call it an old-fashioned view of law.

1. Between Legal Language and Ordinary Language

It may help us uncover some of the tensions upon which legal discourse is built if we think of a day in the life of the lawyer I was preparing to become, starting with the moment when the client comes into our office seeking our help.

This client—whether a person or corporation or government body—will have a story to tell and a language in which to tell it. Perhaps he will tell us about domestic violence that he or his children have suffered; perhaps about an idea that he and two others have for forming a corporation that will create and sell computer software; perhaps about the bank's threat to foreclose the mortgage on his house.

The problem can be mundane and ordinary, or sophisticated and rare, but in any case our client will have his own sense of what is wrong, of what he wants, and of his own incapacity to get it on his own. He will turn to us, after all, only when he sees that he needs help.

His story will be cast in his ordinary language, the way he usually thinks and speaks. Our job is to listen to him talk in his language, and then to ask questions that will prompt him to say more. For our knowledge of the law should enable us to raise issues that he will not have thought of, and in this way encourage a fuller statement of his story in the language of the law.

When is his story complete? When do we have everything we need to know? A very good question. The sea of possibly relevant facts is infinite, and there is no clear way of knowing when we have enough. In such conversations there is a circular dependence between facts and law: the facts determine what law is relevant, the law determines what facts are relevant.[8] In principle we could go on forever, but we stop when we think we have enough to enable us to develop his case.

No rules could tell us when we have reached this point; our sense of completeness is a judgment we gradually make, as we go back and forth between his story and what we know of the law. It rests upon our educated intuition.

Our second task will be to translate what we have been told by our client into legal language. This requires us to go from his or her language to the law and back again, over and over, checking both his story and our translation of it. As with all translations, this process is inherently imperfect and distorting. It cannot be done to a formula or rule, but requires the exercise of an art.

Sometimes the gap between our languages seems on the surface rather small, for example at closing argument, when we are speaking to the jury and do so in a language as close to ordinary English as we can manage.[9] Sometimes the gap is enormous. When our client hears us make an argument about choice of law—maintaining, for example, that Nebraska law should apply, not Iowa law, or federal law rather than state law—she may not see any connection at all with the problem she brought to us. But the choice of law problem, if it is a real one, is one of the ways the law gives meaning to her case. It may even be that what this case will ultimately stand for in the law is a new and persuasive approach to choice of law, something she may not care about at all.

Our first tension in the law, then, is the one between ordinary and legal language. The lawyer has to speak both languages; he or she has to translate, as well as possible, both ways, into the law and out of it, a process that is at every stage defective or imperfect. Sometimes the defect will be fatal: we will simply not be able to say in the language we are given what we think should be said about this case.[10]

This tension can be found not only in interviews with the client, but throughout the process, and in many forms: in the lawyer's examination or cross-examination of lay witnesses, for example; in her closing argument to the jury, who are of course untrained in the law; and even in her arguments with the opposing counsel and to the judge, for it is common there to resort to ordinary life and language for images with which to make a point. Everyone wants to be able to say in ordinary terms what she is saying in legal terms, and vice versa.

The client's story can never fully be told.

This tension is made more difficult by the existence of a related one, between language of any kind at all and the mute world of inexpressible experience. In an important sense the client's story can never fully be told even in ordinary English. There is always a level of experience that cannot be adequately expressed in any language: what a broken arm actually feels like, for example, or the helpless rage and agony of seeing your children hurt by your spouse, or the mute sense of outrage or betrayal at a business partner's disloyalty. Everything that we say, in any language, floats as it were on a sea of inexpressible experience.

So we face not only a tension between legal and other forms of language and expression, but a tension between the world of words and the world of mute experience that underlies it.

These tensions are inherently unstable, never fully resolvable. Responding to them is not a matter of logic, or ends-means rationality, or conceptual analysis, but requires an art, an art of language and judgment.

2. *Between Law and Other Languages*

The tension between legal and ordinary speech is an instance of a larger tension, our second, arising from the fact that legal discourse is itself built upon many different voices, many different languages. It speaks not with one voice but with many voices, and its meaning to a large degree lies in the music that is made among them.

Thus in [the United States], for example, we have the official voices of the legislature, the trial judge, the constitution, the Supreme Court, each speaking in its own way to the others, and to the public too.

We have witnesses, expert and inexpert, each speaking from his or her point of view in the world. The voice of the person who saw the robbery, of the policeman who investigated it, of the technician who tested the blood, of the robbery victim himself; the voice of the defendant, of the psychiatrist testifying on the question of his sanity, of the witness who claims he saw the victim begin the fracas by attacking the defendant; all these are different voices, speaking in different languages.

Suppose for example that our case is a medical malpractice case, in which each side plans to call two expert witnesses—a heart surgeon, say, and an engineer who knows about mechanical heart valves. To prepare our own witnesses for direct and cross examination, and to cross examine the opposition witnesses, we shall need to learn something of the languages of the doctor and engineer. We must be prepared to translate, that is, not only between ordinary language and legal language, but between both of these languages and a range of specialized languages.[11] This activity of translation is both necessary and inherently imperfect, and what it requires in us is the exercise of an art.

It is sometimes thought that the law is a single language of authority, a set of nested commands, running from the general to the particular, all in the same voice of absolute or legislative authority, but as we see here such a view makes little sense. The lawyer or judge must be an artist in translation, prepared to translate between the world of mute experience and the world of words; between ordinary language and legal language; and between both of these and specialized languages as well.

Perhaps we do not teach translation of this kind in law school but we certainly should.

3. Between the Opposing Lawyers

There is a third tension, very different in kind, that is also fundamental to the legal process: the tension that exists between the lawyers on opposing sides of the case. This tension is plain: we want our client to win, he wants his [client] to win, and each of us will do all we properly can to make that happen.

Thus at trial each lawyer will stretch every nerve to present the material of the law, and the facts, in such a way as to fit with the fundamental claims of his client. One is the voice of condemnation or attack, the other of excuse or defense. We are deeply opposed, for each of us is straining to create a sense of the case, and the law, that will lead the judge or jury to decide our way. This is a power struggle in the law, and it creates an inherently unstable tension, one that is by nature both dynamic and dialogic.

Yet there is something odd here: while we and the lawyer on the other side are obviously opposed to each other, we are also in fact cooperating. We agree in a general way, for example, both about the materials of our argument and the way it should proceed. While we are strenuously disagreeing, that is, we are equally strenuously affirming a great deal: the language, the conventions of discourse, the principles or understandings by which we carry on our argument, and certain conclusions too, on questions both of law and fact.

We contest what we can, but we accept what we cannot, and this becomes, for the moment at least, a firm foundation for further thought on both sides. We thus affirm the very constraints of the law within which we find that we, despite our strongest efforts, must operate.

When our joint performance works well—as it of course does not always do—it subjects the material of the law, and the facts too, to the most intense and searching scrutiny. Instead of seeking the single meaning of the statutes, of the judicial opinions, of the

While we and the lawyer on the other side are obviously opposed to each other, we are also in fact cooperating.

regulations, and of other materials of authority, we two lawyers together are demonstrating the range of possible meanings that these texts may be given, and using all our powers to do so. In our hands, that is, the law is not a closed system of significances, but is systematically opened up to new possibilities—opened up, in fact, as far as we can do it. That is one of the points of our work.

This tension between competing voices and perspectives gives a special kind of life to the law. As I just said, it creates a space for newness and creativity in reading the texts of the law, which might otherwise be read in dead and mechanical ways.

It is also a way of being grown-up: learning to live in a world in which people think differently from each other and to respect the judgments of those with whom we disagree. This very process, rhetorical and adversary in nature, creates a related tension, an internal one, moral or ethical in nature, within each of the lawyers. Is what she is doing justifiable, or even respectable?

We are making arguments for our client, on the law and the facts; but suppose we do not think that what we are arguing for is right? Suppose we think that the other side should win? Or, perhaps more likely, suppose we do not allow ourselves to think at all about the right result, about what justice requires, but only about what arguments will work? What have we become?

The most important ethical issue is who we are becoming.

This problem can be swept under the rug by claiming that the adversarial system works to produce justice, so that even if we are not arguing justly, the system will be just—if not in this particular case, most of the time. But that claim rests on an unprovable optimism, and in any event does not address the most important ethical issue, which is who are we becoming when we engage in the activity I describe. Are we just mouthpieces who will say anything to win, whether or not we mean it? Or can we see ourselves as doing something we can truly respect?

A book could be written about this issue,[12] but I hope that you can already see that here is another tension, inherently unstable, deep within the lawyer himself or herself. It is unavoidable by a conscientious person. It is not susceptible of systemic resolution, by resort to a slogan or a rule or a phrase, but must be addressed over and over in the life of the lawyer, in the deep particulars of every argument he or she makes.

4.   *Between Competing but Plausible Readings of the Law*

For our next tension, let us assume that the efforts at negotiation have failed and that the case is headed for court, where the two lawyers will speak to the judge who will decide between them.

If we imagine ourselves for a moment as the judge, we can see that the tension between the lawyers creates, or ought to create, a parallel tension in our own mind, as the two opposing voices are present and alive within us. If we start to think one way, we should find ourselves checked by the other.

The elaboration by the lawyers of arguments on both sides is a way of resisting the judge's impulse to decide too quickly, encouraging her to keep her mind open until she has heard it all, thought through it all—indeed helping her to think it through.

The two sets of arguments, in making explicit the range of possible choices open to the judge, make clear that the judge will have to make her choice and accept responsibility for it—not push the decision off on a statute or other text that is read in a conclusory or unthinking way.

This argumentative process makes plain that the image of the law as a set of clear (and perhaps even self-applying) rules cannot survive a moment's scrutiny. Under the pressure provided by the lawyers' arguments, the scope of judicial choice becomes wide, much wider than one would at first expect. This fact creates a tension right at the heart of the judicial judgment, a tension between rational but opposed conclusions. This is our fourth tension.

If a statute says that "trucks" must travel in the right lane, or that imported "toys" pay only half the usual customs duty, or that an arrest may only be made upon "probable cause to believe the suspect has committed a felony" we have a general idea what is meant to happen, but we also know that elaborate arguments can go about the meaning of the words, *truck, toy, probable cause, felony*, and even *commit* (does it include aiding and abetting another, or being an accessory after the fact?).

Legal categories, whether legislative or judicial in origin, thus invariably carry a substantial range of reasonable possibilities for their meaning, sometimes a very wide range. Among these possibilities the judge will have to choose. How is she to do this?

A great deal has been written on this question, with answers ranging at least across the following spectrum: (1) the uncertainty of meaning creates in her a discretionary power to do whatever she wants; (2) she is to be guided in the exercise of her discretion by her sense of the intention of the rule-maker; (3) she is to be guided by appropriate general principles of moral and political philosophy; (4) she is to be guided by natural law; (5) she is to be guided by analogy to other legal examples; (6) she is to resolve the ambiguity against the drafter of the document, since he or she is responsible for it; and so on.

I will not join in the debate as to which of these, or others, should guide her decision. It is enough for present purposes that it is clear that in her basic task of legal decision the judge inhabits a zone marked by a strong tension between alternative ways of thinking, a tension that is, like the other ones I have described, dynamic, dialogic, and inherently unstable. The resolution of this tension, like the other ones, cannot be achieved simply by reference to a rule or practice or phrase or idea, but must be achieved afresh, in every case, by an art of judgment. This very fact gives life to the law.

As the judge faces this problem, she also faces her own version of what I called before the tension between the world of language and the world of inexpressible experience. This tension arises within her the moment she asks herself how and why the case should be decided.

Here is what I mean. A part of her mind will think in terms of legal arguments of the kind we have been discussing, testing them against each other for their force and power. But beneath that layer of the mind is another, an intuitive center, educated by experience and reflection, that is really seeking the right decision. The judge knows that her written opinion can never express or justify what the center of herself is doing, the secret spring of judgment at her core.[13] This tension cannot be resolved in any *a priori* way by a rule or principle, but must, like the others mentioned, be lived through in detail and addressed anew every time.

5. *Between Substance and Procedure*

A fifth structural tension runs through the law: between what we call "substance," on the one hand, and procedural or institutional considerations on the other.

One of the deepest—and to the lay person, most mystifying—characteristics of legal thought is that the lawyers and judges seem to think about both kinds of questions at once, working as it were in two channels simultaneously. Whenever the lawyers argue about a substantive question, such as the meaning of a statutory or constitutional provision, they are likely at the same time to argue about a procedural question: the requirements for a judgment on the pleadings, for example, or for summary judgment, or for a directed verdict.

This second channel, which I am calling "procedural," is by no means limited to technical matters of judicial procedure, but includes argument of a much more general kind, which might be called "institutional."

Suppose the substantive question is whether one may dump industrial waste water in the river; or whether a school on an Indian reservation may begin its days with the recitation of a sentence that sums up the traditional wisdom of the tribe; or whether one may have a loud party to celebrate one's child's graduation from school, even though the neighbors object. The lawyer or judge facing such substantive questions will at the same time face a set of institutional questions: Who is empowered to decide this question in the first instance, and why? What procedures should this actor be compelled to follow, and why? To what review is the first actor's judgment to be subjected, and why? Or, to reverse the point of view, to what degree of deference is it to be entitled, and why?

Suppose for example in the water discharge case that there is a municipal ordinance on the subject. Here the lawyers will ask what I have been calling the substantive question—whether the ordinance should be interpreted to prohibit this discharge—but at the same time a set of institutional questions: whether the city council was authorized to pass such an ordinance by the relevant statute; if so, whether it followed the requisite procedures; if so, whether this ordinance, even if authorized by statute, meets the requirements of the state or federal constitution. In fact much of what we mean by constitutional law is institutional in just this way, determining what agency should have the power to decide what questions, under what procedures, and subject to what review.

The mind of the lawyer and judge mysteriously works in both tracks at once, and there is an inherently unstable tension between them. Sometimes, indeed, the two lines of thought intertwine in such a way as to make them one. We just cannot think of one without the other. What happens in one line of thought affects the other. It is like seeing that the smooth and rough sides of a piece of cloth each require and imply the other.

There is no way to draft a set of rules for resolving this tension. It must be addressed by an art of language and judgment.

6.   Between Law and Justice

A sixth tension, still different from the others, exists at the heart of legal thought, between the twin demands of law and justice. For in our system the lawyer and judge alike must ask not only, "What does the law require?" but "What does justice require?"

It is a convention of our law—I have never seen plainly stated but seems to me undeniable—that in every case the lawyer on each side must maintain that the result he or she is arguing for is both required by the law and itself fundamentally just. An argument that claimed that the law required the outcome, but admitted that the result was unjust, would be profoundly incomplete. No lawyer would want to be in the position of making such a case. Likewise incomplete would be the sister argument that claimed that justice required the result argued for, but admitted that the law was against it. Nor would a judge happily admit either that her judgment was unjust or that it was against the law.

In this sense ours is a system of both natural and positive law. It is like a chariot being drawn by two horses: they often pull in opposed directions, but unruly and uncooperative as they may be, together they take the chariot in a direction that is much better than that towards which either of the horses alone is pulling it.

In every case the lawyer on each side must maintain that the result he or she is arguing for is both required by the law and itself fundamentally just.

The immense and deep tension between these two claims means that the lawyer or judge must often labor to harmonize them, sometimes to the breaking point. But it also gives both lawyer and judge an opportunity to create something new and alive: not merely the logical working out of rules or premises, but a deep engagement both with the texts of the past and the facts of the present, and what they mean. It is one aspect of the lawyer's great task, which is to bring into one field of vision the ideal and the real.[14]

7. *Between the Past and Present—and the Future Too*

Finally let me suggest one more tension, a temporal one: between the past and the present, and between both of them and the future.[15]

The task of the lawyer and judge is to bring the materials of the past—sometimes recent past, sometimes remote past—to bear on the problems of the present, and in so doing to make something new for the future. The law is thus not a static or timeless system, working out the implications of its premises in abstract or purely logical ways, but a way of functioning in a world dominated by time, seizing the ever-passing moment of the present as the place to join past and future. It is a way of defining experience; learning from experience; shaping experience.

Chris-Havard Berge, June 5, 2010

Shaking hands

This tension is present in all legal argument, but most of all in the special form we call the judicial opinion. This text brings together all that the parties have been able to invoke from the past, and issues the authoritative judgment that speaks to the future. It does not just state or define a rule, but issues a judgment, which it explains, and explains in ways that go beyond the language of the rule itself.

III. The Writing Life of the Lawyer and Judge

I am saying, then, that legal thought is not the top-down elaboration of the meaning of a set of rules, by a process of logic or end-means rationality; nor is it a pattern of conduct that can be adequately represented and understood in the language of social science; rather, it is an activity of mind and language, one that is deeply marked by a set of structural tensions (or clusters of tensions):

— between ordinary language and legal language (indeed between language itself, of any kind, and the mute world that lies beneath it);

— between a multiplicity of voices, speaking from different positions within the legal order, or outside of it, in a variety of specialized and expert languages;

— between the two lawyers, each of whom seems to resist the other at every point, though in another way they are cooperating deeply; and within each lawyer, whenever she asks what it means for herself and the world that she is acting as she is;

— between many conflicting but justifiable ways of giving meaning to the rules and principles of law, among which the judge will have to choose; and also between the reasoning and intuitive capacities of the judge herself;

— between substantive and procedural (or institutional) lines of thought, a tension that runs throughout the law;

— between the imperatives of law and justice; and

— between the past and the present, the present and the future, for law lives in time and out of shared experience.

This is not an exhaustive list, but for present purposes it will do.

Each of these tensions is, as I have said, inherently unstable, that is, not resolvable by reference to fixed rules, principles, or conventions; each is dynamic, not static, thus moving us in new directions that we cannot always anticipate; each is dialogic, not monologic, thus acting with the force of competing voices at work in the world or in the self. These tensions interact, to create fault lines that run through every act of full legal analysis. Their management is essential to the work of lawyer or judge.

1. The Law Is Not the Rules

What happens if we start to think of law in this old-fashioned way? Let me suggest, to start with, that it makes simply impossible the view that the law is a system or scheme of rules that are in practice applied more or less rationally to produce a set of intended or desired results.

This is a view that law students often bring to law school with them. They expect that we shall teach them a set of rules. These are the rules they will apply as lawyers, and knowledge of them is what sets them apart from the non-lawyer, to whom [the rules] are unknown. A large part of a good legal education is disabusing [students] of this view.

If the law is just a set of rules, it won't ask me to change and grow.

There are many reasons that such an image is attractive to the student. It explains the kind of knowledge that the lawyer has, and justifies his role (and his fees). It is also in principle simple, even easy: if all I have to do is memorize a set of rules, even if there are a lot of them, I am confident that I can do it. The work may be dull but it won't be hard. It won't ask of me what I cannot already do; it will not ask me to change and grow. So it is natural for the student to say: "I want the law to be a set of rules!"[16]

But I think the view of law as rules is also at work in the kind of scholarship and teaching that takes as its subject the question, not how lawyers think and should think, but what the rules should be. We see this view at work in policy studies generally, in "law and economics" in particular, in much jurisprudence, and indeed wherever the tendency to abstract or theoretical thinking has taken hold, whether in the analysis of legislative or judicial problems.

2. *The Law Is Not Policy*

The question of policy is of course a legitimate one, and lawyers, economists, social scientists, moral philosophers, ordinary people, and lots of others too, can properly speak to it.

But it is not the essential question for either lawyer or judge, who is instead repeatedly asked to deal with the particulars of a case, whether as adviser, advocate, or decider, and to do so in light of the whole structure of arguably relevant and authoritative legal rules, principles, conventions, precedents, understandings, indeed in light of the whole legal world and culture. This structure, as I have been trying to show, is not a coherent conceptual system but a dramatic and rhetorical process marked by a series of deep and inherently unstable tensions that cannot be reduced to or governed by a system of rules or other directives.[17]

Rules of the standard legislative (or judicial) form do exist, and they serve to guide general expectations and behavior. They are important and can be talked about in such terms. But this is not the level at which the judge or lawyer works, for they are normally called upon only when there is a problem or difficulty, a moment at which the rules collide with reality, or each other, and do not work in the easy way they are thought to do. To put it in a phrase, the judge and lawyer deal not with the "rules" as such, as a discrete conceptual system, but with what happens when that abstract language, and the rest of the authoritative language of the law, meets the world.

3. The Law Is a Set of Possibilities for Original Thought and Expression

For the law is not a system, but a way of managing the relations between what looks like a system and many dimensions of actual life: the experience of the client and lawyer, including the experience that cannot be expressed in any language at all; the multiplicity of languages and voices that make up our world; the conflicts and harmonies between opposing lawyers; the freedom and responsibility of the judge; the idealistic and realistic tendencies of legal thought; the tension between past and present, present and future.

The way in which lawyer and judge think about the moment at which the language of the law meets the world is to engage in a complex process of thought that is built upon and marked by tensions of the sort I have summarized.[18] These cannot be resolved by reference to any set of directives or guides, but must be addressed afresh whenever the lawyer or judge goes to work, and always in light of the particulars of the case in which they are presented. The lawyer and judge do not operate simply at the level of high generality that the rules mark out, nor simply at the level of particularity established by the facts of the case, but always in an uneasy tension between these two levels of thought. They are in this like poets, who also face the tension between particular and general in all that they do.[19]

In saying all this, let me stress, I am trying to define what I see to be the possibilities of life in the law. Of course these possibilities are not attained automatically, and never fully or perfectly, and sometimes they are corrupted. Often lawyers and judges are thoughtless, crude, unimaginative, inarticulate, and dull. Indeed such things are sometimes true of us all. But not always, in every way. My effort here is to offer an image of the activity of law by which we can shape our efforts as we practice or teach it, an image, over the horizon, as it were, which we can keep before us as we do our work: a sense of how things might be if only we could make them so.

The law is a set of possibilities.

The law does not work its way to predetermined conclusions through a process of iron logic, but almost the opposite: it is a set of possibilities for original thought and expression. It is not a totalitarian system, closed and unlistening, but an open system, like a language, not only making creativity possible, but requiring it. The process in which we are engaged is an art of testing and invention.

Every case, every legal conversation, is an opportunity to exercise the lawyer's complex art of mind and imagination. This art is what we teach, what we practice, and what we cherish.[20]

4. *The Law Is an Art of Mind and Language*

In calling what the lawyer and judge engage in an *art*, I have in mind the thought that all art—whether music or painting or architecture or poetry or drama—proceeds by way of tension and resolution: a conflict is stated or hinted at or felt; the tension between opposing elements is developed and expanded; and at the end a resolution is reached—but never a final resolution, only a momentary one. When one poem or sonata is finished, another is to be begun, and so it is with legal argument and legal judgment. The aim of the lawyer, as for the poet, to quote Robert Frost, is to end "in a clarification of life—not necessarily a great clarification, such as sects and cults are founded on, but in a momentary stay against confusion."[21]

The tensions I have been defining are not, then, as some might say, simply "noise in the system," but the life of the law itself.

If I am right, what I am saying here has real consequences: for the sort of education that we offer, which should invite the student to engage in the art I describe, not to learn law as a set of rules; for the ethical and intellectual possibilities of the lawyer's life, which can be seen to be far more interesting, challenging, and ethically alive, than the view of the lawyer as rule-applier; for the expectations that judges can bring to their work and for the ways in which we can evaluate what they do—not simply by political agreement or disagreement with the outcome, but by judging their work as performances of an art, the art of reconciling the ideal and the real.

Law is an art of language and judgment.

This vision of the law is indeed an old-fashioned one, going back to the roots of legal thought in the West, in the study and practice of the art of rhetoric. At its heart it is a vision of law as an art, an art of language and judgment, an art of the maintenance and repair of human community.[22] In another sense, however, it is not old-fashioned at all, but as timely as it ever was. In my view it is necessary to have such a vision if, in our practice and teaching and judging, the law is to fulfill its nature and its promise. This is, perhaps, "an old-fashioned vision of the law for the twenty-first century."

I have been resisting an image of law as rules and policy, but behind those things is a deeper vision: of law as abstract, mechanical, impersonal, essentially bureaucratic in nature, narrowing rather than broadening the human capacity for experience, understanding, and empathy. To focus on the law as a system, and not on what happens when that system meets the world—and the people of the world—is to strip it of its difficulty, its life, its meaning, and its value.

For it is at this moment, when the law meets the world—in the work of lawyer, judge, or teacher—that it becomes most fully alive. This moment contains within it the seeds of resistance to the forces of mindless empire and control, for every case is an opportunity for newness of thought, for creativity and surprise, for the introduction into the world of power an unrecognized voice, language, or claim.

In the moment of speech, or writing, there is always the possibility that one can bring the world into new life.

James Boyd White and his grandson, Oliver

Discussion Questions

1. Reread the first two sentences of Professor White's article. What does he mean by describing the law as "an inherently unstable structure of thought and expression"?
2. Professor White says that law is not rules or policy; rather it is a set of possibilities for original thought and expression—an art of mind and language. What are the seven tensions he identifies as inherent in that legal thought and expression? Might these tensions be the very stuff of our creative work as lawyers?
3. After all our work in this book, does it now make more sense to you to think about law as unstable? Is that instability good or bad? What does it mean for your own life in the law?
4. What does Professor White mean when he says, right before Section I, that law "is a process by which the old is made new, over and over again"?
5. Professor White says that law is an art of mind and language. We have been looking at how that art can be created in briefs. What other roles and activities of lawyering call for this art of mind and language—both in litigation and in all other activities of lawyering?
6. What are you looking forward to most as you anticipate a life in the law? What worries you?

Additional Suggested Reading

Nancy Levit & Douglas O. Linder, *The Happy Lawyer: Making a Good Life in the Law* (Oxford U. Press 2010).

Endnotes

1. Hart Wright Professor of Law emeritus, Professor of English emeritus, formerly adjunct professor of Classical Studies, The University of Michigan. I want to thank Jeanne Gaakeer, Jefferson Powell, Joseph Vining, and Mary White for helpful criticisms of an earlier draft.

2. Simone Weil, *L'Iliade, ou le poème de la force*, first published in *Cahiers du Sud* (December 1940-January 1941), and often republished since then.

3. The *Aeneid*, for example, about the immense value and terrible cost of the Roman Empire; Jane Austen's novels, about the art of judging others accurately and comprehensively by what they say (especially difficult when they speak in formal contexts, where pretense and evasion are so easy to achieve); Thoreau's *Walden*, about the relation between the individual mind and the natural world, the whole universe of energy and life in which we live; and so on and on, throughout the world that the writers of the Western tradition had created.

4. To take Jane Austen's novels as an example, she helps us deal with the fact that we live in a world of false speech of many kinds: sentimental, authoritarian, ideological, racist, dominated by hype and buzzwords and salespitches, by the beating of war drums. How are we to make our way in such a universe? This is what Austen tries to teach us, by exposing falsity and emptiness, manipulation and brutality, for what they are, and offering us forms of thought and speech that are genuine, powerful, and true. Her books offer an education in the difference between false and true, living and dead, in both thought and speech.

5. I was later to pursue at some length the idea that law was a form of translation, in *Justice as Translation* (U. of Chicago Press 1990).

6. If a case was to be settled by negotiation, the hearing still remained the model of legal expression, because at every stage the lawyers were imagining that the case would proceed to trial and thinking ahead of time of the arguments that would be made both ways. Even in drafting documents the same was true: the lawyers were always testing what they were writing by imagining a dispute in court.

7. I have spoken of the life of the lawyer as one of writing, but it was of course one of reading as well. One had to learn how to read texts written in other times and places, on other occasions, by other people, and bring them intelligently and coherently into the present, so that they might speak to the difficulty or dispute we were facing. This kind of reading, like the writing, was an ideal task that could never be performed perfectly, requiring imagination, learning, and intelligence, all of the highest order. And even with all the talents in the world, the coherence would still be imperfect, the argument flawed, the understanding incomplete—a fact that for me opened up a future full of interest and value.

8. I owe this observation to Professor Albert Sacks, who made this illuminating comment in a classroom more than 45 years ago.

9. This appearance can be illusory. Beneath the surface of ordinary English one can often discern important legal judgments and arguments.

10. In such a case we are effectively silenced. I discovered this when I represented a young man who refused induction into the armed services on the ground that the compulsory medical treatment he would receive in the service would violate his religious beliefs. He was not a draft dodger, but a kind of misfit in the law. I imagined myself making a grand argument to the jury, urging them to do justice to his case, then realized that under the relevant statute the only question before the jury would be whether he had refused induction. The issue of the propriety of his classification was for the court, who was in fact required to affirm if it was supported by any basis in fact.

11. An obvious difficulty is that we cannot really learn the language of doctor or engineer with the kind of completeness and depth that only those professionals can have. How then do we face this impossible task? Partly, we are schooled by our own witnesses, and by other advisers as well; partly, we read in the field in question to learn its language as well as we can; partly, we test, over and over, what the expert says by translating it into ordinary language that we can understand.

12. For my own efforts at dealing with this problem, see chapter four of *When Words Lose Their Meaning* (U. of Chicago Press 1984) and chapter nine of *Heracles' Bow* (U. of Wisconsin Press 1986).

13. The opinion therefore, however honestly written, has some of the characteristics of a false pretense: This is why I decided the case as I did, the opinion says; but the judge knows that the true springs of decision are deep within her, and can never be fully known or explained.

14. Consider, for example, the fact that we talk to the judge not as the bundle of prejudices and beliefs and commitments and character traits that form part of his or her character, but as an ideal judge, one who is always seeking to do justice under the law. Likewise, we idealize the legislature, interpreting its words as if they came from a wise and good person, when of course the truth is more complex. We idealize our client in the way we talk about him, presenting him in the best light possible. In this sense we are engaged in work that is explicitly aspirational in character.

At the same time we are required to be realists, about all these actors and about the process too, recognizing that the legislature is a political body, that the judge is biased for us or against us, that our client has all the usual faults of humanity: he may lie to us, or not pay the fine, or our bill; he may skip town.

15. Here are two others one could add to the list: the tension between narrative and theory in the mind of the lawyer or judge (for these modes of thought work in very different ways); and the tension between the particular and the general, a feature also of poetry and other forms of literature. For further discussion, see *The Legal Imagination* 858-926, 624-686 (U. of Chicago Press 1973). One might also consider the tensions that the legislator must face as he or she gives shape to a statute, discussed in the same book, pp.195-242.

16. It was once common for law teachers to think that one of the structural tensions in the classroom was over this issue, as, against resistance, we insisted that we were doing something other than teaching rules, namely how lawyers think, and think well. In teaching criminal law, for example, I handed out the first day a page which had on it all the rules we would learn that term. I told the students that they could memorize them in an hour at most. What this meant was that whatever the rest of the course was about, it was not learning the rules.

17. For a similar argument from a different point of view, see A.W. Brian Simpson, *The Common Law and Legal Theory*, in *Oxford Essays on Jurisprudence*, Second Series (Oxford U. Press 1973).

18. This is true of the teacher as well, of course. When I think of my own decision to teach law rather than practice it, and of the claim, by some, that this is a retreat to the Ivory Tower from the Real World, I want to say that teaching, properly done, is itself a form of practice, a way of facing the set of tensions I describe here. To do this one must regard the cases not simply as instances of theoretical questions or the application of rules, but as pieces of the whole process of legal argument and thought, as I have sketched it here, from the interview with the client right through to the appeal of an adverse judgment.

19. Sir Philip Sidney said that philosophy deals with mere abstractions, history with mere particulars; the poet alone "doth perform both." *The Defense of Poesie* (1595).

20. The voice that says, "I have a theory that answers this and all such questions," is not the voice of lawyer or judge. Those actors must speak in much more complex, tentative, exploratory ways, sensitive, like the poet, to the constant tensions between various lines of thought and meaning.

21. Robert Frost, *The Figure a Poem Makes*, in *Robert Frost: Collected Poems, Prose & Plays* 776, 777 (Richard Poirier & Mark Richardson eds., Library of America 1995).

22. In law as in poetry, the life and quality of one's work inhere in the way in which constraints are faced, tensions addressed and elaborated, complexities recognized. This must be done every time afresh. Think of the way a poem is built: It is a structure of meaning in which many dimensions, each one built on tensions of its own—image, story, meter, rhyme, sentence shape, and so on—interact to create a living whole. There is dynamic tension between or among each of these dimensions, and within them as well, for each presents and responds to a tension between order and disorder. Legal work is like that.

Briefs That Changed the World

History

1. Muller v. Oregon

Linda H. Edwards

In Chapter 14, you read about the famous brief often called "the Brandeis Brief," filed on behalf of the State of Oregon in *Muller v. Oregon*. The Oregon legislature had limited the number of hours women could be required to work at certain physically taxing trades. Curt Muller wanted to require his employees to work more hours in his Portland laundry, so he challenged the constitutionality of the Oregon statute, arguing that it impermissibly infringed upon liberty of contract. Predictably, his lawyer, William Fenton, relied primarily on *Lochner v. New York*,[1] the case that had invalidated a New York statute limiting the working hours of bakery employees. Wanting to invalidate the Oregon statute too, other Portland laundry owners financed Muller's appeal to the United States Supreme Court. The National Consumer League (NCL) came to the defense of the Oregon statute, and the stage was set for a new kind of legal argument.

On behalf of the NCL, Florence Kelley and Josephine Goldmark were working hard to improve the lives of workers, including women and children in the workplace. Kelley was both a reformer and a lawyer, having earned her law degree from Northwestern University. She had drafted the Illinois maximum-hours law of 1893, and when it was challenged, she wrote the brief to defend it.[2] Among other arguments, that brief sought to show the damage caused to women and their families by outrageously long working hours. Kelley also made countless appearances at legislative hearings in many states, presenting sociological and statistical data to support legislation limiting working hours.[3] In 1905, Kelley published *Some Ethical Gains in Legislation*, in which she identified the crucial question of how to persuade the justices of the highest appellate courts about the serious effects of long working hours and bad working conditions on employees and their families.[4] The answer to Kelley's question would soon come, and it would be the very sociological and statistical data she had been gathering and presenting to judges and legislators and anyone else who would listen.

Library of Congress (circa 1909-1923)

Protesters

When the *Muller* case was on its way to the Supreme Court, Kelley, Goldmark, and their NCL colleagues knew it would be an important case, and they wanted an eminent lawyer to defend the statute. Goldmark persuaded her famous brother-in-law, Louis D. Brandeis, to take the case, and Oregon's attorney agreed. Brandeis, Kelley, and Goldmark went to work. They believed that the best defense lay in the presentation of facts establishing the dangers the statute was designed to address, but this new kind of legal argument would be a risky strategy. Perhaps because of the risk, Brandeis submitted another, more conventional brief, relying on legal precedent and traditional legal argument. This second brief was signed by both Brandeis and the lawyers for the State of Oregon.[5]

The more novel brief, however, is the one that has captured legal attention down through the years. Brandeis wrote a scant two pages of legal argument. The rest of the brief consists of the more than 100 pages of findings of social scientists supplied by Kelley, Goldmark, and their team of researchers.[6] These findings showed the pernicious effects of requiring women to work such long hours.[7] The Supreme Court accepted this new kind of legal argument, holding that legislation to protect women workers was reasonable.

Thus, the brief we credit today with saving the Oregon statute also forged the way for a new kind of argument to the Court, one that relies on policy and social science data for its prudential constitutional arguments. There is no doubt that the brief created a startlingly new direction in constitutional thought. Certainly, Louis Brandeis deserves to share the credit for the brief. He was a leading lawyer of great ability, later to have a 23-year tenure as an Associate Justice of the United States Supreme Court. Undoubtedly, his well-earned reputation was a powerful part of the brief's success, and it is his name that appears on its signature line. These are probably the reasons we call it "the Brandeis Brief." But perhaps it would be equally accurate to call it "the Kelley/Goldmark Brief," in honor of the women who were the primary architects of the 100 pages that made the *Muller* brief something truly new.

Endnotes

1. 198 U.S. 45 (1905).
2. *Ritchie v. People* (Ill. Sup. Ct. 1895). Nancy Woloch, Muller v. Oregon: *A Brief History with Documents* 22 (Bedford Books of St. Martin's Press 1996).
3. *Id.*
4. *Id.*
5. *Id.* at 31.
6. *Encyclopedia of World Biography*, Josephine Goldmark Biography, http://www.bookrags.com/biography/josephine-goldmark.
7. Jewish Women's Archive: *Jewish Women—A Comprehensive Historical Encyclopedia*, http://jwa.org/encyclopedia/article/goldmark-josephine-clara.

2. *The Voices Briefs:* Thornburgh, Webster, *and* Gonzales

Linda H. Edwards

Just as the "Brandeis Brief" created a new form of legal argument using social science data, the "Voices Briefs," filed in a series of abortion cases beginning in 1985, created a new form of argument using stories. The lead architect was Lynn M. Paltrow, who wrote the 1985 amicus brief for seventeen abortion rights organizations in *Thornburgh v. American College of Obstetricians and Gynecologists.*[1] Paltrow was counsel for the National Abortion Rights Action League (NARAL). She used hundreds of letters compiled by NARAL as part of its "Silent No More" Campaign, weaving them into the Argument section of her thirty-page brief. The result was a legal argument that helped to place before the Court the realities of women's situations when confronting such a profound and personal choice. In defense of *Roe v. Wade,*[2] the brief makes two points: (1) *Roe* has dramatically improved the lives and health of American women and should be reaffirmed; and (2) overruling *Roe* would deny women their fundamental constitutional rights.

Lynn Paltrow (left) and Marcia Nieman (NARAL staffer/organizer of "Silent No More" campaign) filing the brief in *Thornburgh* (1985)

The first of these points could be thought of as a policy argument; but again, the stories bring the argument home in a more convincing fashion than could statistics alone. The second of these points could be thought of as a more traditional constitutional argument. However, the stories are far more effective than the precedents would be alone. The close relationship between the stories and the precedent is demonstrated. For instance, part of the second argument organizes the stories under the rights and freedoms articulated by the Court in *Meyer v. Nebraska*:[3] (1) to engage in any of the common occupations of life; (2) to acquire useful knowledge; (3) to marry; (4) to establish a home and bring up children; (5) to worship God according to the dictates of [her] own conscience; and (6) generally to enjoy those privileges long recognized at common law as essential to the orderly pursuit of happiness by free men. Thus, the stories are tied directly to constitutional doctrine, and the legal relevance of the stories is clear.

When it was time to file supporting briefs in *Webster v. Reproductive Health Services*,[4] Paltrow was by then at the ACLU Reproductive Freedom Project and working on another brief. So, she asked Sarah Burns at the National Organization for Women to file the *Webster* brief that would continue to present women's stories to the Court. The *Webster* amicus brief was filed on behalf of 2,887 women who had had abortions and 627 friends and family members. It relies primarily on a collection of women's stories supporting the continued importance of *Roe*.

These stories appear in two formats. Excerpts from some of the letters are interwoven throughout parts of the "Argument" section; for instance, under subsections titled "Criminalization and Excessive Regulation of Abortion Endangered the Lives and Health of Women and Hurt Their Loved Ones" and "Only the Woman Can Determine How Best to Meet the Often Sharply Competing Demands Within Her Family."

Many other stories are included in several lengthy appendices filed along with the brief. The first appendix is a 28-page list of the names of the women who submitted their stories. Appendix B includes 42 letters from women who had had abortions. These women describe their situations and experiences in powerful and sometimes heartrending detail. Appendix C includes 23 letters from friends and family members of women who had illegal abortions, many of whom died. Other letters not provided in the appendices were lodged separately with the Court. Taken together, these stories communicate—far better than statistics or policy arguments alone ever could—the need for safe, legal abortions.

In 2006, in the amicus brief for Sandra Cano, the former "Mary Doe" in *Doe v. Bolton*,[5] advocates of abortion restrictions used stories as well. The brief was filed in *Gonzales v. Carhart* on behalf of Cano and "180 Women Injured by Abortion," a clear reference to the amicus women in the *Webster* brief. The in-text sections of the Argument are confined to traditional constitutional argument, but stories appear mostly in footnotes to the authorities and sociological data discussed in the text. In addition, the brief's appendices are devoted entirely to stories. Appendix A includes an affidavit from Sandra Cano, identifying herself as the "Mary Doe" in *Doe v. Bolton* and telling the story of her experience during and since that case. Appendix B includes 178 affidavits telling the stories of other women who had abortions.

No one would argue that stories alone should dictate a legal decision, but more and more, stories are being recognized as one among many legitimate modes of constitutional conversation. Just as the Brandeis Brief used sociological "facts" to support a constitutional principle, so too can the real facts of individual human lives—the individual facts on which the sociological data are based—tell us something important about what our Constitution should mean.

Endnotes

1. 476 U.S. 747 (1986).
2. 410 U.S. 113 (1973).
3. 262 U.S. 390, 399 (1923).
4. 492 U.S. 490 (1989).
5. 410 U.S. 179 (1973).

Equality

3. Brown v. Board of Education

Dean John Valery White
The William S. Boyd School of Law
University of Nevada Las Vegas

In *Brown v. Board of Education*, the United States Supreme Court invalidated the doctrine of "separate but equal" in public education, holding that states could not operate racially segregated schools because "segregation of children in public schools solely on the basis of race, even though the physical facilities and other 'tangible' factors may be equal, deprive the children of the minority group of equal educational opportunities[.]"[1] The decision in *Brown* resolved several consolidated cases from states that required or permitted segregation in elementary and secondary schools. State-sanctioned segregation and a broad system of social and economic segregation on the basis of race had emerged in the decades after the Civil War. *Brown* was the culmination of a line of court challenges to that system of segregation.

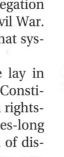

Brown was a momentous decision. Its key significance lay in undermining the legal basis for racial segregation under the Constitution. More broadly, it served as the cornerstone of modern rights-based jurisprudence and launched a more than three-decades-long transformation of American society through the prohibition of discrimination on the basis of race, religion, national origin, sex, age, and disability. If this were not enough, *Brown* stands as a symbol of attaining justice through law and constitutional rights litigation.

Brown consisted of four consolidated cases: *Brown v. Board of Education* from Topeka, Kansas; *Briggs et al. v. Elliott et al.*, from South Carolina; *Davis et al. v. County School Board of Prince Edward County, Virginia, et al.*; and *Gebhart et al. v. Belton et al.*, from Delaware. *Bolling v. Sharpe*,[2] which also accompanied these cases, was decided separately since it involved the District of Columbia, whose practices are not governed by the Fourteenth Amendment but by the Due Process Clause of the Fifth Amendment. For reasons still unclear, Oliver Brown was chosen to represent the plaintiffs in the Kansas case and, consequently, represented the plaintiffs in all the consolidated cases when the Court chose the Kansas case over those

Travis S.'s flickr photostream, March 26, 2011

Virginia Civil Rights Memorial, Capitol Square in Richmond, VA

from the South as the lead case. Mr. Brown was a welder who worked for the Santa Fe Railroad in Topeka and who agreed to participate in the case so that his daughter, Linda Brown, would be able to attend her neighborhood school.

Oliver Brown died in 1961 at the age of 41. However, Linda Brown (Thompson) and her siblings have worked to keep the memory of the *Brown* case alive, particularly focusing on those in the Topeka community who were instrumental in crafting and advancing the case. In particular they point to McKinley Burnett, the president of the Topeka branch of the NAACP, who recruited plaintiffs for the case; attorneys at the Scott, Scott, Scott, and Jackson firm—Charles, Elisha, and John Scott, and Charles Bledsoe—who litigated the case in Kansas; and Lucinda Todd, a school teacher who was the first plaintiff to sign up (on behalf of her daughter), despite the risk that she would lose her job and be blackballed from teaching in Kansas for doing so. As the Brown siblings' efforts to honor the activists behind the *Brown* case in Topeka highlight, each of the cases that became *Brown* emerged from sustained community efforts to confront the broad system of segregation that had relegated black Americans to second-class citizenship under the authority of *Plessy v. Ferguson*.[3]

Brown v. Board of Education overruled *Plessy v. Ferguson*, the 1896 decision that had held that the Constitution did not prohibit segregation. *Plessy* gave legal sanction to the emerging system of segregation that would operate to keep black Americans in subservient status despite the abolition of slavery by the Thirteenth Amendment 30 years earlier. With abolition, former slaves experienced widespread terror meant to restore the pre-Civil War social order and keep former slaves in a subservient status. The widespread violence led to congressional action, notably in the form of a number of civil rights statutes aimed at providing legal protection from terror and discrimination. Disputes over the propriety of these enactments prompted the adoption and ratification of the Fourteenth Amendment, which made clear that former slaves were citizens of the United States and enjoyed the privileges and immunities of that citizenship. The Fourteenth Amendment also guaranteed to all citizens equal protection of the law and due process. It gave Congress the power to enforce the provisions of the Fourteenth Amendment by necessary legislation. Along with the Fifteenth Amendment, which extended to freedmen the right to vote, the Fourteenth Amendment was seen as creating a basis for ensuring freed slaves the opportunity to participate as full citizens in the post-Civil War world. These aspirations would fall far short as the Supreme Court read the new amendments to the Constitution narrowly and found unconstitutional many of the statutes enacted to protect the civil rights of freed slaves and other black citizens.

In *Plessy* the Supreme Court upheld a Louisiana law requiring racial segregation on passenger trains. It found that state-sanctioned segregation did not violate the Thirteenth Amendment since "a statute which implies merely a legal distinction between the white and colored races . . . has no tendency to destroy the legal equality of the two races or re-establish a state of involuntary servitude."[4] While it found that the Fourteenth Amendment did require all exercises of state police power to be reasonable and that the police power could not be used to "annoy" or "oppress" a particular class,[5] *Plessy* held that segregation on the basis of race did neither. First, it was reasonable: the legislature "is at liberty to act with reference to the established usages, customs, and traditions of the people, and with a view for the promotion of their comfort, and the preservation of public peace and good order."[6] Second, it did not impose inferiority:

> [T]he underlying fallacy of the plaintiff's argument . . . consist[s] in the assumption that the enforced separation of the two races stamps the colored race with a badge of inferiority. If this be so, it is . . . solely because the colored races chose to put that construction upon it.[7]

The *Plessy* Court thus created the notion that legislation that imposed segregation was permissible so long as segregated services were separate but equal.

The decision in *Plessy* gave legal support to the growing official and informal segregation emerging wherever there were large populations of black Americans. Soon segregation would be widely enforced, sometimes with sanction of law, always with the implicit threat of violence. *Brown* was the decision that ended this legal support for segregation and replaced *Plessy*'s regime of segregation with a call for equality through rights.

Justice Thurgood Marshall

Brown was the product of a coordinated plan by the National Association for the Advancement of Colored People (NAACP) to take on legal segregation. In that sense, it is also a model for advocacy litigation. The strategy that led to *Brown* was conceived by Nathan Margold in 1930, working as a consultant for the NAACP, and it was implemented by Charles Houston and Thurgood Marshall over the next 25 years. The NAACP carefully selected cases to litigate in state and federal courts with the aim of presenting incremental questions to the court, the decisions in which would chip at the edges of segregation. Over time, this strategy culminated in the ultimate, direct confrontation before the Supreme Court in *Brown*. The success of this strategy is memorialized in *Brown* itself, as the Court summarized its own decisions that necessitated the Court's decision in *Brown*:

> The doctrine of "separate but equal" did not make its appearance in this Court until 1896 in the case of *Plessy v. Ferguson,* supra, involving not education but transportation. American courts have since labored with the doctrine for over half a century. In this Court, there have been six cases involving the "separate but equal" doctrine in the field of public education. In *Cumming v. County Board of Education,* 175 U.S. 528, and *Gong Lum v. Rice,* 275 U.S. 78, the validity of the doctrine itself was not challenged. In more recent cases, all on the graduate school level, inequality was found in that specific benefits enjoyed by white students were denied to Negro students of the same educational qualifications. *Missouri ex rel. Gaines v. Canada,* 305 U.S. 337; *Sipuel v. Oklahoma,* 332 U.S. 631; *Sweatt v. Painter,* 339 U.S. 629; *McLaurin v. Oklahoma State Regents,* 339 U.S. 637. In none of these cases was it necessary to re-examine the doctrine to grant relief to the Negro plaintiff. And in *Sweatt v. Painter,* supra, the Court expressly reserved decision on the question whether *Plessy v. Ferguson* should be held inapplicable to public education.[8]

Gaines, Sipuel, Sweatt, and *McLaurin* were all cases litigated by the NAACP, each of which narrowed the reach of legal segregation until the issue of *Plessy*'s validity could not be avoided.

Brown was, however, neither an easy nor a welcomed decision. The case came to the Supreme Court in 1952 and was set for reargument after the Court first considered the matter. Within the Court, there were several Justices who leaned toward reaffirming

Plessy. Pending rehearing, Chief Justice Vinson was replaced by Earl Warren. Under Chief Justice Warren's leadership, a fractured Court produced a unanimous opinion overruling *Plessy.* That decision focused on the impropriety of "separate but equal," noting that the doctrine was out of line with contemporary social scientific and policy thinking. The Court's foray into the social sciences drew fierce criticism and became a basis for attacking the outcome in the case as well. In the end, the Court's heavily hedged approach to the issues in the case gave the decision great strength. First, the opinion was unanimous. Beyond that, the Court put off the remedial component of its holding until *Brown* [II].[9] Finally, the opinion says little about what equality under law means, confining itself to declaring "separate but equal" invalid.

Brown's hedged approach has produced a contradiction in discussing the case. Most agree it is among the most important decisions of the Supreme Court, certainly in the twentieth century. However, its key accomplishments seem only vaguely connected to the decision itself. As Michael Klarman notes, remarkably little school desegregation followed from *Brown,* at least until congressional action in the late 1960s forced states to comply on pain of losing federal funding for education.[10] Klarman also notes that *Brown* generated such a backlash that it is difficult to assess whether it helped or hurt the then-emerging civil rights movement.[11] Others have noted, especially recently, that support for *Brown's* goal of racial integration was not wide, even among black lawyers. In this sense *Brown's* power lies in its transcendent principle of equality before the law. *Brown* conveys the value of legal equality as a prerequisite to social and economic equality and, with that clarion call, lent support and strength to the civil rights movement. For at least this reason, *Brown* stands as a momentous decision.

Endnotes

1. 347 U.S. 483, 493 (1954).
2. 347 U.S. 497 (1954).
3. 163 U.S. 537 (1896).
4. *Plessy,* 163 U.S. at 543.
5. *Id.* at 550.
6. *Id.*
7. *Id.* at 551.
8. *Brown,* 347 U.S. at 490-492.
9. *Brown v. Board of Education* [II], 349 U.S. 294 (1955).
10. See Michael Klarman, *How* Brown *Changed Race Relations: The Backlash Thesis,* 81 J. Am. Hist. 81 (1994).
11. *Id.*

4. Loving v. Virginia

Dean John Valery White
The William S. Boyd School of Law
University of Nevada Las Vegas

Loving v. Virginia[1] overturned the once widespread prohibitions on interracial marriage that, at the time of the decision, 16 states still enforced. The United States Supreme Court's unanimous decision stands alongside *Brown v. Board of Education*[2] for its significance in ending the widespread public and private segregation that dominated much of the United States for over 100 years after the end of slavery. *Brown* clearly prohibited official segregation, and it implied the invalidation of segregation more generally. The decision in *Loving*, however, expressly invalidated laws that required or enforced private segregation. *Loving* also resolved a potential paradox in antidiscrimination laws: Could a law that applied equally to everyone, without regard to race or identity, but which operated to enforce segregation, stand? *Loving* clearly said it could not. Today, *Loving* is heavily relied upon by advocates of same-sex marriage, who note its emphasis on the impermissible use of race as a condition on marriage, even though antimiscegenation statutes ostensibly applied equally to all races. *Loving*, it appears, continues to resolve the conundrum of equality that emerged with *Brown*.

In 1958 Mildred Jeter and Richard Loving decided to get married. The Virginia residents did what any interracial couple in Virginia, any southern state, and several other states around the country were then required to do: They journeyed to a jurisdiction that permitted interracial marriages, in their case, the District of Columbia, and were married in June of that year. They returned to Virginia and lived as a married couple. In doing so, they had violated at least two aspects of Virginia's Racial Integrity Act. They had violated Virginia's prohibition on leaving the state to evade the Act's prohibition on interracial marriages; they had also violated the state's prohibition on interracial marriage itself. Under Virginia law, their marriage was automatically nullified, without judicial proceedings. In July 1958, they were arrested on an "anonymous tip," and in October 1958, the Lovings were indicted. They pled guilty in January 1959, and were sentenced to one year in prison, with the sentence suspended for 25 years on the condition that they leave the state and not return as a couple.

In 1963, now represented by the ACLU, the Lovings moved to vacate the judgment and sentence, challenging the Virginia statutes as violating the Fourteenth Amendment to the Constitution. Nearly a year later, when their motion had not yet been heard, they filed a class action in the federal district court. They sought a declaration that the Virginia antimiscegenation statutes were unconstitutional and an injunction enjoining state officials from enforcing their conviction. The class action filing perhaps prompted the state court to act. Three months after the class action was filed, the state court rejected the Lovings' request to vacate their conviction. The high court of Virginia also upheld the conviction. The case was appealed to the United States Supreme Court.

Antimiscegenation statutes date back to before the formation of the United States, particularly in Virginia. Historian Winthrop Jordan noted the existence of predecessors to such statutes—severe punishment for interracial sex—in Virginia law as early as the first half of the seventeenth century. Statutes barring interracial marriage were a central feature of post-Civil War American law. Perhaps as significant, efforts to "protect" white women from supposed "animalistic" traits of black men provided a significant rationalization for the system of segregation that relegated black people to second-class citizenship and prompted widespread lynching of black men alleged to have attacked white women. This background made the *Loving* decision especially momentous, not only invalidating antimiscegenation statutes but also undermining hundreds of years of lore justifying those statutes.

At the time the Lovings were married in 1958, a number of states had begun to eliminate their ban on interracial marriage. California's landmark decision in *Perez v. Sharp*[3] launched a wave of state abolition of antimiscegenation statutes, with 13 states—Arizona, Colorado, Idaho, Indiana, Maryland, Montana, Nebraska, Nevada, North Dakota, Oregon, South Dakota, Utah, and Wyoming—in addition to California repealing their prohibitions before the 1967 decision. Sixteen states continued to prohibit interracial marriage, however. These included all 11 states that had seceded in the Civil War—Alabama, Arkansas, Florida, Georgia, Louisiana, Mississippi, North Carolina, South Carolina, Tennessee, Texas, and Virginia—as well as Delaware, Kentucky, Missouri, Oklahoma, and West Virginia. As always, the statutes were efforts to enforce white supremacy by defending racial purity—at least in marriage. Despite the movement toward abolition, Virginia had reaffirmed its antimiscegenation statute in *Naim v. Naim*.[4] In its *Naim* decision, the Virginia Supreme Court emphasized the statute's goal "to preserve the racial integrity of its citizens," and to prevent "the corruption of blood," "a mongrel breed of citizens," and "the obliteration of racial pride,"[5] which the Supreme Court recognized as "obviously an endorsement of the doctrine of White Supremacy."[6] Because the United States Supreme Court had declined to review *Naim*, there was some question as to whether statutes like Virginia's Racial Integrity Act might be constitutional.

stanzak's flickr photostream 2008

Mildred and Richard Loving, 1967

Mildred Loving, speaking years later: "Surrounded as I am now by wonderful children and grandchildren, not a day goes by that I don't think of Richard and our love, our right to marry, and how much it meant to me to have that freedom to marry the person precious to me. . . . "[7]

These issues appear to have been mostly beyond the Lovings. In the few public statements they made, Richard Loving and Mildred Jeter come across as extremely shy and unassuming. They had known each other since childhood. The two had grown up in a racially integrated rural community in Virginia, in which black and white families interacted closely and widely. Moreover, Richard's father had worked for a black landowner and seemed not to have the disdain for black neighbors that many white men of his era did. So when Richard began courting Mildred, nothing stood out. When she was 18 (and Richard 24), he asked her to marry him and she agreed. Once married, they moved into her parents' home, which is where they were arrested.

By all accounts, both Richard and Mildred desired only to live together near their families and to raise a family of their own. When their arrest made living near their families impossible, they moved to Washington, D.C., where they lived with Mildred's cousin. There they began their family and were mostly disconnected from the emerging civil rights movement that was gaining momentum. Mildred was reported to have said that when she saw news reports of debates in Congress over the civil rights act, she wrote Attorney General Robert Kennedy and explained her case. When he received her letter, Attorney General Kennedy referred the case to the ACLU, which took on the Lovings' cause.

With the success of the case, the Lovings were able to move home. Richard built his family a house not far from Mildred's sister, and their children were able to have the rural upbringing their parents wanted for them. Their life together in rural Virginia was short lived, however. On June 29, 1975, Richard and Mildred Loving, along with Mildred's sister, Garnet, were driving near their home when a drunk driver struck their car, killing Richard and blinding Mildred in one eye. Mildred went on to raise the couple's children, only rarely making public statements about the case and her celebrity until her death on May 2, 2008. It is pretty clear from the interviews she did give that she would not have challenged the Virginia miscegenation law if the state had not prosecuted her. In a 1996 interview with a family friend she said:

> We weren't bothering anyone. And if we hurt some people's feelings, that was just too bad. All we ever wanted was to get married, because we loved each other. Some people will never change, but that's their problem, not mine. I married the only man I had ever loved, and I am happy for the time we had together. For me, that was enough.[8]

Endnotes

1. 388 U.S. 1 (1967).
2. 347 U.S. 483 (1954).
3. 32 Cal. 2d 711 (1948).
4. 197 Va. 80, 87 S.E. 2d 749 (Va. 1955).
5. *Id*. at 90, 87 S.E. 2d, at 756.
6. *Loving*, 388 U.S., at 7.
7. June 12, 2007, statement by Mildred Loving issued on the fortieth anniversary of *Loving v. Virginia*.
8. Robert A. Pratt, *Crossing the Color Line: A Historical Assessment and Personal Narrative of* Loving v. Virginia, Symposium: "Law and the Politics of Marriage: *Loving v. Virginia* After Thirty Years," 41 How. L.J. 229, 244 (1997-1998).

5. Hernandez v. Texas

Charles R. Calleros[1]

"Murder is the offense, with punishment assessed at life imprisonment in the penitentiary."[2] So began the opinion of the Texas Court of Criminal Appeals affirming the conviction of Pete Hernandez, despite evidence showing that county jury commissioners had systematically excluded Mexican-Americans from juries, including the grand jury that indicted Hernandez and the petit jury that tried him.[3] Two years later, and two weeks before the landmark decision of *Brown v. Board of Education*,[4] the Supreme Court reversed Hernandez's conviction, finding that the systematic exclusion of Mexican-Americans from juries violated the Equal Protection Clause of the Fourteenth Amendment.[5]

The pending decision in *Brown* overshadowed *Hernandez* even as the Court issued its decision in *Hernandez*.[6] Indeed, *Hernandez* merits study for its nuanced approach to classifications protected by the Equal Protection Clause, an approach that arguably has been overlooked as *Hernandez* receded into the shadows cast by *Brown*.

I. The State Litigation in *Hernandez v. Texas*

On August 4, 1951, Pete Hernandez shot and killed Joe Espinosa in a tavern in the town of Edna, within Jackson County, Texas. Hernandez was represented by experienced attorneys John Herrera, Gustavo ("Gus") Garcia, and Carlos Cadena, along with Herrera's associate, James de Anda, a recent law school graduate. These attorneys revived an argument that Herrera and de Anda had unsuccessfully pursued in a previous case in Fort Bend County,[7] that jury commissioners had systematically excluded persons of Mexican descent from grand juries and trial juries, in violation of due process and equal protection.[8] Hernandez's attorneys relied on the rule of *Norris v. State of Alabama*,[9] which held that proof of absence of African-Americans on juries in criminal cases over many years established a prima facie case of racial discrimination in composition of juries, raising a rebuttable presumption of unconstitutional discrimination.[10] In the prosecution of Hernandez, the trial court twice denied defense motions based on this theory. Hernandez was convicted of murder and sentenced to life in prison.[11]

The Texas Court of Criminal Appeals affirmed the conviction. It declined to apply the rule of *Norris* until the U.S. Supreme Court extended it beyond the narrow facts of *Norris*. Specifically, the Texas court interpreted the equal protection principles of *Norris* to apply only to a two-class paradigm of Caucasian and African-American classes. Drawing on Texas precedent, the Texas appellate court reasoned that persons of Mexican "nationality" were members of the Caucasian or "white" race and thus shared the race of the all-white grand jury that indicted Hernandez and the all-white trial jury that found him guilty. Because the Texas court refused to extend the *Norris* rule to national origin discrimination, and because it declined to find racial discrimination in the exclusion of Mexican-Americans from white juries, it characterized Herrera's claim as an attempt by a subset of the Caucasian race to carve out special privileges that would not be enjoyed by other members of that race.[12]

Herrera's attorneys filed a petition for certiorari with the U.S. Supreme Court, which the Court granted on October 12, 1953.[13]

II. Herrera's Legal Team in the U.S. Supreme Court

James de Anda did not attend the arguments in the U.S. Supreme Court,[14] but he played a critical role in Herrera's success in that forum: De Anda had collected the data that demonstrated the absence of Mexican-Americans on grand juries and trial juries in Jackson County for more than two decades.[15]

The primary drafter of the Brief for Petitioner in the Supreme Court was Carlos Cadena,[16] formerly a law partner with Gus Garcia and later a Professor at St. Mary's School of Law in San Antonio. Garcia described Cadena as "[s]hy, reserved, and retiring," but "the best brain of my generation."[17]

Garcia was anything but shy and retiring. Texas Congressman Maury Maverick described Garcia as "forceful and dramatic" and opined that Garcia likely "would have made just as great a flamenco dancer or bullfighter as he has a trial lawyer."[18] Described by Professor Olivas as "feisty" and a "brilliant orator," Garcia shared the oral argument with Cadena but left the more lasting impression.[19] Although the arguments were not recorded at that date, according to co-counsel Herrera, the Court granted Garcia substantial extra time to continue his argument.[20]

Herrera sat at counsel's table, assisting the orators by managing documents.[21] According to Garcia, Herrera "kept our heads level as we were bombarded by questions."[22]

Sarita Kenedy East Law Library, St. Mary's University, San Antonio, TX

Carlos Cadena

III. The Opinion of the Supreme Court: Defining a Protected Class

The U.S. Supreme Court reversed Hernandez's conviction, finding that his legal team had met its burden of showing a violation of equal protection in jury composition under the *Norris* standard.[23] Before reviewing the evidence of exclusion, however, the Court necessarily addressed the Texas courts' position that Mexican-Americans did not define a class warranting equal protection.[24]

The role of race in *Hernandez* is illuminating. Although this case was decided just two weeks before *Brown*, the members of the protected class in *Hernandez* were not full allies with African-Americans in their quest for equality. Many Mexican-Americans in Texas encouraged the legal view that they belonged to the same race as the white persons who discriminated against them, because they feared that their categorization as non-white would relegate them to the same low social status accorded to African-Americans in their segregated communities.[25]

For years, this strategy bore a bitter fruit: Mexican-Americans still suffered pervasive private discrimination at the hands of the white majority, yet Texas courts condoned their exclusion from juries on the ground that they shared the Caucasian race of the all-white jurors.[26] These two realities collided vividly when Hernandez's legal team stumbled upon a bilingual sign at the courthouse basement in Edna, Texas, signifying the bathroom for non-white men with the words "Colored Only" and "Hombres Aqui,"[27] a fact noted by the Supreme Court when it reviewed evidence of discrimination against Mexican-Americans in Jackson County.[28]

Despite the futility of this attempt to escape the same kinds of private discrimination aimed at African-Americans, Petitioner's Brief in *Hernandez* adhered to the approach of classifying Mexican-Americans as members of the Caucasian race, as did the Texas courts: Although the brief referred somewhat ambiguously to the class of "persons of Mexican descent," it grounded its equal protection claim at least partly on "national origin."[29]

The Supreme Court soundly rejected the Texas courts' binary approach to equal protection: "The Fourteenth Amendment is not directed solely against discrimination due to a 'two-class theory'— that is, based upon differences between 'white' and Negro."[30] In light of largely unrebutted evidence of discrimination against, and segregation of, Mexican-Americans in Jackson County, the Court concluded that the "petitioner succeeded in his proof" that "persons of Mexican descent constitute a separate class in Jackson County, distinct from 'whites.'"[31]

As you read the opinion, try to identify the "separate class" or classes the Supreme Court finds persons of "Mexican descent" to comprise. One easy answer lies in the final paragraph's reference to Hernandez's constitutional right to "juries selected from among all qualified persons regardless of *national origin*,"[32] a reference presumably to "where a person was born, or more broadly the country from which his or her ancestors came."[33] Distinguishing Mexican-Americans on the basis of national origin comported with the strategy of Mexican-Americans in Texas of identifying themselves as part of the Caucasian race and of reaching for the rights and social status enjoyed by the white population.[34]

Unfortunately, this strategy represented a lack of solidarity with African-Americans, with whom Mexican-Americans shared "the bottom rung of the ladder" in the era of *Hernandez*.[35] Moreover, a class based on national origin could not comfortably encompass the U.S.-born descendants of long-time Latino Texas residents; these descendants shared U.S. national origin with the exclusively white jurors but were excluded from juries because of Spanish surnames and likely suffered other forms of discrimination based on their recognizable names, skin color, and facial features.

Consequently, it is significant that the Supreme Court's opinion in *Hernandez* did not limit its equal protection analysis to national origin discrimination. Notice that the final paragraph refers to freedom from discrimination based on "national origin *or descent*."[36] Of course, much of the opinion refers to persons of "Mexican descent," perhaps reflecting the Court's adoption of that term from the Petitioner's Brief, and perhaps suggesting that the final paragraph of the Court's opinion is simply equating "descent" with national origin, as encouraged by Petitioner's Brief.[37]

Earlier in the opinion, however, notice that the Court replaces "descent" with "ancestry": "The exclusion of otherwise eligible persons from jury service solely because of their ancestry or national origin is discrimination prohibited by the Fourteenth Amendment."[38] If "descent" in the sense of "ancestry" is distinct from national origin, what is its intended meaning?

Thirteen years after *Hernandez*, in yet another case dealing with Texas jury composition, the Supreme Court seemed to suggest in passing that Mexican-Americans are indeed properly characterized as defining a racial class: "[I]t is no longer open to dispute that Mexican-Americans are a clearly identifiable class. *See, e.g., Hernandez v. Texas, supra.* . . . [T]he selection procedure is not *racially neutral* with respect to Mexican-Americans; . . ."[39]

More thoroughly reasoned support for this position is provided by the Supreme Court's interpretation in 1987 of a civil rights statute from the Reconstruction era, in *St. Francis College v. Al-Khazraji*,[40] discussed in Section IV.A below. Although a Supreme Court with different composition decided *St. Francis College* more than 30 years after *Hernandez*, it potentially sheds light on the arguments and analysis in *Hernandez*. A more nuanced and contextual analysis of protected classes is found within the *Hernandez* opinion itself, as discussed in Section IV.B.

IV. Conceptions of Race

A. St. Francis College v. Al-Khazraji

Title 42 U.S.C. §1981 has its roots in both the Civil Rights Act of 1866 and the Voting Rights Act of 1870.[41] It provides that all persons shall have equal rights to contract "as is enjoyed by white citizens,"[42] a provision interpreted to prohibit discrimination in contracting based on race, regardless of which race was favored or disfavored in a refusal to enter into a contract.[43] As late as 1987, however, questions remained about the definition of race under these statutes.

In *St. Francis College v. Al-Khazraji*, the defendant relied on an argument closely analogous to the position taken by the Texas Court of Criminal Appeals in *Hernandez*. Al-Kazraji, a college professor, alleged that his college had discriminatorily denied him tenure because of his Arab ancestry.[44] In response, the employer invoked §1981's requirement of racial discrimination and asserted that the plaintiff was a member of the Caucasian race. Because the decision-makers were Caucasian as well, and because the decision-makers held no animus toward members of their own race, the employer argued that the alleged discrimination based on Arab ancestry did not constitute racial discrimination, as required under §1981.[45]

The employer's position received support from twentieth-century scientific classification of all ethnic groups into just three races: Caucasoid, Negroid, and Mongoloid.[46] Under these broad classifications of race Arabs and Europeans were members of the same Caucasian race, allowing the employer to argue that Caucasian decision-makers did not refuse to promote a Caucasian faculty member *because of their shared Caucasian race.*[47] Alternatively, the employer could argue that alleged discrimination in favor of an Anglo-American faculty member and against an Arab-American faculty member would not state a claim of discrimination based on race, because both the favored and disfavored parties are members of the same race.

The Supreme Court rejected this approach by interpreting the 1866 statute in light of congressional intent at the time of enactment, rather than in light of twentieth-century scientific classifications.[48] Legislative history and other historical sources showed that the kind of discrimination addressed by that Congress—when it statutorily distinguished "white citizens" from other persons—was discrimination on the basis of narrow lines of "ancestry or ethnic characteristics,"[49] such as an Anglo-American discriminating against a claimant because of his or her German, Arab,[50] or Jewish[51] ancestry.

Having earlier interpreted §1983 to require "race" discrimination, the Court in *St. Francis College* then roughly equated race with narrowly defined ethnic blood lines, thus multiplying the number of claims under §1981. Discrimination against a person with mixed Spanish and Indian blood from a region in Mexico, and in favor of a person with a mix of German and Irish ancestry, would violate §1981, if the discrimination was based on the ethnic lines of ancestry, regardless of whether the victim and beneficiary of the discrimination would both be considered as Caucasian, broadly defined.[52]

Is it possible that references in the *Hernandez* opinion to "ancestry" and "descent" constitute an early parallel to the analysis of race in *St. Francis College*? If so, *Hernandez* could be interpreted as finding discrimination on the basis of race, narrowly defined, as well as national origin. To the extent that original intent is relevant to the constitutional question in *Hernandez*, as it was to the statutory issue in *St. Francis College*, the same concerns about ethnic discrimination spurring the 1886 statute would presumably have been on congressional minds when Congress proposed the Fourteenth Amendment, and its Equal Protection Clause, ratified in 1868. Viewed in this light, *Hernandez*—albeit in veiled language—arguably supports a conclusion that persons of "Mexican descent" make up a distinct race, in the sense of ethnic ancestry, apart from the Anglo-American "race" of the white jurors.[53]

B. Using Social Context to Define Protected Classes

Regardless of whether one divides racial classifications into a few broad categories or many narrower ones, a more fundamental question arises: Is it futile to search for biological classifications of race? Moreover, even if one can identify biological markers for ethnic blood lines, would they correspond to surnames, physical appearance, or other triggers for discrimination at the hands of others?

Many argue that race and ethnicity are best viewed as social constructs.[54] For purposes of applying an antidiscrimination principle, perhaps the critical factor is whether members of a disfavored group share characteristics that define them as a distinct class in a community and that trigger adverse treatment by others within the broader community. Depending on local context, those characteristics might include such things as physical appearance, language, cultural traditions, national or regional origins, and surnames associated with a region or ethnicity.[55]

If a combination of characteristics "bind a people together as a matter of external perception and internal self-conception," then they may warrant identification as a protected class under antidiscrimination principles.[56] "Race" could then simply operate as a label that connects the classification to an antidiscrimination law, such as §1981. The discrimination along ancestral lines that animated Congress to enact the original version of §1981, for example, might in some cases more closely mirror actual discriminatory behavior—both then and now—than the broader scientific classifications advanced by the defendant in *St. Francis College*.[57]

As you read the *Hernandez* opinion, consider the extent to which the Court advances such a contextual approach to classes protected by the Equal Protection Clause. Take some time to interpret, for example, the following excerpts of the opinion:

> Throughout our history differences in race and color have defined easily identifiable groups that have at times required the aid of the courts in securing equal treatment under the laws. But community prejudices are not static, and from time to time other differences from the community norm may define other groups that need the same protection. Whether such a group exists within a community is a question of fact. . . .
>
> The petitioner's initial burden in substantiating his charge of group discrimination was to prove that persons of Mexican descent constitute a separate class in Jackson County, distinct from "whites." One method by which this may be demonstrated is by showing the attitude of the community. Here the testimony of responsible officials and citizens contained the admission that residents of the community distinguished between "white" and "Mexican." . . .[58]

Unlike §1981, the Equal Protection Clause is not limited to addressing discrimination on the basis of race, so the Court in *Hernandez* had no need to link the class of persons of Mexican descent to the label "race." It was sufficient that they defined a "group[] which need[s] the same protection" as do groups that can more easily show discrimination on the basis of race.[59]

Regardless of whether the Court's reference to "descent" and "ancestry" was intended to refer to a racial classification, does the Court in *Hernandez* embrace a contextual approach, one that views protected classifications at least partly as a factual matter of locally defined social constructs? In *Hernandez*, what evidence of segregation and discrimination persuaded the Court to find that persons of Mexican descent constituted a "separate class in Jackson County, distinct from 'whites'"?

What implications would such an approach have for defining protected classes in other cases? For issues such as affirmative action? To the extent that the overshadowing of *Hernandez* by *Brown v. Board of Education* has caused the approaches suggested in *Hernandez* to indeed fade into the shadows, is equal protection analysis poorer for the loss?

V. The Legacy of *Hernandez*

Hernandez is often cited in cases applying *Norris*'s rule of exclusion in jury composition.[60] In one of those cases, *Castaneda v. Partida*, the Supreme Court relied on *Hernandez* to easily find that Mexican-Americans, and specifically those with Spanish surnames, constituted a protected class.[61] The Court, however, did not further develop its view in *Hernandez* that a protected class can be defined partly by the extent to which others single out members of the group for adverse treatment. In *Castaneda*, the Court noted that "statistics introduced by respondent from the 1970 census illustrate disadvantages to which the group has been subject";[62] however, this passage apparently is introducing the Court's analysis of discrimination in jury selection rather than explaining its identification of Mexican-Americans as a protected class.[63]

In *Tijerina v. Henry*,[64] a case outside the context of jury composition, the Supreme Court passed on the opportunity to apply and extend the *Hernandez* approach to defining a legally significant class. In *Tijerina*, a three-judge panel of the federal district court dismissed a class action in a suit seeking equal educational rights, on the ground that a class was not adequately defined by ethnicity, Spanish surnames, and use of Spanish as a primary or maternal language.[65] The Supreme Court dismissed the appeal without opinion,[66] over a spirited dissent by Justice Douglas, who noted that:

> [T]hose who discriminate against members of this and other minority groups have little difficulty in isolating the objects of their discrimination. And it is precisely this discrimination, as alleged by appellants in their complaint, that presents the "questions of law or fact common to the class."[67]

After reviewing the recognition of a protected class in *Hernandez* on the basis of the discriminatory treatment of Mexican-Americans in Jackson County,[68] Justice Douglas applied the same approach to certification of a class for class action purposes:

> What the Court said in *Hernandez* is, I think, pertinent to the question of establishing the existence of a proper class for a class action under Rule 23. There can be no dispute that in many parts of the Southwestern United States persons of Indian and Mexican or Spanish descent are, as a class, subject to various forms of discrimination. Appellants, as members of that class, brought this action to prevent the continuance of alleged discriminatory actions taken against the class. I do not see how it can be seriously contended that this suit is not a proper class action.[69]

That Justice Douglas stood alone in *Tijerina* is perhaps emblematic of the extent to which *Hernandez* has been limited to its context of jury composition and has failed to emerge from the shadows of *Brown v. Board of Education*.[70]

Nonetheless, *Hernandez* represents an important legal milestone for Mexican-Americans, in the recognition of their status as a protected class, and for the maturation of the Latino bar as well. As summed up eloquently by Professor Michael Olivas,

> [I]n a brief and shining moment in 1954, Mexican-American lawyers prevailed in a system that accorded their community no legal status

and no respect. Through sheer tenacity, brilliance, and some luck, they showed it was possible to tilt against windmills and slay the dragon.[71]

Two weeks later, the Supreme Court decided *Brown v. Board of Education*, the culmination of years of litigation in several school desegregation cases begun by African-American attorney Charles Houston and completed by Thurgood Marshall.[72] Although *Hernandez* stood in the shadow of *Brown*, their dual arrival cast a beacon of hope for those denied equal rights under the law.

Endnotes

1. Professor of Law, Sandra Day O'Connor College of Law at Arizona State University. The author thanks second-year law student Amelia Valenzuela and Assistant Librarian David Gay for their invaluable research assistance on this topic.

2. *Hernandez v. State*, 251 S.W.2d 531, 532 (Tex. Crim. App. 1952).

3. *Hernandez v. Texas*, 347 U.S. 475, 476, 480-482 (1954) (summarizing trial motion, and accepting the proof offered by Hernandez's attorneys about systematic exclusion); Michael A. Olivas, Hernandez v. Texas: *A Litigation History, reprinted in "Colored Men" and "Hombres Aquí"*: Hernandez v. Texas *and the Emergence of Mexican-American Lawyering* 209, 213, 215 (Michael A. Olivas ed., Arte Público Press 2006) (hereafter *Colored Men*) (Hernandez was indicted and tried by all-white juries).

4. 347 U.S. 483 (1954).

5. *Hernandez v. Texas*, 347 U.S. 475 (1954).

6. Arthur Krock, *In the Nation, No Clue to the Separate Schools Case*, N.Y. Times 32 (May 6, 1954) (analysis of *Hernandez* mostly in attempt to predict outcome in pending decision in *Brown*).

7. Olivas, *supra* note 3, at 211-213 (discussing case of *Sanchez v. Texas*, 243 S.W.2d 700 (1951), as well as the crime and the early stages of the *Hernandez* prosecution).

8. *Hernandez*, 347 U.S. at 476-477 (summarizing trial motions of Hernandez's defense team).

9. 294 U.S. 587 (1935); *see also Castaneda v. Partida*, 430 U.S. 482, 501 (in applying *Norris* test, finding that evidence established a "prima facie case of discrimination in grand jury selection" and finding that "the State failed to rebut the presumption of purposeful discrimination"). "While the earlier cases involved absolute exclusion of an identifiable group, later cases established the principle that substantial underrepresentation of the group constitutes a constitutional violation as well, if it results from purposeful discrimination" as required under *Washington v. Davis*, 426 U.S. 229, 239 (1976). *Castaneda*, 439 U.S. at 493.

10. *Id.* at 591-599.

11. *Hernandez*, 347 U.S. at 476-477.

12. *Hernandez v. State*, 251 S.W.2d 531, 534-535 (Tex. Crim. App. 1952).

13. *Hernandez v. State of Texas*, 346 U.S. 811 (1953).

14. Olivas, *supra* note 3, at 217-218 ("as the junior partner, de Anda remained in Texas to mind the store and continue the trials that were still ongoing").

15. *A Cotton Picker Finds Justice! The Saga of the* Hernandez *Case* (hereafter *A Cotton Picker Finds Justice!*) (Ruben Munguia ed.), *reprinted in Colored Men, supra* note 3, App. VIII, at 361 & n.1, 362 (in Gustavo C. Garcia, *An Informal Report to the People*).

16. Lupe S. Salinas, *Gus Garcia and Thurgood Marshall: Two Legal Giants Fighting for Justice*, 28 T. Marshall L. Rev. 145, 169 (2002-2003).

17. *See supra* notes 3-5 and accompanying text.

18. *A Cotton Picker Finds Justice! supra* note 15, at 359 (in Maury Maverick, *Foreword*).

19. Olivas, *supra* note 3, at 216, 218.

20. *Id.* at 218 (citing to letter to the editor written by John Herrera); Salinas, *supra* note 16, at 170.

21. *A Cotton Picker Finds Justice! supra* note 15, at 364 (in Gustavo C. Garcia, *An Informal Report to the People*).

22. *Id.* at 365.

23. *Hernandez v. Texas*, 347 U.S. 475, 480-482 (1954).

24. *Id.* at 478-480.

25. Ian F. Haney Lopez, *Retaining Race: LatCrit Theory and Mexican American Identity in* Hernandez v. Texas, 2 Harv. Latino L. Rev. 279, 287 & n.29 (1997); Clare Sheridan, *"Another White Race": Mexican Americans and the Paradox of Whiteness in Jury Selection*, 21 Law & Hist. Rev. 109, 127, 135-138 (2003); *A Cotton Picker Finds Justice! supra* note 15, at 371 (in Carlos C. Cadena, *A Thumbnail Sketch*) (assuring Mexican-Americans that the Court in *Hernandez* found discrimination on the basis of national origin and did not classify them as "non-white").

26. Lopez, *supra* note 25, at 293-294; Sheridan, *supra* note 25, at 141-142.

27. Olivas, *supra* note 3, at 216 & n.42.

28. *Hernandez*, 347 U.S. at 479-480.

29. *See* Brief for the Petitioner, *Hernandez v. Texas*, 347 U.S. 475 (1954) (No. 406) at 28 (stating in the Conclusion that "[a]ll courts which have considered the question have held that the Fourteenth Amendment forbids discrimination because of national origin"); *see also id.* at 6 n.1 (questioning the Texas appellate court's use of the term Mexican "nationality," which suggests Mexican citizenship, and noting that the brief generally refers to "persons of Mexican descent").

30. *Hernandez*, 347 U.S. at 478.

31. *Id.* at 479-480; *see also St. Francis College v. Al-Khazraji*, 481 U.S. 604, 613 (1987) (distinguishing "place or nation of . . . origin" from race).

32. *Id.* at 482 (emphasis added).

33. *Espinoza v. Farah Mfg. Co.*, 414 U.S. 816, 818 (1973).

34. *See supra* note 25.

35. Olivas, *supra* note 3 at 210.

36. *Hernandez*, 347 U.S. at 482 (emphasis added).

37. *See supra* note 29 (Petitioner's Brief uses the term "persons of Mexican descent" while arguing that the Equal Protection Clause forbids national origin discrimination).

38. *Hernandez*, 347 U.S. at 479.

39. *Castaneda v. Partida*, 430 U.S. 482, 495 (1977) (emphasis added).

40. 481 U.S. 604 (1987).

41. *St. Francis College*, 481 U.S. at 612.

42. Section 1981, divided into three subsections after amendment in the Civil Rights Act of 1991, provides in part:

> All persons within the jurisdiction of the United States shall have the same right in every State and Territory to make and enforce contracts. . . .

42 U.S.C. §1981(a) (2006).

43. *St. Francis College*, 481 U.S. at 609 ("Although §1981 does not itself use the word 'race,' the Court has construed the section to forbid all 'racial' discrimination in the making of private as well as public contracts."); *McDonald v. Santa Fe Trail Transp. Co.*, 427 U.S. 273, 285-296 (1976) (§1981 applies to discrimination against white persons, as well as against non-white persons).

44. *St. Francis*, 481 U.S. at 609.

45. *Id.* at 609-610. Of course, it is possible for someone to discriminate against members of the same race for various reasons. *See, e.g., Castaneda v. Partida*, 430 U.S. 482, 503 (1977) (Marshall, J., concurring) (noting that members of disadvantaged groups may sometimes try to disassociate themselves with those groups, even to the point of adopting the majority's negative attitudes towards the minority). In *St. Francis College*, however, Al-Khazraji apparently did not assert that decision-makers held discriminatory animus toward Caucasians generally; he therefore needed to establish his membership in a different race than that of the decision-makers, a race toward which the decision-makers held discriminatory animus.

46. *St. Francis*, 481 U.S. at 610 & n.4.

47. *Id.* at 609-610.

48. *Id.* at 610.

49. *Id.* at 613.

50. *Id.* at 612.

51. *See Shaare Tefila Congregation v. Cobb*, 481 U.S. 615 (1987) (interpreting companion statute, 42 U.S.C. §1982).

52. In close cases, the analysis in *St. Francis College* does present a challenge in distinguishing between race and national origin. *St. Francis College*, 481 U.S. at 614 (Brennan, J., concurring). National origin refers most clearly to birthplace, whereas race—as defined by *St. Francis College*—relates to ethnic ancestry, which itself may be associated with a specific geographic area that is encompassed within or overlaps the borders of a nation-state. *See generally id.* In some cases, the distinction is easily made: A person born and raised in Britain of parents with ancestral roots in a region in West Africa has a British national origin but a race associated with peoples indigenous to West Africa. In contrast, Al-Khazraji, a U.S. citizen of Arab ancestry born in Iraq, might present a more difficult factual question. If invidious discrimination did occur, would the facts clearly show whether the discrimination was based on Al-Khazraji's Arab ancestry, actionable under §1981, or based on his birthplace within the nation of Iraq, actionable under a modern civil rights statute, but not under §1981? *See St. Francis College*, 481 U.S. at 606 (explaining that claimant brought several claims, including one based on national origin, under Title VII of the Civil Rights Act of 1964, but the Title VII claims were barred under the limitations periods).

53. *See* note 39 and accompanying text. *But cf.* Sheridan, *supra* note 25, at 131 (concluding that "[t]he Supreme Court, however, declined to rule on whether Mexican Americans constituted a race").

54. *See, e.g., St. Francis College*, 481 U.S. at 610 n.4 (citing to several scientific publications concluding that racial classifications are for the most part sociopolitical, rather than biological, in nature; Lopez, *supra* note 25, at 281, 288-289 (race is not biological but is a social construct based on group member's self-conception and on perception of the group by others, and referring to Professor Juan Perera's application of a similar definition to ethnicity).

55. *See generally* Lopez, *supra* note 25, at 281 (setting forth similar list of characteristics).

56. *Id.*

57. *See supra* Section IV.A.

58. *Hernandez v. Texas*, 347 U.S. 475, 478-479 (1954).

59. *Id.* at 478.

60. *See, e.g., Castaneda v. Partida*, 430 U.S. 482, 492, 495 (1977); *id.* at 502 n.1 (Marshall, J., concurring) (citing to other cases, those of which decided after 1954 all cite to *Hernandez*).

61. *Id.* at 495; *see supra* note 39 and accompanying text.

62. *Castaneda*, 439 U.S. at 495.

63. *Id.* at 495-496 (using the 1970 census data to establish exclusion from jury service).

64. 398 U.S. 922.

65. *Tijerina v. Henry*, 48 F.R.D. 274 (D.N.M. 1969).

66. *Tijerina v. Henry*, 398 U.S. 922 (1970).

67. *Id.* at 923-924 (Douglas, J., concurring).

68. *Id.* at 924.

69. *Id.* at 924-925.

70. *See supra* notes 3-5 and accompanying text.

71. Olivas, *supra* note 3, at 222.

72. *See* Salinas, *supra* note 16, at 145-147, 153; *The Road to Brown* (Calif. Newsreel 1990) (documentary film about African-American attorney Charles Houston's litigation of cases leading to *Brown*).

6. Meritor Savings Bank v. Vinson

Ann C. McGinley[1]

Twenty-five years ago the United States Supreme Court decided *Meritor Savings Bank v. Vinson*.[2] In *Meritor*, the Court held that sexual harassment that creates a hostile working environment is illegal sex discrimination under Title VII of the Civil Rights Act of 1964. *Meritor* was a stunning decision that has improved working conditions for many women (and some men). This case, combined with a number of Supreme Court cases that expanded upon *Meritor*'s holding, changed the face of the American workplace for female and male employees and their employers. When the Court decided *Meritor*, only 23 years had passed since Representative Howard Smith of Virginia gleefully added "sex" to the Civil Rights bill in what many presume was an effort to defeat the entire Civil Rights Act.[3] Thus, *Meritor* marks a remarkably rapid change in workplace law, a change that reflected and furthered the swift social transformations of the 1970s and 1980s. These changes resulted from the feminist movement that propelled women into jobs previously reserved for male workers.

Title VII of the Civil Rights Act of 1964 prohibits discrimination in employment because of an individual's race, color, religion, sex, or national origin. The express language of the Act does not mention harassment. Nonetheless, the courts held as early as 1971 that racial harassment constituted illegal race discrimination under Title VII.[4] Courts, however, saw sexual harassment as different. Most denied that it creates a cause of action because of the "natural" and "private" nature of sexual relationships. In 1977, however, the D.C. Circuit Court of Appeals concluded in *Barnes v. Costle*[5] that the plaintiff stated a cause of action under Title VII when she alleged that her job was abolished because she refused to have an affair with her supervisor. Judge Spottswood Robinson, a liberal African-American judge known for his civil rights work as a lawyer and the former dean of Howard Law School, wrote the majority opinion in *Barnes*. He is the same judge who would write the majority opinion in the *Meritor* case when it later would reach the court of appeals. A longtime Republican and Nixon appointee, Judge George

MacKinnon, wrote the concurrence in *Barnes v. Costle*. While the concurrence agreed that the behavior alleged in *Barnes* was illegal under Title VII, he argued that the employer should be liable only if supervisors or managers other than the harasser knew or should have known about the harassment.

Two years later, in 1979, Judge MacKinnon's daughter, Catharine A. MacKinnon, who would soon become the preeminent feminist legal theorist in the United States, published *Sexual Harassment of Working Women: A Case of Sex Discrimination*.[6] She argued that Title VII should treat unwanted sexual requirements on the job as illegal sex discrimination and that employers should be liable for the harassment whether or not they knew or had reason to know of the behavior. MacKinnon's book strongly refutes the arguments made by her father's concurrence that would diminish the employer's liability, but she gives him credit for agreeing with the basic premise that the behavior was illegal.[7] Moreover, she states that perhaps an employer that has no warning about sexual harassment should not be liable for punitive damages.[8]

Catharine MacKinnon coined the terms "quid pro quo" and "hostile working environment."[9] Quid pro quo harassment involves a supervisor's demand for sexual favors in exchange for an employment benefit or a threat of an employment detriment if the subordinate does not comply. A hostile working environment, which can be created by supervisors or coworkers or both, involves an abusive environment that is dominated by sexually or gender-based harassment. The next year, in 1980, the Equal Employment Opportunity Commission (EEOC) revised its guidelines. Following MacKinnon's theory, the new guidelines distinguished between harassment that is directly linked to an economic quid pro quo and harassment that alters the terms or conditions of employment because it creates an abusive environment based on a person's sex. In either case, the guidelines state, the conduct constitutes actionable sexual harassment under Title VII if it has the "purpose or effect of unreasonably interfering with an individual's work performance or creating an intimidating, hostile, or offensive working environment."[10] But EEOC guidelines interpreting Title VII have no binding effect, and it was up to the courts to agree or disagree. After the guidelines were issued, lower courts uniformly held that a cause of action existed under Title VII for a hostile work environment based on sexual harassment.[11] Still, it would take a Supreme Court case to establish the law of the land. Enter Mechelle Vinson.

Mechelle Vinson was a young black woman who began and ended her banking career at Meritor Savings Bank.[12] She had a rocky upbringing. She lived in a poor neighborhood, and because she wanted to escape living with her father, she purposefully got pregnant and married an older man when she was in her early teens. Vinson earned her graduate equivalency degree and worked in low-paying jobs. Thus, she was pleased at the age of 19 to meet Sidney Taylor, an African-American local bank manager, who offered her a job as a teller-trainee. To Vinson, who was always a "go-getter" according to her sister, the teller job was a dream come true. Vinson alleged that, at first, Taylor, who was established in the community and had seven children, mentored her like a daughter. According to Vinson, however, Taylor's behavior soon changed. She alleged that Taylor told her that she owed him for his help and that she had to engage in sexual relations with him. While refusing at first, Vinson gave in when Taylor began to threaten her job. She alleged that over the next two and one-half years, Taylor subjected her to unwelcome sexual relations. She estimated that she had sex with Taylor about 40 to 50 times and that on a number of those occasions the sex occurred in the workplace. Numerous times, Vinson alleged, Taylor raped her forcibly. On at least three occasions, the sex allegedly occurred in the bank vault. Vinson acceded to Taylor's demands because she was uneducated and afraid of losing her job. She also feared for her life. Vinson and other women testified in their depositions that Taylor engaged in similar behavior with other women at the workplace.

Vinson eventually brought suit against the bank, alleging that Taylor's behavior violated Title VII and that the bank was liable for Taylor's behavior. Both sides agreed that Vinson had been promoted a number of times based on merit. There was no economic quid pro quo. Taylor denied having sex with Vinson. The bank asserted that it had no notice of sex that may have taken place between Taylor and Vinson and that the plaintiff's failure to complain to bank officials prevented her recovery even if she had been sexually harassed. The lower court in a bench trial granted judgment for the defendants. The court made no factual findings as to whether sex occurred, but held that if there was sex between Taylor and Vinson, it was voluntary, and therefore there was no violation of Title VII. The lower court also refused to permit Vinson to offer testimony of Taylor's similar treatment of other women employees. In contrast, the federal district judge allowed the defendant to offer evidence of Vinson's allegedly provocative dress and behavior to demonstrate that Vinson voluntarily engaged in sex with Taylor.

On appeal, the D.C. Circuit Court of Appeals reversed.[13] Following an earlier circuit court decision that was decided after the lower court judgment in *Vinson*, the court of appeals held that a plaintiff may have a cause of action for a hostile work environment under Title VII even if there is no economic harm. It concluded that Vinson was not precluded from proving sexual harassment merely because she submitted voluntarily to her employer's sexual advances. If voluntariness were the standard, the court argued, employers would be able to force economically vulnerable women to have sex, behavior that would alter the terms or conditions of their employment. Rather, the court noted, the standard is unwelcomeness. The court of appeals also disagreed with the lower court's ruling that the evidence of harassment of other women is inadmissible. Finally, it concluded that an employer is strictly liable under Title VII for the behavior of a supervisor that creates a hostile work environment even if the employer lacked specific notice of the sexual harassment by the supervisor.

Catharine MacKinnon

Catharine MacKinnon authored Vinson's brief before the United States Supreme Court. The brief argued that a hostile work environment, even absent a tangible economic loss, constitutes sex discrimination under Title VII, for which employers should be strictly liable. The United States Supreme Court affirmed in part, reversed in part, and remanded the case for further fact development. It held that in the absence of economic harm, an employer's creation of a hostile working environment that is sufficiently severe or pervasive as to alter a person's work environment constitutes sex discrimination under Title VII. Moreover, the Court held that even if Vinson's behavior was voluntary, it could still constitute illegal harassment. It agreed with the court of appeals that the touchstone is welcomeness, not voluntariness.

Six years later, in *Harris v. Forklift Systems, Inc.*,[14] the Court held that an illegal hostile working environment occurs even if the severe behavior found in *Meritor* does not exist and even if the plaintiff does not suffer severe psychological harm. In *Harris*, the Court concluded that the environment is illegal under Title VII if the behavior is sufficiently severe *or* pervasive as to alter the terms or conditions of employment from the perspective of the plaintiff and from the perspective of a reasonable person. And, finally, in 1998 in *Oncale v. Sundowner Offshore Services, Inc.*[15] the Court held that harassment by a person of the same sex is illegal under Title VII so long as it occurs "because of sex." *Oncale* made clear that harassment does not have to result from sexual interest, and that the harassing behavior itself need not be sexual in nature. The motives of the harasser may be gender-based instead. For example, illegal harassment of an employee can occur if the perpetrator's motive is to encourage women (or men) to leave the workforce or if the behavior is hostile, but not sexual, in nature.[16] These expansions of *Meritor* are consistent with the purposes of the statute, which sought to forbid sex discrimination rather than sexual repartee in the workplace.

There were, however, some portions of the Supreme Court decision in *Meritor* that retreated from the court of appeals' opinion. First, unlike the court of appeals, the Supreme Court held that evidence of a plaintiff's dress and behavior is relevant to proof of unwelcomeness in a sexual harassment case. Tanya Hernandez argues convincingly in *"What Not to Wear"—Race and Unwelcomeness in Sexual Harassment Law* that the Court's refusal to acknowledge that both Vinson and Taylor are black permitted the unconscious infusion of race-based judgments about black women's sexual availability into the law. Because black women are traditionally considered sexually available and promiscuous, she argues, and none of the opinions mentioned the race of participants, the Court "obstructed recognition of the speech and dress portion of the welcomeness assessment as a problematic racial construct."[17] As a result, all women plaintiffs are now "unfairly burdened with an inquiry into whether their apparel and speech welcomed sexual advances, and this evidence may be used to eviscerate their claims of sexual harassment."[18] Fortunately, however, Federal Rule of Evidence 412 has subsequently been amended to limit introduction or discovery of evidence in a sexual harassment case of the plaintiff's sexual behavior or proclivities.[19] This rule permits the discovery and introduction of evidence only upon a special showing by the defendant of its relevancy. It has, therefore, softened the effect of this portion of the *Meritor* decision.

The Supreme Court in *Meritor* also disagreed with the court of appeals' conclusion that the employer would be strictly liable for the behavior of its supervisory employees who sexually harass their subordinates. In *Meritor*, the Court stated that lower courts should use agency principles to determine whether an employer is liable for a supervisor's actions. After significant confusion in the lower courts, in 1998 the Supreme Court revisited the issue of employer liability in hostile work environment cases.[20] In *Burlington Industries, Inc. v. Ellerth* and *Faragher v. City of Boca Raton*, the Court held that an employer is strictly liable for the sexual harassment performed by a supervisor on a subordinate if there is a tangible employment action such as a demotion or a firing. If there is no tangible employment action, the employer can avoid liability by proving a two-pronged affirmative defense: (1) that it exercised reasonable care to prevent and correct promptly any sexually harassing behavior; and (2) that the plaintiff employee unreasonably failed to take advantage of any preventive or corrective opportunities afforded by the employer. Ordinarily, if an employer proves that it has established a policy that forbids sexual harassment and designates various persons to whom harassment can be reported, and the employer educates its employees about the policy, the employer will not be liable if the employee fails to report the harassment to the employer.

As a result of *Meritor, Ellerth,* and *Faragher,* many employers today take sexual harassment seriously. Seeking to avoid liability for sexual harassment, they institute policies forbidding harassment and regularly conduct training workshops to educate employees about sexual harassment and its repercussions. If an employee is accused of sexually harassing another employee, wise employers conduct prompt neutral investigations, which lead to discipline if the complainant's allegation is corroborated. Moreover, the anti-retaliation provision of Title VII supports these policies. It forbids employers from retaliating against employees who report their good faith reasonable beliefs that Title VII violations have occurred. Thus, Title VII protects employees who complain about harassment at work from employer retaliation.

There is no doubt that *Meritor, Ellerth,* and *Faragher* have produced enormous changes in the workforce. But there is some debate about the efficacy of these changes. While some scholars argue that the courts rely too heavily on the affirmative defense to grant summary judgments to employers where questions of fact exist concerning the reasonableness of the plaintiff's failure to report harassment, others argue that in an attempt to avoid sexual or gender harassment, employers are unnecessarily circumscribing lawful employee behavior. Both arguments are likely correct to some extent. While the courts leniently grant summary judgment to employers, many employers prohibit behavior at work that would never rise to the severity or pervasiveness necessary to prove illegal sexual harassment. But the good news is that as a result of *Meritor,* no employee must suffer the behavior that Mechelle Vinson alleged that she endured at work in order to keep her job.

What happened to the players in Mechelle Vinson's case and to the case itself?[21] Vinson's lawyer, Patricia Barry, was a sole practitioner who took the case from her trial to the Supreme Court. After the trial, Barry moved to California in 1982. She referred to the Vinson case as her "personal Vietnam" because of its apparent endless drain on her legal resources. After the Supreme Court remanded the case, she declared bankruptcy in 1988, and withdrew from the case. Mechelle Vinson, too, declared bankruptcy in 1980 and moved in with her parents. She was blackballed in the banking industry, so she could not get another banking job. She attempted to get a nursing degree, but had to drop out. To raise charitable donations to finish her case, she set up the Mechelle Vinson Defense Fund. After the case was remanded to the federal district court, two lawyers from the Washington Committee for Civil Rights Under Law, a volunteer group, represented her. Sydney Taylor, who had been called a "boy scout" by his lawyer, was convicted of 17 counts of embezzling funds from the bank, and received a jail sentence of 18 to 56 months. When he was paroled in March 1989, the plaintiff's attorneys took his deposition. He admitted that Vinson did not welcome his advances and that she had dressed appropriately except on two occasions. Other witnesses were deposed who swore that Taylor had harassed a number of women at the bank. The parties engaged in motion battles before the federal district court judge. The judge responded to the motions slowly, never setting a trial date. The case finally settled on August 22, 1991, 16 years after the alleged harassment, 13 years after the complaint was filed, and more than 5 years after the Supreme Court decision. The terms of the settlement are confidential.

Endnotes

1. William S. Boyd Professor of Law, University of Nevada, Las Vegas Boyd School of Law.
2. 477 U.S. 57 (1986).
3. Augustus B. Cochran III, *Sexual Harassment and the Law: The Mechelle Vinson Case* 19-21 (U. Press of Kansas 2004).
4. *See, e.g., Rogers v. Equal Employment Opportunity Comm'n*, 454 F.2d 234 (5th Cir. 1971) (race); *Carino v. Univ. of Okla. Bd. of Regents*, 750 F.2d 815, 819 (10th Cir. 1984) (national origin); *Vaughn v. Westinghouse Elec. Corp.*, 620 F.2d 655, 661 (8th Cir. 1980) (race), *aff'd*, 702 F.2d 137 (8th Cir. 1983).
5. 561 F.2d 983 (D.C. Cir. 1977).
6. Catharine A. MacKinnon, *Sexual Harassment of Working Women: A Case of Sex Discrimination* (Yale U. Press 1979).
7. *Id.* at 66, 258 n.48.
8. *Id.* at 93-94.
9. *See* Nancy Levit & Robert M. Verchick, *Feminist Legal Theory: A Primer* 67 (New York U. Press 2006).
10. *See* 29 C.F.R. §1604.11(a)(3) (2007).
11. *See, e.g., Katz v. Dole*, 709 F.2d 251, 254-255 (4th Cir. 1983); *Henson v. City of Dundee*, 682 F.2d 897, 902 (11th Cir. 1982).
12. Facts noted here that do not appear in the published opinions come from Cochran, *supra* note 3; Tanya Kateri Hernandez, *"What Not to Wear"—Race and Unwelcomeness in Sexual Harassment Law: The Story of* Meritor Savings Bank v. Vinson, in *Women and the Law Stories* 277-306 (Elizabeth M. Schneider & Stephanie M. Wildman eds., Foundation Press 2011); Mary Battiata, *Mechelle Vinson's Tangled Trials: After the Supreme Court, Pursuing Harassment Case*, Wash. Post C1 (Aug. 11, 1986); Mary Battiata, *Mechelle Vinson's Long Road to Court: A Disputed Tale of Sexual Harassment in the Office*, Wash. Post C1 (Aug. 12, 1986).

13. *Vinson v. Taylor et al.*, 753 F.2d 141 (D.C. Cir. 1985).

14. 510 U.S. 17 (1993).

15. 523 U.S. 75 (1998).

16. *See generally* Ann C. McGinley, *Creating Masculine Identities: Bullying and Harassment "Because of Sex,"* 79 U. Colo. L. Rev. 1151 (2008).

17. *See* Hernandez, *supra* note 12, at 280.

18. *Id.*

19. For a representative opinion, *see e.g., EEOC v. Bryan C. Donohue, M.D.*, 746 F. Supp. 2d 662 (W.D. Pa. 2010).

20. *Burlington Industries, Inc. v. Ellerth*, 524 U.S. 742 (1998); *Faragher v. City of Boca Raton*, 524 U.S. 775 (1998).

21. For the facts in this section, *see* Cochran, *supra* note 3, at 122-127.

Privacy and Liberty in Intimate Conduct

7. Griswold v. Connecticut *and* Eisenstadt v. Baird

Kathryn M. Stanchi

Griswold v. Connecticut (1965) and *Eisenstadt v. Baird* (1972) are landmark cases for privacy in United States constitutional jurisprudence and were the first cases to establish that certain aspects of intimate relationships are beyond the reach of the government. They were also critical steps in the legal development of the rights of women to control their bodily integrity as well as the legal development of sexual autonomy.

Both decisions invalidated laws that restricted access to birth control and information about birth control. Laws against the distribution of contraceptive information and material were often part of more general laws prohibiting the distribution of obscene and immoral material, which also included pornography and information about abortion. Often referred to as "Comstock laws," after Anthony Comstock, an anti-obscenity crusader and the founder of the New York Society for the Prevention of Vice, these laws were passed almost a century before *Griswold* and *Eisenstadt*, in the aftermath of the Civil War. The laws sprang up in part from the postwar fear accompanying women's changing role in society and emerging emancipation. Underlying the laws was the belief that the changing social order would cause women to become immoral and promiscuous, leading them to forsake their sacred roles as wives and mothers.

The Comstock laws sought to regulate sexual morality, but at their core they were meant to support a particular, and gendered, familial and social structure, with women kept firmly in the private sphere of the home, family, and children. The language, history, and rhetoric of the Comstock laws also reflected the view that law should control issues of sexuality and morality. Privacy was beside the point; the nation had an interest in maintaining a certain order, and law was a way to ensure that women and sexuality were contained within certain acceptable limits. Given their impetus, it is no coincidence that the Comstock laws were used against several early feminists, including birth control advocate Margaret Sanger and suffragettes Victoria Woodhull and Tennessee Claflin.

Margaret Sanger, circa 1910

The laws made it very difficult for women, particularly poor women, to control how often they became pregnant. As a practical matter, the laws not only restricted the flow of information to women, but contributed to the social view of birth control as an obscene and immoral practice. The inability to control pregnancy had a significant deleterious effect not only on women's quest for equality, but also on their health and well-being. During the heyday of Comstockery, a woman could expect to be pregnant more than ten times in her lifetime. This inability to control pregnancy ensured that women were confined to the private sphere of the home and sentenced many women to a life of poor health, poverty, economic dependency, and early mortality.

In later years, court decisions in several states had restricted the effect of the state Comstock laws, but often stopped short of invalidating them. So, as late as 1960, many states as well as the federal government still had laws on the books that, in one form or another, blocked access to contraceptive devices and information. Even though only sporadically enforced, the laws suppressed discussions of sexuality and birth control, even between women and their physicians, and blocked access to birth control, particularly for poor women. In a culture that often stigmatized any talk of women's sexuality or the desire to control reproduction as evidence of promiscuity and immorality, the continued existence of the Comstock laws had a significant chilling effect on women's access to birth control.

Griswold v. Connecticut involved one of the strictest of the state Comstock laws. The Connecticut Comstock law prohibited "any person" from using "any drug, medicinal article or instrument for the purposes of preventing contraception."[1] The law also provided that anyone who assisted or abetted another in committing the offense of using birth control could be prosecuted "as if he were a principal offender."[2] Connecticut enforced the law primarily against birth control clinics that served mostly poor women. The Connecticut courts consistently upheld convictions under the law, refusing, as other states had done, to circumscribe the law or declare it unconstitutional. It was in this climate that Estelle Griswold, a medical technician, came to Connecticut and became Executive Director of Planned Parenthood.

At that time, Planned Parenthood was actively looking for a plaintiff to challenge the Connecticut Comstock law. The office had also been fighting unsuccessfully in the Connecticut legislature to repeal the law. During the efforts for repeal, Griswold met Dr. Lee Buxton, the other party in the *Griswold* case. Buxton was chairman of the Yale Obstetrics and Gynecology Department, and testified before the Connecticut legislature about women who died as a result of their inability to control their pregnancies. Buxton's stories failed to sway the legislature in part because of the powerful moral rhetoric employed by the opposition. The legislative fight to repeal the law was particularly vicious in its judgment of women, with opposition leaders asserting that women who used birth control were emotionally unstable and inferior mothers. Nearly a century after the passage of the original Comstock laws, the core debate about birth control still centered on keeping women in their ordained social roles.

"Planned Parenthood," Feb. 26, 2011

After the failure to achieve repeal of the law, Buxton and Griswold returned to the original effort to have the law declared unconstitutional. In 1943, *Tileston v. Ullman*, an early effort by a doctor to defeat the law in the courts, failed on standing grounds. Buxton and Griswold then collaborated on another challenge to the law brought by both Buxton and his patients. But this case, *Poe v. Ullman*, failed on ripeness grounds. The Supreme Court found that, because the plaintiffs had not been prosecuted or even threatened with prosecution, there was no real controversy to resolve. As a result of the defeat in *Poe*, Griswold and Buxton decided to open birth control clinics in Connecticut. If the law were indeed a nullity, as the Supreme Court had found in *Poe*, the clinics could stay open without state interference. If the law were not dead, then Griswold and Buxton would be arrested, establishing both standing and ripeness for a constitutional challenge.

Shortly after the decision in *Poe*, Griswold and Buxton opened a clinic to much fanfare in the Connecticut press. They held a press conference designed to flout Connecticut's Comstock law as openly as possible. Connecticut's police force was slow to react. However, a single citizen voicing his outrage over the opening of the clinic and the brazen violation of the law eventually compelled an investigation. Police were dispatched to the clinic, and Griswold all but invited them to arrest her by describing in detail the services of the clinic. Griswold refused, however, to disclose any patient records because of confidentiality. That first police visit ended with the officers leaving the clinic after amicably shaking hands with Griswold and Buxton.

Soon thereafter, the police returned and requested the names of two women who had received birth control instructions and supplies from the clinic. Hoping to move the case forward, Griswold called two married patients sympathetic to the clinic and asked them to tell the police that they had received birth control from the clinic. She and Buxton were arrested soon thereafter. They were convicted under the assisting and abetting section of the statute, and fined $100 each for supplying birth control devices to their patients, all of whom were married women.

After losing at every stage in the Connecticut courts, the plaintiffs arrived at the Supreme Court. A deeply divided Court (there were six separate opinions) held that the Connecticut statute was an unconstitutional infringement on the right of privacy of married people. Although *Griswold* was the first case to articulate a constitutional right to personal relational privacy, the opinion by Justice Douglas is quite short and direct. He quickly dispensed with the standing issue and rejected the notion that the notorious precedent of *Lochner v. New York* should be the guiding principle of the case. In rejecting the *Lochner* path, Justice Douglas famously wrote that

the Supreme Court does not sit as a "super-legislature to determine
the wisdom, need or propriety of laws that touch on economic
problems, business affairs or social conditions."[3]

However, in the next sentence, the opinion seems to reverse
course. The opinion does not assert that a law about birth control
is somehow less entwined with economic or social conditions than a
law about bakers' hours, which was the issue in *Lochner*. Rather, the
Court reasoned that the law in *Griswold* was different from the law
in *Lochner* because the Connecticut law "operate[d] directly on an
intimate relation of husband and wife."[4]

The import of this language seems to be that while the Court
should not interfere with *most* laws related to economic, business,
or social conditions, there are some exceptions. The exception
carved by *Griswold* for the "intimate relation of husband and
wife" is, to some degree, evidence of the cultural norms of the
time, which starkly separated the market sphere, which was public,
from the family sphere, which was private. These cultural norms are
evident in Douglas's opinion and the concurring opinions, all of
which locate the privacy right explicitly in the marital relationship,
a relationship they identify as worthy of special reverence and protection. The marital relationship, Douglas wrote, is "sacred" and
"older than the Bill of Rights."[5] Similarly strong rhetoric appears
in the concurring opinions of Justice White and Justice Goldberg.
The *Griswold* opinions can sound like paeans to traditional marriage, an institution that, ironically, the Connecticut law was also
designed to protect and support.

This overlap between *Griswold* and the purpose of the Connecticut law shows that the marital relationship described in and
extolled by *Griswold* was hardly radical at the time. Indeed, the privacy of the marital relationship *Griswold* elevated to constitutional
status was a legal concept not entirely favorable to women. The wall
of privacy surrounding the family often meant that battering, marital rape, and other abuses happened outside the government's
radar. The opinion of the Court and the concurring opinions barely
mentioned the critical importance of birth control to the lives and
health of women, or that the law was primarily enforced against
clinics that served poor women. The opinions also overlooked
that the primary effect of the Connecticut law was to prohibit contraception within the control of women, such as diaphragms, while
condoms were widely available in drug stores. Although the chief
concerns of those who brought *Griswold* to the Court were women's
health and autonomy, the decision is remarkably silent about these
issues.

The *Griswold* opinions also include language that purports to
limit the scope of the privacy right to traditional heterosexual marriage. Justice Goldberg explicitly noted that the constitutionality of

laws against other private sexual acts, such as adultery and fornication, remained "beyond doubt" after *Griswold*.[6] Justice White's opinion noted that government regulation of "promiscuous or illicit sexual relationships, be they premarital or extramarital," is a "permissible and legitimate legislative goal."[7]

But while *Griswold*'s view of the sanctity and privacy of marriage might, in retrospect, look like it echoes the traditional ideals of the Connecticut law it struck down, the decision was nevertheless a significant one for women's health and sexual privacy. Its immediate practical effect was to allow, for the first time in over two decades, the opening of birth control clinics in Connecticut. But *Griswold*'s legacy is, of course, bigger than its impact on Connecticut. The decision provided a foothold for the idea that there is a constitutionally protected right to privacy in intimate sexual relationships.

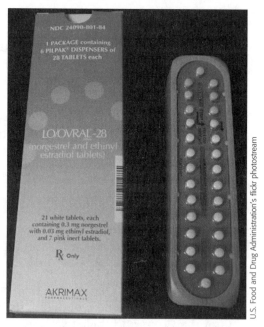

Recalled oral contraceptives, 2012

Within the rhetoric about marriage, the opinion of the Court directly referenced the sexual nature of the privacy right when it noted that allowing "the police to search the sacred precincts of marital bedrooms for telltale signs of the use of contraceptives" would be "repulsive."[8] The example—largely apocryphal, as the law was not enforced by raids on private homes—certainly implies that police intrusion into the bedroom is "repulsive" not only because marriage is sacred, but because of the decidedly private acts that occur in that room.

Griswold also broke new ground in its choice of a legal basis for this foundational idea of constitutionally protected personal privacy. Justice Douglas grounds the right of privacy in the "penumbras" emanating from various amendments in the Bill of Rights (an idea often attributed to William Brennan). The opinion takes a broad view of the Court's precedent, finding that the Court had a long history of recognizing and protecting rights that, while not specifically enumerated in the Constitution, are nevertheless necessary to give the enumerated rights "life and substance." The right to privacy, Douglas noted, is no different, and emanates from the rights in multiple amendments, including the First Amendment's right of association, the Third Amendment's right to refuse to quarter soldiers in one's home, and the Fourth Amendment's right to secure one's house and property against unreasonable searches and seizures.

Griswold was thus a critical first step in what would become a sweeping transformation in constitutional law on the issue of sexual privacy, sexual autonomy, and women's reproductive agency. Though only the concurring opinions of Justices Harlan and White explicitly ground the decision in the guarantee of liberty in the Fourteenth Amendment Due Process Clause, *Griswold* is nevertheless usually seen as the source of the modern substantive due process right. It marked a turning point in the rejection of the idea that law should regulate matters of intimate sexuality. Moreover, *Griswold*'s interpretive approach, that the Constitution is a living document that protects more than just the specifically enumerated rights, but also whatever rights are necessary to make those specifically enumerated rights meaningful, was revolutionary. It began the process that eventually begat transformative decisions in personal sexual privacy like *Roe v. Wade* and *Lawrence v. Texas*.

Griswold's legacy is immediately apparent in its first progeny, *Eisenstadt v. Baird*. While *Griswold*'s effects on constitutional law and social policy were significant, its impact is in some ways exceeded by *Eisenstadt*. Decided in 1972, *Eisenstadt* involved yet another state Comstock law, this time in Massachusetts.

The years between 1965, when *Griswold* was decided, and 1971, when the Court heard the arguments in *Eisenstadt*, were years of social upheaval in the United States. In addition to the burgeoning Peace Movement and the Summer of Love, the second wave of the women's movement, which had just begun when *Griswold* was decided, was in full swing by the time *Eisenstadt* was argued. The National Organization of Women and the National Abortion Rights Action League were founded. The Equal Rights Amendment was introduced in the Senate. California adopted a "no fault" divorce law, the first in the nation. Even the first state laws loosening the more stringent restrictions on abortion were passed.

The issue of birth control was a significant part of this social upheaval, in part because *Griswold* was limited to married people. Also, because of prevailing cultural attitudes about premarital sex, single women and poor women in the United States still faced substantial obstacles to obtaining birth control and information about it. In the late 1960s, the idea of giving birth control to unmarried women was quite controversial. The view was prevalent, even among physicians, that birth control led to promiscuity and that premarital sex was immoral and would lead to cultural decline. As a result, the anticontraception laws that remained after *Griswold* left single women at the mercy of doctors, many of whom were, in the words of one physician, "sticklers for the old morality."

The prevalence of the "old morality" meant that unmarried women who sought birth control were often subject to humiliating moral judgments from their doctors and others in society. While some doctors refused outright to prescribe birth control to single women, telling the women to come back when married, others questioned their patients about their reasons for wanting birth control. One doctor at a student clinic stated that he would pre-scribe birth control only if it were used for "a good solid relationship and not promiscuity." In another case, a doctor required a single woman to sign a pledge that she would soon marry before giving her birth control.

"London at war—birth control," circa 1941

The inability of single women to access birth control made the issue a cause célèbre on college campuses in the 1960s. Within this cause, William Baird was a notorious and controversial figure. In the early 1960s, Baird was employed as a clinical director for EMKO, a birth control manufacturer. While working at EMKO, he witnessed the tragic death of a mother of eight who stumbled into a Harlem hospital, bleeding profusely. The woman had attempted an abortion and had a coat hanger embedded in her uterus. She bled to death in front of Baird.

After witnessing this, Baird became a vocal activist for birth control. Baird's flagrant and audacious tactics often ran afoul of the law and frustrated his allies in Planned Parenthood and the ACLU. Among other tactics, Baird converted a United Parcel truck into a mobile birth control clinic, which he called the "Plan Van," out of which he dispensed free literature and birth control in the poorest cities of New York and New Jersey. He was also a loud proponent of abortion rights, which was a very divisive issue at the time, even among birth control advocates.

But Baird's controversial and imprudent behavior, as well as his outspoken advocacy for sexual freedom, made him something of a hero on college campuses in the 1960s. This led a group of Boston University students to ask Baird to challenge the restrictive Massachusetts birth control law. That law was codified under the title of "Crimes Against Chastity, Morality, Decency and Good Order" and prohibited, among other things, unmarried people from obtaining contraceptives to prevent pregnancy. At this point, Baird was in jail in New Jersey for "indecent exposure of obscene objects" as a result of his dissemination of birth control. Nevertheless, Baird agreed to help, and once he finished his jail sentence, he headed to Boston.

On April 6, 1967, Baird spoke in Boston before thousands of students and a cadre of Boston police officers. Fully intending to provoke his own arrest, Baird spoke about the means and methods for various types of contraception, and displayed devices throughout the presentation. At the end of the lecture, he gave vaginal foam to an unmarried 19-year old female student, and was arrested.

Baird was convicted under the Massachusetts law and eventually sentenced to six months in jail. The challenge to the law was unsuccessful in the Massachusetts courts, and Baird went to jail. Baird's attorney filed a habeas corpus petition, which ultimately went up to the Supreme Court. *Eisenstadt v. Baird* was Baird's first case in the Supreme Court (he was also a party in *Belotti v. Baird*, the Supreme Court case about abortion access for minors).

In *Eisenstadt*, the Supreme Court held that the Massachusetts law violated the Equal Protection Clause of the Fourteenth Amendment by distinguishing between married and unmarried people based on criteria with "at best a marginal relation" to the objective of the law.[9] The Court began by trying to ascertain the objective of the statute. It rejected as pretextual, irrational, or overbroad multiple objectives proffered by Massachusetts, such as discouraging premarital sex and protecting safety by regulating potentially harmful goods. The Court ultimately settled on an objective that sealed the constitutional fate of the law. The only reasonable conclusion, the Court found, was that the purpose of the law was to prohibit contraception. That purpose placed the law squarely within the ambit of *Griswold*.

The Court presented the holding in simple terms: If under *Griswold* the state cannot ban distribution of birth control to married people, then it similarly cannot ban distribution to unmarried people. The Court noted that the state is not allowed to simply "pick and choose" a minority on whom to impose a law. Rather, the law must be applied generally and equally.[10]

It is after stating its rather simple holding that *Eisenstadt* makes a jurisprudential leap from the reasoning in *Griswold*. Justice Brennan began by admitting that the right to privacy in *Griswold* "inhered in the marital relationship."[11] Justice Brennan noted, however, that "the marital couple is not an ... entity with a mind and heart of its own ... but an association of two individuals each with a separate intellectual and emotional makeup."[12] The Court then makes a sweeping and momentous pronouncement about the privacy right announced in *Griswold*: "If the right to privacy means anything, it is the right of the individual, married or single, to be free from unwarranted governmental intrusion into matters so fundamentally affecting a person as the decision whether to bear or beget a child."[13] The pronouncement foreshadows the decision in *Roe v. Wade*, on which the Court had just months before heard oral argument.

With this reasoning, *Eisenstadt* made clear that *Griswold*'s significance would not be constrained to a holding about privacy in the marital relationship—a narrow view embraced not only by Massachusetts, but also accepted by many pro-contraception advocates. *Eisenstadt* took the right of privacy established in *Griswold* beyond the legally recognized zone of the traditional marital unit, and expanded that right to individual people involved in intimate relationships. It established a constitutional right to individual privacy in intimate matters—a radical shift in both social policy and constitutional law.

In expanding the right in *Griswold* to individuals, *Eisenstadt* undercut the enduring legal fiction, supported by *Griswold*, that a married man and woman merged identities and became one person in the eyes of the law. Because traditional marriage was so often a source of oppression for women, *Eisenstadt*'s expansion of the right to privacy to individuals was critical to women's emancipation and sexual autonomy. If *Griswold* took the first step toward the legal recognition of the sexual privacy and autonomy that led to *Roe* and *Lawrence*, *Eisenstadt* took the next leap.

Though it purports to be grounded in the Equal Protection Clause, *Eisenstadt* is often seen as a case that expanded the substantive due process right to privacy. Indeed, Justice Brennan's opinion purported to avoid the fundamental right question reached by the First Circuit. But in dodging the question, the opinion quoted, at length, the First Circuit's damning rationale that the Massachusetts law "conflicts with fundamental human rights" and is "the very mirror image of sensible legislation."[14] The opinion also imposed a level of scrutiny on the Massachusetts statute that seems more intensive than rational basis.

The legacy of *Eisenstadt* as a substantive due process case became apparent in the decisions of *Roe v. Wade* and *Carey v. Population Services International*, both of which cite *Eisenstadt* as support for a general constitutional right to intimate decisions regarding childbearing. By the time *Roe* and *Carey* were decided, in 1973 and 1977, it became clear that the legacy of *Griswold* and *Eisenstadt* would be broader than the freedom to use birth control. *Roe* and *Carey* established that *Griswold* and *Eisenstadt* forbid government intrusion into all kinds of private decisions about family and children.

The road to individual privacy in sexuality and sexual acts took a bit longer. In 1986, in *Bowers v. Hardwick*, the Court declined to recognize that the constitutional privacy right established in *Griswold* and *Eisenstadt* extended to private homosexual acts. The Court's reasoning echoed the more traditional reasoning in *Griswold* regarding marital and family norms. Interestingly, the facts in *Bowers* recall the hypothetical scenario Justice Douglas called "repulsive" in *Griswold*—in *Bowers* a police officer entered the bedroom of a private residence and witnessed sexual activity. Nevertheless, the Court found that this invasion did not offend the Constitution because, unlike marriage, homosexuality was not "deeply rooted in [the] Nation's history and traditions."[15]

But the substantive force of the decisions in *Griswold* and *Eisenstadt* would outlast *Bowers*. It took the Court almost two decades, but in *Lawrence v. Texas*, the essence of the right first articulated in *Griswold* and *Eisenstadt* was fully realized. The Court announced unequivocally that *Griswold*, *Eisenstadt*, and their progeny stood for a liberty interest that broadly encompassed the right to be free to engage in "the most private human conduct, sexual behavior, and in the most private of places, the home."[16] The Court affirmed that the legacy of *Griswold* and *Eisenstadt* was the constitutional protection of a sweepingly expansive liberty interest in matters "involving the most intimate and personal choices a person may make in a lifetime, choices central to personal dignity and autonomy."[17]

The groundbreaking privacy interest announced in *Roe* and *Carey* and the far-reaching liberty interest announced in *Lawrence* owe their existence to *Griswold* and *Eisenstadt*. Close to 50 years after the decisions, the holdings and reasoning of *Griswold* and *Eisenstadt* still resonate with constitutional power. They not only changed the way the Constitution is viewed and interpreted but also were part of a larger transformation in American cultural attitudes toward sexuality, procreation, and women's role in society.

Additional Suggested Reading

Books

David Allyn, *Make Love Not War: The Sexual Revolution, an Unfettered History* (Routledge 2000).

Beth L. Bailey, *Sex in the Heartland* (Harvard U. Press 2002).

Alice Fleetwood Bartee, *Privacy Rights* (Rowman & Littlefield Publishers 2006).

David P. Cline, *Creating Choice: A Community Responds to the Need for Abortion and Birth Control, 1961-1973* (Palgrave Macmillan 2006).

Peter C. Engelman, *A History of the Birth Control Movement in America* (Praeger 2011).

William N. Eskridge & John Ferejohn, *A Republic of Statutes: The New American Constitution* (Yale U. Press 2010).

David J. Garrow, *Liberty and Sexuality: The Right to Privacy and the Making of* Roe v. Wade (U. of California Press 1994).

Elaine Tyler May, *America and the Pill: A History of Promise, Peril and Liberation* (Basic Books 2010).

Richard A. Posner, *Sex and Reason* (Harvard U. Press 1992).

Norman Redlich, John Attanasio & Joel K. Goldstein, *Understanding Constitutional Law* (2d ed. LEXISNEXIS 1999).

Rickie Solinger, *Pregnancy and Power: A Short History of Reproductive Politics in America* (New York U. Press 2005).

Andrea Tone, ed., *Controlling Reproduction* (Rowman & Littlefield Publishers 1996).

Susan Ware, ed., *Notable American Women* (Vintage 2004).

Articles

Bill Baird, *The Politics of God, Government and Sex: A Thirty-One-Year Crusade*, 13 St. Louis U. Pub. L. Rev. 139 (1993).

Anne Bower, *Bill Baird: The 30 Year Crusade: Conversations, Clippings and Remembrances, Part I, The Body Politic* 10 (Feb. 1996).

Anne Bower, *Bill Baird: The 30 Year Crusade: Conversations, Clippings and Remembrances, Part II, The Body Politic* 29 (Mar. 1996).

Ellen Chesler, *Public Triumphs, Private Rights*, Ms. (Summer 2005), *available at* http://www.msmagazine.com/summer2005/birthcontrol.asp.

Gregory C. Cook, *Footnote 6: Justice Scalia's Attempt to Impose a Rule of Law on Substantive Due Process*, 14 Harv. J. L. & Pub. Pol'y 853 (1991).

Janet L. Dolgin, *The Family in Transition: From* Griswold to Eisenstadt *and Beyond, 82 Geo. L. J. 1519 (1994).*

Mary L. Dudziak, *Just Say No: Birth Control in the Connecticut Supreme Court Before* Griswold v. Connecticut, 75 Iowa L. Rev. 915 (1990).

Martha Albertson Fineman, *What Role for Family Privacy?* 67 Geo. Wash. L. Rev. 1207 (1999).

John Killilea, *Time Runs Out for William Baird: State May Be Winning Birth Control Debate*, Harvard Crimson (Oct. 23, 1967).

Steven M. Spencer, *Birth Control Revolution*, Saturday Evening Post (Jan. 1966).

David M. Wagner, *Hints, Not Holdings: Use of Precedent in* Lawrence v. Texas, 18 BYU J. Pub. L. 681 (2004).

Endnotes

1. *Griswold v. Connecticut*, 381 U.S. 479, 480 (1965) (quoting General Statutes of Connecticut §53-32).

2. *Id.*

3. *Id.* at 482.

4. *Id.*

5. *Id.* at 486.

6. *Id.* at 498 (Goldberg, J., concurring).

7. *Id.* at 505 (White, J., concurring).

8. *Id.* at 485-486.

9. *Eisenstadt v. Baird*, 405 U.S. 438, 448 (1972).

10. *Id.* at 454.

11. *Id.* at 453.

12. *Id.*

13. *Id.*

14. *Id.*

15. *Bowers v. Hardwick*, 478 U.S. 186, 192-193 (quoting *Moore v. East Cleveland*, 431 U.S. 494, 503 (1977)).

16. *Lawrence v. Texas*, 539 U.S. 558, 567 (2003).

17. *Id.* at 574 (quoting *Planned Parenthood of Southeastern Pa. v. Casey*, 505 U.S. 833, 851 (1992)).

8. Bowers v. Hardwick *and* Lawrence v. Texas

Carlos A. Ball[1]

One day in the summer of 1982, as Michael Hardwick was leaving the gay bar in Atlanta where he worked, he threw a beer bottle into a trash can in front of the building. Moments later, police officer Keith Torick drove up beside him, ordering him to get into the cruiser. After Torick asked Hardwick what he was doing in the area, he answered that he worked at the bar, a statement that suggested to the officer that Hardwick was gay. Torick then proceeded to ticket Hardwick for drinking in public, despite his protestations that he had not.

The police inadvertently wrote down the wrong court date on the summons. As a result of this mistake, Hardwick did not appear in court on the correct day and a warrant was issued for his arrest. A few hours later, Torick took the unusual step—unusual because the charge was so minor—of going to Hardwick's apartment to arrest him. Hardwick was not home, but when he later learned from his roommate that a police officer had been looking for him, he went down to the county clerk's office, paid a $50 fine to settle the matter, and hoped that he would never see Torick again. But three weeks later, a determined Torick went back to Hardwick's place to arrest him.

When Torick arrived at the apartment, the door was unlocked. The officer made himself at home, walking through the premises to a back bedroom. The door to the bedroom was slightly ajar; Torick opened it further, went in, and saw Hardwick engaging in oral sex with another man. Torick then announced to the startled men that they were under arrest. After Hardwick and his friend dressed, the officer handcuffed them and drove them downtown where he had them booked for violating Georgia's sodomy law.

Hardwick spent 12 hours in jail before being released. Prosecutors, recognizing the questionable legality of the arrest based on an invalid warrant, eventually dropped the sodomy charge. By that point, a lawyer with the local chapter of the American Civil Liberties Union (ACLU) had already contacted Hardwick offering to represent him, and Hardwick readily agreed. On Valentine's Day 1983, the

ACLU filed a complaint on his behalf in federal court in Atlanta challenging the sodomy law's constitutionality.

Sodomy statutes in the United States can be traced back to the English Reformation Parliament of 1533. It was that body which transformed the religious proscription against sodomy into a secular crime (known in England as "buggery"). Although the American colonies enacted laws against sodomy/buggery, those provisions were not aimed at homosexual conduct as such—the statutes prohibited men from having anal intercourse not only with other men, but also with women, children, and animals. American sodomy laws in the seventeenth and eighteenth centuries, in other words, reflected society's strong disapproval of nonreproductive sex rather than a targeted condemnation of those who had sex with individuals of their own sex.

After independence, the original 13 states, as well as most of the states that followed, adopted sodomy statutes. Although a few of those statutes proscribed specific sexual conduct (in particular anal sex), the language of most of the laws simply prohibited "crimes against nature," leaving it to judges to determine the meaning of that vague phrase. Until the end of the nineteenth century, courts for the most part permitted prosecutors to apply the statutes only in cases involving alleged instances of anal sex (both homosexual and heterosexual) or bestiality.

Beginning in the late nineteenth century, and continuing through the early twentieth century, sodomy laws were expanded (either through the enactment of new laws or the judicial interpretation of old ones) to include not just anal intercourse but also oral sex. (In addition, a handful of jurisdictions, in particular some that had large urban populations, for the first time specifically prohibited sexual conduct between women.) Although the category of proscribed sexual acts was enlarged in this way, the statutes were also, as a practical matter, narrowed because when it came to consensual sex, officials began enforcing sodomy laws almost exclusively against gay people. In fact, by the middle of the twentieth century, prosecutors and judges, as well as the general public, had come to understand the word "sodomy" as a synonym for homosexual sex.

The first state to decriminalize sodomy was Illinois, which did so in 1961 following the recommendation of the American Law Institute's Model Penal Code. Ten years would go by before a second state (Connecticut) did the same. The pace of decriminalization quickened considerably after that—by the end of the 1970s, 19 other state legislatures had voted to repeal their sodomy laws. But in the 1980s, the pace of decriminalization slowed. In fact, when Michael Hardwick's case challenging the constitutionality of Georgia's sodomy law reached the Supreme Court in 1986, half the states still had sodomy laws on their books.

For lesbian, gay, bisexual, and transgender ("LGBT") rights activists, sodomy laws were problematic not so much because of their actual enforcement against consensual sex in private—by the 1980s, arrests for private sodomy like that in the Hardwick case were rare—but because of the ways in which they were used to justify laws and policies that discriminated against LGBT people. The mere existence of sodomy laws branded LGBT people as criminals, permitting the government to defend its firing of LGBT employees, landlords to explain their refusal to rent to LGBT tenants, courts to justify their refusal to award custody of children to LGBT parents, and so on. As a result, there was a wide consensus among activists that meaningful equality for LGBT people in the United States would be impossible to achieve until sodomy laws were abolished. If state legislatures refused to repeal their sodomy laws, then activists were prepared to turn to the courts.

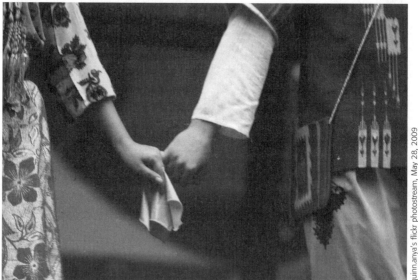

quinn.anya's flickr photostream, May 28, 2009

Holding hands

Michael Hardwick's lawyers had two main constitutional arguments at their disposal. The first was based on the Equal Protection Clause. Although Georgia's sodomy law was gender neutral (i.e., it applied to everyone regardless of the gender of the sexual actors), it was LGBT people—and gay men in particular—who suffered discrimination and harassment as a result of its existence. Hardwick's lawyers, however, decided not to raise an equal protection claim against the law. Many years later, Harvard law professor Laurence Tribe, who represented Hardwick before the U.S. Supreme Court, explained why he did not raise the equality claim:

> I was obviously aware of how even facially gender-neutral antisodomy laws like Georgia's were used principally to harass—and to justify refusals to employ, promote, or extend benefits to gay men (and to a lesser but still troublesome extent, lesbians). I also knew that many of my gay friends and many gay rights advocates saw Michael

Hardwick's lawsuit as an ideal opportunity to topple a major source of the "straight world's" oppression of gays, lesbians, and bisexuals. But the Supreme Court that was sitting in 1986 seemed most unlikely to think of a man getting oral sex from another man as no different from a man getting oral sex from a woman—even if the Georgia legislature saw fit to outlaw both acts in a single breath. If a majority of the Justices were inclined to think of the two acts as intrinsically and profoundly different, persuading them that a facially neutral law was being used to treat homosexuals differently was unlikely to dent their disposition to uphold the law.[2]

Kathleen Sullivan, Stanford Law School

Laurence Tribe in Des Moines, IA, Nov. 17, 2007

The second constitutional argument available to Hardwick, and the one made in the brief covered in this book, was that the Georgia sodomy law violated his substantive due process right to privacy. That right was first recognized by the U.S. Supreme Court in *Griswold v. Connecticut*, a 1965 case in which it struck down a law prohibiting the use of contraceptives on the ground that it violated the privacy rights of married couples.[3] For the next decade, the Court further elaborated on the constitutional right to privacy by including within its scope the right of unmarried couples to use contraceptives in *Eisenstadt v. Baird*[4] and, most (in)famously, of women to decide whether to have an abortion in *Roe v. Wade*.[5]

It seemed clear from these opinions that the Court was determined to protect from governmental intrusion certain personal and intimate decisions made by individuals. Yet, all three of the rulings involved issues associated with procreation, making it possible for some to argue that the constitutional right to privacy in matters related to sexual conduct was limited to that context. Such a limited reading of the right to privacy seemed illogical to others. For example, if heterosexual couples (whether married or unmarried) had a constitutional right to use contraceptives, did they not also have the right to engage in anal and oral sex? And, as LGBT rights activists were asking at the time of Hardwick's challenge to the Georgia sodomy law, if heterosexual couples had a constitutional right to engage in nonprocreative sex, why not same-sex couples?

Despite the fact that Hardwick was arrested for engaging in sexual conduct in the privacy of his bedroom, the Supreme Court ultimately rejected his constitutional challenge.[6] The Court did not accept the argument made by Hardwick's lawyers that its privacy rulings applied to a case involving oral sex between two men. The majority reasoned that its earlier cases had all involved marriage, family, and procreation, and that none of those were implicated by the type of conduct for which Hardwick was arrested. Furthermore, the Court concluded that the long history of sodomy criminalization in the United States meant that there could be no fundamental right for two individuals of the same sex to be sexually intimate with each other.

A crucial aspect of the Court's ruling in *Hardwick* was its rejection of Professor Tribe's argument that the Constitution protected the right of individuals to decide whom to be sexually intimate with. For the Court, the issue was not whether there was a fundamental right of all adults (regardless of sexual orientation) to have consensual sex with other adults. Instead, the Court viewed the constitutional issue raised by the case as a narrow one; namely, whether a particular group of individuals (i.e., gay people) have a fundamental right to engage in a particular kind of sexual act (i.e., sodomy). Given the long history of sodomy regulation in the country, the court dismissed the claim that there was such a right as one that was "at best, facetious."[7]

The State of Georgia argued in *Hardwick* that the legislature could constitutionally express its moral disapproval of same-sex sexual conduct through its criminal laws. (The State's brief claimed that gay sodomy was "purely an unnatural means of satisfying an unnatural lust.")[8] The Court agreed, concluding that moral disapproval of conduct was a sufficient basis to defend the rationality of a law proscribing it.

The fact that the *Hardwick* Court upheld the government's authority to criminalize private and consensual same-sex sexual intimacy was a devastating loss for LGBT rights activists. In the years that followed, a handful of state supreme courts struck down sodomy laws on the ground that they violated their state constitutions.[9] But the best opportunity to return to the Supreme Court in a sodomy case arose in 1998 when the sheriff's office in Houston, Texas, received a phone call about a man who was wielding a gun inside an apartment.

Four deputies, including Joseph Quinn and William Lilly, were dispatched to the scene. Quinn entered the apartment first, announcing the officers' presence by yelling "Sheriff's deputies!" The first thing he saw was an empty living room. One of the other officers went into a bedroom to the left of the apartment's entrance but found no one there. Quinn and the other deputies proceeded to make their way into the kitchen. The officers, who still had their weapons drawn, then noticed that there was another bedroom behind the kitchen area. The door to that bedroom was open, but there was no light inside. Deputy Lilly was the first to enter it, but he apparently became so startled after seeing two men on a bed, that he actually lurched back out of the room. Quinn moved around Lilly and entered the room in a crouched position holding his gun in front of him, with his finger on the trigger.

Michael Hayes' flickr photostream, 2007

Bedroom door

Quinn would later claim that he observed John Lawrence, who lived in the apartment, and his guest Tyron Garner, engaging in anal sex and that the two men continued to have sex for about a minute despite his yelling at them to stop.[10] Lilly, the only other deputy who claimed to have seen the two men having sex, contradicted Quinn by stating that the sex stopped as soon as the deputies entered the room.[11]

In any event, after the deputies barged into his bedroom, an obviously distraught Lawrence began screaming at them, asking why they were in his apartment and demanding that they leave immediately. For his part, Quinn yelled back at Lawrence complaining that he could have been shot. (The officers did not find a gun in the apartment.) Quinn then handcuffed Lawrence and led him, wearing only his underwear, into the living room. Garner, who remained silent during the verbal confrontation between Lawrence and Quinn, was permitted to pull up his pants and to walk into the living room of his own accord.[12]

In the living room, the deputies sat Lawrence and Garner down. They were soon also joined there by Robert Eubanks, a former boyfriend of Garner's who admitted that he had called the police with the false story about a gun because he was jealous that Lawrence and Garner were spending the night together. But Deputy Quinn seemed more troubled by the fact that Lawrence and Garner had, in his view, refused to stop having sex after he had ordered them to do so. In the meantime, Lawrence remained livid at the deputies' conduct, accusing them of acting like the "Gestapo" and as "jack-booted thugs." Lawrence complained that the officers were "harassing" Garner and him because they were gay.[13]

A few minutes later, Sergeant Kenneth Adams of the sheriff's department arrived at the scene. Quinn told Adams that he wanted not just to give a citation to Lawrence and Garner for having violated Texas's sodomy statute, a Class C misdemeanor (punishable by a fine and not imprisonment), but also to arrest them. An arrest was justified, Quinn claimed, because the whole incident almost led to someone being shot.

Quinn then called the district attorney's office and spoke to a prosecutor. The deputy explained what had happened and asked whether it mattered, under the law, that the sex that Lilly and he observed had taken place in the bedroom of a private home. Texas's sodomy statute (called the Homosexual Conduct Law) was different from Georgia's in that it prohibited only sodomy between two individuals of the same sex. But the statute, the prosecutor explained to the police officer, did not make any distinctions depending on the location where the conduct took place.

Quinn proceeded to place Lawrence and Garner under arrest. (The deputies also arrested Eubanks, charging him with filing a false report.) Garner was handcuffed and led down to the police car without incident, but Lawrence refused to accompany the deputies out of his home. The officers then dragged Lawrence down a set of concrete steps, causing parts of his legs to bruise and bleed.

The men were driven in separate patrol cars to the police station. While there, they were fingerprinted, booked, and taken to a large cell that held dozens of male prisoners. Lawrence and Garner remained in that cell for 24 hours, after which they were arraigned and released without bail.

Lawrence and Garner could have pled guilty to the charges, paid a small fine, and gone on with their lives. But neither man chose to do that. Although they were not active in gay rights causes, the two men understood that they had the opportunity to challenge the constitutionality of Texas's sodomy law, and in doing so, that their case might lead the Supreme Court to overrule *Bowers v. Hardwick*. After consulting with their lawyers, the two men decided to plead "no contest" to the charges, which allowed them to pay fines without admitting any guilt, and to challenge the constitutionality of the Texas Homosexual Conduct Law.

The challenge was filed in the state courts, where the emphasis was on the equal protection aspects of the case. The crux of the legal argument was that Texas did not have a valid justification for allowing straight individuals to engage in consensual sodomy but not gay ones. The Texas courts, however, upheld the statute after concluding that it was rational for the legislature to believe that same-sex sodomy is more morally problematic than different-sex sodomy.[14]

After losing their case in the state courts, Lawrence and Garner filed a certiorari petition with the U.S. Supreme Court. A few months later, the Court decided to hear the case, announcing that it would entertain both the equal protection and the due process challenge to the Homosexual Conduct Law. In doing so, the Court noted that it was willing to tackle directly the question of whether *Hardwick* should be overruled. The stage was now set for what would likely be the most important LGBT rights decision in the Court's history.

The lead lawyer representing Lawrence and Garner before the U.S. Supreme Court was Ruth Harlow, an attorney with the Lambda Legal Defense and Education Fund (now known as "Lambda Legal"). As Harlow saw the case, the legal arguments in favor of striking down Texas's sodomy statute could be boiled down to two easy-to-understand principles: first, that the police do not belong in people's bedrooms; and second, that this is as true for the bedrooms of LGBT people as it is for those of straight ones.

Harlow believed that the brief should lead off with a long section on why the Homosexual Conduct Law violated substantive due process rights. The fact that the Court had granted review not only of the equal protection claim but also of the due process one meant that at least four Justices were open to the idea of overruling *Hardwick*. By beginning the brief with the due process argument, Harlow sought to signal to the Court that the two men and their lawyers were confident in their view that *Hardwick* had been incorrectly decided.

One of the biggest challenges facing Harlow and the other drafters of the brief was how to talk to the Justices about gay sex. The *Hardwick* Court had accepted both the notion that gay sex was morally problematic and that homosexuality and sodomy were indistinguishable; or more bluntly put, the *Hardwick* Court had dismissed LGBT people as immoral sodomites. Given its narrow view of LGBT individuals, it was not surprising that the *Hardwick* Court also concluded that there was no constitutionally relevant connection between gay sex on the one hand, and marriage, family, and relationships on the other.

In order to convey to the Court that there was something more momentous at stake in *Lawrence* than the mere right to engage in anal or oral sex, Harlow decided that the brief should use the term "sexual intimacy" rather than "sodomy" or "sex." Using "sexual intimacy," which appeared 23 times in the brief's final version, conveyed the idea that same-sex sexual conduct can be accompanied by commitment and love. The *Hardwick* Court had framed the legal issue in the case narrowly by asking whether the Constitution recognized a fundamental right to engage in homosexual sodomy. It was crucial that Lambda's *Lawrence* brief persuade the Court to be more expansive in its constitutional analysis by viewing the case as one that implicated not only the right to engage in particular sexual acts, but also the right to make the exceedingly personal and sensitive choice of whom to be sexually intimate with.

For several decades, legal advocates had grounded the due process right at issue in cases such as *Lawrence* in considerations of privacy. Harlow, however, did not want to rely too much on the right to privacy in the brief because she feared that doing so might lead her clients' case to get caught up in the deep disagreements among the Justices about the advisability, and continued viability, of *Roe v. Wade*.

The fundamental right to privacy can be thought of as having two components, one spatial and the other decisional. The former relates to the notion that privacy considerations limit the state's authority to regulate what takes place in certain locations (such as the home). The latter refers to the idea that privacy concerns also limit the state's power to legislate in matters that affect personal and intimate decisions made by individuals (such as whether to procreate). The brief made use of the right to privacy in a spatial sense by emphasizing the need to protect the home from governmental intrusion. Yet, when it came to discussing the need to protect the personal and intimate decisions of individuals, the brief emphasized the concept of "liberty" rather than that of "privacy."

One of the criticisms frequently raised against *Roe v. Wade* is that the opinion was grounded in a concept—that of privacy—that is not mentioned in the Constitution. But the Fourteenth Amendment does explicitly protect "liberty," thus providing a textual legitimacy to the brief's arguments about personal autonomy that would have been lacking if it had focused more on considerations of decisional privacy.

The question of which personal and intimate decisions are protected by the Constitution is one of the most intractable and difficult in modern American jurisprudence because, not surprisingly, it often arises in the context of controversial issues such as sex, reproduction, and abortion. The main point made by Lambda's brief in *Lawrence* was that wherever the outer boundaries of constitutionally protected liberty might lie, an adult's choice of sexual partners surely fell within them. As the brief put it, "the choice of one's partner, and whether and how to connect sexually are profound attributes of personhood where compulsion by the state is anathema to liberty. Thus, the essential associational freedom here is the freedom to structure one's own private sexual intimacy with another adult."[15]

The brief also directly challenged the *Hardwick* Court's assertion that there was no connection between LGBT sexual intimacy and marriage, family, and relationships. Harlow knew that in the years between *Hardwick* and *Lawrence*, the nation had become increasingly aware of the ways in which LGBT people go about forming and maintaining families and relationships. Harlow also knew that the Justices were cognizant of the many family law cases involving LGBT parties, including the challenges to same-sex marriage bans, that had been litigated in the lower courts during those years. These cases undermined the old stereotype of LGBT people as individuals who were uninterested in or incapable of maintaining strong and committed relationships with their partners. To further support this point, the brief cited the findings of the 2000 census that identified more than 600,000 households composed of same-sex partners nationally, 43,000 of which were in Texas alone. The brief also pointed to sources that estimated that a large number of children across the country were being raised by LGBT parents.

While the first part of the brief addressed the substantive due process issues, the second tackled the question of equal protection. The brief did not ask the Court to subject the Homosexual Conduct Law to heightened scrutiny under the Equal Protection Clause. Instead, it contended that the law was unconstitutional even under the highly deferential rational basis standard of review.

To defend that position, the brief noted that the Texas legislature in 1973 had repealed the sodomy statute as applied to heterosexuals, while at the same time (and for the first time) targeted LGBT people by explicitly proscribing their sexual intimacy. This unequal legal proscription imposed on them a "badge of criminality" that made them "unequal in myriad spheres of everyday life."[16] The existence of sodomy laws, the brief noted, was frequently used as a reason to deny LGBT individuals the opportunity to have custody of or visitation with their children, to get jobs in the public sector, and to benefit from the protection afforded by hate-crime legislation.

The only justification that the state was proffering for the differential treatment of LGBT people when it came to sodomy was that it was appropriate for the law to reflect the moral views of a majority of citizens. Lambda's brief raised two objections to this argument: First, the state's justification was tautological because it amounted to little more than a contention that the law was necessary because the citizens of Texas thought that it was necessary. Second, the enforcement of majoritarian morality cannot, by itself, serve as a sufficient justification for a law that targets some individuals for criminal prosecution but not others.

Finally, the brief noted that, for several decades now, there had been a steady move across the country to decriminalize sodomy. While in 1960, all 50 states had sodomy statutes on the books, by the time *Lawrence* reached the Court, only 13 jurisdictions still had them (which was in turn about half the number that had them in 1986 when the Court decided *Hardwick*). This showed the growing skepticism across the country about the advisability of regulating consensual sodomy through the criminal law.

The lead lawyer representing the government was William Delmore, the chief appellate lawyer in the Houston district attorney's office. In his brief, Delmore urged the Court not to focus on the more recent trend of decriminalization of sodomy but instead to look to the government's long-standing regulation of consensual sex in the United States, one that encompassed not only the criminalization of sodomy but also of adultery and fornication.

Earlier Supreme Court cases had indicated that in order for a right to be recognized as fundamental, it had to be deeply rooted in the nation's history and traditions.[17] The gradual but incomplete decriminalization that had taken place in the previous 40 years, Delmore argued, was not enough to satisfy this standard. As his brief succinctly put it, "[T]he petitioners mistake new growth for deep roots."[18] Delmore also argued that the conduct for which the defendants were arrested had nothing to do with what he characterized (in a decidedly nonsecular choice of words) as the "sacred choices" of marriage, conception, and parenthood. Not surprisingly, Delmore on this point relied on what he contended was the ongoing constitutional viability of *Hardwick*. Sixteen years was too short a period for the Court to change its mind about whether there was a fundamental right to engage in homosexual sodomy. Delmore also contended that it was legitimate for the government to be concerned with not only the physical well-being of its citizens but also with their moral well-being.

The Supreme Court frequently waits until the end of its term in late June to release its hardest-fought and most controversial decisions. In June 2003, with four days remaining in the term, Harlow traveled from New York to Washington, D.C. It was her intention to sit in the courtroom during those days until the Justices released their ruling in *Lawrence*. Three of the days went by without the issuance of the opinion, meaning that the Court would rule in the case on the term's very last day.

Harlow was guardedly optimistic that her clients would prevail on their equal protection claim, but she feared that there might not be the necessary five votes to overrule *Hardwick*. She was thrilled, therefore, when Justice Anthony Kennedy, in reading the Court's opinion from the bench, started by discussing the ways in which the Constitution protects the rights of liberty and autonomy of individuals to make important decisions about their lives. A few minutes later, as Kennedy explained how the Court had made a terrible mistake in *Hardwick* and how that case had to be overruled, tears welled up in Harlow's eyes. And she was not alone. There were several other LGBT rights supporters in the packed courtroom quietly sobbing as Justice Kennedy spoke. The same Court that in *Hardwick* had dismissed the notion that the Constitution provided protection in matters of sexual intimacy to LGBT people as "facetious" was at that very moment issuing an opinion in which it recognized the basic human dignity of LGBT individuals.[19] The contrast between what had happened 17 years earlier and what was taking place on that June day in 2003 could not have been more stark.

The Court in *Hardwick*, Kennedy explained, failed to understand the extent of the liberty interest at issue in that case. The litigation over the Georgia statute had not been, as the Court had concluded in 1986, about the right to engage in sodomy. To think of the claim in that narrow way was demeaning to Mr. Hardwick in the same way that it would be demeaning to a married couple to suggest that their marriage was only about sexual intercourse. Sodomy laws, in addition to proscribing particular sexual acts, Kennedy explained, also seek to control personal relationships. Kennedy added that the Constitution requires that individuals, in the absence of demonstrated harm to self or others, be allowed to participate in intimate relationships of their choice, especially within the confines of their homes. Kennedy made clear that this constitutional right applied to everyone, including LGBT people.

Most of Kennedy's opinion involved a detailed critique of *Hardwick*. Not only had the Court in that case framed the issue too narrowly, it had also simplified the historical record. There is no long-standing tradition in this country of laws aimed exclusively at same-sex sexual conduct. While it was true that American sodomy laws could be traced back to the English Reformation Parliament of 1533, it was not until the 1970s that some jurisdictions for the first time explicitly criminalized same-sex sexual relations. Prior to that point, Kennedy explained, sodomy laws were aimed at condemning nonprocreative sex in general rather than gay sex in particular.

Kennedy also noted how the *Hardwick* opinion was inconsistent with what he called an "emerging awareness" that adults have important liberty interests in making decisions about their sexual lives.[20] This recognition was reflected in the clear trend among states, starting in the 1960s, to decriminalize sodomy. Furthermore, although the Court in *Hardwick* had relied on what it took to be Western civilization's clear condemnation of homosexuality, Kennedy noted that the European Court of Human Rights had held that the criminalizing of consensual same-sex sexual conduct violated the European Convention on Human Rights.[21]

Finally, Kennedy explained that the Court's substantive due process precedents did not allow the state to criminalize conduct based solely on moral judgments. This was particularly true when the conduct in question implicated the liberty interests of individuals to make decisions about their sexual practices. Those who engage in same-sex sexual conduct, Kennedy wrote, "are entitled to respect for their private lives. The State cannot demean their existence or control their destiny by making their private sexual conduct a crime."[22]

The LGBT community across the country held rallies to celebrate the Court's ruling in *Lawrence*. In Houston, several hundred people gathered in front of City Hall for a celebration that included an appearance by Lawrence and Garner. Celebratory rallies were also held in Boston, Chicago, Detroit, Los Angeles, New York, and several other cities. There was much for LGBT people to be happy about: The Supreme Court had lifted from their collective backs the heavy stigma that came with the fact that, until a few hours earlier, their intimate sexual conduct could be deemed criminal by the state.

Holy Outlaw's flickr photostream, May 12, 2006

Gay rights

In the years following *Hardwick*, LGBT rights opponents had frequently argued that lesbians and gay men were not entitled to equal treatment under the law because they engaged in conduct that the state could criminalize. If the state could put lesbians and gay men in jail for engaging in consensual sex, the argument went, then surely the government could also, in implementing a wide spectrum of social policies, adopt laws and regulations that privileged heterosexuality over homosexuality. One of the most important aspects of *Lawrence* is that, by overruling *Hardwick*, it took away from LGBT rights opponents the ability to defend discriminatory policies against gay people on the ground that the Supreme Court of the United States had given its constitutional stamp of approval to the use of the criminal law as a means to discourage homosexuality.

But *Lawrence*'s importance lies not only in its overruling of *Hardwick*, but also in the way in which it did so. While the *Hardwick* Court summarily dismissed the notion that there was any connection between homosexuality and the types of relationships and families valued by heterosexuals, the *Lawrence* Court spoke of a common human dignity that is implicated whenever individuals make decisions related to sexual intimacy and relationships. Rather than relegating same-sex sexuality to that of the hidden, shameful, and degrading, as *Hardwick* had done, the *Lawrence* Court made it clear that the choices LGBT people make about sexual intimacy are as closely linked to their dignity as human beings as are those of heterosexuals.

Endnotes

1. Professor of Law and Judge Frederick Lacey Scholar, Rutgers University School of Law (Newark). Some of the material contained in this chapter appeared previously in Carlos A. Ball, *From the Closet to the Courtroom: Five LGBT Lawsuits That Have Changed Our Nation* (Beacon Press 2010).

2. Lawrence v. Texas: *The Fundamental Right That Dare Not Speak Its Name*, 117 Harv. L. Rev. 1893, 1951 (2004).

3. 381 U.S. 479 (1965).

4. 405 U.S. 438 (1972).

5. 410 U.S. 113 (1973).

6. *Bowers v. Hardwick*, 478 U.S. 186 (1986).

7. *Id*. at 94.

8. Petitioner's Brief, *Bowers v. Hardwick*, U.S. Supreme Court, No. 85-140, at 27.

9. *See, e.g., Commonwealth v. Wasson*, 842 S.W.2d 487 (Ky. 1992); *Campbell v. Sundquist*, 926 S.W.2d 250 (Tenn. Ct. App. 1996).

10. Dale Carpenter, *The Unknown Past of* Lawrence v. Texas, 102 Mich. L. Rev. 1464, 1482 (2004).

11. *Id*. at 1488.

12. William N. Eskridge Jr., *Dishonorable Passions: Sodomy Laws in America, 1861-2003* 300 (Viking Adult 2008).

13. Carpenter, *supra* note 10, at 1483.

14. *See Lawrence v. Texas*, 41 S.W.3d 349 (Tex. Ct. App. 2001).

15. Petitioner's Brief, *Lawrence v. Texas*, U.S. Supreme Court, No. 02-102, at 12-13.

16. *Id*. at 34.

17. *See, e.g., Washington v. Glucksberg*, 521 U.S. 702, 720-721 (1997).

18. Respondent's Brief, *Lawrence v. Texas*, U.S. Supreme Court, No. 02-102, at 14.

19. *Lawrence v. Texas*, 539 U.S. 558 (2003).

20. *Id*. at 572.

21. *Id*. at 576 (citing *Dudgeon v. United Kingdom*, 45 Eur. Ct. H.R. (1981); *P.G. & J.H. v. United Kingdom*, App. No. 00044787/98 (Eur. Ct. H.R., Sept. 25, 2001); *Modinos v. Cyprus*, 259 Eur. Ct. H.R. (1993); *Norris v. Ireland*, 142 Eur. Ct. H.R. (1988)).

22. *Id*. at 578.

Rights of the Accused

9. Miranda v. Arizona

Gary L. Stuart

Whether innate or acquired early in life, the desire to confess—to take responsibility for a perceived misdeed—is a deep-seated impulse in us all; perhaps we want, as Sartre suggests, to return the world to a "harmony of minds," an agreement on the principles that bind us to the society in which we live. Why we wish to do this seems visceral, as immutable as physical law, and as basic to our sense of justice as the concept of right and wrong. The act of confession, it would seem, restores the world (and our psyches) to a state of balance: For every action, there must be an equal reaction—an eye for an eye, and a tooth for a tooth.

There is, however, a curious aspect to our impulse to confess. We seem to feel that in the act of contrition resides an implicit covenant: If I confess, I will be forgiven by the authority with which I have formed this covenant, for in the confession itself I make restitution. Confess, and all will be forgiven—this is what the police interrogator conveys to the suspect. Not in so many words, but the message is there—in the tone of voice, in the proffered kindness of a cigarette or cup of coffee. And in truth the suspect may be forgiven by the interrogator, whose only real requirement for achieving harmony is the confession. For the higher authority, however, the admission of wrongdoing is not the end. The ancient god of retribution must be served; the wrongdoer must pay for what he did, with his wealth, his liberty, or his life.

— wrongdoer must pay for what he did.

But does the suspect understand this? As he sits in the interrogation room and the hours pass, and the interrogator repeats the same unspoken message over and over, does he think that this whole problem can end if he simply admits to the crime? Does he always know, always remember, and always understand that his problems will only get worse? That what he says can be used against him in a court of law? Does he know that he has the legal right to remain silent and to refuse to answer the interrogator's questions?

416

Do we as a society have the obligation to make sure he knows, understands, and does not forget?

What's more, it is the case that totally innocent people frequently confess to crimes they did not commit. There are many reasons for this, including mental illness, protection of other people, a naive trust that the truth will out, a misperceived need for forgiveness, feelings of guilt for totally unrelated situations. But the single largest explanation is police-induced false confessions. It is also the case that some honest, hardworking police officers become so persuaded of the suspect's guilt that the end (a confession) subsumes the means (coercive interrogation techniques). At the end of 2010, after only a few years of investigation, there were 209 documented cases of wrongful convictions of innocent people based on unquestioned DNA evidence. *Of those individuals, 26% had made false confessions to the crimes of which they were accused.*

The problems with these situations may seem self-evident today, but before the United States Supreme Court handed down *Miranda v. Arizona*,[1] our system of justice operated under a different set of assumptions. Prior to *Miranda*, a well-informed citizen might be aware of the constitutional protection against self-incrimination, but few understood that this protection extended beyond the courtroom. In a very real sense, most Americans—certainly most white, middle-class Americans—assumed that a suspect, once in custody, was probably guilty and that police interrogation could and should continue, in private, isolated from counsel, until the suspect confessed. In general, police held this belief as well and saw no problem with concealing the fact that the suspect's confession would be used to incriminate him. Nor did they see any problem with pandering to the suspect's psychological desire to confess. Scarcely anyone outside the realm of psychology believed a person would confess to something he had not done; and even those who knew better could find comfort in the naive belief that such false confessions would easily be discovered and never used unscrupulously to convict an innocent person.

In the middle of the last century, however, American society began to question deep-rooted assumptions about race, about gender, and about law. The war, to some extent, had desegregated the army, and returning black GIs, having fought for their country, could not help but resent their lack of freedom at home. Then, too, the war effort had brought women into sectors of the workforce long reserved for men. Suddenly they were being asked to surrender their independence and pretend they could not handle a man's job.

Finally, in movies like *The Last Angry Man*, audiences were shown what could happen when the machinery of justice makes the lazy assumption that the accused must be guilty as charged. As the forces of change manifested in the struggle for civil rights and greater social and economic equity, there began a growing demand for higher education. Across the country, the university system expanded to include the children of lower- and middle-class parents, and to provide them the opportunity to enter professions that had been traditionally the province of the upper class—especially the professions of law and academe. As a new crop of lawyers and professors came of age, they pushed for egalitarian reforms, and, for the first time, the state recognized its responsibility to provide legal counsel for citizens who could not afford a lawyer. Soon thereafter, that right was extended to include pretrial procedures. But even so, the suspect had to invoke this right to have a lawyer present, and if he did not know he had the right, well, that was too bad.

- right to counsel

Miranda v. Arizona

Then one afternoon in March of 1963, a Phoenix police detective arrested a young, poor, uneducated Hispanic man in connection with a series of sexual assaults. Within a few hours the man had confessed to the crimes. His subsequent trial and conviction was swift and certain, and it seemed that, like so many others before it, the case would end there.

- Uneducated, ethnically disenfranchized.

Interrogation room 2

But there is, of course, more to this story. What happened that afternoon in the Phoenix police station began a chain of events that came to bear on a central precept of our system of justice and upon a core belief of the American way of life. Ernesto Miranda was convicted of a crime not on the strength of eyewitness testimony or physical evidence, but almost entirely because he had incriminated himself without knowing it, and without knowing that he didn't have to.

Miranda v. Arizona stands as one of the most important events in the annals of American legal history. It came as part of the groundswell for a true and universal recognition of civil liberties and a reinterpretation of that essential tenet of American justice, the right of all citizens to be treated equally under that law. Ernesto Miranda figures centrally in this story partly because he was an uneducated, ethnically disenfranchised citizen with virtually no voice to defend himself. But also, and even more important, he is central precisely because he was so obviously the perpetrator of the crimes for which he was arrested. For it is in cases when evidence and common sense so strongly dictate guilt—when all involved seem willing to waive rights set forth in our Constitution—that the law must step forward to protect the presumed innocence of the accused and provide him with the same legal protection all innocent American citizens can claim. If the system abandons the presumption of innocence in favor of advancing police interrogation techniques designed to close open cases, then the justice system will become little more than a screening door to a mushrooming prison system. Sir William Blackstone said it best in his commentaries on the Laws of England (1765-1769): "It is better that ten guilty persons escape than that one innocent suffer."

This basic tenet had been invoked many times, but never before had anyone drawn such a clear rationale from the various precedents, and never before had the argument been carried so eloquently before the Supreme Court. *Miranda* replaced the vague "totality of the circumstances" test for the admissibility of a confession with a bright-line test. The change was necessary because police interrogation techniques were specifically designed to induce suspects into unknowingly giving up their Fifth and Sixth Amendment rights. It is fair to say that the social and political climate of the day offered proponents of the Miranda Doctrine an environment receptive to their reasoning. Nevertheless, without the dedication of those responsible, and if not for the unique combination of skills they possessed, the chance might have passed, and the course of American justice might have remained unaltered for an unknowable period of time.

The *Miranda* opinion itself contains page after page of examples where police had induced suspects to confess without understanding their situation or the consequences of the confession. The cited cases all shared the same "salient features—incommunicado interrogation of individuals in a police-dominated atmosphere, resulting in self-incriminating statements without full warnings of constitutional rights." As Chief Justice Warren said:

> An understanding of the nature and setting of this in-custody interrogation is essential to our decisions today. The difficulty in

depicting what transpires at such interrogations stems from the fact that in this country they have largely taken place incommunicado. From extensive factual studies undertaken in the early 1930's, including the famous Wickersham Report to Congress by a Presidential Commission, it is clear that police violence and the "third degree" flourished at that time. In a series of cases decided by this Court long after these studies, the police resorted to physical brutality—beating, hanging, whipping—and to sustained and protracted questioning incommunicado in order to extort confessions. The Commission on Civil Rights in 1961 found much evidence to indicate that "some policemen still resort to physical force to obtain confessions."[2]

At the time he wrote the petitioner's brief, John P. Frank sensed that this particular brief would stand the test of time. For several reasons, Frank was perhaps the perfect lawyer for the job and, ultimately, more than any other individual, responsible for the line of reasoning that was to become known as the *Miranda* doctrine. A specialist in constitutional law by the time he joined the Yale law faculty in 1949, Frank had published work in the prestigious University of Chicago Law Review and had just completed the leading biographical sketch of Justice Hugo Black, for whom he had clerked during the October 1942 Supreme Court term. At the time of the *Miranda* appeals, he was working to finish his definitive study of the Warren Court. His extensive scholarship, his impressive faculty appointments, his relationship with sitting Justices, and his annual reports on the Supreme Court's published opinions put the Court well within his personal horizon.

When Frank began to formulate the *Miranda* brief, he was well aware that the argument in favor of a privilege against self-incrimination, as guaranteed by the Fifth Amendment, might be important. Likewise, he knew of scores of cases suggesting a due-process connection to the Fourteenth Amendment. *Johnson v. Zerbst*,[3] for example, had come down in 1938, the same year that Frank had passed the bar. Also, there was *Mallory v. United States*,[4] which had been decided soon after Frank's move to Arizona; and *Escobedo v. Illinois*[5] had given hope just two years earlier than *Miranda*. But Frank saw every one of these as primarily Sixth Amendment cases, which was how he expected all the amici briefs to argue the *Miranda* case. After all, the Warren Court had charted this course with its *Gideon v. Wainwright*[6] ruling three years previously, and in response to the *Gideon* ruling, Congress had modified Federal Criminal Rules 5 and 44, thereby requiring everyone in the criminal justice system to participate in the process of swiftly informing defendants of their right to counsel upon their arrest. As Frank saw it, everyone involved in the appeals would do well to remember that *Gideon* was responsible for the creation of the public defender system in America.

Thus, although in the petitioner's brief Frank wrote that the issue involved both the Sixth and Fourteenth Amendments, his opening brief cites only the Sixth, and consequently, his argument for *Miranda*'s reversal was entirely predicated on what he called the "full meaning of the Sixth Amendment." As a matter of constitutional theory, he contended, a defendant cannot "unwittingly" waive his right to a lawyer during his trial; ergo, even as a suspect, he cannot "unwittingly" waive the right in the police station. Furthermore, he reasoned that, as a matter of practicality, one couldn't know, at the beginning of a case, the precise effect of providing counsel. The precise effect will depend on the case, the lawyer, the client, and the situation. What one *can* know is that it makes little sense to establish an elaborate and costly system of appointed counsel, only to see that no counsel is appointed until it is too late to be effective.

With these basic assumptions firmly in mind, Frank built the brief's line of reasoning on the central question of "Whether the confession of a poorly educated, mentally abnormal, indigent defendant, not told of his right to counsel, taken while he is in police custody and without the assistance of counsel, which was not requested, can be admitted into evidence over specific objection based on the absence of counsel?"

For their part, the 14 amici briefs filed at the invitation of the United States Supreme Court followed suit. Each cited the Sixth Amendment as the only constitutional issue in the case. Only one brief, an amicus brief in *Davis v. North Carolina*, a case joined with *Miranda* for consideration before the Court, relied on a "right to be silent."[7]

Frank understood the importance of the case. Well before he finished and signed the final copy of the petitioner's brief, Frank had decided that the oral argument should be delivered by someone with the presence, passion, and oratory skill to carry home the facts and assertions he had so carefully fashioned in the brief. Luckily, he did not have to look far. No one was better suited to the task than John J. Flynn, Frank's own partner. Flynn argued the Fifth Amendment in response to Justice Potter Stewart's questioning during oral arguments, but until the decision came out, this was the only hint that the Supreme Court would ground *Miranda* on the Fifth rather than the Sixth Amendment.

Miranda's Impact

The sad truth is that before the *Miranda* decision, forced or coerced confessions were commonplace, usually the product of unprofessional police conduct, which was often difficult to prove. Even when it could be proved, it took a lawyer to prove it. What no one could have predicted was that Miranda Warnings would become 30-second tutorials on constitutional law and would be given thousands of times every day in cities and towns all over America.

Vectorportal's flickr photostream, March 18, 2011

Hands behind prison bars

Miranda has continued to guide the development of criminal justice jurisprudence. History was made again in 2004, when the Supreme Court handed down several cases solidifying the Miranda Doctrine in domestic criminal cases and applying the right to counsel to terrorism suspects. The domestic cases dealt with new police interrogation techniques that had been designed to produce confessions by avoiding the strictures set down in *Miranda. Yarborough v. Alvarado*[8] affirmed *Miranda*'s basic promise of protection of Fifth Amendment rights but carefully distinguished pre-custody situations in juvenile cases. *Fellers v. United States*[9] produced a rare unanimous Supreme Court decision that suppressed a suspect's in-custody confession after he had been read and had waived his Miranda rights. His "warned" confession in the police station was suppressed because it came from an earlier confession taken by the same officers at the defendant's home. *United States v. Patane*[10] tested the admissibility of physical evidence obtained by the police as a result of an unwarned confession. *Missouri v. Seibert*[11] involved an "intentional" withholding of Miranda rights by police. The officers who arrested Patrice Seibert consciously elected not to inform her of her constitutional rights as part of a strategy to get the suspect to incriminate herself. One Justice said that strategists cannot use training instructions designed to drain the substance out of *Miranda.* Thus, in these domestic criminal cases, the Court firmly continues to support the uniquely American right to remain silent, the more general right to be informed, and the somewhat global right to be represented by counsel.

The entry of foreign and domestic suspects in the war against terrorism brings an unpredictable consequence of *Miranda*'s legacy. In the past few years, the notion that an individual should have a right to remain silent has spread from police stations in America to custodial interrogations of foreign nationals in foreign countries. The larger question of the extent to which domestic Miranda rights should be respected on foreign soil or on American sovereign territory is the subject of three recent decisions handed down along with the domestic *Miranda* decisions in the last two days of the Court's October 2003 term.

In *Rasul v. Bush*,[12] the Court held that non-citizen detainees held at the U.S. naval base at Guantanamo Bay, Cuba, have a right to file habeas corpus petitions in federal courts to challenge the legality of their detention. In *Hamdi v. Rumsfeld*,[13] the Court clarified American citizen Yaser Hamdi's rights. Hamdi was detained as an "enemy combatant" for two years without access to either courts or a lawyer. The Court held that his detention was proper and may be continued but that he has a right to challenge the justification for his detention (his status as an enemy combatant) before a neutral decision-maker.

We will undoubtedly continue to struggle with how to investigate and prosecute individuals suspected of terrorist activities, but we would do well to remember that if we return to the days when law enforcement was silent on the rights of suspects—be they homegrown simple thieves or foreign-trained terrorists—then those people seeking to destroy democracy itself will have obtained one of their objectives. Justice O'Connor was at the center of the Court and the center of American thought when she wrote in the Hamdi case, "Striking the proper constitutional balance ... is of great importance to the nation during this period of ongoing combat. But it is equally vital that our calculus not give short shrift to the values that this country holds so dear or to the privilege that is American citizenship."

Endnotes

1. 384 U.S. 436 (1966).
2. *Id*. at 444.
3. 304 U.S. 458 (1938).
4. 354 U.S. 449 (1957).
5. 378 U.S. 478 (1964).
6. 372 U.S. 335 (1963).
7. This amicus brief was written by Samuel Hirshowitz and filed on behalf of 29 states, 1 commonwealth, and 1 American territory.
8. 541 U.S. 652 (2004).
9. 540 U.S. 519 (2004).
10. 542 U.S. 630 (2004).
11. 542 U.S. 600 (2004).
12. 542 U.S. 466 (2004).
13. 542 U.S. 507 (2004).

10. Gideon v. Wainwright

Penny J. White[1]

Many lawyers and non-lawyers alike know the story of Clarence Earl Gideon, the 50-year-old self-described "hobo" from Hannibal, Missouri, who, as a *pro se* inmate, successfully pressed a literal interpretation of the words of the Sixth Amendment—"[i]n all criminal prosecutions, the accused shall enjoy the right to ... have the [a]ssistance of [c]ounsel for his defence." Gideon's story was recorded by *New York Times* columnist Anthony Lewis[2] and glamorized by Hollywood, in the 1980 movie starring Henry Fonda as Gideon.

In 1961, when Gideon was arrested in Florida for breaking and entering the Bay Harbor Poolroom with the intent to commit a misdemeanor, the status of the right to counsel in criminal cases was in flux. The Sixth Amendment of the United States Constitution guaranteed the right to counsel, but only in federal criminal trials.[3] Additionally, despite its unqualified language, the Amendment originally had not been interpreted to require counsel for the indigent, but rather guaranteed the right only to those who could afford counsel.[4] But by the 1930s, the Supreme Court had recognized the essential role that the right to counsel played in securing "fundamental human rights of life and liberty" and had held that the appointment of counsel was a "jurisdictional prerequisite to a federal court's authority to deprive an accused of his life or liberty."[5] While the Sixth Amendment did not bind the state courts, the essential nature of the right to counsel and the role it played in securing a fair trial led the Court to require counsel in state cases with "special circumstances"—those in which the accused was incapable of "adequately making his own defense because of ignorance, feeble-mindedness, illiteracy or the like"[6]—and in capital cases.[7]

When a state defendant provided the Court with an opportunity to expand the right, the Court declined, noting remarkably that the "appointment of counsel is not a fundamental right, essential to a fair trial. On the contrary, the matter has generally been deemed one of legislative policy."[8] Adhering to a strong states' rights view, the Court, in *Betts v. Brady*, refused to find that due process "obligate[d] the states, whatever may be their own views, to furnish counsel in

No councel 4 needy

every such case. Every court has power, if it deems proper, to appoint counsel where that course seems to be required in the interest of fairness."[9]

Gideon was not charged with a capital case, but with an uncomplicated breaking and entering.[10] When the case was called for trial in Bay County, Florida, Gideon announced that he was "not ready." When Judge Robert L. McCrary asked why, Gideon responded, "I have no counsel. . . . I request this Court to appoint Counsel to represent me in this trial." Judge McCrary explained that Florida law required appointed counsel only in capital cases,[11] but Gideon replied in his now-famous words: "The United States Supreme Court says I am entitled to be represented by Counsel."[12]

Perhaps Gideon could have persuaded Judge McCrary to appoint counsel by alleging "special circumstances,"[13] but had he done so he would have removed the opportunity for the United States Supreme Court to address the simple question: Does the Constitution of the United States require the appointment of counsel for indigent defendants in state criminal trials?

Ironically, had Clarence Earl Gideon been arrested in any one of 45 states, he would have been provided with counsel. This is because at the time of his arrest, 45 states had constitutional or statutory provisions[14] that guaranteed the right to counsel in non-capital felony cases.[15] In only five states—Alabama, North Carolina, South Carolina, Mississippi, and Florida—were indigent defendants accused of felonies not provided with counsel.[16]

Without counsel, Gideon tried his own case, was convicted, and was sentenced to five years in prison.[17] Gideon did not appeal his conviction, but filed a *pro se* habeas corpus petition in the Florida Supreme Court.[18] Rather than alleging that he was entitled to counsel based upon the *Betts* special circumstances test, Gideon merely asserted the right to appointed counsel. The Florida Supreme Court denied the habeas petition without opinion.[19]

Against this backdrop, Gideon penned his petition to the United States Supreme Court from the Florida state prison at Raiford where inmates regarded Gideon as a "prison legal expert."[20] Some say that Gideon received assistance from another prison legal expert, albeit a more educated one. Joseph A. Peel, Jr., an attorney and municipal judge of West Palm Beach, was serving two life sentences at Raiford for the murder of a Florida circuit judge and his wife.[21] Peel's involvement might explain why Gideon asserted an across-the-board right to counsel, rather than claiming that he was entitled to counsel based on special circumstances.[22]

In his five-page handwritten petition, drafted on paper provided by the Florida Department of Corrections and bearing a list of its "Correspondence Regulations," Gideon wisely grounded his petition not only upon the Sixth Amendment, but also on the Due

Process Clause of the Fourteenth Amendment,[23] alleging that the "lower state court has decided a federal question of substance in a way not in accord with the applicable decisions of this Honorable Court." Gideon relied on and cited two decisions of the United States Supreme Court for the proposition that "counsel must be assigned to the accused if he is unable to employ one and is incapable adequately of making his own defense,"[24] but both cases involved capital offenses punishable by death.

Even if Gideon did have legal assistance from an incarcerated judge, receiving a grant of certiorari was a long shot. As Anthony Lewis, author of *Gideon's Trumpet,* notes, it is uncommon for the Supreme Court to overrule itself.[25] Granting Gideon relief would require the Court to overrule long-standing precedent, which had previously been challenged without success,[26] and to wade into the controversial federal-states' rights thicket.[27] It would also impose huge fiscal burdens and practical challenges for the states.[28]

After seeking a response to Gideon's petition for certiorari from the state of Florida, the United States Supreme Court granted the petition on June 4, 1962, specifying: "In addition to other questions presented by this case, counsel are requested to discuss the following in their briefs and oral argument: 'Should this Court's holding in *Betts v. Brady . . .* be reconsidered?'"[29] On that same day, the chief deputy clerk of the Court corresponded with Gideon, indicating that he should file a motion requesting the appointment of counsel.[30] On June 18, Gideon's motion requesting counsel was filed. The Court appointed Abe Fortas, a partner in a prominent Washington D.C. law firm, the next week.[31]

Library of Congress (photo by Marion S. Trikosko)

Abe Fortas, 1965

Fortas, a 52-year-old Yale Law graduate and editor-in-chief of the *Yale Law Journal*, was a prominent, successful, and committed lawyer described as "angry at injustice."[32] As its spokesperson, the State of Florida chose Bruce Jacob, a 26-year-old lawyer, recently graduated from Stetson Law School, and the "newest and youngest lawyer" working in the Criminal Appeals Division of the Florida Attorney General's office in Tallahassee.[33] Jacob may have been selected because he was the only lawyer in the office who had not briefed or argued a case in the Supreme Court.[34]

The Florida Attorney General's office requested other states to join as amicus protesting that a decision overruling *Betts* "would infringe on the right of the states to determine their own rules of criminal procedure."[35] The request had an unusual effect—two states (Alabama and North Carolina) filed an amicus brief on Florida's behalf, but another brief bearing the signatures of officials in 22 states was filed on behalf of Clarence Earl Gideon.[36]

During the three-hour argument that took place on January 15, 1963, Fortas argued passionately that *Betts* had to be overruled in order to secure the guarantees of a fair trial. He argued that a "civilized nation [cannot] pretend that there is a fair trial" in an adversary system unless both sides have counsel.[37] When pushed to define the limits of the right he was asserting, Fortas carefully expressed his opinion, while maintaining that the exact parameters of the right could be determined in future cases.[38] Jacob, who argued the case for the State of Florida even though he had left the Attorney General's office for private practice, described the oral argument as a "constant rain of hostile questions" and the state's position as "hopeless,"[39] but nonetheless urged the Court to be mindful of the grave consequences of overruling *Betts*: "[T]his court would be requiring the states to adopt socialism, or a welfare program."[40]

Justice Hugo Black authored the *Gideon* decision and as was the Court's custom, read portions of the decision in open court on March 18, 1963. Justice Black's biographer, Roger Newman, described the justice's elocution on that day as "folksy.... Happiness, contentment, gratification filled his voice."

If Justice Black was happy about the decision, he was not kind about what had preceded it. He referred to the *Betts* case as "an anachronism" when handed down. Relying on *Powell* the Court held:

> Governments, both state and federal, quite properly spend vast sums of money to establish machinery to try defendants accused of crime. Lawyers to prosecute are everywhere deemed essential to protect the public's interest in an orderly society. Similarly, there are few defendants charged with crime, few indeed, who fail

to hire the best lawyers they can get to prepare and present their defenses. That government hires lawyers to prosecute and defendants who have the money hire lawyers to defend are the strongest indications of the widespread belief that lawyers in criminal courts are necessities, not luxuries. The right of one charged with crime to counsel may not be deemed fundamental and essential to fair trials in some countries, but it is in ours. From the very beginning, our state and national constitutions and laws have laid great emphasis on procedural and substantive safeguards designed to assure fair trials before impartial tribunals in which every defendant stands equal before the law. This noble ideal cannot be realized if the poor man charged with crime has to face his accusers without a lawyer to assist him.[41]

For Gideon the decision meant a new trial, in which he was entitled to be represented by counsel. After Gideon requested help from the ACLU, corresponding and meeting with famed civil rights attorney Tobias Simon, Simon and another attorney, Irwin Block, interviewed witnesses and appeared on behalf of Gideon before Judge McCrary, the same judge who had originally tried Gideon. Gideon refused their representation, asked for a continuance to request that the trial be moved, and retorted, "I want to plead my own case."[42] The judge asked Gideon if he would agree to the appointment of any local lawyer. Gideon named the lawyer of his choice, W. Fred Turner, who the judge appointed, but Gideon insisted on filing his own motions.[43] Eventually, after the denial of his motions claiming that further prosecution was barred by the Double Jeopardy Clause and Florida's statute of limitations, Gideon was retried and acquitted.[44] After being released from prison, he returned to the Bay Harbor Poolroom, where a reporter asked him if he felt like he had accomplished something. Gideon responded, "Well I did."[45]

Several thousand Florida inmates agreed. Convicted without counsel, the decision meant a new trial for each, but only upon the filing of a petition for writ of habeas corpus. In order to deal with the expected flood of petitions, the Florida courts adopted a rule of criminal procedure directing that petitions be filed in the trial court of conviction.[46] Additionally, Florida's governor called on the legislature to enact a public defender system. Within two months of the decision, the Florida legislature adopted a statute creating public defender offices in each judicial circuit in the state.[47]

Similarly, other states began to adopt measures to comply with *Gideon*'s constitutional mandate.[48] Some states followed Florida's lead and adopted or authorized public defender programs; others devised counsel assignment systems. Their rapid reactions may have been triggered by subtle indications from the Supreme Court that indifference to the decision would not be tolerated. Within a few months of the *Gideon* decision, the Supreme Court set aside and remanded 31 lower court judgments.[49] Among the cases remanded were some in which counsel had been denied not at trial but at a preliminary hearing and many that were completed before the *Gideon* decision was issued. Without specifically ruling on the retroactivity of the decision, the Court set aside judgments and remanded decisions "for further consideration in light of *Gideon v. Wainwright.*"

The fundamental right to counsel that the Court recognized in *Gideon v. Wainwright* did not stagnate with the 1963 decision. The Court expanded the right to apply to criminal appeals (in a case decided the same day as *Gideon*),[50] in juvenile delinquency cases,[51] and in misdemeanor cases.[52] And for the most part, the Court has stood firm against efforts to retreat from the absolute rule.[53] But the promise of *Gideon* has not necessarily been its legacy. As Stephen Bright noted on the occasion of the 40th anniversary of the decision: "No constitutional right is celebrated so much in the abstract and observed so little in reality as the right to counsel."[54] This disconnect between the right and its realization is largely because of the unwillingness of states to devote necessary resources to fulfilling *Gideon*'s promise. If funding the fundamental right to counsel was viewed as a hurdle when *Gideon* was decided, it has become almost an insurmountable barrier to fulfillment of the right to counsel today.

When Gideon died in January 1972, he was still very much a hobo and a pauper who never quite found his way. Years after his burial in an unmarked Missouri grave, a tombstone was added, bearing this epithet: "Each era finds an improvement in law for the benefit of mankind."[55] The recognition of the right to counsel for the accused was indeed a staggering improvement in the law, but the fulfillment of the guarantee remains the task of the present era.

Endnotes

1. Elvin E. Overton Distinguished Professor of Law and Director, Center for Advocacy and Dispute Resolution, University of Tennessee College of Law. I am grateful for the thorough and creative research skills of Joel Hayes, a third-year student at the College of Law.

2. Anthony Lewis, *Gideon's Trumpet* (Vintage 1964) (hereafter *Gideon's Trumpet*).

3. *Barron v. Baltimore*, 32 U.S. (7 Pet.) 243 (1833) (holding that the freedoms guaranteed by the Bill of Rights apply only to the federal government and do not restrict the actions of state government).

4. *See Andersen v. Treat*, 172 U.S. 24, 29 (1898) (holding that the Sixth Amendment guarantees the assistance of counsel of defendant's "own selection").

5. *Johnson v. Zerbst*, 304 U.S. 458, 463 & 467 (1938) (holding that "[s]ince the Sixth Amendment constitutionally entitles one charged with crime to the assistance of counsel, compliance with this constitutional mandate is an essential jurisdictional prerequisite to a federal court's authority to deprive an accused of his life or liberty").

6. *Powell v. Alabama*, 287 U.S. 45, 71 (1932); *see also Betts v. Brady*, 316 U.S. 455 (1942) (holding that due process requires state courts to appoint counsel when circumstances require counsel in order to assure a fair trial).

7. *See Hamilton v. Alabama*, 368 U.S. 52, 55 (1961); *Powell v. Alabama*, 287 U.S. 45, 71 (1932). Although *Powell* was a capital case, it also was a case involving special circumstances.

8. *Betts v. Brady*, 316 U.S. 455, 471 (1942).

9. 316 U.S. at 472.

10. *Gideon's Trumpet*, at 57-62.

11. Bruce R. Jacob, the attorney who argued for the state of Florida in the Supreme Court, suggests that Judge McCrary misstated Florida law, which required appointment of counsel in cases with special circumstances under the *Betts* doctrine and recognized inherent judicial authority to appoint counsel as well. Bruce R. Jacob, *Memories and Reflections About* Gideon v. Wainwright, 33 Stetson L. Rev. 181, 201 (2003) (hereafter Jacob).

12. Jacob, at 200-201.

13. Jacob says that although Gideon had previous experience with the courts, a thorough investigation would have revealed that he had "a serious problem with alcohol" which "might have qualified as a special circumstance under *Betts*." Jacob, at 203.

14. The fact that 12 of the original 13 colonies provided for the assistance of counsel reflected an obvious rejection of the English common-law rule, which provided counsel only to persons charged with misdemeanors. W. Beaney, *The Right to Counsel in American Courts* 8-14 (Praeger 1955).

15. John F. Decker & Thomas J. Lorigan, *Right to Counsel: The Impact of* Gideon v. Wainwright *in the Fifty States*, 3 Creighton L. Rev. 102, 104-105 (1969-1970) (noting that only 5 of the 45 states that provided counsel in non-capital felony cases provided counsel to those accused of misdemeanors).

16. *Id*. at 102.

17. Gideon had four prior felony convictions, including one in federal court in which he had been provided with appointed counsel. *Gideon's Trumpet*, at 98.

18. Jacob, at 212.

19. *Gideon v. Cochran*, 135 So. 2d 746 (Fla. 1961).

20. *Gideon's Trumpet*, at 97.

21. Jacob, at 214.

22. Many years after the decision, Jacob mused whether the state could have mustered sufficient evidence to prove that Gideon was an alcoholic, thereby conceding that Gideon met the *Betts* special circumstances test, and avoiding, or delaying, the overruling of *Betts*. Jacob, at 231.

23. Petition for Certiorari, *Gideon v. Cochran* (http://www.ct.gov/ocpd/cwp/view.asp?a=4087&q=479204).

24. *Id*. at 3-4 (citing *Tomkins v. Missouri*, 323 U.S. 485 (1945)); *Williams v. Kaiser*, 323 U.S. 471 (1945).

25. *Gideon's Trumpet*, at 85 (noting that at the time of Gideon's petition, the Supreme Court had overruled itself "[a]pproximately one hundred times in its history").

26. *Betts v. Brady*, 316 U.S. 455 (1942).

27. Gideon is credited with understanding the magnitude of the issue beyond the particulars of his case. He is said to have commented to a prison visitor, "In *Betts versus Brady* they were trying to allow 'em their states' rights. They gave the state courts discretion, but they don't use any discretion. They just say no. They talk about states' rights. I think there is only one state—the United States." *Gideon's Trumpet*, at 95-96 (1964).

28. The fiscal and practical considerations were considered so significant that the state of Florida appended a study to its brief showing that if the decision resulted in a right to counsel, and was applied retroactively, more than 4,500 of Florida's 8,000 inmates would have to be retried or released. Jacob, at 222.

29. *Gideon v. Cochran*, 370 U.S. 908 (1962) (citations omitted).

30. *Gideon's Trumpet*, at 46.

31. *Gideon's Trumpet*, at 48-49.

32. *Gideon's Trumpet*, at 53-54.

33. Jacob, at 217.

34. Jacob, at 217-218.

35. Jacob, at 223.

36. Jacob, at 223. The state of Oregon supported the amicus brief filed on behalf of Gideon, but filed an additional amicus brief as well. A fourth amicus brief was filed by the American Civil Liberties Union (ACLU). *Id*. at 224. *See also Gideon's Trumpet*, at 146-154.

37. *Gideon's Trumpet*, at 171.

38. *Gideon's Trumpet*, at 173.

39. Jacob, at 244.

40. *Gideon's Trumpet*, at 178.

41. *Gideon v. Wainwright*, 372 U.S. at 344-345 (1963).

42. *Gideon's Trumpet*, at 226.

43. Paul Rashkind reports that Gideon's "stubborn pursuit of the right to counsel was mixed with what is politely described as a quixotic personality." Paul M. Rashkind, Gideon v. Wainwright: *A 40th Birthday Celebration and the Threat of a Midlife Crisis*, 77 Fla. Bar J. 4 (March 2003). Rashkind's description flows from Gideon's request, and then refusal, of the two ACLU lawyers and his rejection of the public defender's office appointed to represent him. *Id*. at 16.

44. *Gideon's Trumpet*, at 224-226.

45. *Id*. at 238.

46. *See Roy v. Wainwright*, 151 So. 2d 825 (Fla. 1963).

47. *Gideon's Trumpet*, at 203.

48. *Id*.

49. Cases from Alabama, Florida, Illinois, Louisiana, Maryland, Missouri, North Carolina, Ohio, Oklahoma, and Pennsylvania were set aside. *Gideon's Trumpet*, at 204.

50. *Douglas v. California*, 372 U.S. 353 (1963).

51. *In re Gault*, 387 U.S. 1 (1967).

52. *Argersinger v. Hamlin*, 405 U.S. 25 (1972).

53. *See Alabama v. Shelton*, 535 U.S. 654 (2002), *but see* David Cole, Gideon v. Wainwright *and* Strickland v. Washington: *Broken Promises*, in *Criminal Procedure Stories* 101, 102 (Carol S. Steiker ed., Foundation Press 2006) (positing that the "real story of the right to counsel is not Gideon's, but that of David Leroy Washington, whose case 'determined the actual content of the right to counsel for the poor'").

54. Stephen B. Bright, *Turning Celebrated Principles into Reality*, The Champion 6 (Jan.-Feb. 2003).

55. Stephen R. Glassroth, *Gideon's Trumpet: The Clarion Call for Justice*, The Champion 61 (Jan.-Feb. 2003).

Punishment

11. Furman v. Georgia *and* Roper v. Simmons

Sean D. O'Brien

The briefs discussed in this chapter were submitted on behalf of prisoners sentenced to death, and are outstanding examples of the use of persuasive narrative writing to overcome formidable obstacles.

The death penalty is the most highly charged legal, emotional, and ideological issue to come before the United States Supreme Court. The Court's reticence to entangle itself with capital punishment can be seen in virtually all of its decisions in death cases. In *Frances v. Resweber*,[1] the Court found no constitutional prohibition against a second attempted execution by electrocution after a first attempt failed. In *Solesbee v. Balkcomb*,[2] the Court saw no constitutional problem with the warden of San Quentin serving as inquisitor, judge, and jury on the issue of whether Solesbee's psychosis rendered him incompetent to be executed. Finally, just a year earlier, the Court in *McGautha v. California*[3] rejected by a vote of six to three an equal protection challenge to capital punishment in spite of the compelling evidence of racial and economic disparity in the imposition of the death penalty. Since that decision, President Richard Nixon's newest appointment to the Supreme Court, William Rehnquist, decidedly tilted the Court to the right, particularly on law-and-order issues.

Even cases decided in favor of prisoners presented obstacles to constitutional attacks on the death penalty. *Trop v. Dulles*[4] established limits on the ability to exclude from capital cases jurors with conscientious scruples against capital punishment and explicitly assumed the right of states to exclude for cause jurors who could not vote to sentence a defendant to death. In *Trop v. Dulles*,[5] Chief Justice Earl Warren speculated, "[I]n a day when [capital punishment] is still widely accepted, it cannot be said to violate the constitutional concept of cruelty." *Witherspoon v. Illinois*.[6] The legal landscape was anything but friendly to a broad-based Eighth Amendment challenge to the death penalty.

If the law was hostile to a constitutional challenge to capital punishment, the grisly facts of individual murder cases presented no
less of a challenge. Consider the crimes of Earnest James Aikens,
a diagnosed antisocial personality with a lengthy criminal history,
who was sentenced to die for raping and stabbing to death elderly
Mary Winifred Eaton after burglarizing her home in 1965. Three
years earlier, Aikens had burglarized the home of 25-year-old Kathleen Nell Dodd in the night while her husband was away and her
two young children were sleeping. After Aikens raped her, Ms. Dodd
attempted to flee, but Aikens overtook her and stabbed her to death
in a neighbor's driveway. Ms. Dodd was five months' pregnant.

Achieving victory in *Furman v. Georgia* and subsequent death
penalty cases was no easy task. Capital punishment seemed solidly
entrenched in American politics, law, and culture. A strong majority
of states (41) had death penalty statutes on the books. The crimes
for which people had been sent to death row were uniformly deplor-
able, mostly murder and rape, and a handful of armed robbers.
Capital punishment was vigorously defended by powerful law
enforcement and government interests. The petitioner's brief in
Furman v. Georgia represents a masterful use of narrative to bring
the Court to a position that previously appeared hopeless, but in
retrospect appears inevitable.

Professor Anthony G. Amsterdam, principal author of the briefs
in *Furman v. Georgia* and the companion case of *Aikens v.
California*, is the main architect of the modern case against the
death penalty in America. He describes his basic approach: "Once
you assume the responsibilities of attorney to client, you do what
has to be done. You leave no stone unturned."[7] In *Furman* and its
companion cases, the challenge was to craft a persuasive narrative
that would guide the Court over and around the sizable obstacles to
arrive at the conclusion that the death penalty should be abolished.
In order to write a credible narrative with the integrity necessary to
achieve this lofty goal, it was first necessary to deal with the officially
established narrative that drove the outcome in the Court (below)—
crimes such as those of Earnest Aikens.

Prof. Amsterdam told the story of Aikens' crime with complete
candor. One could imagine Aikens in his prison cell receiving a copy
of Prof. Amsterdam's brief, and wondering whose side his lawyer
was on. Prof. Amsterdam wrote, "[H]is were ghastly crimes—as any
intentional killing of a human being is a ghastly crime—and were
attended by aggravating features that must necessarily arouse the
deepest human instincts of loathing and repugnance." Yet that concession was essential to Prof. Amsterdam's point that "if the State
may constitutionally punish petitioner's crimes with death, it may
also constitutionally be used to punish murders unattended by the
same features. California's statutes and its courts in fact do so; and

we can conceive of no Eighth Amendment principle which, allowing death punishment in particular circumstances of this case, could confine it to them. *Cf. Furman v. Georgia*, No. 69-5003." With that concession, Prof. Amsterdam acknowledged the ugly facts of Aikens' crime and turned the Court's attention to the plight of William Henry Furman.

Furman's case involved a different challenge because of the paucity of information in the record. Although Furman's trial counsel could have constructed a compelling narrative based upon Furman's tragic life story of poverty, mental illness, and cognitive impairment, virtually no evidence was presented on Furman's behalf. Jury selection commenced at 10 A.M., and at 3 P.M. the same day the case was submitted to the jury for its life-or-death decision. The record was devoid of traditional narrative elements of conflict, action, image, detail, and character. In Prof. Amsterdam's telling of the tale, this weakness became its strength.

Although all homicides are terrible crimes, Furman's crime was far less aggravated than Aikens'. Furman broke into the Savannah, Georgia home of William Joseph Micke, Jr., who was found on his kitchen floor, killed by a single gunshot in the chest. "The bullet which produced this wound had been fired through the kitchen door from the outside while the door was closed. Only one bullet hole was found in the door, which was constructed of solid plywood with no window."[8] There was no evidence that any other shot was fired. Furman's fingerprints were found on a washing machine on the Mickes' back porch, and ballistics matched the fatal bullet to a .22-caliber pistol found on Furman at the time of his arrest. Furman told detectives that Micke tried to grab him, so he fled. Mr. Micke hit the door, which slammed shut, and then Furman fired one time through the door as he ran. Prof. Amsterdam provided a glimpse into Furman's limited intellectual functioning by quoting Furman's own inarticulate address to the jury:

> I admit going to these folks' home and they did caught me in there and I was coming back out, backing up and there was a wire down there on the floor. I was coming out backwards and fell back and I didn't intend to kill nobody. I didn't know they was behind the door. The gun went off and I didn't know nothing about no murder until they arrested me, and when the gun went off I was down on the floor and I got up and ran. That's all to it.[9]

Even if Furman's inarticulate statement were true, the Georgia Supreme Court explained that it would not matter because he would still be eligible for the death penalty under Georgia's felony murder rule. Prof. Amsterdam reduced the court's ruling to its essence. "[A]s the case comes to this Court, it must be taken to be one in which the Georgia courts have permitted the imposition of a death sentence for an unintended killing, committed by the accidental discharge of a pistol during petitioner's flight from an abortive burglary attempt."

Factors from Furman's background and life circumstances suggested that mercy was appropriate, but none were in the trial record. As a sculptor uses negative space to involve the observer, Prof. Amsterdam subtly demonstrated the unfairness of Furman's trial and provided glimpses into Furman's human frailties by accentuating what was absent. He wrote, "The jury which sentenced petitioner to die knew nothing about him other than the events of one half-hour of his life on the morning of August 12, 1967—as just recited—and the fact that he was black."[10]

Prof. Amsterdam painstakingly mined the record for insights into Furman and his mental condition. He pointed out that that Furman was a pauper, and the State of Georgia capped attorney fees and expenses for his defense at $150. From a colloquy between Furman and his lawyer about the defendant's right to testify or make an unsworn statement, Prof. Amsterdam learned that Furman dropped out of school in the sixth grade. According to his unsworn statement to the jury, Furman was 26 years old. The trial record omitted the report of a pretrial mental evaluation by the Georgia Central State Hospital concluding "that this patient should retain his present diagnosis of Mental Deficiency, Mild to Moderate, with Psychotic Episodes associated with Convulsive Disorder."[11] Furman appeared to have difficulty understanding attempts by the trial court and his lawyer to explain his right to testify or make an unsworn statement to the jury. By footnoting this narrative with an explanation of how he gleaned each aspect of Furman's identity and circumstances, Prof. Amsterdam took the Court on the same journey that he had undertaken to uncover evidence of Furman's personal story. The "conclusion" to his telling of Furman's sad tale is not a conclusion at all, but the entry point for the Court to come to Furman's rescue. Knowing virtually nothing about William Henry Furman, an all-white Georgia jury condemned him to die for an unintentional homicide. Thus, the authors of the Furman brief present an unsatisfactory state of affairs that cries out for a remedy. This becomes the backdrop for a broader, more encompassing narrative asking the U.S. Supreme Court to give birth to a vital Eighth Amendment principle striking down the death penalty. Because of the absence of limiting principles in the application of capital punishment, to kill Aikens, we necessarily authorize the killing of William Furman as well.

The effectiveness of the birth narrative in the Furman context lay in the ability to show the steady progression of society's standards of decency and respect for human dignity over time. Undeniable facts, presented with complete honesty and integrity, demonstrated that the use of capital punishment was (and is) steadily and rapidly diminishing in America and in the world. Prof. Amsterdam meticulously analyzed the Supreme Court's capital punishment cases, pointing out that the constitutionality of capital punishment under the Eighth Amendment had never squarely been presented to the Court. The constitutionality of capital punishment had always been assumed, but never decided. There was no mythical dragon to be slain, but it was time to forge a new tool to facilitate the steady march toward enlightenment. It was inevitable that when *Robinson v. California*[12] made the Eighth Amendment applicable to the states through the Fourteenth Amendment Due Process Clause, the Supreme Court would have to come to grips with the Southern institution of capital punishment, the last vestige of Jim Crow. The time had come to strike down the death penalty, and the Eighth Amendment was the right tool at the right time to get the job done.

Professor Amsterdam was driving down the highway when he heard on the radio that the Court had decided in Furman's favor. Because of the arbitrary and discriminatory use of capital punishment, "[t]hese death sentences are cruel and unusual in the same way that being struck by lightning is cruel and unusual," wrote Justice Stewart.[13] Prof. Amsterdam stopped the car. He described the burden of representing condemned men before the Supreme Court: "You represent people under a sentence of death, you're always walking around with a dozen, 50 lives on your shoulders. . . . [Y]ou worry about each and every one separately." Upon hearing the news, "I felt free for the first time in years. I thought, 'That job is done. Those guys are gonna live.'"[14]

Furman stopped the execution of 631 men and 2 women who were then under sentence of death.[15] Demographically, "the typical *Furman*-commutee was a southern male black murderer without a lengthy history of serious violence or repeated trips to prison."[16] The sentence of life without parole was an alternative to the death penalty in very few states, so nearly all of the former death row inmates are eligible for parole, and about half have been released into the community. Only a very small percentage have committed new crimes, very few of which involved violence.[17] Furman himself made parole in 1984, but continued to struggle. In 2004 he was convicted of burglary and sentenced to 20 years in prison. He is incarcerated in Georgia's Wheeler Correctional Facility and will be eligible for parole in 2016, at the age of 76.

Seven prisoners saved by *Furman* were eventually proven completely innocent. Among the innocent were Freddie Pitts and Wilbert Lee, convicted together of a Florida murder. Their appeals had just run out when *Furman* was decided. Because of *Furman*, they were still alive when new information uncovered by law enforcement proved their innocence. Chuck Culhane, after being released from death row at Sing Sing, became an award-winning poet and playwright, and collaborated with Paul Simon on the Broadway musical, *The Capeman*, about a young gang member sentenced to prison. Today Culhane is a college professor in upstate New York. Calvin Sellars, after being released from death row, became a paralegal for a prominent Houston lawyer and is now an evangelical Christian and runs his own business. Wilbert Rideau, sentenced to death in Louisiana in 1961, became a prison correspondent for National Public Radio before finally winning a new trial that resulted in his release from prison 44 years after the crime. Today he works as a consultant with the NAACP Legal Defense Fund, helping lawyers bridge the cultural divide between them and their clients on death row. "I wake up in heaven every day," he wrote in his memoir.[18]

Ken_Mayer's flickr photostream, Dec. 25, 2006

Prison bars and empty bed

Furman stopped short of abolishing the death penalty unconditionally. All nine Justices wrote separately. At 232 pages, *Furman* is one of the longest opinions in the Court's history. While Justices Brennan and Marshall found that capital punishment violates the Eighth Amendment in all cases, Justices Douglas, Stewart, and White concluded that "the Eighth and Fourteenth Amendments cannot tolerate the infliction of a sentence of death under legal systems that permit this unique penalty to be so wantonly and so freakishly imposed."[19] Thus, the door was left open for states to tinker with their death penalty statutes and resume executions. Four years later, *Gregg v. Georgia*[20] gave a green light to a capital-sentencing scheme calling for a second stage of trial in which the jury could impose the death penalty if it found certain aggravating circumstances, unless mitigating factors justify mercy. In this context, "mercy" takes the form of a sentence of life without the possibility of parole, which inmates call "death by incarceration" or "death on the installment plan." In the movie *Shawshank Redemption*, Morgan Freeman's character, Ellis Boyd Redding, explained, "They send you here for life and that's exactly what they take, the part that counts anyway."[21] Some form of this scheme, based largely on the Model Penal Code, was enacted in most jurisdictions that returned to capital punishment after *Furman*.[22]

Several states, including Missouri, Louisiana, and North Carolina, responded to *Furman*'s concern about unguided sentencing discretion by mandating the death penalty for every defendant convicted of murder. Although *Furman* had attacked sentencing discretion, respect for human dignity demanded individualized sentencing decisions:

> A process that accords no significance to relevant facets of the character and record of the individual offender or the circumstances of the particular offense excludes from consideration in fixing the ultimate punishment of death the possibility of compassionate or mitigating factors stemming from the diverse frailties of humankind. It treats all persons convicted of a designated offense not as uniquely individual human beings, but as members of a faceless, undifferentiated mass to be subjected to the blind infliction of the penalty of death.[23]

Thus, *Furman* gave birth to a constitutional mandate of individualized consideration of punishment in death penalty cases. Modern standards of human decency embodied in the Eighth Amendment require a sentencer to consider "any aspect of a defendant's character or record and any of the circumstances of the offense that the defendant proffers as a basis for a sentence less than death."[24] After *Furman*, the scope of mitigating evidence that can be presented on behalf of a capital defendant is "potentially infinite"[25] and includes "anything under the sun" that the defendant proffers as a reason for a sentence less than death.[26] The Court has invalidated statutes, rules of evidence, and jury instructions that preclude jurors from responding to mitigating evidence with a life sentence. For the first time, a capital defendant has a constitutional right to present the jury with any and all evidence that demonstrates his or her intrinsic humanity. *Furman* changed the landscape of capital litigation completely and forever.

Furman also sowed the seeds for chipping away at the death penalty by challenging its application to certain categories of offenses and classes of offenders. The Court struck down the death penalty as disproportionate for crimes that did not involve the intentional killing of a human being.[27] In an opinion that lifted verbatim several passages from Prof. Amsterdam's brief in *Furman*, the Court ruled that the Eighth Amendment prohibits the execution of one who is too insane to understand that he is being executed as punishment for murder.[28] More recently, the Court has exempted persons with mental retardation[29] and juvenile offenders[30] from capital punishment. The brief in *Roper v. Simmons* addresses the latter issue. The Court's limitations on capital punishment virtually all stem from the high value that the *Furman* decision placed on every human being's innate dignity and uniqueness. This steady progression caused Justice Scalia to complain, "There is something to be said for popular abolition of the death penalty; there is nothing to be said for its incremental abolition by this Court."[31]

The second example of briefing against capital punishment is the *Roper v. Simmons* case. When the Court granted certiorari in 2004 to decide whether the Eighth Amendment barred the execution of juveniles, it had been only 15 years since the Court ruled that the Eighth Amendment did not bar the execution of 17-year-old Kevin Stanford and 16-year-old Heath Wilkins. Stanford, a black youth abandoned by his parents, was sentenced by an all-white jury to die for shooting Barbel Poore twice in the head during a robbery. Wilkins, a homeless teenager with a history of psychiatric institutionalization, stabbed Nancy Allen, a 26-year-old mother of two, while robbing a liquor store. Expressing remorse for his crime, Wilkins waived his right to counsel, pled guilty, and asked to be sentenced to death. In spite of his age and mental illness, a Clay County judge granted his request and sentenced him to die. When he arrived on death row in 1986, Wilkins was designated inmate number CP 47, meaning that he was the 47th man since *Furman v. Georgia* to arrive on Missouri's death row. In 1989, the Court decided in *Stanford v. Kentucky*[32] that age alone did not render Stanford's or Wilkins' executions cruel and unusual.

Four years after *Stanford* authorized juvenile executions, Christopher Simmons was convicted of murdering Shirley Crook by binding her hands and feet, wrapping a towel over her face with duct tape, and throwing her in the Meramec River in Eastern Missouri to drown. In his tearful confession to police, Simmons said that he and another teenager, Charles Benjamin, were burglarizing Ms. Crook's home and were afraid that she would recognize them. Under Missouri law, 17 is the age at which all defendants are prosecuted in adult court. The Missouri statute required that the jury be instructed on the defendant's age as a mitigating circumstance, but the prosecutor argued to the jury that his age was not mitigating. "Seventeen years old. Isn't that scary? Doesn't that scare you? Mitigating? Quite the contrary I submit. Quite the contrary." The jury sentenced Simmons to death.

Chris Simmons arrived on death row in 1993 and was designated CP 111. He had never before been arrested or convicted of a crime. The frightened teenager "checked in" to the protective custody unit, postponing his inevitable placement in the death row general population. Fellow death row inmate William Jones was in the adjoining cell, and befriended Simmons. Jones told Simmons that another prisoner on the row, Heath Wilkins, had come to death row under similar circumstances at a young age, and that Simmons should request him as a cell mate. The guards, knowing that Wilkins could and would help Simmons adapt to prison life, granted Simmons' request. When Simmons emerged from protective custody two years older and three inches taller, Simmons was assigned to share a cell with Heath Wilkins. Jones never returned to the general population; he was executed by lethal injection on November 20, 2002.

Neither Stanford nor Wilkins was executed. Kentucky Governor Paul Patton announced that he would commute Stanford's sentence to life imprisonment in June 1993 because "this is a case where the justice system perpetuated an injustice." A federal judge granted Wilkins a new trial in 1999 because his guilty plea was taken in violation of his right to counsel. He was resentenced to life imprisonment, to be eligible for parole in 2011.

Wilkins' reduced sentence resulted in his transfer to an institution with a lower security level. Consistent with prison procedure, the transportation team came to his cell unannounced in the middle of the night. Wilkins begged them to let him say good-bye to his best friend. The guards woke Simmons, told him of Wilkins' request, and asked Simmons, "What is he to you?" Simmons told them, "He was my first cellie, and he is my best friend." At midnight the two young men met on an empty prison yard with guards standing at a respectful distance. They said their good-byes, hugged, shed some tears, and Wilkins said, "I love you, man." Simmons replied, "I love you, too." The guards led them away in opposite directions. Wilkins was taken to the Jefferson City Correctional Center, where he reads books onto audio tape for blind people. Simmons, nearing the end of his appeals, was returned to death row.

Simmons was represented in the lower courts by Patrick Berrigan and Jennifer Herndon, dedicated capital defense lawyers who had left the public defender's office to continue their work in small law practices. They led a detailed investigation into Simmons' life history and challenged the fairness of his trial through federal habeas corpus proceedings. The Missouri Attorney General moved to execute Simmons when his appeals ended unsuccessfully in 2001. Berrigan and Herndon opposed the motion, and filed an original petition for writ of habeas corpus in the Missouri Supreme Court—the legal equivalent of a Hail Mary. They argued that since the *Stanford* decision, a majority of states had abolished the death penalty for offenders under the age of 18, so that a clear consensus against juvenile executions had emerged.

In 2003 the Missouri Supreme Court agreed with Berrigan and Herndon, finding that the Eighth Amendment barred the execution of persons under the age of 18.[33] This was a bold move, considering that the only Supreme Court case on point had reached the opposite result, and Justice O'Connor would later scold them for it in her dissenting opinion. The State of Missouri petitioned for certiorari, and 15 years after turning aside Heath Wilkins' Eighth Amendment challenge to juvenile executions, the Court reached down into the same prison cell to take up the issue once again.

An opportunity to argue a case in the United States Supreme Court comes once in a lifetime to a very few lawyers, never for most. A testament to Berrigan's and Herndon's dedication to their client is their decision to request assistance from an expert in Supreme Court practice to maximize Simmons' chances for relief. Seth Waxman, the 41st Solicitor General of the United States and Tony Amsterdam protégé, co-authored the brief and argued the case before the Court. The brief reflects the fruits of Berrigan's and Herndon's investigation into Simmons' background and character. All the myriad reasons for not executing children—their physical, emotional and neurological immaturity, their vulnerability, their lack of culpability, and their ability to change—could be shown to apply to Chris Simmons. Further, the execution of children is a blemish on our own humanity and inconsistent with our recognition that children need protection. Simmons could not legally purchase a car, get married, buy liquor or tobacco, vote, join the military, or see an R-rated movie without parental consent. By allowing the execution of minors, "[w]e are literally alone in the world," Waxman argued to the Court.

Between the Supreme Court's decisions in *Furman* and *Simmons*, 22 juvenile offenders were executed in America, about 2% of the total number of post-*Furman* executions. The Court's decision to strike down the death penalty for minors removed 72 juvenile offenders from death row in 12 different states. In virtually all of cases, the minor's sentence of death was automatically commuted to life without the possibility of parole. The Court recently extended its reasoning in *Simmons* to declare that the Eighth Amendment prohibits sentencing juvenile offenders to life without the possibility of parole for non-homicide offenses.[34] Approximately 2,225 people are presently incarcerated for life without parole for crimes committed as juveniles, nearly a hundred as young as 13 or 14. Simmons, now designated inmate no. 990111, is incarcerated for life without parole at the Southeast Correctional Center in Charleston, Missouri.

Endnotes

1. 329 U.S. 429 (1947).
2. 399 U.S. 9 (1950).
3. 402 U.S. 183 (1971).
4. 356 U.S. 86 (1958).
5. *Id.* at 99.
6. 391 U.S. 510 (1968).
7. Nadya Labi, *A Man Against the Machine*, The Law School 16 (2007).
8. Petitioner's Brief, *Furman v. Georgia*, Landmark Briefs and Arguments of the Supreme Court of the United States: Constitutional Law 477, 484 (University Publications of America 1975).
9. *Id.* at 485-486.
10. *Id.* at 488.
11. *Id.* at 489.
12. 370 U.S. 660 (1962).
13. 408 U.S. at 309 (Stewart, J., concurring).
14. *Id.* at 14.
15. M. Meltsner, *Cruel and Unusual: The Supreme Court and Capital Punishment* 293 (W. Morrow 1973).
16. James W. Marquart & Jonathan R. Sorensen, National Study of the Furman-Commuted Inmates: Assessing the Threat to Society from Capital Offenders, 23 Loy. L.A. L. Rev. 5, 15 (1989-1990).
17. *Id.* at 23-26. Only two paroled *Furman*-commutees committed another homicide. After being paroled from Texas, Oscar Turner-Bey was convicted of second degree murder and armed criminal action in Missouri, where he is serving a life sentence at the Jefferson City Correctional Center. Keith Allen McDuff was convicted of murder and executed in 1998. Most of the violent behavior among the former death row inmates took place among those who remained incarcerated.
18. Wilbert Rideau, *In the Place of Justice: A Story of Punishment and Deliverance* 330 (Alfred A. Knopf 2010).
19. 408 U.S. at 310.
20. 428 U.S. 153 (1976).
21. *The Shawshank Redemption* (Castle Rock 1994).
22. *See* ALI Model Penal Code §210.6. The American Law Institute recently withdrew §210.6 altogether, explaining the futility of implementing a fair and reliable death penalty. The concerns expressed by the Institute mirror Prof. Amsterdam's arguments in *Furman*. *See Report of the Council to the Membership of The American Law Institute on the Matter of the Death Penalty* (April 15, 2009).
23. *Woodson v. North Carolina*, 428 U.S. 280, 304 (1976).
24. *Lockett v. Ohio*, 438 U.S. 586, 604 (1978).
25. *Ayers v. Belmontes*, 127 S. Ct. 469, 478 (2006).
26. *Lockett*, 438 U.S. at 631 (Rehnquist, J., concurring in part and dissenting in part).
27. *Coker v. Georgia*, 433 U.S. 584 (1977) (rape); *Kennedy v. Louisiana*, 554 U.S. 407 (2008) (child rape); *Enmund v. Florida*, 458 U.S. 782 (1982).
28. *Ford v. Wainwright*, 477 U.S. 399 (1985).
29. *Atkins v. Virginia*, 536 U.S. 304 (2002).
30. *Roper v. Simmons*, 543 U.S. 551 (2004).
31. *Atkins v. Virginia*, 536 U.S. 304, 353 (2002) (Scalia, J., dissenting).
32. 492 U.S. 361 (1989).
33. *Simmons v. Roper*, 112 S.W.3d 397 (Mo. 2003).
34. *Graham v. Florida*, 560 U.S. ___; 130 S. Ct. 2011 (2010).

Index